A LEGACY OF LIBERATION

A LEGACY OF LIBERATION

THABO MBEKI AND THE FUTURE OF THE SOUTH AFRICAN DREAM

Mark Gevisser

palgrave
macmillan

First published in 2009 by
PALGRAVE MACMILLAN®
in the United States—a division of St. Martin's Press LLC,
175 Fifth Avenue, New York, NY 10010.

Where this book is distributed in the UK, Europe and the rest of the world,
this is by Palgrave Macmillan, a division of Macmillan Publishers Limited,
registered in England, company number 785998, of Houndmills,
Basingstoke, Hampshire RG21 6XS.

Palgrave Macmillan is the global academic imprint of the above companies
and has companies and representatives throughout the world.

Palgrave® and Macmillan® are registered trademarks in the United States,
the United Kingdom, Europe and other countries.

ISBN-13: 978–0–230–61100–9
ISBN-10: 0–230–61100–1

Library of Congress Cataloging-in-Publication Data

Gevisser, Mark.
   A legacy of liberation : Thabo Mbeki and the future of the South African
dream / by Mark Gevisser.
      p. cm.
   Includes bibliographical references and index.
   ISBN 978–0–230–61100–9
   1. Mbeki, Thabo. 2. Mbeki, Thabo—Influence. 3. Mbeki, Thabo—Family.
4. Presidents—South Africa—Biography. 5. South Africa—Politics and
government—1994– 6. Political leadership—South Africa—Case studies.
7. Blacks—South Africa—Social conditions. 8. South Africa—Race relations.
I. Title.

DT1975.G47 2009
968.06′6092—dc22
[B]
                                                                2008050763

A catalogue record of the book is available from the British Library.

Design by Newgen Imaging Systems (P) Ltd., Chennai, India.

First edition: April 2009

10 9 8 7 6 5 4 3 2 1

Printed in the United States of America.

To David and Hedda Gevisser
And to Dhianaraj Chetty

CONTENTS

Photographs appear between pages 173–174.

AUTHOR'S NOTE ON THE TEXT

ON PLACE NAMES

Many place names in the Eastern Cape have changed since democracy. This is to bring them in line with the way they are actually pronounced in isiXhosa rather than the way they were transliterated by the colonists. So "Idutywa" is now "Dutywa," "Umtata" is now "Mthatha," and so on. Because most of my informants refer to these places by their former names, I have used only these former names in the text, to avoid confusion.

ON CURRENCY

South Africa used the British pound sterling (£) until it became a republic in 1961, when it changed to the rand (R). This book works accordingly. When the original amounts in the text are in rands, they are reflected in rands and not converted. The rand and the U.S. dollar were roughly equal in the mid-1980s. In the 1990s, there were between 3 and 5 rands to the dollar; this dropped to 7 by the early 2000s, and was at around 10 at the time of publication.

ON SOURCES

Over two hundred people were interviewed for this book. Most were willing to speak on the record, but some preferred to remain anonymous. While unattributed sources are common in journalism, they are less so in serious biography; they are, however, unavoidable in a project of this particular nature, published at this particular time. All quotes from these interviews have been carefully cross-checked and are not cited in the Notes. All other direct quotes, from written sources, are cited in the Notes. In the Bibliographical Notes I provide contextual sources and suggest further reading. With the exception of off-the-record interviews, all materials collected in my research for this book are lodged at the South African History Archives at Wits University: www.saha.org.za.

ACKNOWLEDGMENTS

I am deeply grateful to all of the following:

For archival assistance: Zweliyanyikima Vena and Sandy Rowoldt at the Cory Library at Rhodes University; Stephen Gill at the Morija Mission Archives in Lesotho; Richard Whiteing, Simpiwe Yako, Zolile Mvunelo, and all the staff at the Mayibuye Archives; Sadie Forman and the staff at the ANC Archives at the University of Fort Hare; Stan Ndlovu from the ANC Film and Video Archives; Michelle Leon and the staff at the AVUSA Library; and the staff at Wits Historical Papers, the South African Communist Party Library, and the Missing Persons Task Team of the National Prosecuting Authority.

For access to private collections, and permission to cite from or reproduce material: Thabo and Zanele Mbeki, Epainette Mbeki, Moeletsi Mbeki, the late Linda Jiba, the late Govan Mbeki, the late Norah Moerane, Sophie Moerane, Olive Mpahlwa, Essop and Meg Pahad, Derek Gunby, Mel and Rhiannon Gooding, Tibor Barna, Howard Barrell, Colin Coleman, Gail Gerhart, Barbara Harmel, Shireen Hassim, Philippa Ingram, Tom Karis, Tom Lodge, Tiksie Mabizela, Hugh Macmillan, Mphu Matete, Gabriel Mokgoko, Ann Nicholson, Wiseman Nkuhlu, Tiny Nokwe, Seth Phalatse, Hennie Serfontein, Tor Sellström, Bridget Thompson, and Tony Trew. The Mbeki family also gave me permission to access the Department of Justice files on Govan and Thabo Mbeki in Pretoria.

For assisting me in my travels, sharing ideas and research with me, or reading drafts of my work: Charlotte Bauer, Jonathan Berger, Fran Buntman, Luli Callinicos, Jeremy Cronin, Maggie Davey, Jessica Dubow, Jihan El-Tahri, Andrew Feinstein, Stephen Gelb, Heather Godwin, Derek Gunby, Robert Harvey, Hillary and Tony Hamburger, Barbara Harmel, Gillian Hart, Rachel Holmes, Heather Hughes, Jon Hyslop, Wellington Jansen, Tom Karis, Jürgen Kögl, Reddy Mampane, Achille Mbembe, Kwena Steve Mokwena, Joel Netshitenzhe, Sarah Nuttall, Dele Olojede, Kole Omotoso, Deborah Posel, Helen Schneider, Mark Schoofs, Elinor Sisulu, Carol Steinberg, Raymond Suttner, Ivan Vladislavic, Iden Wetherell, and Claire Wright. I would like to thank, in particular: Colin Bundy, for his intellectual generosity and permission to cite from his unpublished work; Gail Gerhart, Tor Sellström, and Vladimir Shubin for their collegial generosity; Esther Kaplan, who gave invaluable advice for this edition; Shaun de Waal, who edited the first edition of this book; and Jonny Steinberg, the other half of the two-person writer's workshop that has sustained me creatively for nearly a decade now.

For research: Joanne Bloch, France Bourgouin, Collette Fearon, Tumi Makgetla, Boitshoko Mohlabane, Ruth Muller, Felicity Nyikadzino, George Ogola, Sophie Maggs, Rob Skinner, Tymon Smith, Paul Stinson, and particularly Paul Holden. For assistance from the South African Presidency and the ANC: Joel Netshitenzhe, Essop Pahad, Kgalema Motlanthe, Smuts Ngonyama, Ronnie Mamoepa, Bheki Khumalo, Murphy Morobe, David Hlabane, Louis du Plooy, Mandisa Mayinje, and the staff at Mahlamba Ndlopfu.

For agreeing to talk to me: all those I interviewed, and most of all the Mbekis themselves. In particular: Zanele Mbeki, for being so willing a conduit; Moeletsi Mbeki, whose combination of charm, intellect and spirit I can only aspire to; and Epainette Mbeki, who has become a teacher, a mother, and a friend. Three family members have passed away who also helped me greatly: Govan Mbeki, Linda Jiba, and Norah Moerane. I am also deeply grateful to Olive Mpahlwa and Mphu Matete, who have trusted me with their unimaginable pain. Of course, my ultimate gratitude goes to Thabo Mbeki himself, who agreed to spend hours with me and to encourage his comrades, friends, and family to talk to me. There are many others who wish to remain anonymous. I thank you all for your time and insight. The ideas of this book, however, are my own, and no one else should be held to account for them—or my errors.

For helping to bring this book into the world: the *Sunday Times* (Johannesburg), which commissioned the work that began this project; the Wits Institute of Social and Economic Research (WISER) in Johannesburg, which awarded me a writing fellowship in 2001; the Swedish Embassy in Pretoria, which sponsored my European travel; Jonathan Ball, whose faith in me sustained my work for eight years, and all at Jonathan Ball Publishers and at Palgrave Macmillan. I am particularly grateful to my editor, Luba Ostashevsky, whose acuity and equanimity played the key role in getting this book an international readership, and to my wonderfully creative and committed agents, Isobel Dixon and David Godwin.

For their friendship, love, and support over the course of a decade: my family and friends, and in particular Dhianaraj Chetty, who has made a home for and with me, and who continues to nurture and sustain me in every way.

Mark Gevisser
January 2009

A LEGACY OF LIBERATION

INTRODUCTION

THABO MBEKI AND THE SOUTH AFRICAN DREAM DEFERRED

On the night of Sunday, September 21, 2008 a somber Thabo Mbeki, surrender etched into his impassive face, told the world that he was "obliged" to step down as president of South Africa because he had been fired by his own political party, the African National Congress (ANC). This was after a judge had found that he might have interfered with the prosecution on corruption charges of his former deputy, Jacob Zuma, one of his closest comrades and now a bitter rival, whom he had fired in 2005.

The judgment would later be overturned on appeal, but the damage was done: Mbeki's political career was over. His ouster concluded a process that had begun in December 2007, when 4,000 delegates of the ANC met in the bustling northern town of Polokwane and were faced with choosing a leader, usually elected unopposed. It was a rare thing in Africa: a ruling political party dispatching an unwanted incumbent with neither a bullet nor a coup but via the ballot. Mbeki, who had effectively governed the country since 1994 (he was Nelson Mandela's de facto prime minister before becoming president himself in 1999), was defeated by Zuma. It was a moment both exhilarating and brutal: the robust exercise of democracy but also something of a regicide. In his resignation speech seven months later, Mbeki made the point that he had been a loyal member of the ANC for 52 years. He was, in fact, understating things: The son of freedom fighters, Mbeki had in fact been born into the movement, which he considered nothing less than his family. This proud, prickly, and very shy man thus left office not with the dignity of an elder statesman or paterfamilias but utterly humiliated.

Mbeki is, at least as much as Mandela, the primary architect of South Africa's transition to democracy and the postapartheid state; his story provides a key to South Africa's turbulent past, its complicated transition to democracy, and its somewhat perplexing current politics. He was also, in many ways, the architect of his own downfall, and his demise—the tragic denouement to a long, illustrious, but highly controversial public career—signals a deeply contested legacy. The nature of these contestations themselves reveals much about contemporary South African society.

In the ANC's first years in government, Mbeki often cited poet Langston Hughes to voice his anxieties about the crisis of expectation that he believed was building among black South Africans because of the slowness of change: "What happens to a dream deferred?" he asked in parliament, paraphrasing Hughes. "It explodes."[1] Later Mbeki admitted to me that he and his comrades in government had felt deeply disempowered at the time, constrained from their plans to build their new society by factors ranging from the global economic environment, to the recalcitrant civil service they inherited, to their own lack of experience, to the racist "Afropessimism" about the continent that seemed to put a cap on any of its ambitions, to the AIDS epidemic, which, through a terrible coincidence of history, appeared to be decimating the very population they had just liberated. This sense of disempowerment was at the root of much of the dissonance of the Mbeki era: from AIDS to Zimbabwe; from the defensive way Mbeki responded to all criticism to the conspiratorial way he gathered and wielded power. His preoccupation with the "dream deferred" thus seemed to have a personal application as well: His own fantasies of self-determination had been put on hold, even as he sat in the most powerful office in the land.

Now, a decade later, these dreams appeared to have been shattered with his ousting, while the politics around his downfall precipitated not so much the explosion Mbeki predicted as some of the other consequences suggested in Hughes's poem. In the last few years I have witnessed, in my native South Africa, the sagging of a bureaucracy under the heavy load of patronage that is the curse of African politics, in an environment where the state is often the only employer and where jobs are often dispensed rather than earned. I have witnessed, too, the rotten stench of corruption and the way it has been covered up, particularly in the multibillion-rand arms procurement deal authorized by an Mbeki-led government in 1999, which is the fount of the charges against Zuma and of allegations against Mbeki and many others. I have seen the sugary crusting over of dreams with the conspicuous consumption of a thriving new black middle class on one hand and the sore of poverty on the other—a poverty certainly alleviated by Mbeki's welfare policies but festering, nonetheless, due to an unemployment rate that hovers at around 30 percent and a crime epidemic that makes South Africa one of the most violent societies in the world, as well as the AIDS epidemic that has infected around 10 percent of the population. And despite the fact that democracy has brought South Africa an unprecedented period of economic growth and the totally unexpected gift of political stability, I have watched the ideals of an earlier era dry up, like so many raisins in the sun, as the nation's leaders have revealed themselves to be not the demigods of struggle mythology but as flawed and as self-serving as any. One verse, in particular, has stuck with me from Hughes's great poem cycle, and I have found myself repeating it, almost as an incantation: "From river to river uptown to down, there's liable to be confusion when a dream gets kicked around."[2]

The South Africa Mbeki governed was no longer the "Mandela Miracle" of just 15 years earlier, "the world's greatest fairy tale" that seemingly guaranteed a happy ending. South Africans are no longer the "Rainbow Children of God," as Bishop Desmond Tutu delighted in calling us. The reality has dawned: We are a struggling, developing nation in a rough neighborhood, with our own difficult history of conflict and inequality to overcome. Gone, too, is that beguiling myth of the Mandela era, one to which the whole world once seemed to subscribe: that the ANC is a cathedral of morality. No: It is a rowdy town hall of competing interests, driven by patronage and riven by personality, grubby with politics. It is no longer a liberation movement but the ruling party of a young and healthy—messy and unpredictable—democracy. Certainly there is anguish about this end to the era of miracles, but there is relief, too, at the inevitable political maturation of a society that had for too long claimed exceptionalism.

This book sets out to explain how South Africa got to this place and how and why Mbeki ruled the way he did: it understands him as a brilliant but flawed individual with a traumatic upbringing, a difficult past, and a vision for the future that he was not always able to put into practice. The story of the Mbeki family describes a grand arc through the last intense century of South African history: from colonial dispossession and white supremacy, through the struggle for liberation, into the separation and hardship of prison and exile, and finally homecoming, reunion, the ascent to power, and the dream of redemption. Mbeki's own path coincides closely with the tumultuous past South African century, and impacts directly on it. This book tracks back along this path to make sense of the leader Mbeki became and the kind of country he governed for nearly 15 years. It tries to understand the confusion that was South Africa in the first decade of the twenty-first century by looking at the past of the man who carried, on his not particularly broad shoulders, the collective burden of a country seeking to redeem a dream too long deferred.

This is not simply the story of a single man but the epic tale of a dynasty: of a family that was among the first Christian converts in southern Africa; of the riches and status they earned as "black Englishmen" and then of the way they lost it all through a century of willful and brutal dispossession; of their attempts to regain their dignity and their agency through the embrace of communism and the liberation movement; of their incarceration, dislocation into exile, even destitution; of their homecoming and of the difficulties inherent in their eventual empowerment. Mbeki was born to middle-class communist missionaries who had set up shop in one of the bleakest, most dispossessed corners of rural South Africa, and he was schooled in the very last class to receive a mission-school education before apartheid's

Bantu Education came crashing down onto the expectations of black South Africans. He came of age in Johannesburg in the months following the banning of the ANC and its subsequent decision to take up arms, and found his first real home while studying in Britain during the generational rebellion of the 1960s as his father, Govan Mbeki, was beginning a sentence of life imprisonment alongside Mandela on Robben Island. He shuttled, during his two decades of exile leadership, between the Stalinism of the Soviet Union and an ease in Western society that earned him unparalleled access to its corridors of power and enabled him to persuade even Reagan's America that the ANC was an organization of freedom fighters rather than terrorists. With the possible exception of Mandela, no one's role was greater in moving South Africa away from bloody civil war, by talking his comrades in exile out of their notions of communist revolution and talking white South Africans into an embrace of a negotiated settlement. For decades a backroom boy and bag-carrier for ANC elders, Mbeki ran Mandela's government and then struggled to find his own way in the shadow of a living saint.

This is also a story about home and exile, and how these two words describe not physical places but profound states of being not easily reconciled by coming back to the place one was once forced to leave, the place for which one has spent one's entire life fighting. It is a story, too, of political intrigue: of a revolutionary movement struggling first to defeat and then to seduce a powerful and callous enemy; of the battle between unity and discord and the dogged rise and fall of a quiet, clever, diligent but unpopular man who seemed to take little joy in power but had much need for it. It is also a study of patrimony, its fractures and its obligations. It is about Thabo Mbeki, the son of Govan Mbeki, who put struggle before family and taught his children to do likewise; about Kwanda Mbeki, the son of Thabo Mbeki, who never knew his father and who disappeared trying to find him; about Thabo Mbeki, the son and father of the ANC, a movement that was his family as well as the political party he led and that ultimately rejected him.

I began working on this book in 1999, at the time the Mandela presidency was winding down and anxiety was growing about the aloof, obscure, and even paranoid man who was to replace him. Thabo Mbeki had once been the struggle's "crown prince," seducing the world—and white South Africans—into loving the ANC, but now he was described as at worst Machiavellian and at best enigmatic. Both these descriptions had become such media clichés that they had lost their meaning altogether: They were a lazy shorthand to describe a man no one could get a handle on, and Mbeki seemed to encourage it. Even as he became the most powerful person in the country, he shunned a public profile almost entirely, granting only rare and controlled interviews. I felt that if I could understand his history and how it had formed him, and then what had happened to him in the 1990s, I might be able to illuminate the dynamics of change I was living through in South Africa. Perhaps, too, I would be able to bring, into the daylight of democracy, the biography of a man in whose hands my country lay but whose revolutionary ethos impelled him to sublimate his subjective experience to the imperatives of struggle. Unlike Mandela, who made a fetish of his biography for South Africans to identify with ("I was in chains, you were in chains; as I was liberated, so were you; as I can forgive my oppressors, so too can you"), Mbeki denied any relevance of his biography, his subjective life, to the work he did. "I am the struggle, and the struggle is me," he seemed to be saying. "There is nothing beyond or beneath that."

Although this is not an authorized biography of Thabo Mbeki, he agreed to cooperate, and over the course of eight years of research, I had seven interviews with him—usually in a reception room in one of his official residences and on a weekend—lasting a total of about 20 hours. The most substantial of these took place in August 2000, at Mahlamba Ndlopfu in Pretoria, just over a year after he became president. Mbeki had already agreed to cooperate with my project, and I had had two shorter interviews with him in the run-up to the 1999 elections, but now the prospect of an entire Saturday night stretched out before us. He was dressed casually—comfortable house shoes, slacks, a cardigan buttoned over a polo shirt, a well-gnawed pipe in his mouth. But bloodshot, puffy eyes betrayed his exhaustion. He had managed to burst out of Mandela's shadow and into international recognition, not only as the liberating philosopher-king who was beginning to make postapartheid South Africa work and as the first African leader since the *uhuru* independence generation to have a visionary plan for African development, but also as the putative defender of a loathsome tyrant to the north and as an AIDS dissident crank.

Over the previous year I had watched the South African presidency become more logical, more substantive, and more hands-on than it had been during the Mandela era. But I had also watched it contract to a point where it had become nitpicky rather than all-embracing, introverted rather than communicative, too often mistrusting and not often enough inspiring. I had watched Mbeki withdraw into an increasingly sullen and irascible isolation. And, most difficult indeed for a biographer, I had felt that I too had lost sight of my subject. His office had canceled meetings repeatedly. I knew that the bad press he had been receiving had made him more ambivalent than ever about letting an outsider in, and this sense of embattlement had radiated, like an electric shield, around him. When I touched base with his friends and colleagues, I found that even the most considered and independent ones either retreated into prickly caution or soared into manic praise-song. Meanwhile, I was perpetually called on to pronounce on him, in the media and at dinner tables. My friends knew that the surest way to plunge me into a sullen irascibility of my own was to ask me to explain him. It was something I found increasingly difficult to do: In my attempt to understand his position on AIDS, I even lost friends—who saw, in any attempt at empathy, a collusion in genocide. I was convinced that, no matter what my personal feelings, I had to maintain such empathy: The biographer's job, I told my friends and critics somewhat self-righteously, was to see the world the way his subject did.

The expectations were high, then, as I sat opposite Mbeki and watched him carve a space for us, with his pipe-smoking paraphernalia, out of the official residence nowhereland that would be his home for most of the next decade. The perpetual scraping and tapping kept his restless hands occupied, freeing his mind to work, as he conjured with pipe smoke the illusion of home, an intimate study in which we might comfortably sit. We talked about the "disconnection"—his word—of his childhood, and about the way his African Renaissance ideology was powered, at least in part, by his need to reconnect with his roots. We talked about race and social transformation, about the difficulties of governance, about his history in exile. And we talked, for over two hours, about AIDS. I was impressed at his grasp of detail, but although his seductive capacity in one-on-one meetings is legendary, I felt neither seduced nor charmed by him. This was a job, and he worked. He was diligent, thorough, volunteering no more information than was requested and initiating no conversation himself; making no attempt at establishing a connection with small talk or even with more eye contact than was absolutely necessary. The pipe thing, I came to see, was more than just a way of focusing the mind: It created a scrim between him and his interlocutor, allowing him to work with ideas, unhindered by the mess of human interaction.

At some point, Mbeki's wife, Zanele—an elegant, independent, and highly intelligent woman—rode into the room on the warm breath of a day's outing. She was lively and effervescent, engaging and solicitous, excited by the prospect of joining us. I willed her silently to stay, but he willed her, with the greater force, to leave, and so she disappeared into the gloom, reappearing a couple of hours later in a dressing gown—"Oh, are you two still at it? Thabo will keep you all night!"—to offer some refreshment. A waiter subsequently emerged from the bowels of the darkened house, bearing a tray of those cold, fried hors d'oeuvres at which official residences seem to excel. Mbeki waved him impatiently away, and the tray was put just beyond our reach. Finally, at close to midnight, I was running out of tape. I was exhausted and hungry, dying for a toilet but terrified to go in case, in my temporary absence, he realized he had a country to run. If this was an endurance test, he won. I found myself thanking him for his time and terminating the interview.

He saw me out personally, and my last image was, finally, that of a host: a solitary man, snug in his woolen cardigan standing at the hardwood door of the grand gabled Cape Dutch–style residence, offering what seemed to me to be a somewhat regretful half-wave good-bye. I imagined him wandering aimlessly about the huge old pile before finding himself upstairs in the comfort of his study, lost in his books and on the Internet, bathed until dawn in the flickering blue light of his computer screen, a bottle of Scotch and his rack of briars his only company.

As I drove home to Johannesburg, I tried to understand the emptiness I was feeling. This was the president of my country; he was enormously busy. He spoke to almost no journalists, and yet he had given me over six hours of his time. Why, then, was I bothered that he did not ask me a single question, did not wish to break bread with me, did not respond to any of my gambits for small talk? Any portraitist will tell you that while a subject must be posed when being painted, you need to see him move spontaneously in those breaks when he stretches his legs or drinks a cup of tea, to gather up the emotion with which you will then animate the image. Otherwise, it is an entirely formal exercise: You might as well practice your brushstrokes on a bowl of fruit.

It was Mbeki himself who gave me the word "disconnect" to describe his childhood and then his itinerant adult life. Now I wondered, after our time together, whether it was not a condition still very much alive in him. For any returning freedom fighter, coming home must mean the expectation of reconnection and reintegration. For many, the homecoming is profoundly traumatic, for it can never match up to such fantasies for changing and ruling a country. How much more acute that expectation must be—and how much more difficult its lack of fulfillment—for one who felt, as Mbeki did, disconnected to begin with.

From a very young age, Mbeki's response to this condition had been to sublimate all emotions, all relationships, all desires, into the struggle for liberation. He had long made a political career around pragmatism—unusual indeed for a freedom fighter—but at his core he was a revolutionary idealist. He had given himself entirely—as his father did before him—to the ANC, to redeeming the hardship of his life, his parents' lives, the lives of his people, by prosecuting a struggle for the utopian vision his father sold to him as they sat together in the hut that served as Govan Mbeki's study, before he could even read. So much had been sacrificed—father, childhood, son, family, innocence—to the cause of the liberation of his people, a task he has been predestined to fulfill since his youth, and here he was, home at last, free at last, in power, trying to make the grand project of postapartheid South Africa work, against impossible odds and crushing expectations.

Mbeki's biography set me thinking about the politics of redemptive liberation and how it has been both a blessing and a curse to postcolonial Africa: a blessing insofar as it enabled a people to engage in a freedom struggle in the face of unspeakable oppression; a curse because of the way it hitched the newly liberated society to impossible dreams and expectations rather than allowing it to develop according to the more realistic blueprints of incremental development. I found myself reciting the illustrious roll call of Mbeki's predecessors who had fallen off the perch of their ideals, trying to defend their revolutions: Ghana's Kwame Nkrumah, Zambia's Kenneth Kaunda, Kenya's Jomo Kenyatta, Mozambique's Samora Machel, Angola's Eduardo dos Santos, and, of course, Zimbabwe's Robert Mugabe. Could there be a madness visited upon this continent's leaders, not because (as racists might have it) of any pathological defects that make it difficult for democracy and equality to take root in Africa, but owing to the gap that exists between the utopian expectations of revolution and the dystopic reality they have to deal with once they find themselves in power at last? As the current American politics demonstrate, the best leaders of developed countries are, of course, visionaries too—but their vision is tempered by the certainty that their subjects survived before they came along and will get along just fine after they leave. How different it is for an African revolutionary who finally wins his opportunity to govern. The mandate with which Thabo Mbeki came to power was not simply to raise taxes or lower them, to implement national healthcare, or to balance the budget: His mandate was nothing less than the salvation of his people. Against this measure, of course he failed. Of course, his successor will fail too.

In the years following my Saturday night encounter with Thabo Mbeki in August 2000, I had three more interviews with him, the last of which was in January 2006, when he spoke to me off the record about his decision to fire Jacob Zuma and its consequences. During the course of 2007, several scheduled meetings with Mbeki were canceled. We communicated, instead, in a novel way. I would e-mail my questions to his wife, and he would respond to them by talking into a digital recorder. A minidisk would then be delivered to me—sometimes very late at night. In these questions, I asked him to reflect on the succession, but his answers were anodyne; milder versions of his frequent public statements denying any crisis in the ANC and accusing the media of counterrevolutionary agendas for suggesting anything of the sort.

I trailed him, of course, through his Waterloo at Polokwane in December that year, but despite repeated attempts, I did not get to see him again. He withdrew almost entirely from the public eye following his humiliation. Some of his closest friends told me that he was so shattered by his defeat that they believed he was suffering some kind of breakdown. Given how brutal it was—I describe it in the epilogue to this book—I was not surprised. But that he had been surprised about his defeat said something profound about his own disconnection. The self-deception of the Mbeki campaign was astonishing: Despite all evidence to the contrary, his people insisted up until the final announcement that they would prevail. It was a sign of the cult that had grown around him and that had removed him from reality: So regal had he become that his supporters could not countenance his defeat, and everyone, from the ground up, seemed to tell the next person what he thought they wanted to hear, thereby causing Mbeki's entire intelligence network to collapse.

In public comment and in South African media in the weeks following Mbeki's defeat, I argued that his behavior at Polokwane was but the latest symptom of a condition he had suffered all his life and that had compromised his presidency: the same disconnect I had witnessed in that meeting in Polokwane. But Mbeki responded to my assertions in February 2008 by writing me a lengthy letter in which he told me that while he had not yet "summoned the courage" to read the South African edition of my book, he challenged its very premise: "As wrong as it is to interpret my rendition of a poem by Langston Hughes on the basis of some imagined psychological condition, so will it be wrong to interpret all manner of right and wrong things I have done over the decades, on the basis of some penetrating understanding of my 'psychological' make up." On the contrary, he insisted, "I belong among the uncelebrated unwashed masses, offering no rich pickings even for the most highly talented mind reader! Stated simply, all one needs to understand the political Thabo Mbeki is to know the value-system and political programme he inherited from an established movement." He asked me to consider, in this light, his behavior regarding the Polokwane conference: "I would like to assure you that nothing I have done, or not done, in this context, has anything to do with my psychological makeup."[3] Mbeki was not just informing me that he thought I had read him incorrectly, but that I was incorrect in trying to read him at all.

Of course, I disagree with Mbeki's claim that he, like the working classes, has no unconscious—even as I accept that the only person who can truly "know" Thabo Mbeki's story is Thabo Mbeki himself. My starting point is the knowledge that no biographer is omniscient. I attempt, rather, to present a narrative made up of the shards and fragments I have collected along my journey into Mbeki's life, combined with the perspectives of his friends, comrades, relatives, and contemporaries. It would be disingenuous, of course, to pretend that my own perspective does not drive things. But I have endeavored to measure it and balance it with the voices and opinions and subjectivities of others who know Mbeki far better than I do. They exist as guides and characters in the narrative; rather than providing definitive answers, I convene them and let them debate with one another and with me—and with you, the reader.

It would be disingenuous, too, to claim that there is no judgment of Mbeki in this book. But I have been conscious that I am constructing a narrative rather than a polemic, one that attempts to make sense of Thabo Mbeki within his times, and that my work must thus be driven by empathy rather than critique. I have endeavored to sit on the shoulder of my subject and see the world the way he sees it, even if—as in the case of his position on AIDS, for example—I have found myself in a disagreement so fierce that it challenges my capacity for empathy.

The nine years of my research and writing coincided exactly with the nine years of the Mbeki presidency, and in these years I have undertaken an expedition through the landscape of contemporary South Africa. The book might be about the past, but it is set in the present, as I journey through the landscape of contemporary South Africa (and Mbeki's exile), meeting the people and visiting the places that bring to life the story of Mbeki, his family, and the extraordinary century of South African history they inhabited—and motivated.

As I was writing this introduction, I found myself, like so many all over the world, swept up in the 2008 American presidential campaign—wishing fervently, on one hand, that South Africa had a leader as inspiring as Barack Obama, but worrying, on the other, that the United States too might fall victim to the politics of redemptive liberation should he win.

After Obama's victory, I read in a South African newspaper that, on a visit to South Africa in August 2006, he had said that the struggle against apartheid was the issue that moved him "to become politically active and play a leadership role in my community." He told this story, he said, to remind his own compatriots that the United States was not just an exporter of democratic ideals but an importer, too: "We have also been inspired by the struggles in other nations that have, in turn, helped shape and perfect the very freedoms and rights held dear by citizens of my own country."[4]

This led me back to Obama's book, *Dreams from My Father,* where I rediscovered his account of how he had found his political voice. Asked to talk at a rally at his college campaigning for divestment from apartheid South Africa, Obama found himself using the South African struggle to demand that his fellow students choose sides "not between black and white" but between "dignity and servitude," "fairness and injustice," "commitment and indifference," "right and wrong."[5]

Obama's story reminded me of the symbolic significance of the South African story to so many people all over the world, particularly in the United States, where the anti-apartheid solidarity movement inherited the mantle from the civil rights movement as the great moral cause of the late twentieth century. If you, the reader, are 40 years of age or older, chances are you played some role, or at least gave some thought to, or maybe even found your own political voice, in the disinvestment campaigns of the late 1980s.

But Obama's story also reminded me of a paradox I had felt acutely as an undergraduate at Yale at that time: that such language—while deeply inspiring and of inestimable benefit to the South African struggle—voided my country of its specificity. It demonstrated the way South Africa had become something of a figure of speech in the grammar of contemporary politics, a universal metaphor for the battle between fairness and injustice. The real South Africa is, of course, far more complicated—and the work of building a new society is far dirtier. My aspiration, in writing this book, is to tell one of the stories—a very significant one—that demonstrates this complexity. It is a story that is not necessarily as inspiring and as singular as Nelson Mandela's, but it is as complex, and as difficult, and as compelling, as the South African experience itself.

Johannesburg, 2008

1

THE MBEKIS
"THE JEWS OF KAFFIRLAND"

The road to Mbewuleni, Thabo Mbeki's birthplace, takes one up from the commerce of the market town of Idutywa into the hills and the mist. Even on a midsummer's day in January, the landscape is a paradox, both verdant and barren, eerily depopulated in contrast with the teeming settlements strung along the national highway below. Here there is a school, here a motley collection of ramshackle buildings gathered into a compound. Suddenly, in the mist, a woman with a cage of chickens at her side will appear, awaiting a ride into town, or an old man in an unthreading suit and perfectly notched tie will tip his hat as he hobbles along.

It is early 1999, just weeks before Mbeki is to become Nelson Mandela's successor. I am driving to Mbewuleni with his 83-year-old mother, Epainette. Six decades prior, in 1940, she and her husband, Govan—young, educated, urbanized middle-class communist pioneers out to make a Brave New World—had moved here to start their family, to set up their cooperative store, to find a way of living independent of government salaries, and to attempt to put their ideologies of rural improvement into practice.

Their own fathers had been among the elite of the Transkei, the former native reserve, or bantustan, that was the home of the Xhosa-speaking people in the Eastern Cape. Both had been archetypal "black Englishmen," one a schoolmaster and the other a colonially appointed headman. Both had built the first schools and churches in their home communities; both had been converted Christians and severe evangelists; both, too, had been prosperous farmers, the very backbone of the rural economy, and among the first African landowners in the Transkei to build four-walled stone houses. These houses still stand, at the extreme southern and northern borders of the Transkei, sentinels of Western civilization, bookending the region's desperate poverty with their ambitions, narrating the tragedy of a century's battle between these ambitions and a system determined to see them thwarted.

Nowhere is this tragedy more evident than in Mbewuleni, and as we drive up into the highlands above Idutywa, Epainette Mbeki surveys the disused terraces and eroded valleys with a quiet anguish. The desolation of this land, like the difficult life she has led—in poverty, without her husband and sons—signals a failure of the aspirations of both her and her parents, even if South Africa is now a democracy and her oldest son about to become its president.

Eleven miles out of Idutywa, we turn off the road and bump down a sodden track, through the stolid zinc-roofed homes of the *amagqoboka* (Christian converts), past the school, down into a dry riverbed, and up the other side to the Mbeki homestead, which is situated among the conical huts at the entry to the *qaba* (traditional Xhosa) section of the village. Epainette Mbeki, who moved closer to town in 1974, now leases the property out. Decayed by poverty and the weather, it is in a state of disrepair, with a weed-filled yard and broken windows.

But when Thabo was born here, in 1942, the homestead was renowned for its order. "There was nothing here when we arrived," Epainette tells me. "But that was marvelous, because once we set up, we saw how people came to change from their unproductive habits and how they began trying self-improvements." In the beginning, "the locals would just throw off their blankets and offload the goods, naked as they were! But then the men started wearing trousers, and the women discarded the red things and would put a German print on. It was, I am sure, taking an example from us."

For better or for worse, Thabo Mbeki's own approach to leadership would be rooted in this ethos: from his determination to bring South Africa to a negotiated settlement in the 1980s to his questioning of AIDS orthodoxies, to the way he behaved in the political drama that would lead to his 2008 downfall. His grandparents were among the very first Christian converts in southern Africa; his parents became missionaries for a different cause, communism; his own politics were forged by the Leninist notion of "vanguardism"—revolution led by the educated few, always a few steps ahead of their people. He was a third-generation prophet in the wilderness; his own lodestar African self-determination.

As we enter the Mbeki homestead at Mbewuleni, a cluster of women gather diffidently around Epainette Mbeki. There is not a man in sight. Encouraged by her, they have made bread-baking trays out of petrol cans and are looking for a loan to build a bakery. Mrs. Mbeki, who was responsible for sending many of their daughters to school, interacts with them the way her evangelizing parents might have done; the way her son does when he too meets poor, needy people—paternal but not patronizing; schoolmarmish but not disciplinarian. She is with them but not of them, removed, somewhat, by her twinset and her education.

One woman, a retired schoolteacher, has none of the reserve of the others: "Where is that son of yours?" she asks Mrs. Mbeki. "He is our child...we have things to say to him. We have no telephones, no Eskom [electricity supply], no water, nothing. We are struggling. We want to say to Thabo Mbeki that we are getting impatient."

As we get into the car to leave, Mrs. Mbeki shakes her head: "I've told Thabo the villagers want to see him. But he told me that this is the very last village in the whole of South Africa he will ever come to." It is a comment that says much about Mbeki, about his stern disavowal of the sentimentality of ethnic identity and the favor of familial patronage. It says much, too, about the complexity of his relationship with his roots: He has no demonstrable attachment to Mbewuleni or, for that matter, to his family. His modernism does not seem to sit easily with the conventions of being a member of a clan, of having a "hometown" or roots. There is no apparent nostalgia for the tobacco-and-cow dung–scented hills of the Transkei.

A decade later, by the time he was unseated from the presidency, Thabo Mbeki had still not returned to Mbewuleni. Shortly after my first 1999 visit to the village, however, he did go to the birthplace of his father, about 38 miles to the east, at Nyili along the Tsomo River. He arrived by helicopter, to be welcomed home in a ritual that had him draped in beads, eating the inner armpit of a goat, and being rubbed with the resin of a sacred tree. After a life of exile, of wandering, he was being returned to his clan, the amaZizi.

But this was neither a personal visit nor any pilgrimage into his past. Rather, it was a set-piece performance for the election campaign that would lead to his inauguration as president a month later. Photographs of Mbeki participating in the event sought to project the image of an African identity and a connection with rural roots in one too often accused of having neither. A few months later, sitting in the drafty downstairs nowhereland of Mbeki's official residence in Pretoria, I asked him what his relationship was to the tradition he now seemed willing to explore. "We grew up at somewhat of a distance from that kind of thing," he told me. "I've never been to my mother's place, and I only went to my father's place when I came back from exile....So really, we had no connection, it didn't make any impact on us, we were cut off from it."

In Mbewuleni, he told me, "we were sort of disconnected from many things in the surroundings. Growing up among these amaqaba [traditional people], we lived with them, but we were not amaqaba. So in that sense, we were disconnected: You can see it, you live in it, but it is not you." Even though the Mbeki children were baptized, "there was no Christianity in our house," and so they grew up "disconnected," too, from the amagqoboka [Christians] across the valley with whom they went to school. The "detachment" he experienced as a child was "exacerbated by the fact that we went into exile" and that he was forced to stay away from home for three decades. Attempting to salvage some value from his history in the way that exiles and other itinerants do, he concluded that "growing up in this rather disconnected way meant that you could see things from the outside."

Only now, in his late middle age—draped in beads and rubbed with strange resin—did the price of this "disconnection" come flooding over him: "What the old people were saying was that you, as an individual, need to come back. This is where your grandfather was, these are the connections. In a sense, they claim you back."

The amaZizi, originally from the mountains to the north, were part of a group of outsiders within the Xhosa kingdom known as the Mfengu, or "Fingoes." Early converts to Christianity, the Mfengu became British collaborators: soldiers (and buffers) against the Xhosas in the interminable frontier wars of the nineteenth century, and consumers and traders who spread the light of European capitalism into the communalist darkness of Africa. Many, like Thabo Mbeki's grandfather Skelewu, even earned the vote, which was extended to all citizens of the Cape Colony in 1852, regardless of race, as long as they met property or income requirements. The Mfengu would become known by white traders as "the Jews of Kaffirland,"[1] for they were educated, aggressive, and unhampered by the feudal restrictions imposed by traditional hierarchies. They thrived, and soon became an elite: the first Africans to ride horses, to farm commercially, to build four-walled houses. Their children, educated and Christianized, became the region's first African teachers and journalists, preachers, and clerks.

But the story of the Mbeki family, from aspiring gentility to near penury and rebellion, describes the quiet but devastating drama of the black South African rural experience in the twentieth century: the ruthless destruction of the South African peasant economy by the state and the mining industry. The colonial powers might have built up a prosperous peasant class of people like the Mbekis to be their agents and buffers, but as long as Africans could live off the land it would be impossible to gather migrant labor, and so this successful peasant economy was deliberately eroded.

The effects of such policies are evident at the Mbeki farm in Nyili, originally given to Skelewu by the British after the defeat of the Xhosa in 1866. It was once a thriving commercial enterprise, but when I went to visit it in 1999, the fields looked like they had not been worked for a generation, and the handsome old farmhouse was surrounded by the mess of rural poverty: a random accretion of ragged outhouses and rusty old cars and plows. The house had been the very first four-walled one owned by a black man in the entire Nqamakwe district, and was an analogy of the man who built it: its back to the civilization of the Cape Colony, it stares almost defiantly up to the mountains of the Transkei; a beachhead of order and reason, a beacon of civilization, but also a watchtower and a buffer for those behind it.

Govan Mbeki had conjured the bounty and solidity of his childhood, for me, with a description of his father's fine-beveled oak dining table: "If you opened it up it could seat 16 people around it comfortably. *Comfortably!*" Even if Mbeki was a lifelong communist, this table exemplified, for him, his family's upward mobility. And even if he was a lifelong revolutionary, it seemed to hold, for him, the nostalgia of familial comfort. On entering the house in 1999, I saw the table, and insisted on opening it up. It was dull, unpolished, and warped. No matter: It was glorious, its elegantly turned legs in perfect proportion, even if they no longer all touched the floor. It conjured up clean tablecloths, women in calico prints, a Victorian paterfamilias reading to his sons from the family Bible, and it transformed the dowdy room into nothing less than a parlor.

In the years when Govan's father, Skelewu Mbeki, built his farm and homestead, huge changes took place in South African society: With the discovery of diamonds and gold, and with the transition of the Cape Colony into a capitalist economy, it was felt that natives were too comfortable on the land and had to be coerced into becoming the labor force now needed to support the mining industry. The Cape Franchise, which had given men like Skelewu not only their rights but their sense of belonging, began to be eroded, and new legislation restricted the amount of land a black man could own to only ten acres. In 1910, the year both Govan Mbeki and the modern South African state were born, there were only 6,663 African voters in the Cape, compared to over 120,000 white ones.[2] Nonetheless, they were considered threatening, and so, as part of the treaty between Boers and British, black people lost what little power they had. The 1913 Native Land Act gave blacks ownership rights to only 7 percent of the land, and only in native reserves; it abolished individual tenure for black farmers, and forced most black people into migrant labor. "It created overnight," the novelist Bessie Head would write later in the century, "a floating landless proletariat whose labour could be used and manipulated at will, and ensured that the ownership of the land had finally and securely passed into the hands of the ruling white race."[3]

In 1911, a year after Govan Mbeki's birth, Skelewu Mbeki died in shame, dismissed as headman because he had been caught illegally selling oxen over the Kei River. We know from this that he was under considerable financial duress at the time: "I was being pressed for money which I owed," he told the magistrate[4]; the rinderpest epidemic that wiped out 90 percent of the cattle of the Transkei in the first decade of the twentieth century must have affected him severely.

But Govan Mbeki's memories are nonetheless of bounty and solidity. When Skelewu Mbeki died in 1918, he left large separate savings accounts for both his sons, ages 14 and 8, to pay for their educations.[5] Even if the process of the dispossession of South Africa's emerging small commercial farmers was well under way by the time he was born, enough surplus had been farmed, and enough money earned, to ensure the family's continued status as rural middle-class elite well into the twentieth century.

Govan Mbeki told me how, during the Great Depression, destitute Afrikaner farmers would seek shelter in his family home. The memory of assisting landless whites was important to him because it asserted, in contrast, the landedness of his own family. Certainly, all Africans can say that the land belonged to them before it was colonized, but the Mbekis can say that, according even to Western notions of individual tenure, they have owned property for far longer than most white South Africans. With this comes not only a tremendous sense of belonging and entitlement, but also an intense sense of loss.

And so it is no coincidence that Thabo Mbeki first started talking about an "African Renaissance" publicly around the time he first visited Nyili and was "called back home" by the elders of his clan. He could speak of "rebirth" because of his strong sense—from his own family's history—of something having been lost. Mbeki's African Renaissance ideology and all it spawned—Black Economic Empowerment, the New Partnership for Africa's Development (NEPAD), his approaches to AIDS and Zimbabwe—stemmed from a personal project of reconnection, just as the policy of "national reconciliation" that preceded it was both an official ideology and a personal project for Nelson Mandela.

If, then, there was a sense of grievance to the politics of Mbeki—what was often described as "a chip on his shoulder"—it derived from his sense that something profound had been taken away from the legacy of his people, not just their dignity but their material worth, too; that it was incumbent on him to win it back; and that so many of the difficulties he faced during his presidency stood in the way of his doing so.

Thabo Mbeki's understanding of history and his own aspirations must have been formed, even if subconsciously, by the powerful experience in his own family of prosperity followed by loss. The African "nativism" that he embraced during his presidency[6]—sometimes at odds with both his communist past and his worldly modernism—stemmed thus from his own disconnection and his longing to be reconnected. But reconnected with what? The *qaba* or the *gqoboka*? The amaZizi's traditional precolonial rituals, or their history of collaboration with the colonial oppressor? Mbeki's personal African Renaissance cannot but be complicated by the Mfengu legacy: the understanding that while land and prosperity might have been lost through a century of colonial and apartheid depredation, other benefits from the colonial collaboration accrued and were at the very core of his identity: Western education, worldliness, upward mobility, the relative freedom from the feudal constraints of traditional hierarchies, and the calling to save the souls of those around him, if not by Christianity, then by communism and African Nationalism.

2

THE MOERANES
CHEKHOV IN THE TRANSKEI

There is to be found, in the albums of Thabo Mbeki's aunt Norah Moerane, a formal portrait of a country gentleman, his wife, and seven children. This is the family of Eleazar Jacane Moerane, Mbeki's maternal grandfather, captured at his country estate, Mangoloaneng, beneath the Drakensberg in the Mount Fletcher district of the Transkei. Although the costumes are Edwardian, the year is, in fact, 1920. The Moerane patriarch wears the broad-brimmed hat, neatly trimmed beard, dark jacket, and waistcoat of a progressive squire. His wife, Sofi, has the homely demeanor of a squire's wife. Their four sons are dressed in what appears to be some kind of scout uniform: broad lapels, soft cloth caps, and square ties. There is something in the cocky poses of the two older boys, ages 12 and 10, that challenges the future from a position of absolute confidence. Their three daughters are in white calico confections: in the bottom right-hand corner is Epainette, a toddler, the sixth child of Jacane and Sofi Moerane, glowering beneath a floral coronet.

As she showed me the photograph, Aunt Norah ticked off the seven Moerane children. That's Daniel, he was a teacher and took over the farm once the old man died. That's Michael, the renowned educator and composer, the first black South African to qualify as a musicologist. That's Fraser, the first black South African to qualify as a mathematician. That's Manasseh (or "M. T."), Aunt Norah's own late husband, a school principal and the editor of South Africa's largest black newspaper. That's Mphuma, schoolteacher, stalwart of the liberation movement in Lesotho. That's Epainette, teacher, businesswoman, the second black woman to join the Communist Party of South Africa, wife of Govan Mbeki. That's Renee, one of the very first black women in South Africa to obtain a university degree.

There cannot be many black South Africans of Jacane Moerane's generation prosperous enough to be able to send all seven of his children to college. At the turn of the twenty-first century, his grandchildren included businesspeople and professionals, teachers and nurses: a senior health administrator in Washington, D.C., an engineer in Chicago, a senior

United Nations official in Geneva, a senior counsel in Durban, a president in Pretoria. As I looked through Norah Moerane's photos, I tried to superimpose this family's history on the limits that apartheid placed on black aspirations. To call the Moeranes middle class does not begin to appreciate their achievements, or their tribulations.

In the case of Epainette Mbeki, even the photo albums documenting her birthright were taken: brutal security police raids pillaged her home, as was done to many other activists. Thanks to Norah Moerane, however, I now have a record of a family before it was rent asunder: family portraits at Mangoloaneng; Epainette Moerane's wedding to Govan, a dashing, handsome man-about-town; Epainette as a young mother laden with infants, one of whom I was able to identify as her second child, Thabo, at six months. After years of research, this remains the sole image I have found of Thabo Mbeki before the age of 18.

The Moeranes are able to trace their direct ancestry back 15 generations. They are members of the Sotho-speaking Bafokeng, agriculturalists who farmed with iron equipment as early as the 1400s. Their clan, the Mahooana, were traditionally the doctors who officiated at the *lebollo* (circumcision) rituals; and in the mid-nineteenth century, when the king Moshoeshoe was consolidating his Basotho kingdom, Jacane's grandfather Moerane was one of the nation's most renowned healers: "Moerane" is actually the name of a small worm whose silk has powerful medicinal and spiritual value and is still used in the *lebollo* rituals.

Moshoeshoe is correctly regarded as Africa's first nationalist: He gathered together the disparate clans in the mountains of Lesotho in the mid-1800s, and forged them into the Basotho nation. Central to this national project was Christianity: Although he would not convert, he brilliantly used the missionaries' religion (and the literacy it brought) to forge a national identity. In such an environment, the choices facing a man such as the doctor Moerane were complex, and like many in the Bafokeng elite, he hedged: While his first son, Mokele, continued the family vocation of traditional medicine, his second son, Lenare, was sent to the mission station at Morija and given over to the Protestant Paris Evangelical Missionary Society (PEMS).

Lenare would marry the daughter of one of Morija's earliest and most celebrated converts. This man, whose name was Mokhanoi, is immortalized in a biography in the 1888 edition of the PEMS' annual *Journal des Missions Evangéliques*, written by the missionary Arbousset. There is something raffish, even louche, in the accompanying sketch of the convert; he has a hoop through a pierced left ear, and there is, on his right cheek, a prominent circular scar indicating his conversion to Christianity. In his compact, almost feminine features—his fluted nostrils, his rosebud of a mouth, those perfectly almond eyes that interrogate a future lying somewhere to the right of the page—he bears a strikingly intense resemblance to the young Thabo Mbeki.

Thabo Mbeki has a broken right molar, never repaired, which is—as we shall see—something of a war wound, a stigma of his activist past. His great-great-grandfather Mokhanoi gained *his* scar in a battle with a hyena, during which—on the verge of death—he heard the voice of the Lord. Arbousset's biography renders Mokhanoi the archetypal "noble savage," a rough man of the wilds replete with an inner goodness waiting to be released. The sole survivor of his family following a brutal massacre, he was recruited to act as a guide to the first group of PEMS missionaries traveling to the mountains to seek an audience with Moshoeshoe.

When the party finally arrived at Moshoeshoe's kingdom, Mokhanoi assisted the missionaries in the establishment of their station. On Easter Sunday 1841, he was baptized, only the twelfth Sotho to be converted; he took the name Zachea, and became a relentless, unforgiving evangelist. When villagers stoned him and attempted to chase him away because "we have our own gods," he sat down quietly, opened his Bible, and read them into submission. When his own nephew died, he insisted on giving him a Christian burial, over the opposition of the rest of the family, and won their trust by personally guarding the buried corpse against predators every night. "This humble Christian," writes Arbousset, "does not have a single chair in his house, but he has made for the church a little bench of willow-wood, and he often says that he himself is like a bench, hard and worm-eaten, hewn from the tree of a riverbank."

But just as there are hints of something unknowable and potentially dangerous lurking beneath the beauty of Arbousset's drawing of Mokhanoi, so, too, are there shards, in his narrative, of an inscrutable identity, one far beyond the author's ken: "I am the brother of the wolf," says Thabo Mbeki's great-great-grandfather, opaquely, to Arbousset. "We eat together."[1]

In his unpublished memoirs, M. T. Moerane recalls visiting the local shop at Mangoloaneng, all of ten years old, and overhearing two white men talking about him: "Isn't it a shame," one said to the other, "that such good English should come from such a primitive dress?" Moerane comments that "our standard dress, in which I was no different from my peers, including the herdboys, was the loincloth and blanket or sheepskin."[2] Epainette Mbeki confirmed to me that in her childhood, Western dress was worn for only three occasions: school, church, and photographs. Such families straddled the traditional and the Christian worlds far more than we imagine, for we are constrained by the fact that so much documentary evidence of their times was produced by their European interlocutors, thus reproducing only that side of their complex identities they wished the West to see of them.

All Govan and Epainette's children, Thabo included, believe they gained their politics more from their mother than from their father. How, I asked Epainette, did her upbringing at Mangoloaneng educate her? She replied that she only became aware of the budding politics of African nationalism when she went to train as a teacher, in the early 1930s, and she encountered discrimination and the color bar only when she was posted to teach at Heilbron, in the Orange Free State, in the late 1930s. When she grew up in the 1920s in Mangoloaneng, she said, she was entirely without a sense of racial or ethnic identity: "We were mixing mostly with Xhosas and Sothos. There was one Coloured family next door to us, and the whites who ran the shop. But we didn't take them as whites, because they spoke our language. And there was no sense of being oppressed or different at all. How could there be? At home we had so many cattle and so much milk that we would *sell* it to the white man!...He would drink from the pot, the same pot that we drank from. It was normal."

The Moeranes might have been converted to Christianity, but their proselytizers, unlike the Methodists or the Anglicans in the Eastern Cape, were not the agents of any colonial power. And so, unlike the Mbekis, the Moeranes were not colonial subalterns, and they had no experience whatsoever of having been colonized by Europeans. Until the Union of South Africa in 1910, their only fealty was to the Basotho king.

This did not, however, mean that they lived a traditional Basotho life. Jacane Moerane refused to send his sons off for the circumcision ritual, and—like Skelewu Mbeki in Mpukane—would not countenance the payment of a bridal dowry for his girl-children: "My parents didn't talk to us at all about our traditions, or our history as Basotho. Far more important to them was this Christianity business," Epainette Mbeki told me. The politics that she absorbed from her parents were not those of nationalism, or of grievance, but rather the egalitarianism and the impetus for social advancement that fired her father's evangelical mission: "These red [traditionally dressed] people would come home," recalls Mrs. Mbeki, "and my father just took them as ordinary people, so we grew up with that idea that one man is equal to another.... They took this thing seriously of all men being equal before God."

Thabo Mbeki's younger brother Moeletsi visited Mangoloaneng once, as a teenager, in 1962: "There was this enormous stone mansion of my grandparents, and this once-thriving dairy plant, and it was all crumbling away. It was horrendous to watch; there was a feel of it that was Chekhov or Dostoyevsky—the collapse of a grand country manor." Moeletsi's overriding memory is of his uncle—his mother's oldest brother—fighting with his son: "They were at each other's throats, trying to save the farm. The father was trying to save the son's birthright, and the potential loss of wealth was driving them literally crazy."

The policies of the "self-governing" Transkei bantustan collaborated in their impoverishment: the state moved over 50 people onto their property as part of its "rehabilitation" program. The program forcibly clustered Africans in Western-style settlements—supposedly to make it easier to provide services for them, but also to control and tap them for urban labor markets. But the consequence of this and other policies was overgrazing and erosion. And so, recalls Moeletsi, Uncle Daniel and his son Mokhele would get up at three in the morning to drive their cattle higher and higher, into the mountains, to find green pasture. The cattle were Jerseys, purchased and bred because they were better dairy producers than the indigenous Nguni, and thus the mark of Moerane prosperity and worldliness. But "because they were exotics, they couldn't handle the rocky terrain...and they would break their legs on these late-night drives. This is what my uncle and his son were fighting about."

In 1999, I traveled with Epainette Mbeki to the Mount Fletcher district of the Transkei, to visit Mangoloaneng. The homestead Jacane Moerane built was not quite the "mansion" of Moeletsi Mbeki's childhood memory, but it was impressive: three buildings—house, church, and school hall—radiating the honeyed stolidity of Drakensberg sandstone. We were greeted by Epainette's nephew, Majalla, who gave us a rundown of his village's woes: the increasing numbers who returned, having lost their jobs in the city (in whose number he—once a security guard in Johannesburg—counted himself); the cattle-raiders from across the border; the fallowness of the fields owing to lack of capital. To every question I asked, he replied with one word: "Rilithithithi." With the rich, country Sotho intonation of the mountains, he rolled the "r" and spat the "thi-thi-thi" out like machine-gun fire. It was a word he had adapted from the local vernacular. It means "nothingness," "pitch blackness," "darker than dark."

As in the Mbeki homestead down at Nyili, the rooms of the original Moerane homestead were filled with the jetsam of rural poverty, all in a sweaty fog of paraffin and coal smoke. There was a direct analogy here to the Mbeki oak table: a Hammond organ, with rotting and broken keys, lying beneath the junk, carrying the memories of the after-dinner recitals of Epainette Mbeki's youth. It was on this organ that Michael Moerane first began composing the works that made him famous.

I stood with Epainette Mbeki on the threshold and followed her outstretched arm across the grasslands. "*There* were the sorghum fields, and *there*, beyond, the apple orchard. Behind there was the dairy. The maize fields and the wheat fields were a good distance further. Down there was the sheep kraal; that's where we kept the cattle when they were not being grazed up at the mountains. And behind here—oh, the trees have been chopped down now—here was our own orchard." From 130 head of cattle, there are 6. Not a sheep, not a horse. Not a single growing thing—not a stalk of corn, not a tomato plant.

Govan Mbeki actually predicted such devastation, writing with astonishing prescience, in 1945, that settlements formed by policies such as "rehabilitation" would "create a hitherto unknown social group"—a rural proletariat, in effect, and that the villages would become no different from the "ancient markets of the Roman Empire where slaves were sold by public auction."[3] Like Skelewu Mbeki, Jacane Moerane attained his greatest prosperity after the promulgation of the Land Act. But its consequences slowly circumscribed the aspirations of black farmers to such a degree that not only did farming become untenable, but the will to farm—the ethos of self-reliance and initiative that men like Moerane and Mbeki embodied—itself was eroded.

Mrs. Mbeki and I left Mangoloaneng that evening under the dark cloud of her mood. She had run a meeting of villagers at the end of the day, and when I asked her how it went, she lashed out: "It's just too hopeless! I feel like giving up the fight. I was advising them about projects for income generation.... But they won't take it up, I can see.... My son Thabo always says to me, 'Mama, these people come to me for help, but I can't help them if they don't want to help themselves.' Thabo always says, when people complain, 'What are *you* doing about it?' And the answer, all too often, is nothing."

Rilithithithi.

3

THE NEW AFRICANS

There is a captivating image, in Norah Moerane's photo collection, of Govan Mbeki a-courting, standing in the middle of Beatrice Street in central Durban, outside Epainette Moerane's flat, sometime in the late 1930s. The photograph is yellowed and cracked, but nothing can wash the glinting optimism out of the smile that spreads across the young man's handsome, open face. With a jaunty homburg perched on his head, a pile of books and papers clutched under his left arm, and the wind blowing up his jacket to reveal a pair of stylish Oxford bags, he faces nothing less than a brave new future.

The photograph was taken in 1937, the year both Govan and Epainette moved to Durban; they met while teaching at Taylor Street Secondary School. It had been ten years since Govan Mbeki had left the family homestead at Nyili. He had completed his schooling at Healdtown and won a scholarship to Fort Hare, one of only 33 students afforded the privilege that year of entering South Africa's only university for blacks. After four years of study, he had graduated with a degree in political studies and psychology, a card proclaiming him a member of the African National Congress (ANC), a passion for ballroom dancing, a modest collection of Marxist literature, and a first-team rugby jersey.[1] He was among only 500 black students to have passed through Fort Hare in its 20-year history; 157 of them became teachers[2] and he joined their ranks, choosing a job at Taylor Street over the offer of his father's headmanship back home. Now, during his first year as a teacher, he had been hired to edit the *Territorial Magazine*, the only significant black-owned and -run newspaper in the country, and he was writing his first book, *Transkei in the Making*. He was 27 years old.

The object of his affection, Epainette Moerane, was a slight but headstrong young woman, over five years his junior. She had just graduated from Adams College, where she trained as a teacher and was head girl. Norah Moerane (née Fries)—soon to marry Epainette's brother—was her best friend at school, and remembers her as "an introvert, but very dynamic, very intelligent. With strong principles, that she sticks to. The most uncompromising person I had ever met." Epainette was to have gone abroad to study medicine: A teacher spotted her aptitude, and no doubt her humanity, and wished to sponsor her. But Epainette's father would not allow it, for he felt the family would not be able to afford the peripheral costs. And so she was sent to study teaching. Nonetheless, she had as much of a sense of destiny as her handsome suitor: Her family wished her to return to teach at Mangoloaneng, but she chose instead to take a job in Durban, "because I thought I was on a higher level."

By 1937, Epainette Moerane was a thoroughly modern, thoroughly independent woman: She had her own self-contained apartment in the hostel of the American Missionary Society, and when she was not teaching she was fully occupied with activist work. She volunteered for the Child Welfare Organization, she helped organize a rent boycott, and she was an agent for *Inkululeko*, the Communist Party newspaper. She also ran the party's night school—one of communism's most enduring legacies to South Africa, where thousands of illiterate black workers were taught to read.

The 1930s were a time when black South Africans of Govan Mbeki's class began to reject, forcefully, the colonial aspirations of their own parents; they discarded the identity of the "black Englishman"—which, ironically, gave them the personal autonomy to do so—and replaced it with that of the "New African," a phrase coined by H. I. E. Dhlomo, the preeminent black dramatist and essayist of the time. The New African, Dhlomo wrote, "knows where he belongs and what belongs to him; where he is going and how; what he wants and the methods to obtain it"; he was "proud, patriotic, sensitive, alive, and sure of himself and his ideas and ideals."[3] The New African might root himself proudly in the country-side of his parents, but he would take ownership, fully and confidently, of the city and all its promises of transformation. Govan and Epainette Mbeki came of age and came to political consciousness in this moment, a moment that also spawned the ANC Youth League, radical nationalism, home-grown *kwela* jazz, the zoot suit, the shebeen scene, an urban black proletariat, black trade unionism, and the modern South African liberation movement.

Subject to both the popular culture and the political ideologies emanating from black America, the New Africans of Govan and Epainette's generation claimed urban space in an entirely new way: They danced to jazz, they experimented with hairstyles, they mixed with whites as equals, they occupied South Africa's cities not as migrant laborers but as permanent residents. This urban world might have offered personal freedom—away from the constraints of family, church, and tradition—but it also threatened to corrupt, and this threat compelled African intellectuals to look both back to their home cultures and forward to an aggressive nationalist struggle that would restore self-worth. Seventy years later, Thabo Mbeki would mix a call for moral and political awakening with the need to forge identity and autonomy: "We speak about the need for the African Renaissance in part so that we ourselves, and not another, determine who we are, what we stand for, what our vision and hopes are, how we do things, what programmes we adopt to make our lives worth living, who we relate to and how."[4] In this he was very much the child of Govan and Epainette Mbeki: the child of the New Africanism of the 1930s and 1940s.

––––––––––––

Picture Govan Mbeki and Epainette Moerane, he as dashing as she is sensible; he in two-tone brogues, she in running shoes, her four feet three inches to his six foot one, reaching his chest as they walk down Beatrice Street, the heart of black Durban, on a Saturday evening. She has spent the afternoon coaching her girls on the tennis courts behind the Taylor Street School; he has been up to the press outside Verulam to check the pages of his magazine. He does not sleep: He teaches by day, is involved in political organizing in the evening, and only then, once others have gone home to their wives and their children, does he retire to his room to write his essays and edit his newspaper. But Govan Mbeki is also a bon vivant; he loves music and he loves dancing, and it is Saturday night, so he and Epainette go to the movies at one of the mixed-race cinemas on Victoria Street. Perhaps, after the film, they repair to one of Durban's legendary tearooms, Chili's Hotel on Grey Street, or Luthuli's, or the Ngoma Club.

Even now, ten years before the institution of apartheid, leisure time in Durban is segregated. Moneyed black people can attend the symphony concert, but they must sit separately. They can go to the movies, but only in certain theaters and at certain times. Liquor laws forbid black people to drink in any establishment other than the state-owned "native" drinking halls stuck inaccessibly away in the "native locations," but the teetotalling Mbekis can patronize establishments such as Chili's or Luthuli's to drink tea and chat with other young, politically engaged black professionals.

There was a particular openness to the young *izifundiswa*—"educated ones," as professionals like Govan and Epainette were known; an openness that was a product of the sense of opportunity with which they had been raised. They might have spent much of their time organizing workers in dimly lit tenement rooms, but their lives seemed illuminated by the perpetual glow of discovery. Govan became close to a black Edinburgh-trained physician, Dr. Innes Gumede, who introduced him to symphony concerts at the Durban city hall. At first, he recalls, he found the music "all a jumble of instruments played together, but over time...I really began to appreciate it, and I love it and listen to it [to this day]."[5]

One of Govan and Epainette's closest acquaintances was the glamorous Afrikaner trade unionist Bettie Du Toit, who had just returned from a trip to the Soviet Union and had come to Durban to help organize sugar workers.

"We became great friends, Bettie and I," Govan told me. "She would come to school in the afternoon and we would sit together. We would hug and kiss in public, and that was very unusual. Then I would take her back to her flat, walking hand in hand to get there."

Such public affection would have been an extraordinary spectacle in a provincial South African town in 1937; little wonder, then, that the couple soon attracted police attention—even though they had not broken any laws—and threats of intimidation. The way Govan tells it, he and Du Toit defied this intimidation, but Epainette remembers it differently: "The police got hold of him and told him that 'young white people are going to shoot you, because you are dating with a white woman.' And so he said, 'Well, Bettie, we'd better meet indoors from now on—at Piny's [Epainette's] flat!'"

If there was a love triangle at play, Epainette gives no sign that she had a problem with it. In fact, it was Du Toit who recruited 18-year-old Epainette into the Communist Party in 1938, and she recognizes the trade unionist as having played the key role in her coming to political consciousness. "Before I met her, the only white women I knew were my teachers, and naturally they had the attitude of teachers. Now when I meet Bettie, here's a white woman who takes me as an equal, who can sit down with me, who drinks my tea."

From the time of her recruitment, Epainette's primary allegiance has always been to the Communist Party. This was not so much for ideological reasons, but largely because she was attracted to its practical work, "the bread and butter of things," as she put it to me: its night schools, its mobilization of workers, its newspapers and pamphleteering. This activity was, in the 1930s at least, in sharp contrast to the dormancy of the ANC. Epainette is practical before she is intellectual, and the Communist Party gave her something to *do*.

Epainette and Govan arrived in Durban at a particularly volatile time. In 1936, the "Hertzog Bills" of Prime Minister J. B. M. Hertzog were passed— four acts that effectively disenfranchised educated Africans in the Cape and limited economic growth even more severely in the native reserves, ring-fencing the aspirations of elites like the Moeranes and the Mbekis. This was the moment of truth for black South Africans of Govan and Epainette's class and generation: 1936 was the year, Govan Mbeki has said, "that decided the future course of most of us."[6]

After a long dormancy in the 1920s and 1930s, African nationalist politics gathered new energy: the ANC Youth League was formed in 1943, attracting angry young men such as Nelson Mandela, Walter Sisulu, and Oliver Tambo. The league's prime mover was Anton Lembede, a brilliant young lawyer with stern morals and evangelical tendencies, who saw redemption for his people in a return to African values. What differentiated Lembede's philosophy from that of his elders was a faith not only in revolutionary militancy but also in racial exclusivism: Africa, the league declared, was "a Black man's country."[7]

Lembede's ideas came from his reading of the writings by African American W. E. B. Du Bois and Jamaican Marcus Garvey, and had their South African roots in a seminal speech by the lawyer Pixley ka Seme, who had, as a young firebrand in 1906, called for the "regeneration" of the African continent: "I am an African, and I set my pride in my race over against a hostile public opinion."[8] Many years later, Thabo Mbeki would place himself squarely in this Seme-Lembede tradition: "I am an African," he said in 1996, quoting Seme directly, in what has become his most celebrated speech, at the adoption of the new democratic constitution.[9] His particular combination of a call for an African Renaissance and for the moral reawakening of a dissolute people comes straight out of Lembede's mystical, prophetic writings.

Lembede would write in 1946 that "moral degradation is assuming alarming dimensions" and that this degradation "manifests itself in such abnormal and pathological phenomena as a loss of self-confidence, inferiority complex, a feeling of frustration, the worship and idolisation of whiteness, foreign leaders and ideologies."[10] Thabo Mbeki, too, spoke often about the pathological self-hate of the black South African, a "slave mentality" the extent of which, he told me, shocked him upon his return to the country in the 1990s. The corrective proposed by Lembede in the 1940s—one developed by the ANC Youth League, advanced in different ways by the Pan Africanist Congress and student leader Steve Biko's Black Consciousness movement, and then reclaimed by Mbeki—was an aggressive nationalism that would restore to Africans their sense of self-worth and dignity.

The Youth League was virulently opposed to the Communist Party, which it accused of foisting on the African majority not only foreign European ideologies but non-African leadership as well. It tried repeatedly to expel communists from the ANC, and Nelson Mandela was in his youth perhaps its most notorious red-baiter. Certainly there were troublesome racial dynamics in the Communist Party: While the vast majority of the party's membership was African, the leadership remained overwhelmingly white and Indian. The party had waged a long and bloody internecine war over race; there had been purges and counterpurges and even disappearances in Siberia in the battle over whether it should advocate a "native republic" or stick to class struggle. But, despite these tensions, the Communist Party of South Africa remained the only political forum where blacks and whites could work together as equals: It was the crucible of the unique "nonracialism" of the South African liberation movement.

Govan Mbeki was never part of the Youth League that would so strongly influence his son's politics. But even if he was often at loggerheads with the fiery young nationalists in the league, he was by no means immune to the spirit of Africanism in the air at the time. He dedicated *Transkei in the Making* to "the youth of my race" and changed the name of *The Territorial Magazine* to *Inkundla ya Bantu* (The People's Forum), explaining that "our duty has always been, ever is, and always shall be to the African people."[11] In 1941, he launched a new regular feature in the magazine, entitled "The Gallery of African Heroes," to which Epainette would occasionally contribute anonymously.[12]

Epainette Mbeki tells a revealing story about her children's baptism, which demonstrates not only that she and her husband were never to jettison fully their Christian roots but that Govan, at this time, was more driven by the spirit of Africanism than he might later have cared to admit. The Mbeki family was traditionally Methodist, but the only Methodist ministers available to baptize their two younger children—born in 1945 and 1948— were white, "and my husband said, 'No, I will not have my child baptized by a white man!' So they had to go to an Anglican."

Unlike Epainette, who was primarily a communist, Govan saw being a member of the ANC as his primary identification, one that subsumed his belief in communism. He would have in all likelihood agreed with Moses Kotane, the most prominent African member of the Communist Party, who wrote in 1939 that "I am first a native and then a communist... I am born an African with a black skin and inherit all the sufferings and indignities inflicted on my people, whether I like it or not. I cannot escape from being black. But I became a communist by conviction."[13] No statement gives greater insight into the dual legacy of Africanism and communism that Thabo Mbeki was to inherit, and into the decisions he was to make, in the 1980s and 1990s, to jettison his allegiance to communism and to declare the "African Renaissance" the official ideology of his presidency.

In January 1940, Govan Mbeki and Epainette Moerane married, at Mangoloaneng, and moved back to the Transkei of their birth. By this time, Mbeki was studying for his second bachelor's degree, in economics, via correspondence from the University of South Africa. Of the 8,000 Africans registered as teachers, he was one of only 14 with a university degree[14] and the only one qualified to teach psychology. Very few black South Africans were as employable as he and his wife, and the decision of two such educated sophisticates to leave the city—with all its transformative and revolutionary possibilities—and to return to the countryside appears, at first glance, quite startling.

Why, I asked Govan Mbeki, did he make such a decision? He replied by referring me to a passage in *Transkei in the Making*, where he lambasts Fort Hare graduates who obtain scholarships from the Transkei territorial government (as he did) and then flee the countryside for the city: What was "the purpose of educating these young fellows" if they were not to come home and apply the knowledge they had acquired "at so much public cost"? And so he jumped at the opportunity to teach at Clarkebury, the Methodist teachers' training college in the Transkei, if for no other reason than to prove an ideological point he had already committed to print.

Govan found the conservative countryside more difficult than he imagined, and the Clarkebury principal had it in for him from the start. "Before he even offered me a seat on the day I arrived," recalled Mbeki, "he said, 'Have you abandoned your communistic ideas?' I felt insulted! I had been employed because I was the only person in the whole country qualified for the job." Mbeki exacerbated matters by regularly absenting himself from church and refusing to take communion, and by spending his weekends doing political mobilization rather than coaching the students at sports, as was expected of him. He was fired after 18 months, on the pretext that he refused to lead his students in prayer at the beginning of class.

Clearly, he all but instigated his dismissal. He had become involved with a group of young Transkei intellectuals turned on by the idea of cooperative societies as a means for rural development, the vogue in leftist thinking in Europe at the time, and were determined to apply it to the Transkei. The ideology of self-help is at the root of nineteenth century African nationalism—specifically in organizations like the Zenzele movement, of which both Epainette and her mother were stalwarts, and in African breakaways from the church, such as the Order of Ethiopia and Independent Methodists; it took hold again in the late 1930s, now with a Marxist application.

Fired from Clarkebury, Govan received immediate offers to teach at both Lovedale and Adams, but turned them down to blaze a trail in the wilderness in the Idutywa district. There a local politician found a job for Govan on the Idutywa Cattle-Dipping Committee while he attempted to start his own cooperative society, the basis of which would be a rural general dealer's store. For a black man to start a business in the Transkei in 1940 was no easy matter. Africans could open trading stores as long as they were not within five miles, by the shortest route, of any of the 700 white-owned shops currently in business[15]; by 1941, only a few dozen licenses had been granted to African traders, none in the Idutywa district. Mbeki eventually determined that there was a space for the shop at the village of Mbewuleni, on the road between Idutywa and Engcobo. He put together a consortium of investors and applied for a license.

Mbeki originally intended to erect the shop on the main road, on the gqoboka (Christian) side of the village, where there would be more traffic. But the nearest white storekeeper, a Mr. Lyndhurst, complained that this would be in violation of the five-mile rule, so Mbeki applied to put his shop farther down in the village. Another white trader objected, and the license Mbeki was finally granted permitted him to trade only on the *qaba* (traditional) side, in Kwa-Tenza. The shop was the first black-owned enterprise in the Idutywa district, and the first black-owned cooperative store in all Transkei.

By becoming a black rural trader, Mbeki was disrupting a very powerful and very established relationship between modern white capital and black precolonial society. Protected by monopolies, traders were at the same time the sole purchasers of agricultural produce, the sole sellers of manufactured and dry goods, and the sole creditors available to rural black people in the Transkei. They were also recruiting agents for the mines, an activity that generated most of their income: They were paid per man but were subject to a financial penalty if they did not provide the agreed quota of able-bodied workers per year. To reach this quota, they often stimulated recruitment through active debt inducement: offering loans and credits to their black customers and then forcing them into migrant labor when they defaulted.[16]

And yet trading stores became nothing less than the community centers of rural black life, and—in the beginning at least—Govan Mbeki made the most of this. A 1941 article in Mbeki's newspaper, *Inkundla ya Bantu,* describes the new proprietor of the Mbewuleni store thus:

> The man behind the counter has much work, wrapping, weighing, cutting, measuring, selling, persuading and last but not least, speaking to the people. His is a strenuous job, he must speak to the people about their lowly location affairs in a friendly spirit, encourage them in their undertakings, and some- times he is even asked to give a review of the international situation. This store has the fortune of being run by a man interested in the people and in world affairs as well, so he is at no loss under the circumstances.[17]

This article is without a byline but it was probably written by Mbeki him- self, so perfectly does it embody his self-image and his credo. He purveys not only dry goods but new ideas; like their parents and grandparents before them, but with a very different agenda, he and his wife are nothing less than evangelists, bringing progress and enlightenment, communism and com- modities, a vision of New Africa, to the rural poor.

4

MBEWULENI

"A PLACE OF SEED"

In one of his more arresting images, Thabo Mbeki referred to the almond-and-thornbush hedge that was planted by the Cape's first white settler, Jan van Riebeeck, in 1652, "to ensure the safety of the newly arrived white European settlers by keeping the menacing black African hordes of pagan primitives at bay." As Mbeki put it: "Black and white had to be kept apart, circumscribed by an equation which described each as the enemy of the other, each the antithesis of the other." Mbeki was speaking to the Report of the Truth and Reconciliation Commission in parliament in February 1999; that almond hedge, he said, has existed throughout the three and a half centuries that whites have settled southern Africa. It surrounded the native reserves; it separated black townships from white suburbs; during the years of apartheid repression its thorns were "the bannings and the banishment, the torture, the assassinations, the massacres, the weapons of mass destruction and the sustained propaganda and indoctrination."[1]

Being South African has meant, always, the perpetual negotiation of frontiers, the marking of territories, us and them, the known and the unknown, the safe and the fearful. And on my trips to the Transkei, as I visited the birthplaces of Thabo Mbeki and his parents, it occurred to me that the Mbeki dynasty itself had come into being on that very almond-and-thornbush hedge. Thabo Mbeki's grandparents, his parents, himself: All three generations were born and bred on the frontier between two civilizations, two ways of being, and if, during his years of public life, it sometimes seemed that Thabo Mbeki was too acutely aware of the hedge that divided South Africa, perhaps it is because it was lodged so deep in his own psyche. He could see it as few others could, for he was born amid the sweetness of its blossoms and the sharpness of its thorns.

———————

When they set up shop in Mbewuleni in 1940, Govan and Epainette Mbeki built their homestead high on a hill at the entrance to the *qaba* (traditional) side of the village, looking across the dry riverbed to the corrugated-zinc schoolroom and the *gqoboka* (Christian) homesteads beyond. They were thus at the frontier of Western civilization and traditional Xhosa culture, directly between the school—the last outpost of civilization to the west—and the traditional people to the east. In Mpukane to the south and Mangoloaneng to the north, virtually the entire communities had become Christian during the eras of Skelewu Mbeki and Jacane Moerane. At Mbewuleni, however, most remained tied to traditional authority and animist religion. There were literally two worlds, two ways of being, living side by side. Even today, the social topography of Mbewuleni is deeply inscribed upon the landscape. The dry riverbed still separates *qaba* from *gqoboka*, "traditional" from "Christian," even though these days the division is far more about class than about creed.

With money lent by comrades, Govan supervised the building of a large, rectangular five-room house. Across the back, facing the *qaba* village, was the shop. Through a door behind the counter you entered the Mbeki living area of four rooms. In time, three conical thatch-roofed huts would be added, and Epainette would create a prickly-pear border against stray cattle and goats and plant corn, cabbage, and tomatoes.

The Mbekis paid £3 a year for a general dealer's license and another £2 for a patent medicine license, allowing them to sell the regular sixpenny line of teething powders, painkillers, castor oil, cough mixtures, and the like. As the shop grew, the Mbekis expanded their line to include clothing and blankets.[2] Olive Mpahlwa, the daughter of the local schoolmaster who would become Thabo Mbeki's teenage sweetheart and the mother of his child, recalls that you could see the shop "from miles off, all whitewashed among the mud huts, like a beacon of light." For Moeletsi Mbeki, the shop was "big, bustling, rambling, the center of small-town life.... There were agricultural equipment outside, piles of grey blankets stacked to the ceiling, bags of maize, people coming and going." It was a credit bureau, a postal agency, a place where you would come for advice, where you would have your letters read and written, first by Govan and Epainette, and later by the Mbeki children.

But it soon became clear to the Mbekis that the Transkei to which they had returned was very different from the one into which they had been born. The state's native reserves policies had all but collapsed the rural peasant economy that had provided the comforts of their own childhoods. These were the war years too, boom years for the white South African economy, and thus there was more call than ever for migrant workers. New legislation eroded the rural black agricultural economy entirely, rendering the Transkei little more than a reservoir of cheap labor. Malnutrition and illnesses such as tuberculosis were endemic, and the authorities themselves reported that the majority of the population was living "very much below the bread line."

In such an environment, the odds were severely stacked against a trading store owned by a black man without collateral or a credit record, or the willingness to be a recruitment post for the mines. And once it became clear that his store would not succeed, Govan Mbeki lost interest and found other arenas for his irrepressible desire to reform and organize the territory of his birth. Ever since his return to the Transkei in 1939 he had been intimately involved in local politics, and it was to this that his interests now turned fully. The Transkei, he wrote to the new African National Congress president, Dr. A. B. Xuma, in 1941, was "in midnight slumber." His plan was to awaken it.[3] The upsurge of militancy in the 1940s was an almost entirely urban one. There was, however, a parallel (if more modest) radicalization in rural politics, one brought about by men like Govan Mbeki. And it worked along the vector of commerce: Together with a Fort Hare classmate who had set up shop in a nearby village, Mbeki became an agent for Prosperity Insurance. The two men acquired a two-tone blue Nash car, and selling insurance to well-to-do Africans provided them with a perfect alibi for cross-country mobilization and the recruitment of people into the ANC.

Govan Mbeki's political activities in the 1940s were such that he was hardly ever in Mbewuleni. And on the rare occasions he was around, he was more often than not holed up in the hut that served as his study: He was still a prolific journalist and pamphleteer. And so the responsibility for running the shop, and for raising their four children, fell to Epainette. Linda, their only daughter, was born in 1941; Thabo, on June 18, 1942; then Moeletsi and Jama in 1945 and 1948.

When we met in 2000, three years before her death, Thabo Mbeki's older sister gave me a powerful memory of her brother's early childhood. Father and son, she told me, would sit together conspiratorially in Govan's study-hut. "I would often see them there, poring over documents. They weren't newspapers, and you knew they were dangerous, because they would be hidden when you came in. Mommy would be busy in the shop, and I'd be back from school, doing housework, and Thabo would be in the room with my father. This was from a very young age." There is something in this image of induction that encapsulates the nature of Thabo Mbeki's patrimony: Completing the revolutionary work of his father was their only emotional connection.

Linda was the only Mbeki child who did not become involved in politics. Diffident and hardworking (she ran a tavern in Butterworth), she lived her life, with great resentment, in the shadow of the public lives of her father and brother; in 1976 she spent a year in detention for no other reason than that her surname was Mbeki. Epainette's own intellectual and political life, too, became seriously constrained after she married, because of her need to keep the shop running and to raise the children. Communism had initially attracted her, at least in part, because of the possibilities it gave women to work side by side with their male comrades; clearly, a more conventional gender regime crept into the Mbeki marriage once it relocated to Mbewuleni.

———————

What links Thabo Mbeki to his parents and grandparents is not just a missionary zeal and an impulse to progress, but also the notion that work is a form of redemption. "Life wouldn't be life for them without work," Olive Mpahlwa said to me. "They know no other life. I don't mean to say that they hide behind it, but I do see that it's good for them, because it does take them away from every other problem." Growing up in Mbewuleni, the Mbeki children were, like their parents, always busy: If they were not doing their schoolwork, they were doing housework or helping in the shop. Clothes had to be washed and ironed—by the children themselves—every day after school; each had a wooden box in which possessions were stored and which had to be kept immaculate. With his characteristic hint of mischief, Govan Mbeki told me how "Thabo was a voracious reader, and for that reason he was not popular with my wife, [who] felt he spent too much time at books and did not help in domestic chores. 'That son of yours,' she would complain to me, 'he's just like his father!'"

In much the way she had been brought up in Mangoloaneng, Epainette Mbeki governed her brood with a combination of discipline and openness. "My children did well in school because they knew I would not take failure lightly," she recalled. "Even when they were very young—Jama could not have been more than two or three—I would collect the four of them together and say, 'Listen here, children...if any one of you does not wish to go to school, you should tell me now. If any one of you wishes rather to go and work on the mines, or to work for white people in their kitchen, rather go now and do not waste my money. There's the door!'"

Epainette Mbeki's love was a tough one that made little concession to a child's need for play and fantasy: The world she wished her children to occupy was free of the affect, both the fear and whimsy, the ghosts and fairy tales, that conventionally populate childhood—and of the religious beliefs that animate rural African life. Witches and demons are very much part of the Xhosa cosmos, but Epainette Mbeki would have none of them: She deliberately terrorized her children by striding fearlessly through gullies reputedly populated by dog-demons and would sometimes deliberately fabricate tasks that forced them to pass trees during the night where witches were feared to reside, so as to exorcise them of irrational fears.

The Mbeki children were taught "to communicate freely, but always with respect," recalls Fezeka Mabona, an Mbeki relative brought up by Epainette. Once Mrs. Mbeki chastised her grandson Kwanda—Thabo's son, whom she also raised—for becoming too heated in an argument: "You can debate as much as you like," she told him, "but you are *never* to point a finger at me. You are to use your ideas, not your body, if you wish to fight me."

Most villagers remember two things about the Mbekis: that Govan's two-tone blue Nash was the only motorcar in Mbewuleni, and that their home was filled with books. According to Govan, the library was "small, but significant. There were novels, the English poets, quite a few Marxist books." These children were not reared on *Biggles*: "The very first book I ever attempted to read," recalls Moeletsi Mbeki, "was a Maxim Gorky novel, which I pulled off my father's bookshelf." The volumes his older brother pulled off the bookshelf in his early teens included Dostoyevsky's *Crime and Punishment*, a biography of the Ghanaian educator James Aggrey, and Bunyan's *Pilgrim's Progress*.[4]

During his presidency, Thabo Mbeki's intellect was marked, often to a fault, by perpetual questioning. When I asked him about the roots of this intellectual approach, he went straight back to his parents: "You see, we grew up with books around the home, and whenever we were together with the parents...you could say anything, and it would be discussed." If you are brought up with books, he believes, "you begin soon enough to understand that there are many ideas in the world, and that it's not shameful not to know about something. In fact, it would be shameful if you didn't try and find out." He did not say it to me specifically, but he was clearly signifying his reasons for plunging so deeply—and so controversially—into the science around the etiology of AIDS, as is explored later in this book.

Thabo Mbeki began his education in the one-roomed hall that was the village schoolroom. His mother recalls that her son "didn't have many friends of his age. Let me say he was not very communicative. On the reserved side." She remembers him, from the age of six, rushing to the wireless whenever he heard the radio news. If she asked him what he was listening to, he would reply, "World affairs, Mommy. You wouldn't understand." Her son, she says, "had grown-up ideas from a very young age. I don't know how he sucked them from us."

But if Thabo was to be found sitting in the shop after school rather than running around the village with his agemates, this was only in part a function of his solitary and introverted nature. It was also largely due to his upbringing: all of Epainette's children had a reputation in the village for staying very close to their mother's skirts. For even though the Mbeki family had "crossed over" onto the *qaba* side, they had not—for want of a better phrase—"gone native." "There was to be no lolling about the village with other boys," Mrs. Mbeki says firmly. "No aimless roaming about. The idea of football clubs was not acceptable either. They were to come straight home after school, or to a couple of families we were friendly with, and that's all." These families were, of course, other educated *gqoboka* families like the Mpahlwas.

The Mbekis might have lived on the wrong side of the dry riverbed, but they nonetheless formed part of a powerful network of learned, Christian families. Epainette would take her children to church every Sunday morning, "not for any religious reasons, but for the cultural ones." Of course, given their class, the Mbekis had more in common with the people they met in church or at political meetings than with their customers and neighbors. Like other educated families, they sent their children on second-class tickets to boarding school, they ate cheese, they used cutlery, they read the *Daily Dispatch*, they motored down to the seaside for holidays in large family cars. But whereas other Christians disparaged illiterate peasants, the egalitarian Mbekis adulated them. Govan could often be seen singing and practicing traditional dances with his neighbors outside the shop; Epainette Mbeki made extra money by sewing up traditional *icayi* skirts. These activities were embraced, quite deliberately, to make the point that traditional custom was legitimate.

But therein lay a paradox, one articulated clearly to me by Linda Jiba's memory of what their mother would say to them if they complained about going to school: "If you don't go, you are going to grow up to be...like *them!*" Epainette had a very clear sense of her children's destiny being different to those of the villagers around them, even as she insisted on respecting them and educating them. This could not but "disconnect" the Mbeki children—to use Thabo Mbeki's language—from their environment, placing them in a no-man's land between the two cultures: they were able to mix in both worlds but belonged, ultimately, to neither.

Epainette Mbeki describes her son, no more than seven years old, behind the counter of the shop: "There are no customers, so of course Thabo opens his book. Someone enters. If it's a *gqoboka* [educated] somebody, he attends politely to that person but gets straight back to the book as quickly as possible. But the moment a 'red' [traditional] person comes in, he puts his book down and they go on communicating, for ages, about this, that and the other. The person feels free."

This memory moves Epainette Mbeki deeply: "When he speaks, now, about 'the poorest of the poor,' it's because of his experiences in the shop. That's where he discovered that these people need to be uplifted. That's his"—she struggles to continue, but eventually finds an immensely revealing word—"his ministry."

As a young boy, Thabo was a letter-reader and letter-writer for the illiterate adults in his community, privy to all the news communicated between migrant laborers in the cities and the people they left back home: their emotional pains and marital infidelities, their physical hardships, their longings, their aspirations and the impossibilities of ever attaining them. He was by no means the only child in the Transkei who read and wrote letters for illiterate peasants—his contemporary and rival in the ANC, Chris Hani, was doing the same thing at the same time in another part of the Transkei. But Mbeki seems to have responded to it in a particularly intense way.

His mother recalls that he once came to her and said, "Mama, I should not be reading other people's letters"; "I told him it was fine," she says, "as long as he kept their confidence." He thus carried, at an unnaturally early age, the burden of confidentiality. Imagine being seven years old, reading to a distraught woman that her mineworker husband has died of lung disease; or taking dictation, from a mother to her migrant son, that his wife is pregnant with another man's child, and then reading back to the wife her husband's chastisement.

Both Mbeki's parents told me that they believed this had a profound effect on him. Not only did he come to understand, in a powerful and subjective way, just how tragically the migrant labor system warped the lives of rural black people, but he was, his father said, "hearing about things at an age when [he] should not have been." The experience, his father believed, robbed him of his childhood.

If Govan Mbeki is correct, and Thabo Mbeki was indeed forced by his circumstances to grow up very quickly, then this must also have been because of his early understanding of the dangerous life his father led—and thus because of the attendant responsibilities he thus took on, as the eldest Mbeki son. The trade unionist and veteran communist Ray Alexander, a close comrade of Govan Mbeki, told me once about her memories of visiting the Mbeki shop in 1950: "There, [sitting] behind the counter, was a little boy whose feet did not even touch the floor. 'Where's your father?' I asked, but he would not tell me. He was so serious, and he knew not to trust a stranger, particularly not a white one."

How does one begin to assess the effects on this perceptive little boy of the weight of the understanding of his family's precarious condition, coupled as it was with the acute human suffering that he observed in his role as letter-writer? If Govan Mbeki's mode of revolutionary behavior was passionate and even somewhat reckless, then Thabo's would be exactly the opposite: He would carry on the fight, but with the diligence and caution of an eldest son who lives with the perpetual fear that his parents will be taken away from him. His lifelong commitment to struggle would be one of joyless responsibility.

5

FAMILY

"What a joy it is to be alive these days when history is being made all around us." Govan Mbeki wrote these words to the African National Congress president, Dr. A. B. Xuma, in 1946, paraphrasing one of his favorite Wordsworth verses.[1] But the pleasures Mbeki took in his political activism do not appear to have been matched, at all, by those of domesticity: "We didn't have fun, not at all," he told an interviewer in 1992, when asked about his family life in the Transkei, resorting once more—as he habitually did at moments of stress or emotion—to English poetry, this time Rossetti: "Does the road wind uphill all the way?" "Well," he said, "the road that was going uphill all the time was our marriage."[2]

Perhaps Mbeki used his activism to take him away from an unhappy marriage and the difficulties of his Mbewuleni enterprise. Epainette Mbeki found herself in an isolated and undeveloped corner of the Transkei, miles away from family or friends, with a largely absent husband, a business to run, and—by 1948—four children under the age of seven. This at the same time that the Nationalist Party (NP) government began its aggressive program not only of segregation but of political suppression. The NP had won the 1948 general election in no small part by enlisting the aid of the communist bogeyman. In 1950 it passed the Suppression of Communism Act, which made the party illegal and gave the state the power to declare any kindred organizations unlawful, to "name" members of such organizations, and to remove them from any political or social activity. This act had a direct effect on the Mbekis' lives: The newspapers on which Govan served were banned, thereby depriving him of a small but dependable income, and Epainette Mbeki was also "named," making it all but impossible for her to seek any form of paid employment.

Family legend has it that Govan Mbeki left the Transkei to take a teaching post in Ladysmith following two devastating acts of God. In the summer of 1954, a tornado blew the roof off the Mbewuleni shop and destroyed all the dry goods; the following year, a fire gutted the premises. Like most black traders, the Mbekis were not insured. To make matters worse, the tornado struck just after Epainette had returned from her mailbox in Idutywa, laden with remittances from migrant laborers to their families, all of which were destroyed. The Mbekis found themselves, overnight, with no goods and in heavy debt to their customers. But the shop's financial difficulties and the problems in the Mbeki household long predated these natural disasters; Govan Mbeki had in fact already left home when they happened. Despite the illusion of prosperity, Mbeki found himself by 1950 on the verge of bankruptcy.

The Mbekis were caught in the double bind familiar to many black traders: too close to their black customers to exploit them; too distant from their white suppliers to ask for favors. But it was not just the shop's failure that plunged the family into financial difficulty. Govan had fallen out with his political comrades in the Transkei and resigned from the Bhunga—the territory's parliament—thereby losing a dependable annual income, and had also entered into two disastrous business ventures: a store in a neighboring village, and a tearoom in Idutywa, both of which collapsed.

And so, at the end of 1952, Epainette Mbeki made up her mind to leave Mbewuleni: " 'I can't tolerate this any longer. I'm a qualified teacher. I'm going to teach,' " she said to her husband, offering to "take the children or leave them, as you please." When he argued against breaking up the family she decided to consult the children, ranging in ages 5 to 12, themselves: "I called them together and I said to them, 'Look, you see things are not proper. I'm opting out. I'm going home.' The older three were quiet, but Jama piped in. 'Have you got a mother?' he asked. I said, 'No.' 'And your father?' 'You know, my child, that I do not have a father.' He says, 'What's at home for you then? Your nephews will be excited that you are bringing provisions home, but after two or three days you'll be a burden.' The others just kept quiet, but Jama said, 'No, Ma, you'd better stay with us.' So I stayed."

And Govan Mbeki left: first to Ladysmith, where he taught for one and a half years before being fired once more for political activism, and then to Port Elizabeth, where he worked as an ANC organizer and an editor for the liberation journal *New Age*, reviving his career as an activist of national importance. He was never to return to Mbewuleni.

That apartheid is the villain in the breakup of the Mbeki family, as in the breakup of so many African families during the course of the twentieth century, is a given. The new order made it more difficult than ever for African families to stay together, and certainly the system played a role in ensuring that Govan Mbeki left Mbewuleni without his wife and family in 1953. Not only might the Mbekis have forfeited all property rights had Epainette accompanied him, but the new legislation would have declared her an "illegal squatter" outside the Transkei unless she was gainfully employed herself—an increasingly unlikely situation, given that she was now a listed communist. But Govan Mbeki made the decision to leave the Transkei not only because the family financial situation dictated it but because he had reached a dead end there: politically, financially, and domestically.

———————

"Family life suffers" if you are a revolutionary, Govan Mbeki told me. "If you don't live with your family, there's so much your family has to learn to live without. Especially your wife. Sexual relations are broken, and because your wife is not certain what you're doing... [she] becomes jealous. This man leaves without even having his dinner and comes back after midnight. It arouses suspicion, unfair suspicion." Then, when the children ask where their father is, "the mother says, 'I don't know.' That must have had an effect on them."

Govan Mbeki once told an interviewer that he "never really had time for the children. Not that I didn't like them, not that I didn't love them. But I was doing writing and reading so I didn't have time to be playing about with them. I pushed them to their mother. I do not know how they feel today. Probably they feel that I didn't pay sufficient attention to them as children. I can't blame them if they feel like that."[3]

Unlike Govan Mbeki, Nelson Mandela has publicly castigated himself for not having been a better parent and husband. His biographer Anthony Sampson writes that Mandela "blames himself" for the fact that he had "sacrificed" his family "for his political purpose" and says that he underwent some kind of redemptive process while in jail: "He learned about human sensitivities and how to handle the fears and insecurities of others, including his Afrikaner warders. He was sensitised by his own sense of guilt about the family and friends he had used during his political career."[4] It was this sensitization, says Sampson, that led to Mandela's extraordinary capacity for reconciliation upon his release.

Perhaps it is unfair to compare Govan Mbeki and Nelson Mandela: The latter's life project of personal reconciliation is unique, and Govan Mbeki was far more typical of his class and of his generation in not going through a similar process of remorse—and thus self-knowledge. Unlike Mandela, who after his release talked either with sadness or with love about his family, Govan Mbeki carried, to his death, deep and unresolved emotions on the subject, emotions he found hard to articulate.

Govan Mbeki was as ideological and intellectual as Mandela was intuitive and emotional. He found impenetrable refuge in the struggle, with its Marxist understanding of affective family relationships as sentimental, bourgeois, and ultimately distracting from the revolutionary matter at hand; of "the family" as a political rather than a biological unit. When I asked him, for example, how he coped with the fact that both his youngest son, Jama, and his grandson, Kwanda (Thabo's son), disappeared without a trace while supposedly in exile in the 1980s, he responded once more with literature. He could not remember the exact lines of the poem, but he was clear on the sentiment: "When you go into war, if your comrade in front of you falls off his horse, you must not stop and weep. You jump over him into battle. You learn not to weep."

Similarly, when Govan Mbeki went off with other members of the internal leadership in January 1990 to meet the ANC-in-exile in Lusaka, he was asked by a reporter at Johannesburg's Jan Smuts airport how he felt about seeing his son Thabo. "Not much finer than seeing the others," he retorted. "You must remember that Thabo Mbeki is no longer my son. He is my comrade!"[5] A son is a mere biological appendage; to be called a comrade, on the other hand, is the highest honor.

The Mbeki children were brought up to understand, from a very early age, that it was "the system" that was the villain and not their father, and to believe that if they had lost their father to the struggle, this was because he was liberating their people, and thus themselves. But even if their diffidence and discipline prohibited them from articulating it, the acceptance of such an explanation could not have come without emotional cost. Robyn Slovo, the youngest daughter of South African freedom fighters Joe Slovo and Ruth First, has spoken about how she experienced something similar: to express fear or to ask "What about me?" was not only "extremely weak" but actually "injurious" to her parents, because it weakened their commitment to struggle by forcing them to pay attention to their own children. Her own pain had "no validity.... There are always others worse off than you are."[6]

The Mbeki children were not only taught the same thing, but they witnessed it daily, by living amid the poverty of the *amaqaba* in Mbewuleni. The pain of the family breakup remained invalidated; so many other children were far worse off. What do you do with your own pain if you are not permitted to articulate it?

Perhaps one strategy is to slot it into the freedom fighter mythology that your parents have provided for you, and Thabo Mbeki has been adept at this. He was sent away to live with his uncle in Queenstown in 1951 at the age of eight, and he understands this solely as a function of his parents' political activism. He and his siblings did not grow up at home, Thabo has said, "because there was a decision taken by both parents... that sooner or later... one or both of them would be arrested and possibly sentenced to long periods, and therefore that it was necessary that the children should learn to grow up without them."[7]

But in fact an absence of educational facilities in Mbewuleni was the driving cause for his move to Queenstown. The Mbekis believed it made sense to get their children into more formal schools as early as possible, and in this respect, the Mbeki children were little different from most other *gqoboka* families—or white farming families, for that matter—who lived in the countryside and sent their children away to school. Instead of offering this simple explanation (or the more difficult one about his parents' broken marriage and financial difficulties), Mbeki says that his parents sent him away because of the dangers and the uncertainties arising out of their involvement in the struggle. Of course there is some truth to this: Govan and Epainette *were* in danger because of their activism, and they *did* believe in self-sufficiency and independence. But his way of dealing with the distance of his parents is to turn it in on itself, into a virtue, an act of self-sacrifice that, far from damaging him, actually prepared him for the difficult times ahead. And thus for his leadership: the experience of being sent away so young, we read in his official biography, "helped to reinforce the attitude of self-reliance and sufficiency which Mbeki would need as he became involved in the struggle to liberate his country."[8]

Nelson Mandela, Oliver Tambo, Govan Mbeki, Thabo Mbeki: Leadership of the South African liberation struggle is built on the myth of men who sacrificed personal and family life for the benefit of their people. Yet Walter Sisulu, who was jailed on Robben Island with Mandela and Govan Mbeki, was as dedicated an activist as they were (and perhaps even more effective), but he had a very stable and fulfilled home life: He found as much joy in bathing his children as in running a revolution.

Perhaps the answer to this difference is to be found in the way political prisoners describe the roles they played in the "family" created on Robben Island: Mbeki was "Oom Gov," the stern but beloved uncle and teacher; Mandela was the patriarch, adored and feared; Sisulu was the mother, the behind-the-scenes nurturer who held the family together. If Walter Sisulu's maternal qualities arose out of his ability to break the traditional gender roles ascribed to leaders, then perhaps Mandela's and Mbeki's paternal qualities—stern, emotionally distant, heroic—had less to do with their being freedom fighters who had sacrificed their personal lives in the name of struggle than with the simple fact that they were men. They were men of a certain age and culture, from a tradition that validated the soldier's battlefield (or the intellectual's study) over the hearth as the forge of masculinity.

Govan Mbeki's total commitment to the freedom struggle took him away from home and children. But if Govan was an absent father, this is not necessarily just because he was a revolutionary. Epainette Mbeki recalls a conversation she had with her husband about his own childhood: "I asked him, 'How old were you when your father died?'" When he replied that he was just an infant, "I got a reply to a question I've been wondering about—why he didn't adopt a more fatherly attitude to his children. I realized, for the first time, that it's because he doesn't have the background of a father. He has no idea of what a father is supposed to be." Absent fathers, and not simply revolutions, beget absent fathers.

Epainette Mbeki recalls her son Moeletsi telling her, "Mum, I'm not going to follow Thabo and my father.... Politics is abstract, I want to do something practical." Moeletsi developed a work identity independent of the liberation movement, as an engineer in Tanzania and a journalist in Zimbabwe, and his younger brother Jama became a lawyer in Botswana. While their sister Linda eschewed politics altogether, both Moeletsi and Jama were to remain deeply engaged, although they did so outside of—and perhaps in reaction to—the all-consuming ideology of their father and their eldest brother. Moeletsi was associated with the anti-Soviet new left that was in perennial conflict with the South African Communist Party, and Jama became an activist of the strongly pan-Africanist Basutoland Congress Party and a cadre in its Lesotho Liberation Army, at war with the ANC in the 1980s. Both married non-South Africans and drew professional salaries; both led lives within the shadow of the ANC but were neither dedicated to nor dependent upon it.

Thabo Mbeki's trajectory has been altogether different. He followed his father, step by step. According to Fezeka Mabona, Mbeki once told his wife, Zanele, "I'm not like the other sons. I've never worked for my parents"—in other words, sent money home to support them, as African children are always expected to do—"but what I'm doing here [in exile], I want to do in the best way I can. I want to excel at it and complete the work of my father." He appears to have turned his anger outward, at the system that robbed him of a father. Rather than rebelling against or resenting his father, he would compete with him within his own realm of intellect and politics, of the liberation struggle, and win.

Epainette Mbeki recalls him asking, when he was young, "Ma, what class has my father passed?" "I said, 'He's a BA.' He said, 'Only a BA? I'm going to be something higher than that.'" Then, when he got his master's degree from Sussex he wrote to his mother and asked her tell a local lawyer that he was no longer the only man from Idutywa with an MA: "He wanted to prove what he was capable of on his own. He wanted to show everyone that he was just as good as or even better than his father"—not just in terms of academic qualifications, but in terms of "uplifting the people too."

Thabo Mbeki has always been prickly about being identified as his father's son ("I am *not* Govan Mbeki," he pointedly told new friends when he arrived in Johannesburg in 1960), and resented the inference that he climbed so rapidly in the movement because he comes from one of its dynastic, "royal" families. Perhaps as a counter to this, perhaps as a denial of the father who neglected him, perhaps as a consequence of his years in exile, he would embrace even more rigidly than his father the concept of "family" as a political, rather than a biological, designation. Like being a son, being a father would be, for Thabo Mbeki, an entirely political experience.

6

QUEENSTOWN
THE AFRICAN SPRINGTIME ORCHESTRA

In 1951, Govan Mbeki recalled, he arrived unannounced at the Queenstown home of Michael Moerane a few months after Thabo, aged eight, had moved there to continue his schooling: "I found my brother-in-law sitting at the piano, and his six children plus Thabo all with an instrument of his or her own. I just crept in without them noticing and listened. It was beautiful! These sessions used to happen almost every night." The family group was called the African Springtime Orchestra: Each child was given a different musical instrument to learn, and Thabo's was the flute.

Michael Moerane, Epainette's older brother, was music master at the local black high school. He lived with his large family in a rambling old house with a red zinc roof on Scanlan Street, on the eastern fringes of town. Thabo attended the Moravian mission school with his cousins, who remember him as a quiet but humorous child who made them laugh by putting his own satirical words to a hymn they sang, "Every Time I See the Spirit."

His cousin Sophie, a year older than he, became particularly close to him, and told me that she was devastated when, two years later, his parents sent him to school in Butterworth, closer to home. "I have never got over it," she repeated several times during our few hours together. She conjured his absence with a page of musical notation, Mozart's Symphony No. 39 in E Flat, on which she had drawn an arrow to a line of notes and written "Thabo—Solo flute." The symphony was the favorite set piece of the African Springtime Orchestra. So impressed was Michael Moerane with Thabo's musical aptitude that he arranged the second theme of the third movement as a flute solo for his nephew. "When Thabo left," Sophie recalled, "there was always a gap when we performed it, because no one ever replaced him.... We would just have to hum it and imagine Thabo was there."

Queenstown, like so many places in Thabo Mbeki's life, was a frontier town—on the border between the native reserves and white farmland—and also a way station for migrants on their way from the reserves up to Johannesburg. Later in the decade, under the Group Areas Act, the Moerane family would have their land expropriated and be forcibly removed to the new black township, but in the early 1950s, when Thabo lived with them, his relatives were part of precisely the kind of mixed and fluid society that apartheid intended to eradicate.

Known as Jazz Town, Queenstown was also the center of black musical life in the Eastern Cape; the birthplace of black South African jazz. In the 1950s, the big man in town was Meekly Matshikiza, whose Dixieland jazz band entertained whites and middle-class Africans at "soirées"[1] and who had "seven sons who played the piano like nobody's business."[2] One of these sons, Todd, would become one of South Africa's most celebrated composers and journalists. The Matshikiza family lived right next door to the Moeranes, in tenuous counterpoint: Michael Moerane, upright and classical, thought the jazzy Matshikizas were dissipated ne'er-do-wells, and the Matshikizas, no doubt, returned the favor by viewing the Moeranes as teetotalling prigs. But, there, on Scanlan Street, you had black South Africa's two great musical traditions living side by side, for Queenstown was as renowned for its choral and classical music scene as it was for its jazz, and Michael Moerane was at its very center.

Stern, righteous, and ambitious, Michael Moerane was perhaps the most formidable of Epainette's illustrious brothers. His music is still part of the BBC's classical repertoire, and his songs are standards on the South African choral scene. Like many black schoolmasters from the Cape, he belonged to the Non-European Unity Movement (NEUM), a radical rival to the African National Congress. Govan Mbeki later described the NEUM as "a clique of phrasemongers" whose "empty vapourings" have "bedevilled" South Africa's liberation struggle.[3] Not surprisingly, he and his brother-in-law did not get on. And Michael Moerane's uncompromising approach was to provide Thabo with his first lesson in politics, too.

On the morning of April 6, 1952, Thabo Mbeki was at home doing gardening duty with one of his cousins when they heard drums rolling from the agricultural showgrounds just down Scanlan Street. Through the fence of the showgrounds—"we had to remain outside, as it was 'Whites Only'"—they watched a small-town pageant celebrating 300 years of white settlement in South Africa. The boys looked on as the white citizens of Queenstown enacted the arrival of the Dutch at the Cape; the Great Trek into the interior; the covenant with the Lord before the Battle of Blood River; the bringing of civilization and light—of ox-wagons, lacy bonnets, and brass bands—to the darkness of Africa. Part carnival and part religious devotion, these were the kind of popular mythmaking events at which the Afrikaner nationalists excelled.

While they were standing at the fence, recalls Mbeki, "my uncle rode past on his bicycle. We dashed home, but not in time. He was waiting for us, and there were many lashes on our bottoms with his belt." Michael Moerane's rage was not so much over the fact that they had forsaken their domestic responsibilities but that they were "collaborating" in this celebration of white supremacy and Afrikaner nationalism.

In response to the tercentenary, Nelson Mandela launched his Defiance Campaign, which would mobilize thousands of ordinary people into defying the system by going through whites-only doors, traveling on whites-only trains, and breaking curfews or pass restrictions. Over 8,000 people would be arrested in the following six months. Thabo Mbeki, then ten years old, was determined to be one of them—and he describes this, lightheartedly, as the beginning of his career as a political activist. He and his cousin decided to enlist, "but to volunteer you had to join the ANC, and this cost two and six-pence. We collected used bottles and sold them to the Chinese shopkeeper, and arrived at the recruitment center with our two and six each, but we were told to go away because we were too young. 'Next time,' they said."

Even without Mbeki, the campaign was spectacularly successful, particularly in Queenstown. But it was disparaged in the Moerane home, and for the young Mbeki, such uncompromising harshness became associated with the thrashing he got from his uncle, which he has never forgotten. When he arrived at the Lovedale mission school a few years later and needed to make a choice between the ANC Youth League and the NEUM's youth wing, the thrashing came back to him: "My uncle, being Unity Movement and acting in that sort of way, put me off. I felt 'This is the wrong political approach. Why didn't you rather come and talk to us? We were conscious enough to reason with.' " How typical for Mbeki to see a parental act of discipline, or perhaps cruelty, as "the wrong political approach" rather than something painful and simply unfair.

In 1953, the Mbekis moved their son from Queenstown to Butterworth, where he lodged with an amaZizi acquaintance of the family. His sister Linda told me that it was because his mother wanted him to be closer to home—perhaps because her husband was leaving. Mbeki has said of his departure from the Moerane household that "it was my parents' decision, but it was a bad one. I had none of the things at Butterworth, such as a piano, that I had had at Queenstown."[4] This piano, we can assume, stands for many things: song, the security of a family, intimate friendships with his cousins, the urbanity of Scanlan Street with its jazz legends and its Defiance Campaigns; and the attentions, no matter how severe, of a father figure. The Moerane family may have lost the flute solo for Mozart's 39th Symphony, but Thabo Mbeki lost an entire orchestra of accompanists. He was only to find another, many years later, in the ANC.

7

LOVEDALE
"AFRICA'S BEST AND BRIGHTEST"

I f South African literature is characterized by journeys, by migrations, by the crossings and recrossings of frontiers, then one of the most compelling must be that which takes children from their homes in the rural areas and deposits them, with blazer and school bag, beneath the arch proclaiming "Lovedale," at the iconic white wooden gates of the mission school that was known as the "Eton of Africa." In 1955, by the time Thabo Mbeki passed through these gates and up the avenue of oaks that led to the somber stone building with its severe gables and crenellated bell tower, black students from all over the continent had been attending Lovedale for over a century. The first South African high school to admit blacks, it was founded in 1841 by the Scottish Presbyterian church in a fertile, sheltered valley alongside the Tyume River at Alice. The University of Fort Hare would be built on the grassland just across the river. The Tyume Valley thus became the center of black education in southern Africa.

"Oh, we were the best and the brightest!" exclaimed Zweliyanyikima Vena, for four decades the librarian of the Cory Library at Rhodes University in Grahamstown when I met him in 2000. Lovedale's records are held there, and so Vena—who was expelled from Lovedale, with Thabo Mbeki, after the 1959 students' strike—had become custodian of the school's history. "But there was a contradiction. While we had the same sort of pride in ourselves as our white contemporaries at St. Andrew's or Kingswood—we wrote the same exams and got the same results—we knew we would never have the same opportunities as them. It was that 'you may not' that motivated us. That's where our activism came from."

Vena remembers his classmate Thabo as "formal" and "properly dressed" but "not stylish. You could see from his style of dress that he was rural." Students at Lovedale were divided regionally and ethnically, and when Mbeki arrived he was placed, along with the other Transkeians, in Shaw House. The Transkei boys were known as *moegoes*—country bumpkins—by the more sophisticated Eastern Cape city boys in other houses. Whereas they wore their formal clothing with the propriety learned from their small-town-teacher parents, their classmates from Port Elizabeth and East London were freer and looser with style, taking on the jazzy fashions and attitudes of the era. And while the Transkei boys played soccer, the Eastern Cape boys were devoted to rugby. Determined to shuck his *moegoe*ness, Thabo Mbeki chose rugby, and doggedly stuck to it throughout his time at Lovedale, despite the fact that he was never very good at it: He never made it beyond the lowest division.

Like all the schools Mbeki had attended previously, Lovedale was a mission school, a private institution set up by the church. These were the incubators of the black political elite and intelligentsia, and when the National Party was elected into office in 1948 it decided to scrap them and integrate them into its "Bantu Education" system, which would teach blacks, as apartheid architect H. F. Verwoerd so infamously put it, "that equality with Europeans is not for them."[1] While Mbeki was at Lovedale, control of the mission schools was finally transferred from the church to the state, and so his education took place in a curious interregnum—a time of ferment and contestation but also of the last glimmerings of possibility—between the colonial and apartheid systems. He would, in fact, be in the very last class to be allowed to follow the same standard curriculum as white students.

Dr. R. H. W. Shepherd, Lovedale's principal when Thabo arrived, epitomized the school's paternalism. "Despite their barbaric customs," he had written, the natives of the region were "a fine race of people, and nothing but religion and civilisation were wanting to exalt them in the scale of being, and to raise them to the true dignity of human nature."[2]

Such sentiment was not matched by the conditions in which students lived—which were more primitive than what these largely middle-class children experienced at home. There was constant complaint over the food: "I gave up eating meat altogether," Sigqibo Dwane, an Mbeki classmate, told me. "It was often rotten, not stuff you would even want to smell. We had samp [crushed corn] and beans once a week...otherwise it was just bread and porridge." But even if the fare was starchy at best and rotten at worst, it had to be eaten properly. "Table manners!" exclaimed Isaac Mabindisa, another classmate of Mbeki's. "Nothing was more important. You had to eat at table, in absolute silence, with a knife and fork.... And at the head of each table was a prefect whose sole responsibility during the course of the meal was to make sure that you had table manners."

But "the true dignity of human nature" meant something a little more profound for many of the students: as the fulcrum of black intellectual life and aspiration in South Africa, the Tyume Valley was the place where young middle-class Africans found their politics. Govan Mbeki had became enamored of communism at Fort Hare, and Epainette Moerane, too, had obtained her first understanding of oppression while she was at Lovedale. This understanding came not only from interacting with other students, but from observing the racial dynamics of the school itself. There were very few things, in elite black South African society in the 1950s, as prestigious as becoming a teacher at Lovedale, but seeing the slights their black teachers had to suffer, and observing the glass ceilings on these teachers' aspirations, had a profound effect on the more politically minded students at the institution.

In 1956, Lovedale was put under the authority of the new Bantu Affairs Department. By 1959, after his son was expelled, Govan Mbeki would write about how "in less than six years the Nationalists carried out acts of reckless destruction of work that had taken more than a century to build." The library had been closed; "students are discouraged from reading outside their prescribed work" and are not even permitted "to stand in a group and engage in discussions"; "informers are planted in every dormitory," and "even the literary debating society is no longer there. Instead, most of the time after class is taken up with manual work, while . . . a great deal of time is taken up with scripture teaching in which the emphasis is placed on loyalty."³

Still, it would take a few years for the apartheid system to strip Lovedale of its mission-school ethos. The racism only really set in, Thabo Mbeki recalls, once Bantu Affairs started placing its own officials at the school: He remembers the children of one taunting the boys as they went down to the fields to play sport in the afternoon, singing *"een kaffer, twee kaffers, drie kaffers"* [one kaffir, two kaffirs, three kaffirs] as they passed. This, Mbeki told me, was his first direct experience of racism.

In 1958 Mbeki passed his Junior Certificate examination and was enrolled in the academic stream toward university matriculation. His subjects were English, history, mathematics, Latin, biology, and chemistry, and his prescribed texts were Austen's *Northanger Abbey*, Conrad's *The Nigger of the Narcissus*, and Shakespeare's *Macbeth*. I asked Mbeki's history teacher, Ruth White, what it was like teaching colonial and apartheid history to black students: "You *did* do these wars," the 90-year-old recalled, "and they got quite angry sometimes, especially when the prophetess [Nongqawuse] said whites would be driven into the sea! 'That's a lie!' the children would say to me. 'She never said anything like that!' Well, I wasn't going to argue with them. All I said was 'You are writing an exam. You'll be corrected by the people who wrote these books, so stick to the book.' It may not have been correct teaching, but it got them their As after all. I used to say 'Be practical about it!'"

Thabo Mbeki could have been taught history differently, by Mac Makalima, a historian who was the senior black teacher at the school, but

Makalima was barred from teaching the subject because of his political activism. As it was, Makalima used his Xhosa-language classes to educate his students politically about their responsibilities as black society's elite. Zweliyanyikima Vena recalls that "[Makalima] used to say to us, 'When you leave this school and go out into the world, don't reject the people you grew up with.'" To make this point, he would hold out his open hand "and compare us to his fingers, which he called the black nation. There is the short finger, the pointing finger, the thumb. He would say, 'You may be the longer finger, but you will not be able to hold on to life if you do not work together with the other fingers. The hand only functions when all the fingers work together.'"

Meanwhile, for English, Mbeki's class landed with one Mrs. Webb, an avowed Afrikaner nationalist who made no bones about her politics. The class decided to protest, but Mbeki argued strongly against it: "We've only got two years with her, so let's put up with it." He did not rock the boat, Vena recalls; he preferred not to be noticed.

In fact, although Mbeki was already on the executive board of the ANC Youth League's Lovedale branch as its secretary, and had quickly become a student leader, he was not noticed as such by the teachers. When I met him in 1999, Makalima remembered Chris Hani vividly as a student leader and hothead, but his recollection of Mbeki, a year behind, was hazy: "He was Govan Mbeki's son, and he was one of the brighter young fellows, usually first in the class. But he gave no impression of being a leader. One didn't notice anything in particular about him. He gave no impression at all except that of being a diligent, quiet boy."

When I told Vena that Mac Makalima had no memory of Thabo as a student leader, he was not surprised: "That's the thing about Thabo," he said. "You could never identify his role. Now, it was different with Chris [Hani], because Chris was political-minded; he would go out and oppose something. But Thabo kept quiet. He just worked behind the scenes. That's what we liked about him. Through his quietness and deep thoughts, we were able to plan something with him constructively, and it will hatch out when it's ready."

Any discussion of politics was illegal at Lovedale, but when lights went out in the dormitories each night, the Lovedale boys pulled out their copies of *New Age* and had fierce, whispered debates about the merits of the Congress versus the Non-European Unity Movement (NEUM); about whether the Freedom Charter was correct in stating that South Africa belonged not just to black South Africans but to whites too; about whether the ANC was guilty of "adventurism," as the NEUM liked to put it. "Oh, there would be very strong disagreements!" recalled Sigqibo Dwane. "We behaved like gentlemen, but we were tough with each other." On weekends, Lovedale students stole across the Tyume River to meet at Fort Hare with older activists; there they listened to student leaders and collected literature, or they met with organizers from the cities.

In this way, Mbeki and his classmates followed the forced removals of 58,000 people from Sophiatown and their 1955 resettlement in Soweto. They also followed the buildup to the June 1955 multiracial Congress of the People at Kliptown, outside Johannesburg, which laid out a manifesto for equality that was to power the liberation movement for decades to come. Thabo Mbeki might not have known for certain that his father was one of the 2,884 delegates to the congress, but he must have suspected it and worried about Govan's well-being when he read in his father's own newspaper about the police raid on the gathering.

Then, at the end of 1956, just as Lovedale's students were beginning to pack up to go home for their Christmas break, something happened that shattered once and for all the illusion that these students, even if they were black South Africa's "best and brightest," could in any way be exempted from the saga of repression and resistance that was playing itself out in the rest of the country. After the removal of Coloureds from the voters' roll and the extension of the passbook system to African women, the ANC launched a Million Signatures Campaign in support of the Freedom Charter. In response, the state swooped down: In one day, between the hours of four and five o'clock in the morning, police all over the country knocked on doors and arrested 140 people, charging them with high treason. One of them was the most venerated man in the Tyume Valley: the acting principal of Fort Hare, Professor Z. K. Matthews. The subsequent treason trial was to drag on for five years until, finally, in 1961, the last 30 accused were acquitted. On trial were all the major political figures from the Congress movement—with the notable exception of Govan Mbeki. (His detractors cite this as evidence of his lack of importance in the movement in the 1950s.)

Meanwhile, beyond South Africa's borders, "a new world had emerged," Thabo Mbeki was later to write, with both the Ghanaian and the Egyptian independence movements and with a Soviet Russia standing up "in defence of the threatened African motherland" over the Suez Canal crisis. It was at this time that "we started at school discussing what this 'Russian bear' which the papers talked about was. The branch chairman had to answer many questions. Impatiently we waited to enter the higher classes when we would be taught about the French Revolution, the American Revolution and the Russian Revolution."[4] The moment of Ghanaian independence, in March 1957, was particularly memorable. As Mbeki would later say: "We were mere schoolboys when we saw the black star rise on our firmament, as the colonial Gold Coast crowned itself with the ancient African name of Ghana.

We knew then that the promise we had inherited would be honoured. The African giant was awakening!"[5]

Inevitably, the students began to see the school as some kind of microcosm not only for South African society but for the battle against colonial oppression being waged across the African continent. And in this they were encouraged not just by the racism they experienced and the iniquities to which they saw their black teachers being subjected, but also by the official attitude to student politics: "We were doing things as if underground," recalls Sipho Makana, who was to become one of Mbeki's closest comrades, going into exile with him. "The school paid students to spy on us, so we had to recruit members very carefully." Thus, when he was only 13, Mbeki knew what it meant to hold illicit ideas and work for an underground organization—even if "underground" meant torch-lit meetings in a corner of the dormitory and "work" entailed little more, at this stage, than distributing, reading, and discussing struggle literature.

By 1957 it was impossible to insulate Lovedale's student community from the surrounding turbulence. Johannesburg was racked by a bus boycott, a rural uprising was beginning in Pondoland in the Transkei, and the state had introduced new legislation to forbid contact between the races at political gatherings. Throughout 1958, Mbeki and his classmates plotted to strike; by January 1959, they returned to the school from their Christmas break ready for confrontation. The pretext came in the first week of March, when the students at the junior hostel organized a petition about the quality of food: Worms had been found in the porridge! The authorities responded with severity: Four "ringleaders" were identified and summarily expelled.

The students launched a strike in reaction and the whole thing was, the way Vena describes it, extraordinarily civilized, "all silence, discussion, suggestion. The idea of toyi-toyiing [the ANC's martial dance] is something recent. We didn't have banners, we were just sitting there, talking." A list of demands, drawn up by Mbeki and the branch executive, were dispatched: no more rotten food, no more overnight expulsions, no more spying on students. The students remained barricaded in the gymnasium all weekend until, on the morning of Monday, March 9, the authorities called a general assembly. Buttressed by an official from Bantu Affairs and the local magistrate, they laid down the law: If the students did not go back to classes immediately, they were to pack their bags and leave.

And so, on the morning of March 10, Mbeki and nearly 300 others were marched to the station at Alice, accompanied by grim Lovedale officials and the local constabulary, and boarded onto trains. The school was shut down. Some students were expelled outright, but most were permitted to return at the end of the month if they signed loyalty letters saying that they would never again participate in student politics or challenge the school's authority.

The fact that so many students did not return—despite the value of an education, despite the way they had struggled to get scholarships or their parents had struggled to pay the fees—gives some indication of how turbulent the times were and of just how rapidly the school's reputation had plummeted since its transfer from the church to the state four years previously. The March 1959 strike signaled the end of Lovedale's status as the country's leading black South African educational institution; the end, too, of a century of mission schooling.

The Mbewuleni to which Thabo returned, in March 1959, was very different from that of his childhood. His father was away, as were all his siblings: Linda was working in Cape Town, and Moeletsi and Jama were being brought up by Epainette's sister, Mphuma, in Lesotho, where they had been sent to escape Bantu Education and to become eligible—as apartheid entrenched itself—for non–South African citizenship. During school holidays, the boys would return to Mbewuleni, but for the most part Thabo was alone at home with his mother and his young cousin Fezeka Mabona. Mabona's strongest memory of the young man who returned from Lovedale was that he taught her and the other children struggle songs he had learned at school, paeans to Albert Luthuli and to Patrice Lumumba, the man who would lead the Congo to independence in 1960 and whose handsome, bookish face was the icon at the time of the freedom that people of Thabo Mbeki's generation had come to believe was their birthright.

Back in his home village, Mbeki was in a quandary. Unlike his friends, he had not been expelled outright, as the authorities failed to recognize that he was the strike's primary organizer. And so he was offered the "loyalty" letter, and the option of return. If he did not sign the letter, his expulsion could preclude his readmission anywhere, and he might thus not be able to graduate from high school and proceed to university. He was following Govan's lessons—acting on principle, resisting the oppressors—and yet he got no help from his father, who simply wrote to him that he had to make his own decisions and arranged for him to continue his education through a correspondence college under the tutelage of his mother.

Like the others expelled, Thabo Mbeki was not a natural rebel: They were good boys, the Eastern Cape's best and brightest; that is how they got to be at Lovedale in the first place. The expulsion marked a dramatic transition: a possible end to their families' aspirations of professional careers, but also the entry into another world: that of the freedom struggle. For country boys like Mbeki, there was also the new veneer of urbanity: He was no longer a *moegoe* but the organizing secretary of the ANC Youth League, Lovedale Branch, one of the leaders of a significant political action. Mbeki arrived in Lovedale in 1955 a quiet, diligent little boy whose intellectual precocity meant he had very few friends among his agemates. Four years later, he had grown into his long trousers. His upbringing in Mbewuleni had given him an aptitude for political analysis and a facility in political organizing that had afforded him status and respect among his peers. Within the world of the Youth League, he had found a community that valued him; his comrades had become his friends, his family. He had taken the place of his father: nearly 17, he returned home to Mbewuleni an activist, a man.

8

FATHERHOOD

"Good has brought Thabo back, but he has taken Kwanda away," says Olive Mpahlwa. It is shortly after Mbeki's inauguration in 1999, and we are sitting in the Reverend Wellington Jansen's evangelical Bread of Life Ministries, in a shopping complex in Bethelsdorp, one of the bleak Coloured townships that tumble across the scrubland north of Port Elizabeth. The room has a midweek torpor to it: Last Sunday's floral arrangements are wilting, and the sweat of that day's exertions lingers in the air.

Mpahlwa has chosen this room for our meeting place because it is here, under the Reverend Jansen's pastoral care, that she has been healing herself. Here she tells me about the wreck of her life: about how the man she loved was forced into exile, about how their son followed him and never returned. For the past decade she has been trying to trace her son, Kwanda Mbeki, from whom she last heard in 1981. In desperation, she eventually turned to the Truth and Reconciliation Commission (TRC): In May 1996 she testified publicly before the commission's Human Rights Violations Committee, where she likened her search to a battle against a "faceless monster." She had been "weeping and crying for 16 years," she said; she had been stricken with a series of stress-related illnesses and was forced to take an early disability pension from her nursing work.

She knew, she told the TRC, that Kwanda's "interest in the ANC [African National Congress] was double-pronged, to fight for the liberation struggle and meet his father in exile. My son would never let me worry like this if he was alive. He was brilliant, he was loving, he was considerate, he was my joy."[1] But by 2006, no one had come forward, from either the South African security forces or the liberation movements in exile, to offer any information about Thabo Mbeki's only acknowledged child.

Mpahlwa shows me the only two photographs she has of Kwanda, the two she submitted to the TRC: his Bantustan identity book and a photograph bearing the rather grandiose pretensions of a small-town studio—a backdrop of billowing floral curtains, a foreground of silk flowers, a 14-year-old boy pressed stiffly between them in his smart Sunday clothing, angled forward to please the camera. If the studio photograph captures the diligent and well-behaved child, compliant yet reserved, then the passport photograph of the 20-year-old—a brush with officialdom—betrays the slightest flicker of anger. The eyebrows are slightly arched, and although he has the same open, inquiring aspect his father had at that age, there is defiance as well in those eyes, around the mouth. This is a young man who has lived through the 1976 student uprising, who has embraced liberation politics, and who is soon to experience, sharply, the whip of racial discrimination upon his own back. He has just graduated from a technical high school with excellent grades in metalwork and welding, and he is on his way to the industrial region of the Vaal Triangle to look for an apprenticeship. But soon he will write to his mother to say that he has been rejected over and over again because of the small quota of skilled jobs reserved for blacks—and that he believes the name "Mbeki" has something to do with this. She will see him once more, seemingly dissipated and unreachably distant, at her brother's home in Umtata, then she will never see him again.

As the offspring of Mbewuleni's two leading *gqoboka* families, the Mbeki and the Mpahlwa children had grown up with one another. Geoffrey Mpahlwa and Govan Mbeki, schoolmaster and shopkeeper, were close friends: Olive recalls that she or one of her siblings would run up the hill every afternoon to the Mbeki shop to collect the *Daily Dispatch* for her father once Govan was through with it.

The romance between Thabo and Olive started in 1958, when both were in their penultimate years of high school, although Olive was three years older. He seduced her with his family's passion for intellectual activity: "I'd come into the Mbeki shop to collect our family's post," she recalls, "and you could hear noise and laughter coming from the kitchen. There they would be, together with their mother, and they'd grab me and say, 'Help us! We're struggling over how to analyze this sentence!'"

They would see each other over the holidays, at Mbewuleni: "I found him quite interesting, even though he was younger than me. He was compelling. He could pick things up quickly, look at something and come up with an answer. He was a shy boy, but he covered it up with laughter. He laughs a lot, as you know, and laughter is a great cover-up for shyness."

The South African school year begins in January, and Kwanda was conceived just before Thabo returned for his final year at Lovedale in 1959 and Olive went off to the prestigious Ohlange Institute outside Durban to complete her schooling. In March, at the same time Thabo was expelled and sent home, Olive's pregnancy was discovered when she went into the hospital for a minor ear operation. She was immediately put into confinement at a cousin's home in Durban. The Mpahlwas were staunch Christians, and termination was out of the question; given that Thabo was still a minor and in no position to pay dowry, marriage was no option either. And so the two families were compelled to go through the arduous traditional motions of negotiating a solution, a process made more difficult by the fact that Govan was not around. Geoffrey Mpahlwa and Mrs. Mbeki agreed on terms: She would pay him the standard fee of five head of cattle in compensation—an onerous obligation, given her financial situation—and the child would be raised by the Mpahlwas.

Monwabisi Kwanda Mpahlwa was born in Durban on October 8, 1959. At Christmastime that year, a traumatized young mother returned with her son to Mbewuleni: "I was told that the child must never call me 'mother.' He must call me 'aunt,' because I am unmarried." Thabo was living in Mbewuleni at the time but was not permitted to see his son—and was also no longer welcome in the Mpahlwa home. A lot of this attitude, says Olive Mpahlwa, was no more than social custom, put on to preserve the good names of the families.

In late October 1959, just after his son was born, Mbeki went to stay with family friends in Umtata, to sit for his examinations at St. John's College. The Queenstown years still lingered: He remembers that he chose the subject "On Learning to Play the Piano" for his English composition, drawing on his experiences in Michael Moerane's household. He received his results during the same fraught days that Olive and her baby returned to Mbewuleni: He obtained disappointing, but perfectly respectable, grades.

The 17-year-old Mbeki had other things on his mind at the time: The year was one in which he led a rebellion and was expelled from school; it was the year he fathered a child. It was also a time in which—strange as this might seem in hindsight, knowing as we do that South Africa was hurtling toward the Sharpeville slaughter, where 69 protesters were killed, and the repression that followed it—black South Africans believed they might topple the still-young apartheid regime. This, after all, was the moment of *uhuru*— freedom—the great African independence movement. "*Afrika!*" was the new rallying call. If Thabo had been permitted to acknowledge his paternity, he might have christened his boy Jomo or Kwame (after Kenyatta or Nkrumah), as so many were that year. With a dozen or more countries planning their independence, 1960 was frequently declared "the Year of Africa."

The African independence movement and Thabo Mbeki thus came of age at exactly the same moment. To the extent that his "African Renaissance" is nostalgic, it looks back not to a mythical precolonial time when Africans were free and happy but to December 1959, when both the continent and a young man in Mbewuleni saw limitless possibilities—the progress, power, and self-sufficiency of adulthood—before them.

In 1960 Thabo Mbeki would be sent to Johannesburg by his family, and the movement, to do his A levels, which would enable him to study abroad.

He would be integrated into the very bosom of the liberation movement. Two years later, after a harrowing flight into exile, he would be shuttled off to Sussex University in the United Kingdom on a scholarship, for four years of cosseted, stimulating university education. The contrast between this experience and that of his son—who was last seen living as a migrant manual laborer in the brutal world of the single-sex hostels of the Transvaal—is stark. It is a contrast that tells the story of a South Africa that had drastically limited the possibilities for black South Africans of the Mbekis' class: All evidence is that Thabo Mbeki's boy was also intellectually gifted, but there was no longer a Lovedale to send him to. It also tells the story of diminishing paternity: No matter how distant Govan Mbeki was, he intervened—as we shall see—to ensure that his son got the best possible education and mentorship, in a way that Thabo could not do when it came to his own son. But most of all, it tells the story of the devastation wreaked, on one family, by the brutality of apartheid and the imperative of struggling against it. It is nothing short of a tragedy.

Kwanda spent his first years with no knowledge that he was an Mbeki, tainted by the shame of unknown paternity. In 1969, when he was 10 years old, Epainette Mbeki decided she wished to reclaim him, as she thought that it would be better for him to know where he came from. She was lonely, too. Through a male intermediary in the village, she set about another complex series of negotiations, assisted by correspondence from her husband in jail on Robben Island, to gain custody of her grandchild. She prevailed, and the little boy changed his name to Mbeki and moved up the hill to her shop. She sent him first to board at the Mariazell mission school, where she and her siblings had gone, then to a technical high school in King William's Town.

Kwanda adored his new grandmother. Olive Mpahlwa told me how, whenever he came to visit her in Cradock—where she had obtained work as a nurse—he would be itching to get back to Epainette: "We have work to do," he would say. "We have things to build and gardens to tend to." His mother was also struck by his discipline—"He would never go out to join the other boys without asking my permission, and only then after having done all the dishes"—and yet there was an edge to him: "He was very angry about his heritage. Epainette told me that he would sometimes throw a tantrum, wanting to know where his parents are. She would say, 'I am here. Here I am for you!' but he would say 'I need my parents!'" Epainette Mbeki confirms this: "Sometimes, for no reason, he would say 'Grandmother, you say Thabo is my father and Nokwanda [Olive] is my mother. Where are they?' He would ask that question in a grudging way, as if they had deserted him."

Testifying before the TRC, Olive Mpahlwa used the story of a watch, sent from abroad, to evoke the triangle of longing, impotence, and absence that stood in place of a happy family for Kwanda and his parents. The boy had been sent the watch by his father, inscribed with his name at the back: "He gave it to me and I tried everything to get it working. I took it to the best jewelers…but they could do nothing about it. I remember when I gave it back to him and I told him it could not work he just could not believe it. The way he looked at me he showed that it seemed as if I did not know how much he was hurting inside. It showed I was not giving enough. I was not aware [until this moment] of how much he idolized—this person, his father."[2]

As Kwanda grew older and angrier, he spoke more frequently about wanting to meet his father. The last Epainette Mbeki had heard from him was in 1981, when he had written to tell her that he had finally got a job, at the huge building materials company Everite. In one of her last meetings with her grandson, he had asked her how to find his father and she had given him his uncle Jama's contact details in Botswana. When she stopped hearing from him, she assumed he had gone into exile

Olive Mpahlwa also saw him last sometime in 1981, when she heard he was staying with her brother in Umtata. He was "discouraged and despondent. He didn't seem to have any intention of going anywhere, and he had given up on the Vaal Triangle." Shortly thereafter, also in 1981, she wrote a letter to him, at the address he had given her in the Vaal, to tell him she was getting married. It was returned, addressee unknown. And so she, too, assumed he had left the country.

When the ANC was unbanned in 1990, Epainette Mbeki and Olive Mpahlwa waited in vain to hear from Kwanda. Olive began to make inquiries, and heard from a returned exile, an Idutywa homeboy named Phumelelo Rulumeni, that he had met her son in Tanzania in 1985. Rulumeni suggested that Kwanda might still be alive but said that he was not able to give her any further information. She passed this information on to Thabo Mbeki in 1992; he promised to make inquiries and asked her to keep in touch with Govan, as he was too busy to handle the matter himself. In 1994 Govan contacted the Mpahlwas and told them the Mbeki family had decided that it was time to give up the search on all three of their family members who had disappeared—Kwanda, Thabo's youngest brother Jama, and a cousin named Phindile Mfeti—and declare them dead. There is no evidence to corroborate Rulumeni's claims that Kwanda was in exile; all available evidence suggests that he disappeared while working in the Vaal during 1981.

In 2005, the Missing Persons Task Team set up by the National Prosecutions Authority to investigate people who had been reported missing to the TRC announced that it was looking into the disappearances of both Kwanda and Jama Mbeki. I made contact with the team and gave the investigators my notes on both cases. Two years later, in 2007, Pule

Zwane, an ace senior investigator on the team, did an intensive search for Kwanda in the Vaal area and found several people who had known him when he was there, including his girlfriend, several work colleagues, and, most important, an old school friend of Kwanda's, Zakhele Nikelo, whom he had hooked up with when he arrived in the Vaal in 1981. The two men found jobs together on the night shift in the pipe-making section at Everite; Kwanda rented a room in a backyard in Sebokeng Zone 3 and then moved to Everite's private hostel.

Nikelo confirmed to Zwane that Kwanda was deeply interested in politics and that he often spoke about trying to find his father. Kwanda was apparently a quiet young man, highly intelligent and clearly overqualified for the manual labor he was doing at Everite. In July 1981, two months after he and Kwanda started working at Everite, Nikelo was sentenced to seven months' imprisonment for possession of marijuana. When he was released in February 1982, he looked for Kwanda but could not find him and assumed he had returned to the Transkei. Zwane also found Kwanda's girlfriend; the woman, who wishes to remain anonymous, told the investigator that she had last seen him in August 1981.

On the basis of the evidence he found, Pule Zwane identified three paupers' graves in the Vaal area where unidentified black men Kwanda's age were buried in late 1981, but as this book goes to print, the bodies have not yet been exhumed to conduct DNA testing. Whether there is a positive identification from these exhumations or not, the evidence shows that Kwanda Mbeki's disappearance was due neither to the authorities' harassment of the Mbeki family or to exile intrigue, but to something more everyday in apartheid South Africa: a callous system that drove a "lost generation" to disintegration and then did not even bother to mark the passing from this world of those who eventually succumbed. Was Kwanda stabbed to death in a mugging or fight? Run over by a speeding car? Killed in a taxi accident or lost to alcoholism? Is he still alive, perhaps confused and disoriented, somewhere on the fringes of the Vaal townships? While the TRC revealed the hundreds of families of activists unable to bury their loved ones, its terms of reference were such that it could not tell the stories of tens of thousands more who were not necessarily assassinated but who merely disappeared into the voids created by a system that devalued black life and all too often dumped it, unidentified, in an unmarked grave.

Thabo Mbeki has seldom publicly referred to the disappearances of his family members. In 1999, at that ceremony at Nyili where he was welcomed back into the amaZizi clan just before he became president, he mentioned the disappearances within the context of a family shattered and needing to be reunited. And five years earlier, in 1994, just weeks after they were inaugurated as Mandela's deputy presidents, Mbeki had a set-to with his fellow deputy, F. W. De Klerk, on the subject.

In his speech to the closing session of a World Economic Forum meeting in Cape Town, De Klerk had warned that the impending Truth and Reconciliation Commission might open the wounds of the past. Mbeki had retaliated with uncharacteristic emotion: Like the ANC, he said, his family was not looking for retribution or revenge, but merely for an answer to what had happened to their loved ones, so that they could bury them and become part of the national process of reconciliation. No one who was there will ever forget the cold rage covering his emotions as he looked directly into De Klerk's eyes.[3]

Mbeki told me that he did make efforts to follow up rumors that his son had been spotted in exile but that he was firm in his belief that Kwanda could not have left the country, or he would have heard about it. Besides, he added, it would have been "inappropriate" to "broadcast" his family's personal tragedies; doing so would have given the impression that his approach to the Truth and Reconciliation Commission was motivated by a personal agenda. What he left unsaid was that it would also have been a contravention of the family ethos for him to have demanded, as an ANC leader, any fast-track or special privilege in finding out what happened to Kwanda, over and above all the other families looking for lost children or siblings. Remember Govan Mbeki: "When you go into war, if your comrade in front of you falls off his horse, you must not stop and weep. You jump over him into battle." The dead are soldiers who died on the road to liberation; nothing more, nothing less.

But Olive Mpahlwa has difficulty accepting this. "Surely your blood comes first?" she asks, incredulous. She has been deeply disappointed at Mbeki's inaccessibility since his return from exile in 1990; at what she perceives as his lack of interest in finding out what has happened to their son and his unwillingness to use his position to solve the mystery. She remembers Mbeki, as a young man, telling her that it "caused him pain that he never had a chance to be with Kwanda." When I express surprise at this, given Mbeki's renowned emotional reserve, she responds: "I think the attitude of being repressed, secretive, closed off, must have been a consequence of exile, because the Thabo I remember was much more open. The laughter I remember from him, from the days that I met him, it was an open laughter."

"God has brought Thabo back, but he has taken Kwanda away." This is not quite true: For Olive Mpahlwa, Thabo Mbeki never returned either.

After leaving her infant with her mother in Mbewuleni, Olive moved to Johannesburg at the beginning of 1960, to study nursing at Baragwanath Hospital in Soweto. Later in the year, Thabo Mbeki followed, to begin studying for his A levels. He would, in time, become a lodger at the home of Duma Nokwe, the ANC secretary-general; in the beginning, however, not having any family in Johannesburg, he stayed at the Soweto home of Olive's uncle. Olive lived in the nurses' hostel at Baragwanath, and the two continued to see each other. He did not tell her, two years later, that he was going into exile, but it was her impression that when he left they were still together. There was a part of her that believed—perhaps because they shared a son— that he would return to her. As the years went by, she heard that he had married in exile, and she continued her life: She qualified as a nurse, met and married another man, and bore two more children. But something primal, something first kindled in her adolescence in Mbewuleni, remained unresolved.

Olive Mpahlwa is a naturally diffident person, but she is not without tenacity. After testifying before the TRC, she became determined to meet the father of her child, to have her say. She managed to get through to him and tell him this, and he responded that a meeting would be arranged, but it never was. When she read in the newspaper that he would be visiting Port Elizabeth on Soweto Day, June 16, 1998, she decided that he would not leave the city without seeing her. She spent the day following him, awaiting her opportunity. At a morning session at a high school, she sent a note to him, via his bodyguards, saying that she wished to speak to him; she noted, throughout the day, that he was aware of her presence. Finally, as he was leaving to catch his plane back to Johannesburg, "he turned around and saw me, and waved. I took this as a signal, and moved forward to him. Of course, there was no privacy. I complimented him on the good work he was doing, and then I said, 'I've come to bid you farewell...I am trying to break away from the past and say farewell to that. I want to go on, go forward in my life.' He smiled, as he always does, and nodded. He didn't say a word back. And then he was whisked off."

That was it: the first and the last time she has seen him since he went into exile in 1962, surrounded by his inevitable buffer zone of bodyguards and aides, rushing to catch a plane. But of course, saying good-bye to your first love who now happens to be president is more easily said than done: He visits you every night, like it or not, mediated by the flickering blue lines of your television screen.

9

JOHANNESBURG
FRINGE COUNTRY

If his father had had his way, Thabo Mbeki would have become a doctor. Because Fort Hare had been turned into a "Nationalist indoctrination camp,"[1] as Govan Mbeki was to describe it, his alma mater was no longer an option, but Govan was nonetheless adamant that his son obtain a university education and enter a profession. And he was determined that this profession be medicine. He tried to arrange for Thabo to go to medical school in India, but in an unusual act of rebellion against parental authority, his son resisted, telling his father that he "didn't like that idea...of cutting up people, the blood and all that." He also wanted to stay close to the fire: If 1960 was to be "the Year of Africa," he wished to be part of it.

In South Africa, at least, the Year of Africa started brutally. In January, nine policemen were killed during riots outside Durban. In February, the British prime minister, Harold Macmillan, spoke before the South African parliament, warning that the "wind of change" blowing through the continent could not be ignored. By March, the breakaway anticommunists of the Pan Africanist Congress (PAC) launched their demonstrations against black people having to carry passes; at Sharpeville, 69 protesters were shot dead, mainly in the back as they were running away, and another 186 were seriously wounded.

In one heady, terrifying week, the country seemed to unhinge. Tens of thousands heeded the call to stay away from work; there were mass burnings of passes and marches, a severe hemorrhage of capital out of the country, and a wave of immigration applications by white South Africans at foreign embassies. The state responded through a massive clampdown. On March 30, 1960, a nationwide emergency was declared, allowing for arrests and detentions without trial. A week later, the ANC was banned for the first time in its five-decade history, along with the PAC. By this point, 2,000 activists across the country were detained—among them Govan Mbeki, picked up from his lodgings in Port Elizabeth's New Brighton township. Thabo Mbeki, back in Mbewuleni after having taken his examinations, read about the arrests in *New Age*. The situation must have been terrifying for him: He would have had to consider the possibility that his father might be locked up for a long time or even killed and that he—all of 17—would now become the head of the struggling family.

In the midst of all of this—a week after Sharpeville and two days before his father was actually arrested—Thabo received a telegram requesting his presence at an interview in Johannesburg.[2] The previous year, Govan Mbeki had asked Walter Sisulu's advice about his son's education, and Sisulu had suggested that he apply for a scholarship from the South African Committee on Higher Education (SACHED). SACHED had just been formed to train young Africans, handpicked by the ANC, for future leadership by preparing them for A-level examinations so that they could register to do British degrees by correspondence and thus avoid the apartheid-controlled black universities; Sisulu agreed to put the young Mbeki's name forward.

And so, in early June 1960, with the acrid gun smoke of Sharpeville still in the air, Thabo Mbeki traveled by train to Johannesburg for an interview; it was his first trip outside of the Eastern Cape. From this first meeting, SACHED's founder, Ann Welsh, told me that she recognized the potential of Govan Mbeki's son: "You could see that he tested things," she told me in November 1999, a year before her death. "It was obvious that he was able and ambitious and very exploratory-minded. He was quite brave with ideas, not frightened at all by new ones."

Welsh—an economics lecturer at Johannesburg's Witwatersrand [Wits] University—was to become one of Thabo Mbeki's most significant benefactors, ultimately arranging for him to go to Sussex University. Because SACHED had been struggling to find students advanced enough to do A levels, the young Mbeki was a godsend: highly intelligent, well educated, and an ANC blueblood to boot. Mbeki got the SACHED scholarship and moved to Johannesburg, where he attended Britzius College on Plein Street. He stayed in Soweto, first at the home of relatives of Olive Mpahlwa and then with the family of Duma Nokwe, the ANC secretary-general.

SACHED's meticulous records are studded with plaudits to the young Mbeki. On Friday, July 22, 1960, he presented himself at Britzius for his first tutorial and quickly became star student: He was, his reports note, "an excellent student," the only one in the whole college "who has been able to keep up to date with his Course."[3] By 1962 he had passed his A-level examinations and become the organization's first student to be accepted by London University, into its Bachelor of Science in Economics correspondence degree. SACHED made a substantial investment in Mbeki over two years: Records show that it had spent R310 on tuition at Britzius for him, R138 on private tutorials, and R105 on stationery and textbooks—a total more than double that of the next student.[4] Clearly, the committee thought its money was well invested: When Mbeki applied for a monthly living allowance of R8, it was unanimously approved.

Ann Welsh understood immediately that Thabo Mbeki was not in Johannesburg simply to study and that enrolling at Britzius was, at least in part, a cover for political work: "There was this thing about getting permits [or passes, to stay in Johannesburg], and I had to learn how to lie on behalf of the students. I remember signing things for Thabo...I became conscious that I had acquired a new sense of obligation—to mislead the authorities."

In 1960, a staggering one in ten urban African adults was convicted for pass offenses—for not having permits to be in the city. In Johannesburg alone, there were an average of 162 arrests a day.[5] Until this time, Mbeki had not had to worry about passes: He had been under 18 and—but for his two years in Queenstown—he had spent his entire life in the bantustan reserves of Transkei and Ciskei. But now, in the city without any identity papers, he was vulnerable.

Apartheid legislation also meant that, outside of private colleges such as Britzius, there was almost no public space in downtown Johannesburg for black students to work and study, or even to read and relax. With its curfews, its whites-only leisure spaces, and its strict enforcement of the pass laws, Johannesburg had redesigned itself to accommodate black people as laborers and transients, certainly not as aspiring intellectuals and professionals preparing for A levels and British university degrees. The public library was for whites only; the only reading and studying spaces available to black students were the information service libraries of the British and U.S. consulates.

Welsh managed to secure a little common room for SACHED students in the Anglican Church's old Amen Court building. She took Mbeki, one Saturday morning in 1961, to choose a print to "cheer up" the room: "I always remember the one Thabo chose, because it spoke volumes. It was a painting by a French artist of a lot of people in a train, sitting sort of huddled on their way home from work. It was a vivid characterization, it gave a sense of the people—their toughness and their weariness. He clearly didn't just want the picture to be there for decoration. The idea was to have something that meant something; that could speak."

The fact that the public libraries were closed to black students meant that, for young and hungry students like Mbeki, it was difficult to access a literary world beyond textbooks. There was, of course, the Vanguard Bookshop in Joubert Street, run by the indefatigable old Trotskyist Fanny Klenermann. Vanguard had a formidable collection of left-wing periodicals and literature, even after such literature was banned, and it became an important rendezvous for black and white people after many other mixed-race venues shut down. But Mbeki could not afford its wares, so he raided the bookshelves of older comrades. "Because Thabo was so very wide awake," Welsh told me, "so very interested in reading, I used to acquire books that I thought would interest him....When Thabo came in for his tutorial, he would say 'Hi' with one eye, while the other eye was looking towards the bookshelf to see what was new there!"

In September 1960, once Duma Nokwe was released from detention, Thabo Mbeki moved into the home of the ANC's 35-year-old secretary-general, who lived with his wife and daughter at his parents' home at 7044 Westcliff in Orlando, one of Soweto's oldest neighborhoods. Mbeki would be part of the Nokwe household for two years, until he went into exile in late 1962, and Duma Nokwe would become his first real mentor. Much of Mbeki's political education took place in Nokwe's doughty Ford Prefect, driving to and from Soweto every day.

The Nokwe home was a standard government-built four-room "matchbox," with unplastered brick walls, unpainted asbestos roof, no indoor plumbing, and—although the cooling towers of Orlando Power Station loomed over the township, supplying energy to white Johannesburg—no electricity. As with all matchboxes, you entered a small front room, off which led three doors: one to the kitchen, and one to each of two bedrooms. The Nokwe parents lived in one bedroom; Duma and his wife, Tiny, and their daughter lived in the other. Whoever was lodging at the time slept on sofas in the front room. For much of his Johannesburg sojourn, Mbeki shared this room with another Eastern Cape migrant, Sindiso Mfenyana: They were expected to wake up before the rest of the household, put their bedding away, and prepare the room for its daytime obligations.

Nokwe was a well-paid lawyer, the only black advocate at the Johannesburg bar. Yet not only was he denied chambers at court, he was not allowed to own property in Johannesburg, classed like all blacks (in H. F. Verwoerd's notorious term) a "temporary sojourner." As part of its project of developing the buffer zone of a black middle class, the state finally allowed well-to-do Africans to purchase a 30-year lease on a title deed in Dube Native Village; "the beginning of a new Native suburbia," as the media put it; "Beverly Hills," the home of "highbugs," "tycoons," and "socialites."[6] Nokwe's widow, Tiny, does not specifically recall Thabo Mbeki moving with them into Dube in 1962, but the police do. According to the Justice Department file opened on him when he left the country and scrupulously maintained for the three decades of his exile, his "address at the time of departure" from South Africa was 1695 Dube South.[7]

Duma Nokwe had a quick wit, an explosive personality, and a sometimes-swaggering urbanity that was in many ways contrary to the man with whom he worked most closely, his predecessor as secretary-general, the cautious and gentle Walter Sisulu. Whereas Sisulu was an uneducated man who had become a realtor through tenacity alone, Nokwe seemed to revel in his status as one of the most highly qualified black professionals in the land. Like Thabo Mbeki in later years, he was averse to the populist instinct, and was often caricatured by the rival PAC—as Mbeki would be by his detractors in later years—as an elitist professional alienated from his mass base. He did not suffer fools, and many found him uppity; because of both outspokenness and inefficiency, he was not an effective secretary-general in exile, and he lost his place in the ANC leadership in 1969.

Despite their marked differences in temperament, the 18-year-old Mbeki must have seen in the sharp 35-year-old something close to his own aspirations: a bon vivant, an urbane professional, someone who could hold his own among his white peers. Tiny Nokwe described the relationship between her husband and Mbeki to me as an "older brother—younger brother" one; she recalled her lodger from Idutywa as "a very serious-minded young man, serious about his studies, serious about his politics."

After their release from prison following the 1960 state of emergency, Duma Nokwe and Walter Sisulu continued to run the now-illegal ANC from Macosa House, the Transvaal Indian Congress (TIC) headquarters on the corner of Commissioner and Bezuidenhout streets in Ferreirasdorp, at the western fringes of town. This was the one place in central Johannesburg where racial boundaries remained somewhat blurred. Here, beyond the handsome golden facades of the mining houses, in the hinterland of the magistrates' court, the white business district slid into Chinatown—whose inhabitants occupied a netherworld of race classification—and bumped up against the Indian area of Fordsburg. Here you could find, among the colorful stalls of the Gujarati traders that crowded the Victorian colonial arcades, the few venues that would accept all races as patrons: the Crescent in Fordsburg, renowned for its all-race Sunday afternoon jazz sessions, and Kapitans Café—Nelson Mandela's lunchtime hangout—on Kort Street.

When he was not at Britzius College, a few blocks to the east on Plein Street, Mbeki would meet Sisulu and Nokwe at Macosa House and do errands for them around the city. Another young man doing similar things was Joe Nhlanhla, who was to become Mbeki's first minister of intelligence. Nhlanhla explained to me how youths such as Mbeki attained status—and became "insiders"—far more quickly than an earlier generation might have done: "A Walter Sisulu could not move down the street unrecognized. A Thabo Mbeki could. So a Thabo would start doing the work, in public, for a Walter. And that's where Thabo learned the value of something that has stood him in good stead all his life—the value of keeping a low profile."

On the top floor of Macosa House was a common room that went by the name of "The Rand Youth Club." This was Walter Sisulu's brainchild, formed after the ANC ban as a social cover for political activism. Although people of all races gathered there, it became a particularly important hangout for African youths because of the scarcity of recreational and public space for black people in town. To an uninformed observer, recalled Sindiso Mfenyana, it looked like a dancing school: "We charged five shillings a month, brought in a record player, and an ANC supporter who was a professional dancer taught us, so that we looked convincing when we were giving dancing lessons. But really, this was a cover, so that we could carry on our work as youth leaders and activists."

It was here that Mbeki met the Pahad boys, Essop, a handsome and bumptious Wits student—some black students were still allowed there, under special circumstances—and Aziz, still in high school; they would become lifelong friends and counselors. Essop Pahad's recollection of his new friend was of "an exceptionally charming fellow, good-looking—lots of women used to run after him, of all races and colors—and someone who was clever and confident." Pahad recalls their forays into the white northern suburbs: "You always borrowed somebody's car.... You'd play the going music of the time, dance, you'd be drinking, you'd have political discussions—never leave the political discussions behind!" The boisterous group would sing struggle songs, or add rousing words to popular hits: Pahad remembers Mbeki mimicking Harry Belafonte, "Take-o, Take-o! We'll take the country the Castro way!"

A youth choir, the People's Choir, practiced out of the Rand Youth Club, and singing became Mbeki's major extracurricular activity. He became friendly and then romantically involved with the one white woman in the choir: an art student named Ann Nicholson. Nicholson lived in Norwood, in the garage of white activists Eve and Tony Hall. The Hall home was something of a commune, and Tony Hall remembers Nicholson (who would spend three years in jail before going into exile in 1968 and becoming an art teacher in Vancouver, Canada) as "a gorgeous, vivacious young woman, ready to laugh and full of spirit. She had the kind of character of throwing herself into things, boots and all, and within no time she was deep into Congress politics."

The relationship between Mbeki and Nicholson was to carry on, in fits and starts, throughout the decade. Nicholson told me that she did not see it in any way as an act of defiance or of experimentation; they were bound, rather, by their shared political ideals and the sense that their relationship was one of the forges of the utopian new order for which they were striving: "This is how we lived, in a multiracial group to which we were all dedicated. It was our whole life. We didn't have other lives. And it was thus natural that we made friends and had sexual partners across the color line." But there was a darkness to it all. The most difficult part of the relationship, Nicholson told me, "was when you had to leave each other. Because of the curfew and because you were going home to different areas. Then there was a sense of isolation. I'll never forget the loneliness, walking home in the dark on my own, for the bus in Fordsburg."

Sharpeville put an end to the "infinite hope and possibility," as the journalist Lewis Nkosi put it, of the 1950s. But still, a twilight lingered, one that would only be extinguished fully four years later, following the Rivonia trial in which Mandela, Govan Mbeki, and others were charged with treason. Thabo Mbeki arrived in Johannesburg on the cusp of two eras. When Todd Matshikiza's film *King Kong* opened to a mixed-race audience in 1958, Nkosi gushed that the city "seemed on the verge of creating a new and exciting Bohemia of mixed-race co-operation."[8] Nkosi was writing in *Drum*, the vibrant magazine whose black writers captured the dynamism of Johannesburg in the 1950s; he might have been overly sanguine, but there still existed a place that the magazine's other prodigy, Nat Nakasa, named "Fringe Country":

> a social no-man's-land, where energetic, defiant, young people of all races live and play together as humans....Some people call it "crossing the colour line." You may call it jumping the line or wiping it clean off. Whatever you please. Those who live on the fringe have no special labels. They see it simply as LIVING. Dating a girl. Inviting a friend to lunch. Arranging a party for people who are interested in writing or painting, jazz or boxing, or even apartheid, for that matter.[9]

Did Thabo Mbeki consider himself to be part of "Fringe Country"? When I asked him this in 2000, he told me a story to draw the distinction between himself and the world Nat Nakasa represented. One day, driving back to Soweto, he and Duma Nokwe came across Nakasa and offered him a ride. But the writer, perhaps drunk, proved unable to direct them to his home. Nokwe was disparaging: "This person no longer belongs here, he doesn't even know his home." Mbeki's point was that "yes, there was something of a rebellion, of a refusal to be identified, to be ghettoised, to say 'no' [to apartheid's restrictions]. But then there's a small problem—you get a Nat Nakasa who doesn't even know where he lives."

So assimilated had Nakasa become—so global, so rebellious—that he had forgotten his roots. But "forgetting where you live" is also a euphemism for behaving like a bourgeois, for succumbing to passion, for falling in love, for forgetting your duty to society; Mbeki thus also meant that Nakasa had taken his eyes off the ball; lost his head to his heart; confused a contempt for the segregating laws of apartheid—which Mbeki would have shared— with real revolution. For many in the *Drum* generation, the collaboration across the color line—personally, sexually, and artistically—was an end in and of itself, a creative act with its own integrity rather than a means toward the "greater" end of national liberation. Things could not have been more different for Thabo Mbeki: No matter how far he roamed, no matter how assimilated he might have appeared to become—or how much his detractors accused *him* of forgetting his roots—his own sense of self was that his primary allegiance was to the struggle, his family.

Perhaps, then, it is not surprising that Thabo Mbeki articulates so strong an antipathy for Nat Nakasa and his ilk. The *Drum* writers were as hungry for freedom as Thabo Mbeki, but they defined it in a different way: They wanted to get on with it, and to hell with the consequences. Certainly freedom meant the right to vote and the chance to work, but it also meant living the way one chose to rather than according to the prescriptions and restrictions of either the racial supremacists or the struggle ideologues.

Interestingly, although there was a great deal of casual sex across the color line among young political activists, Thabo Mbeki was one of the very few black comrades involved in a long-term relationship with a white woman. Given his family background, he told me, "You just couldn't avoid" mixing with people of other races. Remember Govan Mbeki's friendship with Bettie du Toit: The difference was that in the 1930s, it was social convention that proscribed such relationships. Now, a generation later, the younger Mbeki was not simply being worldly and "progressive" by dating Ann Nicholson; he was breaking the law. By the time they became involved, "Fringe Country" was more of an underworld than a state of possibility. The few remaining public places where blacks and whites could socialize were shut down, and in 1960 alone, 427 people were convicted under the Immorality Act, which forbade sex across the color line.[10]

Drum-era writer Lewis Nkosi has noted that "in order to survive and in order to conceal their scars," he and his peers "laughed, clowned, mocked and finally embraced their 'outlaw' condition": They gave in to a state that Nkosi terms "underworldism,"[11] and most of them degenerated into alcoholism and early death. After the Sharpeville massacre, the ANC was banned and forced underground, and young activists like Thabo Mbeki were, at their very moment of coming to adulthood, forced into a different kind of underworldism. They too had no option but to become outlaws—but in a very different way from the *Drum* intellectuals; without the artful play and the self-destructive humanism, but with an impulse that was ultimately far better for survival: a mission.

10

BECOMING
A COMMUNIST

"AN HONOUR BESTOWED
UPON ME"

With the possible exception of 1976, it is hard to imagine a more turbulent time in which to have been a 19-year-old black South African student than the early 1960s. Yet Thabo Mbeki appears to have prospered, organizing his new student movement while at the same time writing and passing his A-level examinations in economics, British economic history, and British constitutional law.

Mbeki sat for his first paper on Saturday, June 17, 1961, the day before his nineteenth birthday, just over two weeks after the Verwoerd government declared South Africa a republic. The prime minister, H. F. Verwoerd, cynically framed his republicanism within the African independence movement of the era, and state propaganda made much of the need for blacks to cast off the blight of partial westernization and to take pride instead in their tribal identities. Meanwhile, in a classroom at Britzius College in downtown Johannesburg, a young man found himself sweating over an examination that was nothing less than his passport into the very society that white South Africans had just rejected: Passing his A-level exams well could give him access to a British education at a British university.

As Thabo Mbeki was writing his second examination paper on June 24, African National Congress members from across the country—his father included—were making their way to Stanger, the district in northern Natal to which ANC president Chief Albert Luthuli was restricted. There, after an all-night debate, they approved Nelson Mandela's proposal to establish Umkhonto we Sizwe, "the Spear of the Nation," known as "MK," and to begin a campaign of armed sabotage against the South African state.

Six months later, on Friday, December 16, 1961, ten explosions ripped through electricity substations and government offices in Johannesburg and Port Elizabeth. They were small bombs, carrying more symbolic weight than dynamite. December 16 was the Day of the Covenant, a public holiday commemorating the 1838 victory over the Zulus, where the Almighty proved to Boers that they were his chosen people. More prosaically, the public holiday was also the traditional beginning of the Christmas break. Whites began their annual seaside holidays, and blacks returned to the reserves until after the New Year. The explosions of December 16 thus shattered the promise—for whites at least—of the first republican Christmas.

In the crush of people traveling out of Johannesburg that long weekend was a group of young comrades, led by Thabo Mbeki. They were on their way to Durban to launch an organization they had spent most of the previous year planning: a new association for African students that would serve as a cover in black schools and universities for the now-banned Youth League. Just one day after MK exploded into existence, Thabo Mbeki was elected the first national secretary of the African Students' Association (ASA).

Two weeks later, Thabo Mbeki published his first piece of political polemic in *New Age*, explaining why the ASA had been founded. Given that the African student was "lettered among his people," he wrote, he would have to take the lead as "the intellectual elite of a people [suffering] from subjection by a minority government."[1] There was a gangly adolescence to Mbeki's first attempt at propaganda, but his conceptualization of the role of African students in their society and struggle was sophisticated and literate, a prescient foreshadowing of the Black Consciousness (BC) movement of a few years later.

On one of his trips to Durban during 1961, as he traveled about the country setting up the ASA, Thabo Mbeki had hitched a ride with Ronnie Kasrils, an irrepressible working-class Jewish comrade who would become a minister in his 1999 cabinet and one of his staunchest supporters in the battle against Jacob Zuma. So struck was Kasrils by "this extremely pleasant, well-dressed, well-mannered, self-confident young man" that he invited Mbeki to a party at his home: "We made one hell of a noise with our singing and dancing," Kasrils told me. "Blacks, whites, it was totally mixed, but my cottage was, of course, in a white area.... Eventually the police raided it, took names, broke the party up." Kasrils, knowing Mbeki's parentage and his involvement with the ASA leadership, was particularly anxious about what might happen to his guest, "but Thabo was terribly cool about the whole thing. In fact, he was terribly cool about everything. He wasn't exuberant and exhibitionist on the dance floor the way the rest of us were. He was more of a guy who talked to people."

Kasrils recalls that his new friend's favorite accessory was a Lenin pin on his lapel. Just as his parents had been attracted to communism in Durban in the 1930s, Mbeki was inevitably drawn to it in Johannesburg in the early 1960s. But by then the South African Communist Party (SACP) had been underground for over a decade, and the consequences, for Mbeki's generation, were profound: While his parents forged their egalitarian ideals in an environment open with possibility, he came to understand these ideals in a world under siege, where the penalties were imprisonment, even death.

Many young activists would have classed themselves as socialist, but only a select "vanguard" would be card-carrying party members, recruited through a highly secretive process that protected the SACP's elite status within the liberation movement. And so Mbeki's friends and comrades in the liberation movement might have surmised that he was a member of the Communist Party but could not have known for sure. Even Ann Nicholson, a party member herself, did not know whether her new boyfriend was a comrade until many years later. The stated reason for this level of secrecy was, of course, security: If you did not know who other comrades were, you could not give them away. But it also allowed the party to introduce, undetected, socialist content into mass-based organizations—and its "democratic centralism" allowed for taut control of comrades from the center. Secrecy was more than a necessity—it was a cherished virtue and a mark of the true revolutionary.

The pull for an ambitious young man was, in part, one of status: Only the very best and the very brightest were tapped for this elite vanguard. As Mbeki himself would later write: "I felt that an honour had been bestowed upon me."[2] Membership in the SACP not only put him into the very elite of the liberation movement, but it also put him into a thrilling new world of ideas. While you might learn about apartheid and colonialism in the ANC, Mbeki told me, "being a member of the Communist Party with its Marxist-Leninist philosophy takes you a step further to say 'Let's study societies!' Not just apartheid society, but the evolution of all societies." When legal, the party had required all members to be part of formal study groups. Now this tradition continued on a more ad hoc basis underground.

As it had for his parents in an earlier generation, the party opened up new worlds, wider horizons, for the 20-year-old, not least by putting him into cells and study groups with white activists and intellectuals. Mbeki was tutored primarily by Bram Fischer, the Afrikaner communist lawyer who would defend Govan Mbeki and Nelson Mandela at the Rivonia treason trial and then land in prison himself. He also became close to Michael Harmel, the intense and disheveled SACP chief ideologue, who introduced the young Mbeki to romantic poetry and specifically to Yeats. Harmel's daughter Barbara told me that "like most revolutionaries of his generation," her father was "not always the most engaged or present parent. All of his emotional energy was poured into his relationships with younger black comrades, whom he adored and cherished, and mentored. And number one among these was Thabo."

Thabo spent much time at the Harmel home, at 47 High Road, Gardens: Just down the road from the Halls, it was another gathering place in the white northern suburbs for black activists. The Harmel household was anarchic, scruffy, and bohemian: Books and papers covered every surface, and, in a thumbed nose to bourgeois respectability, there were Indian-print cushions on divans rather than couches in the living room. Harmel would die in Prague in 1974, after a life of depression and, in his later years, severe alcohol abuse. Rusty Bernstein, an SACP leader, remembers that he was "not easy to work with. He kept up an undergraduate lifestyle, working erratic hours, often sleeping till noon and then working late into the night. . . . Method and detail escaped him, but he had high standing in the party for his original and critical mind and his total dedication."[3]

One could not imagine a personality more different from Mbeki's biological father. Fascinatingly, although Govan had played so significant a role in finding an academic placement for Thabo, he had little to do with his son's admission into organized communism. In fact, the first time Govan Mbeki knew for certain that his son was a member of the SACP was when he heard, while in jail, that Thabo had been sent to the Lenin Institute in Moscow, in 1969. Thabo Mbeki's pedigree meant that he arrived in Johannesburg with immediate access to the movement and without really having to prove his loyalty, but while it was a given that the children of leaders were part of the ANC "family," they often found themselves there by circumstance or necessity rather than volition. It is thus incorrect—and perhaps unjust—to accuse Thabo Mbeki of having been born with a "red spoon" in his mouth. He may have been Mbeki's son, but had he not proven himself, he would have remained ANC "family" the way Tambo's or Mandela's children were: loyal, coddled, and made into icons, but not given powerful positions.

Ultimately, by becoming a member of the Party—a "family" forged by a shared commitment—Mbeki found an environment that was, quite literally, familiar. It was a world where personal emotions were dismissed as sentimental bourgeois attachments; where effect was more important than affect, and productivity more valued than intimacy. The true revolutionary vanguardist, Lenin wrote, forsakes his family and his class and becomes one with the masses he is to lead. Thabo Mbeki thus found himself in a world that elevated emotional detachment and the repression of personal desire into essential traits of the revolutionary personality, into nothing less than ideology.

11

INTO EXILE

Through the years of his presidency, Thabo Mbeki had a photograph hanging in his private study. In it, a group of 27 well-dressed young men and women are descending from an East African Airways Dakota DC-3 and are advancing in an exhilarating V toward the camera, their triumph captured by the silvery hyperreality of the print, as if Africans have found themselves in some black-and-white Hollywood epic. It is November 1962, and the young people—all refugee students from South Africa—have just landed in Dar-es-Salaam, capital of the newly independent African state of Tanganyika. They almost did not make it: They had come through two months of hell, spending most of the time in a Rhodesian jail expecting to be deported back to South Africa and certain long-term imprisonment.

You would never guess, if you did not know, that their leader is that serious young man in the second row, bomber jacket over a T-shirt. He is not participating in the performance of arrival and liberation; he is frozen, rather, in a moment of connection, listening, with a slight skepticism creasing his brow while he looks straight at the camera—as if the photographer has broken his concentration but must nonetheless be acknowledged. His interlocutor is immediately recognizable, by his heavy horn-rimmed half-moon spectacles, as the African National Congress leader in exile, Oliver Tambo. The young man next to him is Thabo Mbeki, and this is his first-ever meeting with the man who would become his political mentor and patron.

By the time we see Mbeki in this photograph, he is already precious cargo. Partly because of his family's credentials, partly because of the precocity of his intellect, he has already caught the eyes of "the elders." In South Africa, they had given him the responsibility of forming a new African students' association and of leading this, the second group of ANC students to go into exile; now, as the students disembark, Tambo makes a beeline for the young Mbeki. Soon he will see Mbeki off to London, arranging for him to fly with the Zambian liberation movement leader Kenneth Kaunda, to take up his scholarship at Sussex University. With so manifest a destiny laid out for him, the 20-year-old Mbeki is worlds away from his comrades in the photograph, none of whom has any idea of the next move. All the rest of them have is the vague promise that they will get scholarships to study; they will be shunted through Ethiopia and Algeria, and most will end up in obscure, icy outposts of the Soviet bloc. Given how many of them will die, disintegrate, defect, or simply drift away during three decades of exile, there is something moving, even tragic, about the hope in their open faces.

Thabo Mbeki did not, in the beginning, want to leave the country at all. His mentor Ann Welsh was determined to get him out of South Africa, he told me, because she could see he was going to be distracted from his studies if he stayed: "So she went to Duma Nokwe and Walter Sisulu, and she said, 'That man must go!'" But Mbeki wished to remain at the barricades, fighting for liberation. This was June 1962, the time when the Algerians had finally won their liberation struggle; it was the time, too, that Che Guevara's *Guerilla Warfare* and Frantz Fanon's *The Wretched of the Earth*, with their ideas of revolutionary violence as a "cleansing force," were making the rounds among Mbeki's comrades in Johannesburg. Mbeki bluntly informed Nokwe that he was refusing the scholarship.

At the time, Govan Mbeki was in hiding with the rest of the high command of the ANC's armed wing, Umkhonto we Sizwe (MK), at Lilliesleaf Farm in Rivonia, outside Johannesburg. He heard of his son's refusal to leave and demanded a meeting. Together with Nokwe, he laid down the law. When the young man tried to argue his position, he was told that if he insisted on staying, "You're on your own. If you get arrested, please don't come back to us." The family had made its decision, and Mbeki understood that if he rebelled, he would no longer be considered part of it. He agreed to leave, but only on the condition that the decision could be reviewed at the end of his first year in Britain. He had obviously not internalized the reality of the fact that he was going into exile: return would be possible only with liberation.

I asked Govan Mbeki why he took such a strong line on his son, given that he himself was on MK's high command and an avid adherent of armed struggle. "I didn't approve of him joining MK," he said resolutely, "or of him staying in the country. All the young people were excited about fighting, but we elders knew the other side. We realized that not everyone was going to be a soldier." Perhaps, then, Govan Mbeki's hard line with his son masked a deeper perceptiveness: He knew enough about Thabo to understand that his destiny was not as a soldier on the barricades but as an intellectual. There was a different world of engagement in the struggle awaiting him abroad, one that would suit him far better and take him much farther.

Thabo Mbeki came of age at a time in which a new phase in the ANC's history had begun, one that had its locus not in the townships and the rural villages among the people but beyond the country's borders, in exile. In the 1950s, the ANC had attempted to shift from being an elite group of professionals to being a mass-based organization. Now, in 1962, in response to bans and repression, it would once more become an elite preserve, this time of two select groups: guerrillas mounting armed struggle and international lobbyists and propagandists. Perhaps Govan understood that the latter was where Thabo's considerable talents would come to the fore; he would rise in that part of the movement—the dominant part, it would turn out—that suited his character and personality. Ironically, had the movement been able or willing to foment the internal mass-based insurrection his father so passionately advocated, Thabo Mbeki may well have been unable to find the trajectory that would take him to leadership.

By 1962, the number of people leaving South Africa had increased dramatically. Thousands of whites emigrated either because they could no longer tolerate apartheid or—more often—because they feared an ever-escalating conflict. Blacks, too, were leaving in large numbers, for the first time in the country's history. But, without access to the resources, rights, and networks that whites had, they had a far more difficult time of it. Those who did make it across the border in the early 1960s tended to be middle class (like Mbeki's Moerane relatives), and were convinced there was now no possibility of feeding their aspirations in South Africa. Others left with the express intention of joining a liberation army in whose triumphant phalanxes they planned to return, sooner rather than later, to the land of their birth.

On the ANC side, the very first to go was Oliver Tambo, with the express mission of setting up a movement in exile. One of his primary functions was to find the means to bring young people out of the country for military training and education, and by the end of 1961, he had secured commitments for both, from the Soviet Union and its satellites. And so, for the first half of 1962, Thabo Mbeki's primary work had been to travel the country under the cover of his African Students' Association, recruiting young people who would leave the country to take up scholarships at Soviet bloc universities. The first group of these students left in early 1962; the second, which Mbeki would join, was scheduled to leave toward the end of the year.

Thabo Mbeki left Johannesburg in a flatbed truck, along with 26 others, late one night in September 1962. The ANC had briefly formed a South African United Front (SAUF) with the other liberation movements, and so the group was split between the ANC and the Pan Africanist Congress (PAC). There remains, to this day, a dispute among those who were in the SAUF as to whether Mbeki was its leader: The ANC people are emphatic that he was; some of the others are equally emphatic that he was not and that he imposed himself upon them as part of the broader ANC strategy of marginalizing other voices in exile in an attempt to prove to the world that it alone was the legitimate voice of oppressed South Africans. His major opponent in the group was a PAC activist named Mosebejane Malatsi, who told me when we met in 1999 that Mbeki was far too rigid and doctrinaire a young communist to lead so disparate a group, for he harbored "an ideological fanaticism that simply would not accommodate another person."

The students' plan was to cross illegally into Bechuanaland—still a British protectorate—and from there make their way up to Dar-es-Salaam, where the exiled South African liberation movements had their temporary headquarters. Most of the group had been kicking around Soweto for nearly two months waiting to go and were bored and restless, so they ignored Duma Nokwe when he told them that they were inadequately prepared and warned them to delay their departure.

It was, indeed, a spectacularly ill-planned adventure. Thabo Mbeki and Sipho Makana—Eastern Cape boys who did not know the way—sat up front in the cab with the driver, which resulted in frequent wrong turns and delays. By 2 a.m., when they stopped for gas at Rustenburg, still in South Africa, they attracted the attention of some patrolling policemen who thought they were drunk because they were making so much noise. When Mbeki and Makana were asked their purpose, they said they were a football team on the way to a match, but they had no equipment to back the story up. Unsurprisingly, the whole group was detained.

After a night in prison, they were—astonishingly—released, and they returned to Johannesburg, because they feared the police might follow them to the border. Back in the city, Mbeki and Makana received a reprimand from Nokwe, who accused them, Makana recalls, of impatience and "misplaced militancy." For about a week, the group hung around Soweto while plans were made for a more effective departure. Joe Modise—an underground operative who would become MK chief in exile and then minister of defense—took charge, and a more sensible approach was decided on. The students would cross the border legally at Lobatsi, saying that they were going to the funeral of a prominent chief. Scores of black South Africans were streaming through the border for the same reason, and Mbeki and his group were allowed to pass through unchallenged.

Once in Bechuanaland, they used their savings to hire a truck to take them to the Rhodesian border, where they made contact with guerrillas of the Zimbabwe African People's Union (ZAPU), who helped them cross into Rhodesia, from where they hoped to take buses overland to Tanganyika. But the plan failed: The Rhodesian police apprehended them as soon as they crossed the border and charged them with illegal entry to the country. And once the Rhodesian authorities discovered their links to the South

African liberation movements, they announced that the "terrorists" would be returned to South Africa to face the law at home.

The clerk of the court was a man named Cyril Ndebele, later to be the speaker of the Zimbabwe parliament. A ZAPU man, he went to see the prisoners. Mbeki left "a deep impression" on him, he told me, as the only one who understood the gravity of the situation: "The rest of the group did not seem very worried, but Thabo never smiled like the rest. He was serious, incisive in his analysis of the problems, and his instructions were precise." Ndebele advised the South Africans to buy time by appealing the deportation.

In the six weeks' wait until the case would be heard, things started to fall apart in the Grey Street prison, where the students were being held. There was a never-ending supply of marijuana, and most of the prisoners passed the time in a stupefied haze. Although the Rhodesians were, Makana told me, "quite gentle with us," the confinement—and the dashing of their expectations of freedom—took a heavy toll. What Mbeki had understood from the start slowly dawned on all of them: They would be returned to South Africa and certain long-term imprisonment. Some in the group became quite unhinged, and it did not take long for sectarian arguments to break out between PAC and ANC supporters.

Finally, on Thursday, November 8, the group appeared before the Rhodesian chief magistrate. They lost their appeal and were told they were to be returned to South Africa the following day. But their counsel, a prominent human rights lawyer, had found a precedent that required the Rhodesian authorities to return the refugees to the country from which they had entered, so the group was put on the Bechuanaland train, with no armed escort, rather than being sent directly back to South Africa. The students could not believe their luck. On the night of November 9, they jumped off the train at the siding of Palapye—the hometown of the ANC-supporting Bechuana leader, who had been alerted to their arrival and was waiting for them at the station.

But their troubles were far from over: They found that they were not welcome. The local chief ordered them out of his district by the next morning. They managed to make their way to Gaborone, and after a four-day wait they received permission to remain in the protectorate until transport could be arranged to take them to their original destination, Dar-es-Salaam. Their travails, documented by the South African daily media, made them minor celebrities back home: On November 15, the *Star* published a photograph of the group, leaning out of a train departing from Gaborone, giving the thumbs-up. They were being sent to the northern town of Francistown, where they were to be granted asylum until the ANC could arrange to fly them out.[1]

The Francistown governor was not sympathetic. "He led us to a barren piece of bush that was two miles by two miles, and he said, 'This is your asylum,'" recalls Manto Tshabalala-Msimang, later Mbeki's controversial health minister. "There was nothing there for us. Not even shelter." That night it rained heavily and they were drenched, but the next morning a tent miraculously appeared along with some cooking utensils. Contact was finally made with the ANC, and, with help from international supporters, the movement organized a plane—but it exploded mysteriously on the tarmac overnight (the possible work of South African saboteurs), and it took two more weeks for another to arrive. Meanwhile, the refugees sat in their four square miles of asylum and waited. Tshabalala-Msimang remembers that a group of them, out of boredom, decided to brew pineapple beer. Mbeki thought this was inappropriate, given their tenuous status and, in his characteristically unaggressive way, suggested that they stop. It was the way he handled this—and his particularly attentive approach to the women in the group—that persuaded her of his capacity as a leader and led to her four-decades-long loyalty to him: "To me he has always been a person who cared for women, who had this feeling that women needed to be protected."

The South African journalists who went to Francistown to cover the story brought food but also introduced a dilemma: How was the group to present itself to the wider world? Mosebejane Malatsi and his PAC comrades were enraged that Mbeki appointed himself as their spokesman and portrayed the group as an ANC one: "Before the media came," he said, "we were arguing left and right but in a collegial way. But now the division was clear, and acrimonious." Things got so bad that the ANC and PAC leadership organized a formal debate, and here Malatsi felt he got the measure of the man who was later to become the ANC president and South African leader: "As an opponent, Thabo was not aggressively loud—like I was! But when you believe you have won the debate, and you leave it at that, in no time he organizes in a very surreptitious fashion, and before you know where you are, he has taken the rug from under your feet...the end result is that you discover he has outmaneuvered you or outmarginalized you."

This is a fascinating early account of the reputation for opacity and back-room dealing that Mbeki would earn throughout his political career: "You would sit and discuss, but you would realize, over and above this, there was another decision which was taken outside the formal way," Malatsi said. If Mbeki was not able to convince his opponents, "he would more or less keep quiet, and then still do what he wanted to." It was this sleight of hand that would make Mbeki such an excellent propagandist for the ANC in exile and would also draw such criticism once he became South Africa's president, and play so significant a role in his downfall.

Finally, the ANC managed to arrange for a Russian-crewed East African Airways flight to land in Francistown and pick up the students, and for Mbeki and his comrades, stepping off the plane into Dar-es-Salaam's muggy maritime air was nothing than less stepping into freedom. They arrived just before the newly decolonized country's first democratic elections—in which Julius Nyerere would win by a landslide—and its transition to full independence.

The Tanganyikan authorities allocated a residence for Mbeki and his group when they arrived, a rough place out in the bush on the city's outskirts. Manto Tshabalala-Msimang remembers it as "really very pleasant...because we moved into a structure. For the time I was there, I really enjoyed myself. I was happy-go-lucky, just looking forward to where I was going to settle." But Vincent Mahali, another in the group, quickly felt undersold by "Free Africa": "The climate was extremely hot and conditions rather primitive by our South African standards.... You considered yourself lucky if you managed to get two slices of bread a day. Meanwhile, the leaders had their usual three meals a day and none of them even considered that we existed."[2]

The PAC comrades were given the choice of scholarships in the West; with the exception of Mbeki, however, all the ANC comrades were told they would be going to the Soviet Union and other Eastern bloc countries. Mbeki did not stay long in Dar-es-Salaam: He had been expected at Sussex in early October, and he was already several weeks late. Neither knowing that he had a preexisting scholarship nor understanding why he alone was being sent to the West, Mbeki's contemporaries in exile harbored resentment about his early departure to Britain that was to fester for years. Vincent Mahali believed that the "pre-existing scholarship" story was concocted by the ANC to cover the fact that Thabo was being given "special treatment" because he was Govan's son; that this released him from the "months and even years of deprivation...that most of us 'commoners' would have to go through."[3] The impression would linger, and cast a long shadow over his ambitions.

12

SUSSEX MAN

When Thabo Mbeki arrived in London in November 1962, he was put up at Catholic Community of the Resurrection. He found himself at dinner the first night, he remembers, "discussing pornography! We sat for hours and hours, it was the first time I had been exposed to a discussion like this, very explicit language, but very serious in the sense of a debate, that these are human activities that have to be looked at. *So* different from our discourse back home. Open, unrestricted. Among priests!"

After his few nights in London, Mbeki was sent to the Sussex country home of Nicholas Mosley. Mosley, the anticolonialist son of the fascist Oswald, outfitted the young South African in a wardrobe of genteel finery and reintroduced him to the pleasures of the pipe, which he had first discovered while in South Africa. Little wonder that Mike Yates, Mbeki's housemate at Sussex for two years, remembers him as "very proper compared to the rest of us. We read the *Manchester Guardian*; he took *The Times*. We dressed like students in jeans and donkey jackets; he chose to wear clothing that was quintessential Sussex 'county'—cloth tweed caps, and, of course, the pipe! He arrived looking like a country squire, and never quite lost it."

The world around Mbeki was the Beatles and the blues, the Mersey poets, chili con carne and spaghetti bolognese, Beckett and Sartre, antinuclear marches and the anti-apartheid movement, pitched battles between the communists and the Trotskyites, coed student digs. The good burghers of Brighton might have been flocking to *The Sound of Music* at the Regent cinema, but Sussex students preferred Schlesinger's *Terminus* and Buñuel's *Los Olvidados*, screened at the university's Friday night film society. In the first week of December 1962, the week Mbeki arrived at Sussex, art historian Quentin Bell gave a lecture titled "Truth in Art," and the university's Socialist Club hosted a talk by the editor of the *New Statesman*. A Sussex student could be busy every night at some political gathering or other: at the Student Union, the Socialist Club, the Labour Club, the Campaign for Nuclear Disarmament, or the Anti-Racism Movement.

Sussex University was an icon of the optimism of its era, expressed in its high-modernist vanguard architecture, its pink brick and cantilevered concrete arches, its eschewal of straitjacketed curricula, its spirited jab to the guts of Oxbridge. It caught the public imagination: By 1966 the *Sunday Times* would say that the university deserved "its many reputations: for brilliance, for laxity, for awareness, for its sense of adventure, occasionally for sheer hollowness. Sussex has no sense of occasion, but neither does it have any pomp."[1] The same year, the *Sunday Telegraph* did a sensational exposé of moral laxity at the university, citing statistics that one in ten students lived in sin.[2] The tabloids got hold of it, and Sussex University became "the University of Sex."

There might not have been the orgies of Fleet Street's febrile imagination, but there was a sexual openness that, if new and exciting to middle-class British students, would have been an utter revelation to the child of socially conservative African communists, schooled at upright, uptight Lovedale. Certainly, unlike his classmates, Mbeki had fathered a child already, and there might have been the stirrings of sexual liberation during his years in Johannesburg when he began to date white women. But Mbeki now found himself at the front line of a generational war over morality; an early portent of the great era of sexual liberation that was about to sweep across the Western world.

Thus began Thabo Mbeki's 1960s, his years of opening up. But it would happen slowly, and along a different path from that of his peers, as he sought—and occupied—an adult identity, away for the first time from the strictures of his father and the liberation movement but inextricably bound to them in a way his classmates never were to their own roots. His Sussex peers defined themselves, in one way or another, through generational rebellion, an uprising against the grim, nose-to-the-grindstone postwar years of reconstruction in which they had been raised. One of Mbeki's greatest friends at Sussex was Meg Shorrock, whom he later introduced to the man she would marry, Essop Pahad. She arrived at Sussex from a very sheltered, conservative northern English middle-class family in 1963, a year after Mbeki, and her world exploded: "Sussex was an absolute *wow* for me. Jazz, blues, sex, fashion." There was an urgency, she told me, to her generation's rebellion: "We couldn't wait. We couldn't tolerate all the things our parents had brought us up with. We wanted to make the world a better place.... We wanted to change the world, overthrow corrupt governments. We had been told so many lies when we were growing up, in our official histories at school, that we tended to discount anything told to us from any form of authority."

But here was the difference between Thabo Mbeki and his Sussex friends: While they were fighting against their parents, he was fighting for the freedom of his people. He might have been a revolutionary, but he was never, really, a rebel.

Upon arrival at Sussex, Mbeki was billeted to Wentworth House, a classic English seaside guesthouse on Marine Parade. He was several weeks late for the beginning of term but made an immediate impression. Mel Gooding, a resident at Wentworth, was quickly seduced by "his charm, and a very luminous personality, a sense of subtlety and intelligence. He worked his charm: He could look at you and laugh and disarm you. I was intrigued." Mbeki often was the passive party in friendships, the pursued rather than the pursuer. Rhiannon Gooding—Mel's wife, also in their class at Sussex—recalls that, beneath the charm, he was "incredibly watchful and reserved, from the start, and would keep his own counsel, very much so in situations where he was not familiar."

Nonetheless, the Goodings and a few others became the closest Mbeki would come to having intimate relationships based on emotion rather than political commitment. "I hope the years won't wear the affection away both from you and from me," he wrote to Derek Gunby—another student living at Wentworth—in 1963, just months after they had met.[3] Five years later, sitting in isolated, unfamiliar Moscow, Mbeki wrote a series of letters to Rhiannon Gooding in which he confessed to being "'home'-sick" for England and "a pint of bitter," fantasizing about being a jazz pianist rather than a revolutionary, and gave free and emotional rein to a passion that he would later hone into his carefully crafted speeches and public writings: "That we did become friends is due to you," he wrote. "It is a great strengthening thing in the sense in which Khrushchev made the statement—'Show me your friends and I will tell you who you are.'"[4]

Mbeki had a remarkable ability to cut across class lines and social cliques. If his core group of friends were the campus radicals, he had no qualms mixing, too, with the children of the feudal and capitalist elites against which he and his comrades had set themselves so firmly. He was also a ladies' man, particularly popular with and responsive to his female classmates, and his exposure to the sexual mores of liberal Britain in the early 1960s gave him a far more sophisticated and subtle heterosexual male identity than his South African peers. Meg Pahad recalls, for example, that Mbeki was a frequent visitor at the flat on South Street that she shared with the Goodings from 1964 onward, and that on several occasions he would crash in her bedroom, which doubled as the living room. When, the following year, Thabo Mbeki introduced her to Essop Pahad and they began to date each other, she mentioned this to her future husband, who immediately jumped to the conclusion that she and Thabo must have slept together. "When I told him we hadn't, he was incredulous: 'Do you expect me to believe that?' There was this thing among the South Africans that if you were a man, aggressive and macho, you were supposed to go around chatting up women all the time, if you didn't there was something wrong with you. But Thabo wasn't like that; we liked the unconventionality of men and women sleeping in the same room and not having sex. We made a point about *not* being bothered about any sexual conventions."

Mbeki would have many liaisons and relationships at Sussex, but the most serious would be with Philippa Ingram, an intensely intelligent slim brunette, whom he would meet in 1964 when he was in his final undergraduate year and she in her first. The two would move in together, and Ingram's memory of Mbeki's gender consciousness is somewhat different from that of Meg Pahad: both Ingram and Mbeki, she recalls, were tied to traditional gender roles. Mbeki, by then an ANC youth leader, traveled frequently while she took care of all the domestic responsibilities; she "never thought it should be otherwise." Their relationship ended acrimoniously, and she told me that she felt, in retrospect, that part of its difficulty was grounded in "cultural differences." In his worldview at the time, "it was all right if you were assisting or playing an ancillary role in the struggle, but you definitely had your place. He didn't like displays of independence."

Being a South African male freedom fighter brought with it a certain swaggering machismo intrinsic to the martial revolutionary code. But Mbeki was soft-spoken, slight, cerebral, even somewhat effeminate: He was never at home in archetypal maleness, which is one of the reasons why he never really found his way into the ANC's military structures or became "one of the boys" in exile in Lusaka. This does not mean for a moment, however, that he was a sexual innocent: He arrived at the university with a precocity unusual, in Britain at least, for a man of his age. Not only had he had several girlfriends in Johannesburg, but he was also (even though he told almost no one about it) the father of a three-year-old boy back at Mbewuleni. Later in his career, he would become a champion of equality for women, insisting on gender equity in ANC leadership and his cabinet; he would also develop a reputation for being a ruthless womanizer. In the 1960s, however, it is not clear whether he eschewed that South African way of "chatting up women all the time," or whether he simply refined it.

In February 1963, only three months after his arrival on campus, Mbeki was elected to the Student Union. Three months later he embarked on what would be, in effect, his career for the next three decades: mobilizing international support against apartheid. The South African authorities had just passed a law allowing the state to detain people without charge or trial for 90 days, and Mbeki led a successful motion in the Student Union to condemn it and join the boycott of South African goods. The young Sussex student asserted, in the student newspaper, that the South African government's new restrictions were a form of fascism: "It is therefore our view that the students of this university could not stand aside while another Nazi Germany is arising in our midst."[5]

With three years of membership in the South African Communist Party and the personal tutelage of Bram Fischer and Michael Harmel under his belt, Mbeki was, almost from the beginning of his time there, Sussex's

Marxist oracle in residence. "At the end of our first year, much of what we knew about Marxism we knew from Thabo," Derek Gunby told me. Although Mbeki's personal friends vigorously deny it, others who were at Sussex at the time believe that Mbeki's status was due in no small part to the fact that he was one of only two black students at the university. The other, a Nigerian woman, was crowned Rag Queen—a beauty competition—in 1964. Mbeki's political and social preeminence might well have stemmed from a similar fetishizing impulse: Rod Kedward, then a tutor and later a professor at Sussex, believes that "given the spirit of the times, any black student immediately became iconic, symbolic, and seen as the natural leader of any kind of discussion on race or politics. We would naturally defer to them whether they were worthy of that deference or not."

In the autumn of 1963, however, another formidable and well-read student arrived on campus: Alan Woods, son of a Welsh steelworker and a passionate Trotskyite. His presence precipitated nothing less than a struggle for the soul of the Socialist Club. Woods quickly identified Thabo Mbeki as his only serious competitor and set out to eliminate him. Woods had a trump card he delighted in playing: Unlike everyone else at the university, he was not cowed by Mbeki's race or revolutionary provenance, and he dismissed his adversary, stridently and frequently, as "the black bourgeoisie." Mbeki, for his part, began to hone what would become a lifelong antipathy for the "ultraleft." "There were very antagonistic debates between them," recalls Derek Gunby. "Thabo would get angry. He's usually so cool, but he lost it with Alan."

Also in the autumn of 1963, Mbeki decided to rent an apartment with Mike Yates and Derek Gunby. It took about ten applications, Yates told me, before they found one willing to accommodate them. Yates and Gunby had been enraged by the racism of Brighton's landlords, and were struck—once more—by how unfazed their black South African friend was by such prejudice. Eventually, in January 1964, they found a place in Hove, on Landsdowne Place, and moved into the rather grubby three-bedroom ground-floor apartment behind a grand terraced Regency facade, just a few yards up from the waterfront. Mbeki would remain in this slightly dilapidated neighborhood for the rest of his time at Sussex, and a key part of his social life would be the Star of Brunswick, a pub around the corner. "We immediately made it our own," Yates told me. "When we got there it was kind of dead, a saloon bar, very chintzy, with old Hove types drinking gin-and-orange. Then we made it happen—and suddenly there were students pouring in at the end of the day drinking beer like there was no tomorrow....No wonder the landlord liked us. He was particularly fond of Thabo." Yates recalls a particular Mbeki ritual: As soon as he entered the pub, he would light his pipe. This was the landlord's cue to get him his pint, which had to be placed in front of him before the match went out. He would then drop the burnt match into his pint: "That way he knew which his glass was." Gunby says that "we were such regulars they'd cash checks for us there. It was a home from home for us. And it was one of the few places in Brighton where Sussex students actually integrated with the locals. We'd play darts against them, but our passion was bar billiards. We'd play it endlessly."

At closing time, the group would return to somebody's flat and, recalls Yates, "that's when the Monopoly board would come out! A most unsocialist pastime, but we'd go at it for hours. We'd never get to bed before 2 or 3 a.m., and then we'd sleep until midday." Rhiannon Gooding recalls late-night pursuits more lofty than Monopoly: "Everyone would come back to our place, we'd open a bottle of Scotch, play music, and read poetry." Most often, says Gunby, "we listened to music, discussed, laughed a lot, plotted and so on." Here is where Mbeki developed his love for Brecht and for Shakespeare, where he deepened his appreciation of Yeats. Here, too, is where he discovered the blues—Mel Gooding had one of the best collections around—and through it the poetics of black American life.

Meanwhile, in the classroom, Mbeki and his fellow students were being intensely challenged by their avant-garde lecturers. Most famous was Patrick Corbett, who taught a mandatory course on moral thought that began with the declamation "There is no God!" Nothing thrilled and shocked the sensibilities of his sheltered middle-class first-year students more. In his economics coursework, Mbeki was equally challenged; in his March 1963 final exam paper for the mandatory Economics and Social Frameworks course, he was faced with this question: "Why are dustmen, who do unpleasant work, paid less than university teachers, who do congenial work?"[6]

The course was taught by the Hungarian émigré Tibor Barna, who was, according to Mbeki's official biographical sketch, "one of the greatest influences" on the young student.[7] It is fascinating that Mbeki accords Barna this honor, for the economics professor was also in exile: After having sat on the Hungarian Central Planning Commission for several years, he defected to the West and became a forceful critic of communism. Outside the classroom, Mbeki remained a doctrinaire Marxist-Leninist, but inside he was taught an entirely different school of thought: the iconoclastic and pragmatic approach of ex-Marxists like Barna and his deputy, Guy Routh, the South African exile who was Mbeki's undergraduate tutor. He was not to question Marxist orthodoxy until much later, but this grounding gave him the intellectual tools to do so—tools to which his comrades schooled exclusively in the Soviet bloc or Africa had little access.

During his first English summer, Thabo Mbeki lodged with the Tambo family at their Cholmely Park home in north London. While he was staying there, in July 1963, the news came through that his father had been arrested at a raid on Lilliesleaf Farm, together with Walter Sisulu and five others. They were to be charged together with Nelson Mandela, already in jail, for plotting to overthrow the South African state; the death penalty was expected.

Adelaide Tambo, Oliver's wife, remembers talking to Thabo after the arrests: "I remember saying to him that...it is a big blow to the organization, because these are people—Govan, Nelson, Walter—that we cannot replace. And Thabo's response was, if I remember correctly, 'The revolution produces leaders all the time.'" Such a response points, perhaps too easily, to the oedipal nature of Mbeki's own struggle with his father: What do you mean my father is irreplaceable? *I* can replace him. But to make further sense of it, seemingly so callous in the face of such personal misfortune, we need to understand more clearly the 21-year-old's contexts: not only the revolutionary ethos of the insignificance of individuals in class struggle and the pick-up-the-spear-of-the-fallen-warrior bravado learned from his father, but also the immense helplessness he must have felt, so far away, from both the struggle and the family for which he was now, as the eldest son, expected to be responsible.

Such repression of his own emotions—and its abstraction into righteous triumphalism—was characteristic of a man trained from infancy to sublimate personal need to the imperatives of struggle. It is evident, too, in an extraordinary two-page note he wrote to Gunby just after the Rivonia arrests. He began by thanking his friend "for your condolences on my father's arrest. It was a very hard blow to the ANC, but they can't stop us Derek. They can't stop humanity. The ANC is in the habit of recovering from such blows." Not "a hard blow to me" or "a hard blow to my family," but "a hard blow *to the ANC.*"[8] There is no sense of a son's grief or pain, of a 21-year-old's fear that his father has been arrested and will in all likelihood be hanged, upon realizing that he is now, barely out of his own youth, the "father" of the family.

But then Mbeki's letter to Gunby goes on to betray the deep anger and distress the young man must have felt: "To come to the core Derek," he writes, "I won't be returning to Sussex....I am going home and I am glad you see my reasons for doing so. I don't know when I am leaving this country. Please keep this to yourself, especially when you are in London among my friends. This is instructions. This is decided and final, Derek and I won't pursue it any further." And then the delightful coda: "When SA finally becomes free, contact the embassy here & ask about me. They'll probably know where I am."[9]

Of course this letter was no more than fantasy: not only because it was impossible for any South African exile to return home under any circumstances, but because Oliver Tambo had emphatically denied his request to leave Sussex. Thabo Mbeki insists, to this day, that he was absolutely certain the deal made with his father and Duma Nokwe permitted him to make this choice at the end of his first year—and that they had communicated it to his new guardian, Tambo, who decided, against his ward's will, to break the deal and refused Mbeki permission to leave his studies. Mbeki's determination to leave Sussex and join the ANC's armed wing at the end of his first year is a rare moment, in his life story, where one discerns the violent beating of a heart, the impetuousness of youth, the flare of militancy. Perhaps he got over his desire to leave Sussex and settled in; perhaps, now that he had displayed the required militancy to his superiors, he could amble back to student life with impunity. More likely, though, he found himself strung between two powerful and contradictory urges. On the one hand, there was the impulse to grow, intellectually and emotionally, among his newfound soul mates, an impulse that could not but unhinge him from the single-mindedness of the liberation struggle. But on the other hand, there was the impulse to follow his destiny, even to the death; to prove himself a worthy fighter—and a worthy son of a father now facing the prospect of the gallows.

And so Mbeki returned to Sussex for his second year and threw himself into organizing in support of the Rivonia accused. In April 1964 he traveled to London to give evidence before a delegation of the United Nations Special Committee Against Apartheid. His statement was one of the finest pieces of polemic he was ever to pen, shot through with emotion carefully worked into righteousness: "I should like to add my testimony about the character of the men that the South African government would have the world believe are criminals," he said to the delegation. "They are not only men of the greatest integrity that responsibility to their families and friends would demand, men who would be welcomed by any civilised country, but also men who would grace any government in which they served."

Mbeki asked the delegation to "be so kind as to take this message to the nations of the world from one who may be about to lose a noble father and a noble leader." The man who was to become South African president nearly four decades later spoke publicly, for the first and only time, of his father, from the perspective of a son—but he was quick to turn the categories of "father" and "son" into political rather than biological ones:

If the butchers have their way, we will draw strength even from the little crosses that the kind may put at the head of their graves. In that process we shall learn. We shall learn to hate evil even more, and in the same intensity we shall seek to destroy it. We shall learn to be brave and unconscious of anything but this noblest of struggles. Today we might be but weak children, spurred on by nothing other than the fear and grief of losing our fathers. In time we shall learn to die both for ourselves and for the millions.[10]

Two months later, after the Rivonia defendants were found guilty, Mbeki was interviewed in the local Brighton newspaper, saying he was "intensely proud" of his father, whom he declared to be "guilty of the same crime as all those who struggled for freedom in the European resistance movements to defeat Hitler and the Nazis." The article was headlined: "In Bid to Save His Father's Life, Thabo Will Lead Night March to London."[11] By this point, the trial had become something of a cause célèbre at Sussex: Mbeki and his friends had set up an Anti-Racism Movement and managed to collect 664 signatures—almost the entire Sussex University community—to protest the imposition of the death penalty, which seemed inevitable. The plan was for Mbeki to lead students on the 50-mile march from Brighton to London and to deliver the petition himself to 10 Downing Street.

"Wet and Weary but Trekkers Plod On" read the headline of Saturday's *Evening Argus,* as it described the marchers' passage through the pouring rain and their arrival 24 hours later at Westminster Bridge.[12] By this point the crowd had swelled to 1,500 people; singing "We Shall Overcome," they were met outside the Houses of Parliament by a delegation of sympathetic Members of Parliament. The group then marched on to Trafalgar Square, where they held vigil outside South Africa House. "Well we made it!" wrote Derek Gunby to his fiancée, Jenny, "telly and all. The march was tough and our feet were sore, but I think we made our point. Everyone was tremendously brave and very cheerful."[13]

By the time the Sussex crew joined the demonstration at Hyde Park Corner the next morning, word had spread that the Rivonia accused had been sentenced to life imprisonment rather than the gallows. "It *was* something special," says Mel Gooding of their night march to London, "and we were enormously proud of it. It was only a small gesture, really, but it was noticed, and we did feel—I still feel—that it was part of something that happened all over the world, something that was taken notice of by the South African authorities." Later that day, Bertrand Russell would tell a crowd of about 20,000 gathered in Trafalgar Square that "the lives of Nelson Mandela and his brave colleagues have been saved by worldwide outcry."[14]

Sitting next to the great philosopher/activist, on a pedestal overlooking the square beneath huge portraits of Nelson Mandela and Walter Sisulu, was Thabo Mbeki. It was the young South African's day. Media eyes were trained on him as he marched from Hyde Park Corner to Trafalgar Square and then on to 10 Downing Street beneath a banner declaring "Brighton Against Apartheid," his signature cloth cap on his head, a Mandela badge on his lapel, his mouth open in full protest, and three people always at his side: Derek Gunby, Peter Lawrence, and Dorothy Lewis—an Anti-Apartheid Movement activist from London who would later marry his brother Moeletsi. Mel Gooding (who was, with Meg Shorrock, just behind the front line) puts his friend at the very center of things: "Thabo was at the head of it the whole way, completely identified with it," he recalls. "For him, I'm sure, this was child's play—a march through the Sussex countryside and the West End— but the rest of us felt incredibly tense, and he was clearly the glue that held us together, the galvanizing force of our organization."

The *Daily Worker*, a Socialist paper, carried a photo of Mbeki and his Sussex comrades on the front page. Beneath the banner proclaiming "Brighton Against Apartheid," they stride forward, their mouths wide open in angry sloganeering.[15] The previous evening, Independent Television News broadcast a segment on the protest, showing Mbeki leading the Sussex marchers to Downing Street. At the black door of Number 10, the iconic gateway to power, they stop short—and Mbeki moves forward to raise the famous lion's-head knocker. As he waits, he removes his cap and puts it under his arm. A functionary in a dark suit emerges, barely crossing the threshold, and Mbeki leans forward to shake his hand. A few words are spoken, and Mbeki deferentially hands the petition over.[16] The door closes. Watching this footage today, I am unexpectedly moved—not only by the huge sweep of emotion carried in so banal and bureaucratic a transaction, but also by my subject's politesse. Even now, after having spent two days in the pouring rain marching up to London—and after having heard that he will in all probability never see his father again, after the days of anguish and mobilization and fiery sloganeering—the 21-year-old student from Lovedale has not forgotten his manners. He has removed his cap.

Back in Brighton, Mbeki celebrated his twenty-second birthday at a big bash at Guy Routh's home—a thank-you party, really, for all those who had participated in the march. Then, while his friends went home to their families and summer jobs, Mbeki secretly flew to Moscow to meet the comrades he had last seen in Dar-es-Salaam after going into exile with them. It was his first visit to the Soviet bloc: He led the ANC delegation to a youth festival, giving a memorable paper and organizing his comrades into the performance of a mock trial of apartheid leaders. According to Sipho Makana, the other South African students in the ANC delegation jibed their leader that he was in the wrong place: "We all felt that Thabo should come and study in Russia. We said to him, 'Come! Come to where the future *really* is.' But he said, 'No thanks, I'm all right where I am.'"

By November 1964 Mbeki had disappeared again—this time to Algiers, as the movement's student representative at the celebrations marking the tenth anniversary of the beginning of Algerian Revolution. The trip was something of a rite of passage for the young activist: his first visit to Africa since leaving Dar-es-Salaam two years previously, and his first international field assignment. There is no question that such work inspired him and gave him a sense of purpose of an entirely different order from that of his classmates: His excitement is palpable in the report he wrote to ANC headquarters after his trip to Algiers.[17]

But this component of his life was entirely shielded from his friends and comrades—as was his membership in the Communist Party, despite his status as the leading Marxist student intellectual on campus. Derek Gunby is struck by the difference between Mbeki's easygoing social aspect—"He was humorous, free, easy, able to talk to everyone, at the pubs, enjoying himself"—and his political one, which was far more closed: "He was politically canny, because he had to be. It took a long while for people like me to realize the position he was in." When Gunby was tapped for recruitment into the British Communist Party, he naturally went to Mbeki for advice. Laughing, his friend replied, "Join, of course!" "That's where *you* are, right?" Gunby asked tentatively, to which Mbeki responded, "If you understood where I came from, you wouldn't ask me that question. But if you listen to what I have to say, you'll know."

Ultimately, despite their intense undergraduate closeness, Mbeki's friends knew little about who he was, about the work he did for the ANC, or even about his life before he went into exile. Most of them read this diffidence, as he urged them to, as a necessary political imperative rather than an emotional condition, but his friend Veronica Linklater—later a liberal peer in the House of Lords—did pick up the consequences of Mbeki's very atomized identity: "There was a sort of shadowiness in him. He had a calmness and gentleness, but also...an elusiveness." Being uprooted meant that he seemed not to have "a core...to which everything is linked"; because he had to straddle "very different worlds," "he kept his worlds in different compartments, and they never really met." The mission marked out for him "must have put him into a kind of limboland. While there was this destiny for him, he would never or could never articulate it. So despite the impression of a life and a world populated with friends and people, he was alone."

13

FAVORITE SON

From his first year in England, Thabo Mbeki spent his summers with the Tambos in north London, first at Cholmely Park and then at Muswell Hill in Highgate. The Tambos had been in London since going into exile in 1960, but Oliver Tambo himself—who traveled the world continually.—was rarely there. Adelaide Tambo found work almost immediately as a nurse, and was determined to make a home not only for her own three children, but also for other young exiles studying in Britain. "We never educated them to think they were alone," she said to me, of the young exiles in London. "We were their parents. Christmas in England is a family day, and my home...was where they came. They all congregated there and they sang freedom songs, and we cooked for them, and then on Boxing Day they would go out and visit their friends, while we took the turkey from the previous day and curried it."

Tambo insisted to me that she had no favorites among the students, but Ann Welsh, Mbeki's South African Committee on Higher Education sponsor, remembers that the matriarch paid particular attention to him: "Adelaide was determined to keep him on the straight and narrow." "I'm not going to have Thabo lying around and sticking around the Azizes and Essops [the Pahad brothers] and so on," she told Welsh. "They'll lead him astray. I see he gets up in the morning."

Clearly, too, Mbeki's budding role as heir apparent afforded him certain rights. "In exile he was like my firstborn," Tambo told me. And he behaved accordingly: He was diligent, respectful, and dependable. For a short while, he had a job at Abbey National Bank, and unlike the other youngsters who filled her apartment during holidays, "Thabo brought me some money at the end of every week. And that brought tears to my eyes. Here was this child who needed everything that he earned, to buy himself clothes like any other student, and yet he found it necessary to share some of his little earnings with me, [because] I was looking after all of them. None of the others did it."

In southern African families, where wage-earners so often have to leave their families, the sending home of a remittance is perhaps the prime marker of filial responsibility, particularly in a firstborn son. But Epainette Mbeki told me that of her four children, Thabo was the only one who almost never did this. She noted this with neither rancor nor recrimination, but with the understanding that her oldest son—who was never a professional and never really earned a salary—had transferred his filial allegiance from her to the liberation movement. And yet, if Adelaide Tambo's recollections about Mbeki's contributions to her household's coffers are correct, they give us some insight into the young man's need to play the eldest son within an environment of revolutionary camaraderie, to reconfigure old ways of kinship even within the struggle paradigm of family.

There was no question when Thabo Mbeki arrived in exile that his guardianship was to be passed from Duma Nokwe to Oliver Tambo. This was not because he particularly needed coddling, or because he was the son of a prominent and illustrious ANC leader: Max Sisulu was not handled in the same way, and neither were Mbeki's brothers. Rather, there was an understanding that, as a designated future leader, Mbeki would be Tambo's ward and apprentice. The relationship became dynastic—in its intensity, in its aspirations, and in the way it was interpreted by those around them. "When I look at Thabo, I look at my husband's son," Adelaide Tambo said in a speech at Mbeki's sixtieth birthday celebrations in 2002. "Physically, they bear a striking resemblance—the height, or lack of it, the goatee and the twinkle in their eyes.... They are both perfectionists, but without the intolerance that comes from many who share that quality. They are loyal and true. They are their own harshest critics...." Mrs. Tambo explained that she spoke of her late husband in the present tense because "when I look at Thabo, I see so much of him. As long as Thabo is with me, Oliver isn't really passed on, he has simply merged. God blessed me with two sons. Their father lives on in both of them. Thabo is my son."[1]

There is no gainsaying the intimacy of their relationship, and no doubt that Mbeki learned his political art at the older man's side. Nothing formed his career as much as this primal relationship, and—most important for South Africa's history—the African National Congress's paradigm shift to negotiated settlement arose in large part out of the dynamics of their very fertile communion. But Essop Pahad believes that the partnership was so successful precisely because neither man allowed it to be limited by the "emotional straitjacket" of familial intensity, by the rivalry that Mbeki's relationship with Govan Mbeki appears to have occupied. In this way, the Tambo-Thabo liaison was exemplary in revolutionary terms: a father-son relationship able to reach its fullest potential *because* there were no genetic strings attached.

———————

When Mbeki graduated with his bachelor's degree in economics in May 1965, Govan and Epainette Mbeki obviously could not attend. And so Adelaide

Tambo and Michael Harmel drove down to Brighton to stand *in loco parentis*. In a photograph taken after the ceremony, we see Mbeki standing between the "mother" to his right—wearing a voluminous floral concoction topped with a straw hat—and the "father" to his left, all wild hair and spectacles. The young Sussex graduate, the pride of his family, was sandwiched not only between the excessive grandeur of a mother figure and the disheveled distraction of a father figure, but between the two strands of the movement: the son of both Mother Africa and Father Russia, if you will. For Mbeki was, in the London of the 1960s, in the unique position of being the Favorite Son of both the nationalists and the communists. Being Favorite Son of both these demanding parents, so often mistrustful of each other, undoubtedly facilitated Mbeki's precocious climb up the ladder of the hierarchy of the ANC. But the dual allegiance would also be the source of much mistrust of him, particularly within the South African Communist Party, as he began to backslide from it in the 1980s and sidestepped it altogether in 1990: Was he being as expedient in dumping communism in the late 1980s, it was asked, as he had been in embracing it in the early 1960s?

In February 1965, Mbeki gave his girlfriend, Philippa Ingram, a volume of African poetry for her birthday and inscribed it: "The African poet Senghor is undoubtedly the leading negritude poet in Africa. The godfather of them all is Aimé Césaire, the giant." Césaire, from the French Caribbean island of Martinique, was the originator of the philosophy of negritude; he had quit the French Communist Party—of which he was an elected representative—in the 1950s because of its unwillingness to acknowledge race as a social determinant. Senghor—the poet-liberator of Senegal—had also renounced Marxism, saying it did not speak to the African's experience. Mbeki would have viewed such sentiments as heresy, but his gift to Ingram reminds us that he not only read the philosophers of negritude in the 1960s, but admired them greatly. He may have adhered rigidly to Marxism-Leninism, but he also engaged, deeply, with the ideas of Césaire and Senghor, of W. E. B. Du Bois and Marcus Garvey, of Malcolm X and Frantz Fanon. Much of Mbeki's Africanism has its roots in identity politics: Even at Sussex he was imbibing the Africanist canon and integrating it into his worldview.

These were the 1960s, after all, the decade in which that profound and abiding slogan of the Women's Movement would take hold—"The personal is political"—and activism would be driven by identity; a high-water mark in Africanism that would culminate, ultimately, in the Black Power and its South African sibling, the Black Consciousness movement. In Mbeki's final two years at Sussex, Mobutu Sese Seko, backed by the West, would seize power in the Congo, and two of Africa's most legendary freedom fighters, Ahmed ben Bella and Kwame Nkrumah, would be deposed in coups. The years 1965 and 1966 were, in a way, the African independence movement's fall from innocence, the beginning of the shame Mbeki would attempt to expunge with his African Renaissance in the 1990s. But even back in the 1960s, he was trying to read the dirty reality of postcolonial Africa against a redemptive ideology of African nationalism that was—whatever his Marxist study groups said—about freeing the black man from his chains rather than the poor man or the working man.

Yet, very much the ideological acolyte of white South African communists such as Joe Slovo and Michael Harmel, Mbeki identified himself as an early and passionate defender of "nonracialism," arguing for the need to work with non-Africans. In 1966, the year the ANC upheld its decision to remain racially exclusive, Mbeki engineered the first ever admission of non-Africans into an ANC structure. Essop Pahad remembers accompanying Mbeki to see Oliver Tambo, to argue for the admission of any South African student who supported the ANC's policies into the movement's Youth and Students Section (YSS), regardless of race. Tambo agreed, and the YSS became the first nonracial arm of the ANC. The ANC army, Umkhonto we Sizwe, had always been nonracial, but it was a partnership between the ANC and the SACP.

Still, Mbeki remained very close to both the moderate African nationalists, such as the Tambos, and the more radical ones, such as Robert Resha. Indeed, it was his very acceptability to the ANC's nationalist mainstream that made him so attractive to the communist leadership in the first place. Understanding that their race meant that they would never be able to lead the liberation movement themselves, SACP leaders such as Slovo actively sought a younger generation of African leaders to groom who would lead South Africa to the "second stage" of the revolution: socialism. Mbeki seemed to fit the bill perfectly. Not only was he a stellar intellectual passionately committed to the Marxist-Leninist cause; he was the darling of the African Nationalists—the protégé of Oliver Tambo.

And so he was, as another South African exile at Sussex at the same time, Kenny Parker, puts it, "the King over the Water"—a reference to the exiled Bonnie Prince Charlie of the eighteenth century. Mbeki was the heir apparent, in training, in exile, awaiting the right moment to return. And if he had been sent abroad to safeguard his person in 1962, the events of 1963 and 1964 had sealed this destiny. After the Rivonia trial, the ANC's leaders did not expect to live to see a liberated South Africa. A younger generation of heirs thus had to be developed, and one above all had to be groomed as their leader.

But the outcome of this process was by no means foreordained, as ANC *grande dame* Frene Ginwala made clear to me when I asked her, in 1999, whether she thought Mbeki embodied Tambo's legacy. Ginwala—who had been Tambo's personal assistant and one of his closest confidantes—discerned a critical difference between the two men and their approaches to power: "Thabo's style is more closed than O. R.'s [Tambo's]. O. R. was never competitive...[but] Thabo has had to fight for leadership, consciously or unconsciously, and therefore he is much more of a closed person." To understand Thabo Mbeki and particularly his downfall, one needs to recognize that he carried the scars from these battles all the way into his presidency and that he developed, as a result, a shell of guardedness, even paranoia.

Mbeki's correspondence from the 1960s demonstrates that, even if he was the movement's crown prince, he exercised his authority self-consciously, somewhat brusquely, and not always with ease. Typical of his tone is a sharp response to the ANC's propaganda chief Alfred Kgogong, whom he reprimands for giving him a last-minute assignment: "I must...try and impress [on you] the fact that short notices do sometimes catch one occupied with other matters. The habit should where possible be stopped."[2] Justified as such irritation might have been, it did not win him many friends. From the very beginning of his professional career as a revolutionary, Thabo Mbeki's primary experience of the world of work was that of being the most competent person in the room. All the way up to his presidency, this would lead to a vicious cycle of mistrust and contestation, and the single most defining factor of his political development: the fact that he had to fight for a position he did not necessarily want but had been led to believe was his birthright.

In the 1960s, Mbeki's greatest detractors were the discontented cohort of ANC students at universities across the Soviet Union. Unlike the military trainees who were safely sequestered, usually in large groups, in camps on the temperate Black Sea, academic students were often isolated and subjected to extreme racism and resentment. Many, too, were not even communists: It did not take long before they rebelled against the strictures of both Soviet society and the movement in exile. Mbeki, as the leadership representative, attracted the brunt of this resentment—a position exacerbated by the fact that he was based in Britain: How could he be telling *them* what to do when they were in real revolutionary territory while he lived in the bourgeois, imperialist West?

In April 1967 Mbeki was sent to Moscow to assess the grievances of ANC students placed there. But the students condemned him as a leadership stooge and refused to meet him. Matters came to a head in the early hours of one morning, when two drunken student leaders threatened to beat him up and told him, he later wrote in a report to his superiors, that they were "keeping a record of everything we were doing overseas, and that as far as I (personally) was concerned, I should resign myself to permanent exile, as I would never be able to return home after the revolution"[3]: a veiled insinuation that he would be exposed as a counterrevolutionary or even a double agent. It was to be his first real encounter with the poison of internecine conflict that tore most exiled liberation movements apart—an infection against which the ANC, unlike the Pan Africanist Congress, had largely managed to immunize itself.

Perhaps in response to the allegations that he was soft because he was educated in the West, Mbeki and his allies have made much of the assertion that he would have preferred military to academic training. Both the memories of his Sussex community and the ANC's own records reveal that there is more than a little mythmaking to this recapitulation of youthful militancy. Mbeki's girlfriend, Philippa Ingram, recalls that the only time she saw Mbeki devastated to the point of loss of control was when he was told, in his final undergraduate year, that the time had now come for him to join the army. He had, in fact, written to the ANC in October 1964, pleading with the movement to allow him to continue with graduate studies. In the ANC archives, there is a letter from him to the leadership in Dar-es-Salaam, reminding them that his course is about to end and asking for permission to enroll in the master's program: "May I point out here," he writes in support of his petition, "that my tutor [Guy Routh] is of the opinion that I should perhaps stay on.... He appears to have strong arguments...and presumably we could then go about finding the money and getting the British government to allow me to stay on for another year."[4] These are not the words of one itching to forsake lecture halls for those of war. On November 30, the ANC executive member responsible for youth affairs, J. J. Hadebe, wrote back: "We are agreeable that you should stay on for another year to pursue your studies leading to a master's degree."[5]

And so, in October 1965, Mbeki returned to Sussex for a final year, to do his master's in the Economics and Development program, led by Tibor Barna. There were nine other students in his class, and Barna's records offer a sense of what Mbeki was exposed to: Two students were working in India, and an Arab student—the only woman in the program—was working on the oil economy in Iraq. The remainder had chosen African topics: Mbeki worked on the location of industry in West Africa; and Peter Kenyatta, the son of Jomo Kenyatta, focused on manpower training in East Africa.

Mbeki and his girlfriend Philippa Ingram found a place at 3 Sillwood Street, around the corner from the Star of Brunswick pub, and moved in together. His friend Peter Lawrence, who lodged with them, recalls that "we still had good drinking sessions, partying and dancing, and Thabo took part in that. And of course we had our pub, which we frequented religiously, every night. But my most abiding memory of Sillwood Street is the three of us sitting in the living room, each in our own armchairs, reading, with some intense classical music playing..." This sobriety might have had to do with the presence of Ingram, whom Rhiannon Gooding remembers as "very together and organized and serious" and whom Lawrence recalls as "rather sharp and difficult," but, like all of Mbeki's Sussex girlfriends, "highly intelligent and self-confident."

The relationship was not an easy one, not only due to a significant cultural gulf in attitudes about how men should treat women, Ingram thinks, but to his "loathing of open conflict": "When he was annoyed about something, he'd never say it," she told me. "He'd just go really quiet. You'd have to divine it by the fact that he was no longer speaking. He might be absolutely furious but you were expected to be sufficiently sensitive to figure out why, and then amend your behavior." By May, Ingram had broken up with him and moved out. "I should not include this here, but I will," wrote Mbeki to a friend in Sweden. "England is both hot and cool for me at the moment. Work and work, and niggling personal problems, nothing very serious. I have broken up with Philippa. All for the best I think. Please write."[6] This was tacked on as a footnote to an official letter Mbeki had written, in his capacity as chair of the YSS, and offers a rare admission of the tension the writer felt between his identity as a disciplined revolutionary and his need for intimacy. "I should not include this here, but I will": Mbeki is explicitly acknowledging that the articulation of any personal emotion or difficulty, even if it is no more than "niggling," transgresses the revolutionary discourse in which he has been schooled.

In 1965 Thabo Mbeki reconnected with Essop Pahad, the South African of Indian descent he had become friendly with in Johannesburg. Pahad had gone into exile with his younger brother Aziz after having been banned for five years in December 1964, and met up with his old friend within days of arrival in Britain. If Mbeki was Favorite Son, Essop Pahad was at his side from the very beginning. The two men became inseparable in the first half of 1965, and in September of that year Pahad enrolled in the master's program in African politics at Sussex.

At the Star of Brunswick, Mbeki introduced his old comrade to his Sussex friend Meg Shorrock; she decided she fancied him and invited both men over for dinner. She "went to extensive lengths" to impress the man she would later marry, she recalls, making a big meal that reached its grand finale with *poires Hélène*. "I hope these pears aren't South African," said Pahad huffily, and when Shorrock admitted sheepishly that they were, he threw a temper tantrum and threatened to leave. Essop Pahad had arrived at Sussex.

The relationship between Mbeki and Pahad—which was to become the primary one during Mbeki's years in power—is epitomized by the respective roles they played at a demonstration against Ian Smith's Unilateral Declaration of Independence in May 1966, when they organized a demonstration at the Clock Tower in Brighton's central square. Kenny Parker recalls that when the members of the local branch of the Socialist Workers Party tried to disrupt things, "Essop was in charge of keeping the Trots at bay, and when one of them...[started] yelling 'Arm the workers!' Essop just floored him! But afterwards, the police came up to Thabo, who was the organizer, and thanked him in that polite English way for a very orderly event."

Parker's point was that far from being impervious to image, as the presidential Mbeki claimed himself to be, he was always "very conscious of the fact that he was representing South Africa...as if to say 'Look how good we are; look how civilized we are. How can people like *us* be discriminated against back home?'" But, clearly, Mbeki was able to behave with such propriety only because there was someone on whom he could rely to keep the enemy at bay, to bash heads backstage while the constabulary complimented his civility.

When people in the Sussex set attempt to describe Thabo Mbeki's political style, they invariably do so by measuring it against that of Essop Pahad. "Thabo moved quietly," Peter Lawrence told me. "He didn't declaim. He treated people with extraordinary politeness. He was no Essop." Pahad would stand up and shout if you said something he disagreed with, they recall, while Mbeki would sit down and listen, trying to make sense of your arguments so that he could find a rational way of responding to them. Perhaps more important, he was willing even then to engage the other side in the South African conflict. Extraordinarily, he even participated in a debate with a representative from the South African embassy, held at Lancing, a public school in Sussex, shortly after the Rivonia trial. "At the end of the debate," recalls Lawrence, who accompanied him, "he actually went and shook this guy's hand. I was quite shocked!" Twenty years before Mbeki was to lead the process, within the ANC, of talking to the other side, he was testing his skills as a negotiator.

And so, while Mbeki might have been an archetypal Stalinist to those in the New Left, Lord Richard Attenborough summed up the general collective memory of his Sussex contemporaries when he said, while awarding him with his honorary doctorate from the university in 1995, that the young freedom fighter's style, when at university, "eschewed bullying and bombast, choosing instead to make his mark with charm, humour and sweet reason."[7] Meg Pahad, who had arrived at Sussex politically illiterate, remembers how, unlike the other lefties on campus, "Thabo didn't make you feel stupid and ridicule you or call you bourgeois. He would listen to what you had to say, where you were coming from, and try and edge you towards his point of view. He never saw anyone as a lost cause, which is why he had so many friends across the conventional lines. I have since met many other people who have noticed Thabo's ability to put himself in someone else's shoes and move them towards strategic goals. It is more than a skill—it's an empathetic ability that is very rare." But Philippa Ingram counters that this was strategy rather than flexibility: "I never felt that his willingness to engage was evidence that he was keen to understand; rather that he was keen to manipulate. And to do that he had to understand where *you* were coming from first." Ingram's point is that while Mbeki might have been more canny than his voluble friend Essop Pahad, he was no less fervent.

One way or the other, Mbeki played his constituency right, for in the 1960s era of antiheroism he came across as eminently reasonable, calm, and reflective rather than wild-eyed and demagogic. Despite his heroic exile and the dramatic, tragic fact of his father's imprisonment, there *was* something antiheroic about him. "He was rather low key," recalls Rod Kedward, the Sussex academic, "and I think that's what I found so appealing about him. I identified with him immediately. He didn't seem to have a Joan of Arc complex."

Everyone who has known Thabo Mbeki has a different take on whether he was ruthlessly ambitious or simply fulfilling a preordained destiny. Adelaide Tambo recalls that Mbeki used to show her correspondence received from his mother: "Her letters were always encouraging him about the struggle," she says. "She would tell him what was going on at home, and one sensed she was doing this so as to say 'Don't play out there. Things are not good here. Use whatever opportunities you have so that one day you can come back home to help your people.'" Such a reading of Thabo Mbeki emphasizes duty over ambition as his driving force. Sobizana Mngqikana, one of his closest comrades for many years, says that "he did have a sense of responsibility, of trying to carry others with him. But he didn't have any overt signs of ambition....In fact, I used to get irritated, often, by his indifference to leadership struggles."

Certainly he had the mantle of crown prince bestowed upon him by Nokwe, Sisulu, and then Tambo. But there are those in the ANC who dispute the notion that Mbeki was Tambo's chosen successor. Tambo, they say, was preoccupied to the point of obsession with the development of a cadre of young leaders who would take South Africa to freedom. He was fanatical about not showing favoritism, and he thus treated all the men of Mbeki's generation equally. If this is true, how then did Mbeki so quickly streak ahead of the others? Some believe that Tambo quickly identified not only Mbeki's brilliance and usefulness but his vulnerability: He noticed that it was precisely Mbeki's competence and efficiency that was rendering him unpopular, and thus took him under his wing to protect him.

Others maintain that the protégé himself was more than a little instrumental in securing his mentor's patronage: "O. R. nurtured and handpicked many young people," recalls an exile leader. "But of all this cluster of people, Thabo was the most personally ambitious. He was by no means the only one in O. R.'s office, but the smart money had it that he deliberately spiked the others' guns." Another of Tambo's protégés recalls that "O. R. would give all the young men an assignment for the morning, and then Thabo would say, 'Come, let me stand you all a drink at the pub before we get working.' None of us could say no to a pint, so off we went. But then while the rest of us got plastered, Thabo remained sober. And while we rolled into bed, he sat up all night doing the work!"

Ann Nicholson, who knew Mbeki in all three of his 1960s environments—Johannesburg, Britain, and then Moscow—observed that her ex-boyfriend's approach to power was extremely conservative: "Always take the safe road. Don't rock the boat. Do what is necessary. Always act responsibly, like a leader. Everyone knew how leaders should behave in the movement; there was this kind of leader culture that people talked about a lot. If you were a leader your life was not your own. You belonged to the people. You didn't have personal life. Political work came first." She did note, however, that with Mbeki, leadership "didn't seem like a passion. It seemed like a strategy."

"We knew Thabo was one day going to be president of South Africa," Rhiannon Gooding told me. Her husband, Mel, added: "Long before we all left Sussex it was clear that he was going somewhere. People would come to Sussex to talk to him, to discuss things with him. These people were themselves quite ambitious, and Thabo seemed to be the person they came to consult. Almost as you might the godfather.... Perhaps the apparent lack of ambition came from the sense that he didn't need it. Things were invested in him from so early on."

And then, as only a very old friend can, Mel Gooding came as close as is possible to an understanding of the relationship of ambition and destiny in Mbeki's political makeup: "It's as if there were expectations of him, and he had to live up to them very quickly. Perhaps what drives Thabo is the satisfaction of being or doing what was expected of him. It's a very different thing from ambition, but it's an immensely powerful motivation."

14

SWINGING LONDON
OLD LEFT, NEW LEFT

Thabo Mbeki moved to London to work for the African National Congress full time, in the organization's propaganda section, in October 1966; he lived out of the Pahad, Tambo, and Gooding homes and rented (for a while) a tiny apartment in Bayswater. This was the height of "Swinging London": "London is switched on," declared *TIME* magazine in its definitive cover piece in April of that year, describing "a dazzling blur of op and pop...alive with birds (girls) and Beatles, buzzing with minicars and telly stars, pulsing with half-a-dozen separate veins of excitement."[1] The ANC's European headquarters at 49 Rathbone Street, just north of Oxford Street, could have been universes away, filled as it was with purposeful, somewhat down-at-the-heel comrades edging their way around ungovernable masses of pamphlets, books, and papers. Around the corner on Goodge Street was another office used by the movement, unofficially the South African Communist Party headquarters: a single room in a "poky building," recalls Ronnie Kasrils, containing "three old desks, a couple of odd chairs, nondescript carpeting, bookshelves and a battered filing cabinet....Photographs of Mandela, Sisulu, J. B. Marks, and Kotane hung imperfectly on the walls under a ceiling that sagged. A bust of Lenin and piles of Party journals."[2]

Even those comrades who did not work at the ANC offices would gather there, and so there developed a "Little South Africa" in the warren of narrow streets around Charlotte Street. In 1966 South African jazz burst onto the Swinging London scene—mainly through Chris McGregor and his Blue Notes, who were regulars at the city's hottest jazz club, Ronnie Scott's. The ANC exile community, craving the sounds of home, congregated around them, and a pub called the Duke of York on Rathbone Place became the informal center of a blossoming South African music scene. It seemed as if every renowned South African musician passing through London jammed there; many waived their fees to help the ANC. It was here that Thabo Mbeki began to become a serious aficionado of the music he had encountered in Johannesburg in the early 1960s.

Exiled South African writer Lewis Nkosi was also part of this scene, and in a 1966 essay called "Jazz in Exile" he wrote that South African jazz was "a music which has its roots in a life of insecurity, in which a single moment of self-realisation, of love, light and movement, is extraordinarily more important than a whole lifetime."[3] This is the jazzman's definition of exile: a surrender to the present moment. The other is that of the revolutionary, for whom the future is all there is. The jazzman's view can lead to intense creativity, but also to abject dissolution: Alcoholism was a major problem among exiled South African communities, and Mel and Rhiannon Gooding, who were pulled into the scene around the Duke of York, told me how saddened they were to see so many of their friends felled by drink. They were struck, however, by how different Thabo Mbeki was in this respect, in that he did not succumb to this endemic illness of exile. Mbeki might have listened to *kwela* jazz, but he did not do so drowning his sorrows in drink, longing for a country to which he could not return. "He never developed an exile mentality and complex," Mel Gooding said to me. "There was no sense of exile, of being in constant pain. I don't think he felt that sort of pain. He was just here, doing a job and making the most of it. For some of the others, exile became an internal condition that shaped and affected the way they saw things. It was never like that with Thabo."

Mbeki's time at Sussex had taught him that young Europeans craved authenticity, anything that gave them the pulse of the anticolonial revolution rather than its dry theory. And so, during his years in London, he pioneered one of the ANC's profound innovations: its use of culture to promote anti-apartheid activism. Mbeki and his friend Sobizana Mngqikana approached The Manhattan Brothers—one of South Africa's foremost *kwela* ensembles, living in exile in London—to train them in gumboot dancing, and a group was set up. They also revived the Macosa House choir from Mbeki's Johannesburg days. "It became the core of our social life," Mngqikana told me. "Thabo used to sing bass; he was a beautiful bass." The group, which was mostly white, soon attracted the attention of Tambo, a serious choir aficionado, who was "amazed," Mngqikana recalls, "that we had managed to teach the whites to sing African freedom songs so well."

One of the choristers was Mbeki's old Johannesburg girlfriend, Ann Nicholson, who had gone into exile in 1967 after a traumatic imprisonment in South Africa. Following "rest treatment" in the Soviet Union, she was sent to London, where she worked in the ANC office. The two rekindled their relationship, but it did not last: A newcomer to London, she tended to mix with other South African exiles, and when she did accompany Mbeki to his English friends' homes, she felt uncomfortable. She was very conscious of not being "as sophisticated" as Mbeki and his British friends: "The whole group seemed very English. And Thabo fitted into this group very well, I suppose because he had been to university with them." She found it strange that "Thabo was more English than me," given that she was born in England and had English relatives.

In fact, Mbeki seems to have kept only a few of his Sussex friendships once he moved to London, perhaps because they had scattered, perhaps because many of them were drifting into the New Left and were thus considered "unreliable"; perhaps because he found it more difficult than ever, now that he was a full-time functionary of the movement, to maintain the secrecy required. He remained as close as ever to the Goodings, however, and often stayed with them in their home in south London, which became something of a gathering place for young South African exiles. But he also had a set of black South African comrades and friends with whom his Sussex set had little or no contact. It is a measure of how compartmentalized his life was that this was also the time in which he met and began dating his future wife, Zanele Dlamini: Very few of his British friends knew about her, let alone had met her, until their marriage in 1974.

Dlamini had arrived in London in 1966. She was 28, more than three years older than Mbeki; a stylish and highly intelligent woman, shy but poised, determined to advance her career as a social worker; a keen tennis player and a lover of ballet. She, too, had a university degree—in social work from Wits University in Johannesburg—and had been employed, for three years, as a caseworker at Anglo-American's Nchanga mine in the Zambian copper belt, before moving to London. Her older sister Edith, a glamorous former *Drum* cover girl, had married an upper-class English foreign office official, Wilfred Grenville-Grey, whom she had met while working for the YWCA in Northern Rhodesia—a union that had caused a frisson of scandal in the Fleet Street tabloids. With the Grenville-Greys receiving her, the air that Zanele Dlamini breathed when she first arrived in England was thus not the smoky, jazzy atmosphere filled with freedom talk at the Duke of York pub, but rather that of the British aristocracy.

Like Mbeki, Dlamini was also of the African elite, one of six girls born to a prominent Methodist cleric from Alexandra township outside Johannesburg. But unlike Mbeki, she went into exile not primarily to join the struggle but to develop herself intellectually and professionally in a way that was impossible back home. As any intelligent, thinking young black person in exile would be, however, she was quickly drawn into the world of the liberation movement. She was taken under the capacious wing of her relative by marriage, Adelaide Tambo, who introduced her to Thabo Mbeki and told me that Mbeki and Zanele Dlamini "were together before he went to Moscow for military training, and the relationship grew stronger while he was away: Dr. Dadoo [the SACP chairman] was the one who received Thabo's letters for Zanele, and he used to pass them on to her. Nobody knew where he was, but Zanele knew. Then, when he came back, she had already left for the United States, following her studies. Oh my God, my poor boy!"

Mrs. Tambo has a vivid recollection of her surrogate son standing by the telephone waiting for a call from Boston, but no one else I have spoken to from Mbeki's 1960s London world—South African exiles and British alike—has much sense at all of their strong relationship, nor does there seem to have been any clear commitment between them when they went their separate ways at the end of the decade before reconnecting five years later.

In 1968, "the sixties" finally exploded, blasting the rock of postwar stability apart and sending shards of rage and love, of intense generational and social rebellion, all across the globe, from trippy Haight-Ashbury to the flaming barricades of the Paris *événements*; from the race riots that wrecked Newark and Detroit to the fervent hope of Dubček's Prague Spring; from the Black Panthers in Oakland to Red Rudi in Berlin. The birth control pill had given women more freedom over their reproductive systems and thus over their relations with men; frustration at the slowness of change wrought by civil rights reform in the United States had given way to the radical Black Power movement; by the next year even homosexuals were rioting, following a police raid on the Stonewall bar in New York's Greenwich Village. Within two searing months in the spring of 1968, both Martin Luther King and Bobby Kennedy were assassinated. Suddenly—and it *was* suddenly—the old way was over in the West, and there were new rules governing the way women dealt with men, the way blacks dealt with whites, the way young people dealt with their elders.

The wild, unpredictable energy that arose was perhaps most extreme in the United States, where the Vietnam War had mobilized an entire generation of young Americans against the smug, Cold War–inspired imperial identity of the post–World War II United States and where Black Power and Motown conspired together to give black Americans a new and powerful sense of their own agency. Middle-class campuses and inner-city ghettoes alike were aflame. Vietnam offered a compelling enactment of the drama of anticolonial liberation as the Vietnamese communists held the massive military might of the United States at bay, finally wearing it out. Not surprisingly, Mbeki and his comrades were immensely inspired.

Mbeki, we read in his official biography, "knew many of the student leaders who participated in the student uprisings in Western Europe in 1968, once during this exciting period of change sharing a platform in Amsterdam with [student leader] Rudi Dutschke."[4] This puts far too easy a gloss on what was, in fact, a profound ambivalence Mbeki and his fellow ANC youth activists had toward *"les événements"* and the student movements of Western Europe, which were as anti-Soviet as they were anticapitalist. After the Soviet invasion of Czechoslovakia in August 1968, for example, Mbeki and his ANC comrades became known as "tankies" because they supported the tanks rolling in to Prague. The ANC's statement on the matter actually praised the Soviet Union for having "normalis[ed] the situation in Czechoslovakia" and accepted the disinformation that Alexander Dubček's Prague Spring was "deliberately engineered by right-wing counter-revolutionaries with the support of imperialism."[5]

But even if Mbeki's official biography attempts to burnish his 1960s credentials by putting him on the same platform as Red Rudi, it is correct when it goes on to state that in Britain, "Mbeki also busied himself with the struggle for nuclear disarmament, the protest against increases in fees for foreign university students, and solidarity struggles with the peoples of Zimbabwe, Greece, Cyprus, Spain, the Portuguese colonial territories, Iran, Iraq, and, in particular, Vietnam."[6] The involvement of the ANC Youth and Students Section in the anti-Vietnam war movement was, in fact, spearheaded by Mbeki, over the objections of some of the elders, who held that ANC members should not get involved in other causes. But on the basis of his experience as an activist at Sussex, Mbeki "knew how to project the ANC in international solidarity work," Mngqikana told me, "by becoming involved with all the student and youth organizations centered in London..We would lobby to get invited to a meeting and then we would get a friend, someone who was part of the Anti-Apartheid Movement already, to nominate one of us onto the steering committee. That's how we made the ANC known through the youth movement."

And Mbeki was, once, at the barricades in 1968: On the morning of March 17, he participated in the huge anti-Vietnam march—20,000 strong—that ended in chaos and violence outside the American embassy in Grosvenor Square. "It was huge, tense, and exciting," recalls Mel Gooding, "and the word spread that, yes, they do have machine guns behind the door, and if anyone tries [to storm the embassy] they'll use them. So when they brought the mounted police to clear the square, people scattered, it was absolutely terrifying." When, a little later, the Goodings and the Pahads regrouped, they noticed that Thabo was missing. "He wasn't even making a noise," recalls Essop Pahad. "*We* were the ones chanting slogans. But somehow or other they pulled him out as we were walking away"—perhaps because he was black. When he tried to resist, he was punched in the face and was hauled, bleeding, into a police van.

But what happened in this van, Pahad told me, was the essence of Thabo Mbeki: "What does he do? He engages this young British policeman who punched him and arrested him in a political discussion! And in the end he makes the chap feel so sorry that he'd arrested him, that the chap is apologizing, saying 'I'd like to let you go. What can I do?' If it was me, I would have reacted with rage. I would have told the policeman to piss off! But he engaged the man, he made him feel sorry for him." Along with dozens of others, Mbeki was arraigned, but he was not one of the 246 charged. He was released, with his flawless record of civility intact, but less one shoe—the other had been left behind in Grosvenor Square—and a broken upper-right tooth, which he has never repaired. When he smiles it reveals itself, like a jagged trophy, providing a hint of the street to his otherwise urbane features.

Moeletsi Mbeki, Thabo Mbeki's younger brother, who had arrived in Britain in 1965, gave me the sharpest understanding of the effect of the era on his brother, offering his own experiences in contrast. "In the sixties," he told me, "a section of the ANC got locked into the Soviet Union, and that sapped them of their ability to innovate. Soviet Marxism was reduced to formulae, and they found themselves locked into this.... The sixties was such a magic period, and many ANC leaders and future ANC leaders missed that period. They missed the intellectual probing, the depths of the discussions, the expositions of a Herbert Marcuse and a Paul Sweezy. They missed Nyerere's experiments and Shivji's critiques of them; they missed China's Cultural Revolution and the French Marxist theoreticians who supported it; they missed the Black Panther Party, Malcolm X, and the crisis of the Negro intellectual; they missed Samir Amin and the theories of the 'dependency school.'" Although he would never say it, the implication is clear: Both Mbeki boys spent the 1960s in Britain, but while Moeletsi was swept into the currents of the New Left rebellions of the time, his older brother was so deeply involved in the South African Communist Party and the leadership hierarchies of the ANC that he all but missed the revolution itself.

Moeletsi had been forced to leave Lesotho—where he had been raised by an aunt—because of his political activism. Adelaide Tambo recalls that the younger Mbeki complained to her, shortly after his arrival in London, that his brother always seemed to be surrounded by other students and did not make time to talk to him about home and their parents. "I could see that Moeletsi was homesick," recalls Mrs. Tambo, "so I spoke to Thabo about this. But Thabo was firm. He said, 'No, Ma, we are all students together. We are all in the same situation.' He did not wish to make something special with Moeletsi."

So firmly had Govan raised his son within the ethos of the supremacy of the political family that it is unsurprising Thabo would respond in such a way. But the movement-as-family ideology masks, at least in part, more complex familial dynamics for which there is evidence in Thabo Mbeki's sibling relationships. Epainette Mbeki remembers both her first and second sons, as children, comparing themselves to their father. But while Thabo set himself up to compete with Govan on the same turf, Moeletsi decided to leave the playing field altogether. Unlike his father and older brother, he wanted "to do something practical, to build things"—and so decided to study engineering.

On the surface, the brothers are uncannily similar, not just in their physical features but in the ways they express themselves and in their very vocal qualities. Both combine the plangent, water-over-gravel timbre of the Mbekis with the deliberate fluency of the Moeranes. Both mask their tenacity with an often-charming self-deprecation and diffidence; both also share a laugh—rich, deep, and comfortable—inherited from their father. But in Moeletsi Mbeki's throat, the laughter is not only easier but also often swollen with mischief. If Thabo Mbeki is Isaiah Berlin's hedgehog, "who knows one big thing" and who relates "everything to a single central vision, one system less or more coherent or articulate," then his brother Moeletsi is Berlin's fox, "who knows many things" and who pursues "many ends, often unrelated and even contradictory."[7] The foxy Moeletsi Mbeki's diffusion stands in clear counterpoint to the single-minded hedgehoggery of his older brother—and, for that matter, of his father. Moeletsi Mbeki can be described as television executive, property developer, journalist, railroad engineer, political analyst for financial houses, talk show pundit, foreign-policy wonk, perpetual dissident, freethinker, intellectual dilettante, *flâneur*, self-declared ultraleftist and arms manufacturer, chance-seeker, questioner, rebel, *mensch*: a delight. In short: a second son. And a constant thorn in the flesh of his diligent, serious, and cautious older brother.

Moeletsi Mbeki understood the ANC—his family—as a middle-class organization whose innate conservatism, entrenched by its relationship with the bureaucratic Soviet Union, has prevented it from ever being fully committed to revolutionary activity or transformation—or, later, from taking action against a tyrant such as Robert Mugabe. He came to see his brother's ANC government as an elite protecting its own interests, the political arm of a voracious new capitalist class. During the Mbeki presidency, he was one of his brother's most articulate and most righteous public critics, particularly when it came to Zimbabwe—where he once lived—and "Black Economic Empowerment." The latter was Thabo Mbeki's cornerstone transformation policy, which Moeletsi proclaimed an unmitigated disaster, a form of legal corruption that encouraged cronyism and political patronage and stifled entrepreneurship.

When Moeletsi went into exile in 1964, one of the first things he heard about the brother he had last seen over five years earlier was a complaint. He told me that somewhere in Tanzania, awaiting his papers, "I hitched a lift with these three MK [Umkhonto we Sizwe] guys, and when they heard my name, they told me they were very unhappy about Thabo's position in the youth leadership. Their view was that I was also going to be groomed, was also going to get the privileges and the leadership position that he got, just because I was the son of a leader."

This attitude profoundly affected the way Moeletsi saw himself—and comported himself—back in the ANC family. Perhaps it not surprising, then, that he took so different a tack to his older brother. In 1965, he enrolled at technical college to do his A levels, and like his brother before him, he campaigned for Harold Wilson in 1966. But he and a group of classmates became professional hecklers, dogging the local Tory candidate who also happened to be the chairman of the board of governors of his school. He was, not surprisingly, expelled.

This was to be the first of a series of acute embarrassments for his brother, responsible as the leader of the Youth and Students Section for ANC students in Britain. Moeletsi would argue passionately at YSS meetings against the ANC's relationship with the Soviet Union; he was, recalls Sobizana Mngqikana crisply, "the one who caused all the trouble." Among Moeletsi's many breaches of discipline, Mngqikana told me, was a contravention of ANC policy forbidding exiled comrades to join the political parties of their host countries: He defiantly became a member of the British Young Socialists. Mngqikana maintains that Moeletsi Mbeki's case proved the validity of the ANC's policy, for "he quickly became a troublemaker in the eyes of the youth wing of the Labour Party, and they came to complain about him to us."

Moeletsi visited Sussex one weekend, played a Nat King Cole album incessantly, and got paralytically drunk at a social: "Thabo thought this wasn't cool; that Moeletsi wasn't in control, that he was letting the side down," recalls Mike Yates. "He got very angry indeed." Moeletsi concedes that "we were an embarrassment to the Sussex set. We'd go down there, and they were behaving like the next generation of leaders—Thabo, Essop, Peter Kenyatta. And then I'd arrive with my friends, a Malay South African, a Turk, all of us unkempt, unruly, rebellious.... They were leaders, they were going to save Africa; we were a bunch of youngsters testing the limits and having a good time."

In 1966 the brothers would have a serious confrontation over a personal decision of Moeletsi's of which Thabo did not approve. "You can't do this," the older brother said. "The leader of an African Nationalist movement can't do this." Moeletsi Mbeki comments that "he was right, of course. But the difference was, I was not the leader of an African Nationalist movement. And I had no interest in becoming one."

How, I asked Moeletsi Mbeki, did he understand this difference in perspective between himself and his older brother? He answered quickly, without needing to think about it: "My father was the dominant person in Thabo's life, whereas he was not around when I was growing up. For me it was my mother." Epainette Mbeki was "much more radical, socially, than my father. She was also this lone MoSotho in this world of the Xhosa elite, so outside of the traditional institutions. She *likes* rebels. She might have thought I was misguided, in fact I'm sure she did, but she nonetheless encouraged me. She understood rebellion; it was what she needed herself to raise her children by herself, with her husband absent; to remain in a hostile Transkei."

And so Moeletsi and their younger brother, Jama, escaped much of the pressure that their father brought to bear on their older brother. "Of course," Moeletsi told me, "there's a stronger socialization and pressure on the eldest son than on the younger ones. He is the heir. He is conditioned from an early age to conform to the norms of society. He is the carrier of the culture unto the next generation. The reinforcer of the next patriarchy. The younger son, on the other hand, is never going to inherit. You're never going to be the new patriarch. So, in a way, you're free."

While Moeletsi Mbeki was indisputably ANC royalty, he was not indentured to the family the way his older brother was. "I was not dependent on the ANC emotionally," he told me. "I had my independence. If an ANC leader disapproved of me, I didn't suffer the depth of fear. I was like a British kid, doing British things—taking summer jobs, trying to find cheap flights to Italy for summer holidays." The irony is that this freedom from the political family of the ANC allowed Moeletsi to develop relationships of affection with his blood family in a way his older brother never could: while the baggage of primogeniture appears to have had the effect of estranging Thabo from his father, upon return to South Africa, Moeletsi quickly developed an intimate and loving relationship with the man he had barely known.

The key to understanding the development of Thabo Mbeki's ideology, and the apparent disjuncture between his New Left sensibilities and his Old Left politics, is in his bifurcated experience of the 1960s. He was both the son of a liberation movement and a questing undergraduate. In his consciousness, two sets of revolutionary politics were brought into play: those of a people fighting for their freedom and those of a generation looking for answers. Much of Mbeki's energy, in his 20s, seems to have been dedicated to finding a way to advance his single-minded objective within that reality. It was an environment, ultimately, that benefited him. He might have been a "tankie" but, unlike his peers at universities in the Soviet Union, he was forced to engage with Alan Woods in the Student Union, with Tibor Barna and Guy Routh in the classroom, with Rudi Dutschke on a platform in Amsterdam. He had, in other words, the intellectual space to consider the Prague Spring and to reason with those of his comrades who supported it. "Things like flower power, hippies, the drug scene, as far as Thabo was concerned, that was all petit-bourgeois rubbish," one of his contemporaries within the ANC told me. "But he was nevertheless a beneficiary of the 1960s. It gave him the space, and as a result of this space created by the New Left, he moved on. It could no longer be 'I disagree with you, so off to the Gulag!'"

Ann Nicholson, who touched base with her ex-boyfriend intermittently through the 1960s, avers that the effect of the decade on Mbeki was "more like layers settling upon him than something growing within him." Despite his doctrinaire Soviet partisanship, during his time in Britain the seeds of critical thought were planted in Mbeki, seeds that would germinate into his breathtaking creativity in the 1980s, when he led the ANC toward a nego- tiated settlement and away from socialist economics. Certainly a man of greater courage or broader vision might have forsaken Stalinism earlier. But was it simply a question of courage? If Mbeki had been won over to the New Left, as so many of his Sussex friends and his brother were, he would have been lost to the leadership of the ANC. That was not an option.

And so, in late 1969, the SACP central committee decided—with Oliver Tambo's assent—to parachute Thabo out of Swinging London and to land him in an extraordinarily different world: the Lenin Institute in Moscow, the ideological training center for generations of Marxist-Leninist revolutionar- ies. None of Mbeki's London friends can recall precisely when he left Britain, and none of them—not even his fellow South Africans in the YSS—knew, at the time, where he was going. But they all remember the atmosphere of his departure.

A group gathered at the airport to bid him farewell: "People were so emo- tional," Sobizana Mngquikana told me. "Everyone knew he was leaving. The Goodings were there too. The scene was at the terminal. People were crying!...Nobody talked to anybody. You just saw tears. It was a moving thing."

While the Goodings "didn't know where he was going," Rhiannon told me, "we could see in other people's demeanors how worried they were.... There could be something perhaps dangerous. That's why everyone was so hys- terical." Her husband recalls that "we wept copiously. We sort of knew he was going to the Soviet Union, and that he was probably en route to South Africa." How had Mbeki himself dealt with the emotion? "Oh, very calm and sweet," according to Rhiannon Gooding. "He wasn't crying. He was very sweet and, you know, affectionate."

From Moscow, Thabo Mbeki would write to Rhiannon Gooding that he was " 'home'-sick."[8] Certainly he was beginning the journey home. But he was also leaving home.

15

MOSCOW MAN

Thabo Mbeki arrived in Moscow to study for ideological leadership training at the Lenin Institute in February 1969. The institute was an imposing, neoclassical Stalinist edifice on Leningradsky Prospekt about three miles north of the city center. Set up by the Soviet state to train communists from all over the world in Marxist-Leninist ideology as part of its imperial ambitions, it had been running since the 1920s, and Mbeki was one of three South Africans enrolled in 1969, along with 400 other students. The other South Africans were Ann Nicholson, his old girlfriend from Johannesburg, and Ahmed Timol, a young Indian comrade also from Johannesburg, who would die while in detention back home four years later. Because the South African communists were "underground," their presence at the institute was kept secret, even from other ANC students in the city. The South Africans were given noms de guerre, Rhodesian identities, and elaborate covers: Mbeki was "Jack Fortune"; Nicholson "Jenny Wood."

The African National Congress itself was never communist, but through its relationship with the South African Communist Party, it had developed a strong relationship with the Soviet Union: the Soviets were the movement's most significant international funder, supplying military training and arms, academic scholarships, and humanitarian aid to exiles living in other African countries. Inevitably, then, the ANC was a Moscow client—although Mbeki, as we shall see, would play a key role in changing this in the 1980s. But his own skepticism about Soviet imperialism (and ideology) was still to come: right now, he needed revolutionary training. He would spend the better part of the year at the Lenin Institute and then another doing military commander training just outside Moscow. Sussex might have opened him up intellectually and exposed to him to the workings of liberal, Western society, but his time in the Soviet Union would prepare him for actual leadership of a liberation movement. Once he was done, he would be sent back to Africa, to work out of the ANC's headquarters in Lusaka, Zambia.

Mbeki imbibed both the ideology and the practice of Soviet communism while in Moscow. Although he never refers directly to the effect of his Moscow training on his thinking, it was clearly profound. The imprimatur of the Lenin Institute training could be seen during his presidency, not only in his fluid grasp of the Marxist-Leninist canon but in his obsession with organizational politics and his abiding faith in Leninism's core strategic precepts: the notions of *iskra*, "the spark" of vanguardism, and of democratic centralism, the assertion of tight central control over the process of transition. Mbeki's attempt to apply such notions to democratic, twenty-first-century South Africa would be marked, most of all, by his faith in a newly empowered black bourgeoisie, and in the way he would try to develop the postapartheid ANC into an elite cadre of trained change agents rather than a mass movement. These were the fundamental lessons of his ideological training, but his inability to adapt them to a twenty-first-century electoral democracy would be a key part of his failure toward the end of his presidency.

Fascinatingly, despite his own political journey away from communism over the years, Mbeki's memories of Moscow remain rose-tinted: "You'd walk around the streets of Moscow without a fur hat," he told me, "and old women would approach you and berate you very strongly: 'You must understand, young man, you're still young, you don't feel the cold, but you need to wear this hat, because the cold seeps into your head and it's going to affect you.' So you thought, 'Here's a society that cares. People don't walk by.'" For a young communist like Mbeki, Moscow was the romantic center of the universe, and his memories reflect this: "You'd get onto the underground train in Moscow, and three-quarters of the coach would be reading, and this [observation] translated very quickly into thinking, 'Yes indeed, this is socialism, because this is part of the thinking—the all-round development of the individual!'"

Ann Nicholson had a similar response: "I had never ever before in my life been treated as well," she told me. Because the Lenin School students were an elite "vanguard," their experiences were vastly different from regular South African students in the Soviet Union. The institute staff rigorously checked the foreigners' clothing before they went out to make sure they were dressed warmly enough, and students at the Lenin Institute were called to the doctor if their lights were seen to be on late at night. If they said they had been partying, they would be slapped on the back and sent on their way; if they said they had been studying, they would be lectured on the importance of balancing work and leisure. Lenin Institute staff not only took care of their wards' ideological training, they supervised their eating habits, insisted on the restorative qualities of fresh air even in the dead of winter, and even tested and quarantined Nicholson's entire floor in the hostel when she came down, once, with diarrhea.

This might sound like a deranged nanny state to the contemporary reader, but for people like Nicholson and Mbeki, who had been traumatized by underground life, exile, dismembered families, and (in Nicholson's case) a few years in prison, there was—as she puts it—something "emotionally bonding" about the experience: not least being in a place where, for the first time, you did not need to be secretive or defensive about your ideological affiliation. At last, it was acceptable to be a communist, and this was like "coming home," Nicholson told me.

The coursework at the Lenin Institute was demanding. Students took five courses: Philosophy, Political Economics, Theory and Tactics, Soviet History, and Social Psychology, all taught in English or with English translators. The last had been introduced into the curriculum only in 1967 and was considered very "reformist," Mbeki's lecturer, Shura Rodianova, told me: It was "all about getting people to cooperate and work together by recognizing their individual personalities." In reality, it was a practical course in propaganda: Students learned how to produce and disseminate underground literature. In one of the institute's more bizarre innovations, they would hone their oratorical skills in a soundproof basement room, painted with murals of crowds at a rally, against the simulated sounds of the cheering—or heckling—masses.

Mbeki's teachers and classmates confirm that he excelled in both his coursework and in extracurricular activities such as public speaking; Nicholson recalls that he addressed the Lenin Institute's weekly assemblies far more often than most other students. Such stellar performances, however, clearly rubbed some of his classmates the wrong way; although they were impressed by Mbeki's ability, recalls Paul Bjarnason, a Canadian at the institute who would later marry Nicholson, "his colossal ego became wearying after a while." Bjarnason says the Canadian group was particularly irritated by his claim that "he was going to be the first black prime minister/president of South Africa. In 1969, this ambition, coming from a 25-year-old communist, struck us as more than merely optimistic."

The days at the institute followed a set routine: classes in the morning, "self-education" (as study was known) in the afternoon, and leisure time in the evening. Nicholson recalls that Mbeki's leisure activities were sedentary—chess and dominoes—and she does not recall him using the gym or doing any sport; when Rhiannon Gooding sent him tapes via secret SACP post, he wrote back that he liked to "jig and jog" to them, but only in private: "For the exercise I lock all doors."[1] After a few hours of "self-education," groups of students would gather in a room for tea "and probably a bit of vodka or Cuban rum," recalls Nicholson. And for the Russians they hung out with—usually their younger professors—"anything was occasion for a party."

Lenin Institute students had almost all their needs catered to: There was a huge library of over one-and-a-half million books and magazines, a large subsidized shop, and access to subsidized tickets to any theater or concert hall in the city. Many would attend concerts at the huge Tchaikovsky Concert Hall, built by Stalin, and would return to South Africa with a love of classical music. The Lenin Institute students were also given a stipend of 180 rubles a month, double that of students at other universities and twice as much as the average white-collar worker.[2] "That was another thing that blew our minds," says Nicholson. "Not only was education free in the Soviet Union, but you actually got paid to be a student."

That Nicholson and Mbeki felt so positive about Moscow is all the more striking given that they arrived only seven months after the Soviet invasion of Czechoslovakia. This was the height of the Brezhnev era's descent into what is often termed neo-Stalinism: There was none of the mass terror and genocide of the Stalin years, but political prisoners continued to be subject to inhuman incarceration, and there was a marked increase in censorship, surveillance, and the ostracism and exile of those few who dissented. The South Africans might not have been conscious of the hardship most ordinary Russians faced, but they were aware and critical, Nicholson told me, of the repression of independent thinking in the Soviet Union. Obviously, they discussed it only among themselves, and Nicholson recalls that while Mbeki "did not come across as very doctrinaire," neither was he "very questioning. I can't remember him saying anything politically that was either really different or shocking. I think he had a talent for *not* doing that."

This is not surprising: Mbeki was already well along the route to party leadership and had access even to the Soviet leadership that his classmates could only dream of. Since his graduation from Sussex, he had been impressing SACP leadership by his contributions on the editorial board of the *African Communist*. Now, while studying in Moscow, he was given his first major leadership test, when he was chosen—above many senior to him—to be secretary of a high-level four-person SACP delegation to the International Conference of Communist and Workers' Parties in Moscow, in June 1969. The highlight of the visit, for the South Africans, was a rare meeting with Aleksei Kosygin. When the Soviet premier asked about the conditions of mineworkers in South Africa, the delegation leader, J. B. Marks, referred the question to the 26-year-old Mbeki, an extraordinary display of confidence in the young man.

Mbeki had been earmarked for leadership, but one could not, of course, lead a liberation movement if one did not have military training. And so upon completion of his Lenin Institute course, he was transferred to Skhodnya, a military camp northwest of Moscow, to join a group of about 25 South Africans for a course in advanced guerrilla warfare. The course was usually only for those who were already in Umkhonto we Sizwe (MK): that Mbeki was the only one in the group who had not yet undergone basic military training was a sign—certainly to his peers—of his future prospects. The group studied guerrilla formation management, underground organization, radio communications, explosives, topography, intelligence, and security; it was here that Mbeki learned to use a gun.

But Mbeki raised eyebrows among his comrades, says Sipho Makana, who was also taking the course, because "he was always reading political and not military works; he was interested in revolutionary theories rather than in studying the calibers of weapons." Max Sisulu's overriding recollection of Mbeki at Skhodnya is of his diligence: "He wasn't one of those you would see out on the field playing soccer. He'd spend his spare time reading. That was the one thing he clearly loved." Sisulu thinks that Mbeki found Skhodnya taxing, not just because he was not particularly athletic but because of his free-spiritedness and advanced education: "He [just] didn't find it easy being told what to do and what not to do. He was too well educated and independent-minded for that.... I could never imagine Thabo as General Thabo. I could only see him then as a political leader, but not as a military one."[3]

For his part, Mbeki told me that the elemental lesson he learned at Skhodnya was that "a gun is not something to be proud of or boast about, because it does a *bad thing*"; that weapons were "manufactured, created, designed, to kill people, and it's not a normal human thing, this wanting to kill people.... If you speak to any of our people trained as soldiers in the Soviet Union, you'll find a very common respect for weapons." But respect did not mean pacifism. Later Mbeki would become a strong advocate for a negotiated settlement rather than armed struggle, but in his early public utterances as an ANC leader, he displayed a deep commitment to violent struggle—not just as a strategic imperative, but, following Fanon (and Lenin), as a tool for redemption. By 1978 he was saying on American television that the only way a black man was ever going to equal his oppressor was by carrying a gun.[4]

Mbeki's peers at Skhodnya might have disparaged his military prowess, but that did not hinder his rapid ascent into the elite SACP leadership. In June 1970 he was whisked, without the knowledge of his fellow trainees, to a dacha in the woods outside Moscow, where a meeting of the SACP's Central Committee was to be held. The dacha had belonged to Stalin—he had actually died in it in 1953—and was now a guesthouse of the Communist Party of the Soviet Union. Up to this point, party leadership had been largely non-African, aging, scattered around the world, and barely in touch with the realities of life on the ground in exile—particularly in the MK camps. Now several Africans were added, including Thabo Mbeki and Chris Hani, both celebrating their twenty-eighth birthdays at the meeting and the youngest members ever on the committee.

The two new additions were exact contemporaries: Separated in age by only ten days, they had been at Lovedale together, and were to be rivals and competitors all the way until Hani's murder by right-wing assailants in 1993. Hani was a protégé of Govan Mbeki's, but—unlike Thabo—was earmarked for the army, and sent to the Soviet Union for military training in 1963. He had led the ANC's heroic but quixotic Luthuli Detachment into Rhodesia in 1968 and spent most of the year in a Botswana jail. After his release he would exhibit his immense bravery once again, when he submitted to the ANC leadership a memorandum of complaints considered so treasonous that it nearly got him executed. Prominent was a grievance about "the practice of nepotism": "Virtually all the sons of the leaders" had been sent to universities in Europe, he wrote, "a sign that these people are being groomed for leadership positions after the MK cadres have overthrown the fascists." He mentioned Mbeki by name, disparaging him as a leader of the "bogus" ANC Youth and Students Section.[5]

Later in life, the intellectually gifted Hani often complained that he would have loved the academic opportunities afforded to Mbeki. There is something biblical about the sibling relationship between these two men: They were, in effect, both sons of Govan Mbeki, each carrying a different set of aspirations for their shared father, and the first arena for this rivalry was within the SACP, where both young men were potential future leaders. Initially Mbeki was considered the diligent insider while Hani was the unpredictable militant. But by 1972, when Hani was elected assistant general secretary of the party, this had changed. It is possible that this was because the SACP leadership considered Hani's populist action-man persona to be more valuable than Mbeki's aloof ideas-man one; and possible too that Mbeki was being deliberately kept out of the senior party leadership so that he could remain acceptable to a broader base within the ANC and thus be Oliver Tambo's successor. But one of the main reasons for Hani's unexpected ascendancy over Mbeki within the party had to do with Joe Slovo, the larger-than-life Jewish lawyer who was one of the founders of MK and who, from exile in London, was the ANC's preeminent strategist.

In the years to come, Mbeki's movement through the ANC and his rise to power would be defined, in many ways, by the difficulties of his relationship with Slovo: It would be Slovo and those close to him, such as Hani, who would oppose Mbeki most vigorously, both in exile and back at home. The relationship between the two men was fraught with intellectual competition and riven by ideological mistrust, but at the heart of it was a personality clash. In London, Slovo never mentored Mbeki in as direct a way as Tambo or Michael Harmel, although they had held a mutual if somewhat distant admiration for each other. But a confrontation took place between the two while Mbeki was at the Lenin Institute, and Slovo believed that this was the root cause of the bad blood.

Slovo told several of his confidants that, while Mbeki was in Moscow, the SACP Central Committee received a complaint about the young man's personal conduct in regard to a woman. Slovo was dispatched to Moscow to discipline Mbeki, a task that was particularly difficult not only because of Mbeki's status but because of their budding mentor-protégé relationship. No one but the most senior leadership of the SACP knew about this event, and Slovo believed, until his death, that it marked the turning point in their relationship; that he had either injured Mbeki's pride or exposed him, and from this moment their relationship cooled.

During his stay at the Lenin Institute, Mbeki sent a series of letters to his friend Rhiannon Gooding, in which he confessed to longing for England and wrote with intimacy (and perhaps the help of vodka) about Shakespeare, Brecht, Beethoven, and utopian idealism. He shared his excitement at having "discovered" Shakespeare's *Coriolanus* and tried to convince his British friend that the Roman general was not the tyrant he was generally considered to be in the West, but rather the very prototype for the modern-day revolutionary, not unlike Che Guevara. This is a particularly eccentric reading of one of Shakespeare's darkest tragedies: *Coriolanus* is generally considered to be a lesson in the dangers of tyranny, its eponymous hero tragically flawed by his own pride and driven by hubris to war against his own people in vengeance for their having exiled him from Rome. But Mbeki saw the general's contempt for "the rabble, the unthinking mob," as he put it to Gooding, as part of his heroism. And if purging the rot required destroying the state of Rome, well, then, so be it—that was what made a true revolutionary!

Such was the ideology—and the sense of purpose—that Mbeki imbibed in Moscow. "In everyday life," he wrote to Gooding, "you and I tend to denigrate [the qualities] of truthfulness, courage, self-sacrifice, absence of self-seeking, heroism, optimism.... We shrink at 'hero-worship.' But to think of revolutionary struggle is to think of heroic feats of individuals, who...carry all the qualities above." Such a person was not only "infinitely preferable to the existential non-hero," but fought "for revolutionary socialist transformation of the world."[6]

The principles of antiheroism and existentialism; the importance of self-expression and individualism; the joy of knowledge or creativity for its own sake; skepticism about "hero worship": These were the values that drove Thabo Mbeki's education at Sussex. The "incorrectness" of populism; the counterrevolutionary nature of blood ties over political comradeship; the value of martyrdom; the illusion of democracy in liberal multiparty states; the vanguardist notion of doing what is right for the people even if they do not know it themselves; the heroism of struggle: These are the values with which he had been raised, strongly reinforced by his time in Moscow.

Certainly, in the long run, the lessons of Tibor Barna were to prove more influential on him than those of his Lenin Institute teachers. But the lessons from Moscow were profound, for they offered him a road map for how he might spend his life transforming the world. The two educations Mbeki received in the 1960s would struggle with each other for prominence throughout his political career, albeit often in different guises and complicated by the march of other ideologies onto the battlefield: "Third-way" Sweden would soon present itself to mediate between them and then, later, the mythical army of the African Renaissance would appear and attempt to vanquish them all. During the Mbeki presidency, the war would often seem to be raging not only in the presidential head but in the body of the ANC he led: a struggle between the principles of liberal democracy and the vanguardist, centralist methods of Leninism.

But back in 1970, after nearly two years of training in the theory and practice of revolutionary warfare, Mbeki clad himself in the armor of a hero and looked bravely to the future. He could not, he wrote to Rhiannon Gooding, submit "to the feeling that we are the idle bourgeoisie or part of it." The choice was clear: become a revolutionary, or submit, "in the most primitive way ... to events, phenomena, nature, and when all else fails, God." "Yes indeed the bitch is in heat again," he wrote to her, paraphrasing Bertold Brecht's famous lines about the perpetual recurrence of authoritarianism in society; it was his duty to slay it.[7]

16

"NOT QUITE HOME"
LUSAKA AND MARRIAGE

Following his military training, Thabo Mbeki returned to sub-Saharan Africa in April 1971 for the first time since his flight into exile over a decade earlier. He was billeted to the ANC's new headquarters in Lusaka; the torpid and dusty Zambian capital would be his base until he was able to return to South Africa nearly 20 years later. Here his wife, Zanele, would set up home, and here he would work full time for the movement: as the administrator of the new Revolutionary Council (RC), tasked with finding a way to get South African freedom fighters home; as an envoy to several other African countries; and, from 1978 on, as the political secretary to the African National Congress president, Oliver Tambo, and as the movement's propaganda chief. The peripatetic Tambo brought his protégé to Lusaka to be his eyes and ears and ultimately his proxy. This would give the young Mbeki great power but would also attract much resentment. In effect, Mbeki would run the movement in exile and, as the 1980s progressed, its negotiations strategy. His greatest achievement would be as the articulate and charming face of the struggle, engaged in a double seduction: getting the West to accept the ANC as a legitimate liberation movement rather than a terrorist organization and getting white South Africans to come to terms with the inevitability of black leadership.

But that was to come. The bitter truth was that, in 1971, the ANC was farther than ever away from home, separated from the front line by a buffer of other white-run countries—Angola, Namibia, Rhodesia, and Mozambique—and by independent states bludgeoned into hostility against the ANC by economic dependence on South Africa and the threat of punitive action. There was no contact at all between the ANC and comrades back home, and Joe Slovo would later admit that, by 1975, the ANC had not fired "a single shot in South Africa" in 14 years.[1]

To make matters worse, ANC comrades were at this point unwanted guests in their host countries. The organization had just been thrown out of Tanzania because of internecine conflicts in the ruling party there; their current Zambian hosts were somewhat ambivalent, too. On one hand, President

Kenneth Kaunda built his profile as a postcolonial African colossus by offering sanctuary to the entire cohort of southern African freedom fighters. On the other, his responsibility for Zambia's own security meant that he felt compelled to restrict the activities of his guests for fear of provoking the ire of South Africa on whom the country depended economically: The Anglo-American mining group owned 49 percent of Zambia's copper mines, the mainstay of its economy. Kaunda could not be seen to be launching acts of violence against South Africa and so forbade any military activity out of Zambia. At the same time, he was powerless in preventing attacks by South Africans on his guests. For both these reasons, ANC comrades lived covert double lives and a culture of paranoia took root, one exacerbated by the constant threat of double agents and infiltration. Learning to wield political power in such an environment was to have a profound effect on Mbeki's psyche and career.

Mbeki's assignment to the RC meant that he was billeted to a safe house in Makeni, an agricultural area southwest of Lusaka, upon arrival in Zambia. Without even regular transport to take them to the city, let alone communications into South Africa, the cadres posted here felt utterly disconnected, and spent most of their time reading revolutionary theory or working in the garden to supplement their rations. "There were terrible shortages of food," Sipho Makana, who also lived there, told me. "Nothing but beans and *stywe pap* [dry corn porridge], except for tin fish and meat occasionally, from the Soviet Union."

With the help of the Soviet Union and other Soviet countries (most notably East Germany), the ANC would build an army of over 10,000 soldiers over the next two decades, based mainly in camps in Angola. But despite the overwhelmingly militaristic culture, which held the movement together with its imperatives of armed struggle even if it was singularly unsuccessful in the field, the main business of the ANC was actually the provision of social services to an ever-increasing population of exiles and refugees. The ANC became something of a state within a state in Zambia, with its own schools, clinics, stores, and even police force. Being part of this state meant becoming a dependent rather than a citizen, relinquishing one's own agency, almost entirely, to the common cause, even if the South Africans were scattered all over town, woven into Lusaka's fabric by the stuff of day-to-day living: by the bed, the bar, and the street. When I visited Lusaka in 1991, as the exiles were preparing to go back to South Africa, the world I encountered was fractious, apprehensive, and suspicious, articulated in a language of shadows and circumlocutions. No one ever spoke of going "home" or even allowed the name of their country of birth to pass their lips. South Africa was "that side" or "southside," and anywhere else was "this side" or "outside." Perhaps, I wrote at the time, this was to avoid having to call either side "home."[2]

Thabo Mbeki would live in this liminal world for the better part of two decades. I once asked him whether he ever considered Lusaka to be home or whether it was just another experience of the disconnection he had known since he had been a little boy: "Not quite disconnection" was as much as he would allow, "but not quite home either."

In 1971, the year Thabo Mbeki returned to Africa, Zanele Dlamini won a scholarship to the doctoral program in social welfare at Brandeis University outside Boston. The program was small, with only 15 to 20 students a year. She quickly made her mark and is still remembered as one of the brightest students ever to have passed through it. In 1974 she submitted her PhD proposal, on the position of African women under apartheid, but never completed it—she left the United States shortly thereafter to marry Mbeki and move to Lusaka.

Once it became clear that the two were going to marry, the ANC connected Dlamini with the International University Education Fund (IUEF), a Swedish-funded organization that found scholarships for black South Africans. Tasked with setting up its Africa office in Lusaka, she moved to Zambia in early 1974. With the assistance of the movement, she found a spacious three-bedroom terraced house to rent on Roan Close—or Martin Luther King Close, as it would be renamed—in the formerly white inner-city suburb of Kabulonga, and set about furnishing it. The house, one of a row along a secluded leafy lane, became the Mbeki home for nearly two decades: as close to a hearth as he had ever known, and clearly a refuge for both of them.

The residence was chosen for the Mbekis because of its excellent security: A pair of solid black steel gates, over six feet high, blocked its driveway. To enter, one needed to open the big outer gate, then a smaller inner gate, and finally cross a small front garden before reaching the front door. The Mbekis kept the yard bare as a sort of Zen-garden security precaution: The sand would be raked into a pattern every night and then examined for disturbances in the morning. Their friends remember the home's modest interior as simple and elegant in the hands of Zanele Mbeki. "Neatly ordered," their then-neighbor Hugh Macmillan recalls, "with [Mozambican artist] Malangatana pictures and sculptures and books and a coffee table; comfortable chairs." There was a main living area under a steeply pitched ceiling with sliding doors that opened up onto the yard and a blue-and-white-tiled kitchen at the back. Up a flight of wooden stairs were the master bedroom and Mbeki's study.

Only those few comrades with hard-currency jobs were lucky enough to have their own homes in the affluent inner suburbs; for the most part,

South African exiles lived on the periphery of Lusaka, in its hardscrabble townships. The homes of those who lived in suburbs like Kabulonga were thus often gathering places: Near the Mbekis, for example, the residence of Billy and Yolisa Modise was perpetually full of people meeting, practicing choir, eating, or just hanging out. But Tor Sellström, a Swedish diplomat who was one of Thabo Mbeki's closest friends in Lusaka, told me that the Mbeki residence "was not a gathering place at all. It was their home. In fact, the only time I think I ever saw Thabo annoyed was when someone came in unannounced and disturbed him. He came to *you*; you didn't go over to him." Not even Mbeki's closest comrades spent much time there, and when they did, it was to work or consult.

Or, perhaps, to listen to jazz. One of these was Victor Moche, who, like many people, draws a distinction between Oliver Tambo and Thabo Mbeki through the way they appreciated music: "O. R. used to have choirs for relaxation," he told me. "You'd go over to Billy Modise's house and all sing together. Thabo also had musical tendencies, but not for public display. He was happiest in a small group of people, spending the afternoon listening to jazz records. Thabo and Zanele were very private people." If you arrived at the Mbeki house "at any time of the day or night," said Moche, "there would invariably be some music playing, and he would be upstairs, working quietly." Even during his presidency, Mbeki's desk would be covered in CDs; he listened to music as he wrote, and it seems likely that this was an aural equivalent of that Zen garden in Kabulonga: a barrier against the very exposed world he inhabited for decades.

Thabo Mbeki and Zanele Dlamini decided to marry in London, not Lusaka, in November 1974. After the couple signed papers in a North London registry, Adelaide Tambo hosted a huge party, more of a bash than a ritual, at her Muswell Hill home. Although many of Mbeki's British friends and diplomatic connections attended, this event was an ANC one, with the buzz, song, and copious alcohol consumption that characterized such gatherings in exile.

A few days later, a smaller group gathered for a religious ceremony at Farnham Castle in Surrey, the twelfth-century pile built by William the Conqueror's grandson Henri de Blois. Originally the residence of the Bishop of Westminster, it was now the home of Zanele Dlamini's older sister Edith, whose husband, Wilfred Grenville-Grey, ran a training center for foreign-service diplomats out of the castle. For Mbeki's Sussex friend Veronica Linklater, the experience of a traditional African ceremony in the castle's medieval chapel was "surreal": "There was a minister, and he was singing, and then the congregation was taking up responses. It was absolutely fantastic, so beautiful but also so bizarre, like a film set really, in this ancient English castle." After a formal dinner, the party proceeded into one of the castle's great halls, where Linklater remembers "an old man with a stick singing a Zulu praise song, getting more and more carried away until by the end of it he threw his stick away and only had the back of a sofa to cling to."

The rituals, like the guest list, were a concoction only someone like Mbeki could conjure: Home Counties Gentry meets Third World Revolutionary, with a smattering of Sussex Lefty thrown in. Filling the bijou chapel's pews were African communists flown in from the southern African front line, unkempt (and not entirely approving) academics and artists from Mbeki's university set, and titled personages no less than the Duchess and Earl of Richmond, Grenville-Grey's sister and brother-in-law. The Anglican wedding rites niggled at some of Thabo Mbeki's British friends: "Meg [Pahad] and I thought this was awful," Rhiannon Gooding told me. "Everybody was dead set against any kind of religious thing." They approached Dr. Dadoo, the SACP chairman, to object: "We're *not* kneeling down!" He laughed, betraying South African communism's idiosyncratic ease with religion: "But you *have* to do it, for Thabo."

The traditional African rites were potentially as contentious. Govan Mbeki would have approved of his new daughter's provenance. Not only was she from the elite black middle class too (her father was a prominent cleric), but she was even, distantly, of the same clan as the Mbekis: The amaZizi claimed descent from the Zulu Dlaminis and, in fact, traditionally greeted each other as "Dlamini." But the imprisoned Mbeki patriarch strongly opposed the payment of *lobola*, or bride price. The condition of exile, however, happily deferred the issue, and *lobola* between the Mbeki and Dlamini families was never negotiated. (Thabo Mbeki did not share his father's modernism in this respect: When he later became the family patriarch, he would insist on the payment of *lobola* in the marriage of his niece, the daughter of his deceased brother Jama.)

If the photographs at the London registry signify the modern, secular community inhabited by the bride and groom—Mbeki is groovy in cream bell-bottoms and his favorite polka-dotted shirt; the only evidence that Dlamini is a bride is the little corsage she holds—then the formal portraits at Farnham Castle tell a different story: the coming together of an Anglicized African aristocracy. In the absence not only of Govan and Epainette Mbeki but also of Oliver Tambo, Adelaide Tambo and Mendi Msimang stood *in loco parentis* for the groom; Essop Pahad was best man. Thabo wore his favorite swirling psychedelic tie beneath sober pinstripes and Zanele was in fairy-tale ivory, but the focal point of the photographs—indeed of the entire event—was Adelaide Tambo. Wrapped in swirls of apricot and carrying a traditional carved stick, she had taken on a ceremonial role. Leopard skins are no doubt hard to come by in north London and so, in a moment of inspired creativity signifying the two worlds of this wedding, she had substituted for traditional chiefly hides a luxuriant mink border on her gown and a matching headdress. Mbeki's English friends will never forget the way she disrupted the dulcet Anglican tones of the ceremony with a booming ululation, as if Thabo Mbeki's ancestors were rattling the stained-glass windows ŏf an England that could no longer encase him, claiming a son of Africa back for the soil through the medium of a mink-clad chieftainess.

For Veronica Linklater, something that had been hovering inchoately in her mind about Mbeki since their first year together at Sussex suddenly gelled: her sense, in the theatricality of the event, that Thabo Mbeki's own identity might have been staged rather than internalized and that the disjuncture of the event represented "that lack of a core from which everything emanated" within him.

Call it disjuncture or call it creative reconciliation: The hybrid energy in the wedding of Thabo Mbeki and Zanele Dlamini gave the event not only its character but its meaning. Although the young ANC leader was no longer based in England, he continued to spend much of his time there, shuttling between the insecurity of Lusaka and the familial comfort of the Goodings' south London hearth, where he would usually put up. The world of Farnham Castle was one with which—rather unusually for an African communist revolutionary—Mbeki was familiar, due to some of his Sussex friendships. And yet it was a world so far away from the reality of the duress of life in exile on the front line and the situation of Mbeki's own parents—Govan imprisoned on Robben Island and Epainette in bantustan penury—that it beggared belief. If all weddings are performances, public masquerades of their participants' aspirations and values, then this was the living out of a fantasy, a willful act of the self-definition that characterized the new Black Consciousness movement sweeping South Africa. It said: "We are not refugees, not the oppressed, not victims. We are the rightful rulers of our dominion."

That was the other element of this wedding noted by Mbeki's British friends: its aura of dynastic union, its role in sealing Mbeki's ascendancy by pairing him with the kind of spouse suitable for an heir apparent. Zanele Dlamini came from a prominent family, was educated, articulate, connected, beautiful, committed, and Zulu to boot—a factor not insignificant in an ANC leadership keen to mitigate the perception that it was dominated by Xhosas. There was also the need to counter the suspicion, already whispered, that Mbeki was a deracinated "black Englishman." This was something to which Mbeki had acceded even while at Sussex. Living with Philippa Ingram in Brighton, he had told a close friend of hers: "Of course I could never marry Philippa, because I must have an African wife."

Many people who have known them over the years describe the union of Thabo Mbeki and Zanele Dlamini as a "partnership." Ann Page, an

Anti-Apartheid Movement friend who was at the wedding, was "very struck that it was Zanele and not an Englishwoman. It looked like an alliance." Another friend remembers thinking, upon hearing of the impending union, "Well, he would do that, wouldn't he? Although he had English girlfriends, I think we knew he would never marry them. We always knew he would marry the person who would be the *right* person to marry. If you're going to make an impact on the world, you're not going to choose an unsuitable wife."

The movement had strict regulations on marriage: Permission had to be applied for, and granted, before one could take place. The ANC, after all, *was* the family for those in exile: All human emotion had to be sublimated into struggle; marriage could be allowed only if it enhanced, rather than detracted from, the revolutionary work of the cadre. This was one of the areas of social regulation (the others included drink and casual sex) that was to plague the movement through its years in exile, as comrades tried to negotiate the space between individual agency and communal responsibility and as leaders, charged with enforcing the rules, acted inconsistently and capriciously. Finally, in 1988, the ANC set up a long-planned Subcommittee on Marriages, which tried to set fixed hurdles rather than leave the matter in the hands of individuals: Men had to be older than 35 and to have been ANC members for 10 years; women had to be older than 25 and to have been members for 5. Marriage to non–South Africans was to be discouraged, with permission to be granted only by the secretary-general himself.[3]

Although she did not deny her role in bringing them together, Adelaide Tambo insisted that the marriage between Thabo Mbeki and Zanele Dlamini was a love match, and had many stories about Mbeki pining for his beloved when she was studying in Boston. The way she tells it, Mbeki's decision to marry Zanele was taken alone and somewhat in rebellion against the ANC ethos of always placing the struggle first. When, on a trip to London in early 1974, Mbeki told her that he planned to marry, she asked whether he had obtained permission to do so from "Papa"—her husband.

He had not. "Listen, Ma," he told her, "if *Ou Tata* ['old father'] and the leadership refuse to give permission, I will remain a bachelor for the rest of my life."

Permission, of course, was granted. Would it have been if the request had been to marry Ann Nicholson or Philippa Ingram? Unlike Thabo, neither Moeletsi nor Jama so much as thought to request permission to marry their spouses, and both married non–South Africans, outside the ANC "family." The fact (in Adelaide Tambo's retelling, at least) that Thabo Mbeki's only option was to remain a bachelor, were *"Ou Tata"* to refuse permission, signifies the depth of his allegiance to the family; he is the diligent son who would never risk disinheritance by marrying against his parents' wishes.

Mrs. Tambo sent telegrams to Epainette in Idutywa and Govan on Robben Island, announcing the wedding. Both responded with salutations.

Following tradition, Epainette Mbeki gave her son's bride a new name, which she sent back to Mrs. Tambo: Mamotlalekgotso, "she who brings peace"—a signal, surely, not only of Epainette's wishes for South Africa, but of her hopes for a daughter-in-law's healing powers over a shattered family. Indeed, there was not one Mbeki at the wedding. More than ever, there was only one family, the political one: Zanele Dlamini was not becoming the daughter of the Mbeki clan; rather, she was being confirmed as a daughter of the movement.

This was not an identity with which Zanele Mbeki seemed fully at ease. During the exile years, she seemed perpetually to be renegotiating the boundary between marriage to the movement (and its favorite son) on one hand and some kind of individuated subjectivity on the other. She was renowned as a freethinker, often articulating radical and independent positions. Many highly trained professionals, particularly in the service fields, worked full time for the ANC rather than pursuing their own careers; Zanele Mbeki tried to find a way to do both, seeking work outside the movement that expressly benefited ANC exiles. In Lusaka, she was elected to ANC Women's League structures, most notably the editorial committee of its publication, *Voice of Women*, and yet in her professional career she was required to be strictly nonsectarian: Her mandate at the IUEF required her to assist all refugees, regardless of their affiliation.

In 1981 the IUEF was closed down after the sensational exposure of Zanele Mbeki's boss, Craig Williamson, as a South African spy. Zanele lectured at the University of Zambia for two years, and then took a job with the UN High Commissioner for Refugees out of Nairobi. A friend recalls a disagreement between the Mbekis after Zanele was offered the job. Even more so than with the IUEF, working with the UNHCR would require her to be visibly nonpartisan, and her husband argued that the job would take her out of the "ANC family." She seems to have found the balance, though: To other ANC comrades, there was no doubt that she was a stalwart, and yet most of those in the diplomatic world who worked and socialized with the Mbekis remember her as assertively nonpartisan, going out of her way to demonstrate that she was not beholden to the ANC.

Easily one of the most competent and qualified of the returning corps of exiles, she would decline nominations for political office or appointment to the new ANC bureaucratic elite, choosing instead to set up her own enterprise, the Women's Development Bank. In 1995 she resubmitted her doctoral proposal to Brandeis and was reaccepted. But these were precisely the years of her husband's ascent to power: Once more she put her academic career on hold and failed to complete her studies. This tension between being her own woman and the wife of a leader was reflected in her ambivalence, from 1999 onward, toward the position of "first lady." She played the role with grace and poise—no doubt living up to the expectations of the family who accepted her as bride in 1974—but resisted being typecast or identified as such, even to the point of refusing to be interviewed for this project: She made it clear that she was a professional in her own right and not an append-age to her husband, and thus did not see the reason for being included in a biography about him. Despite the fact that there was "Spousal Office" in Mbeki's presidency and that Zanele frequently played a formal role at the taxpayers' expense, she steadfastly refused to be interviewed or profiled in any media; so seriously did she take this stand that she would not even release a curriculum vitae.

Vernon Mwaanga, then Zambia's young foreign minister, had been a tennis partner of Zanele Dlamini's when she first moved to Lusaka. He remembers vividly the day she announced that she was planning to marry. According to his recollections, she told him that she understood that the life of a freedom fighter was unpredictable and dangerous but that because she was a South African who supported the ANC, she was going into it "with her eyes wide open." In case the new Mrs. Mbeki had any doubts about the unpredictability of her life to come, it must have been brought home very strongly by her new husband's departure to Sweden immediately after the day of their wedding at Farnham Castle. Over the next 16 years, until their return to South Africa, Thabo and Zanele Mbeki would be apart as often as they were together, often living parallel lives but returning always to their "not quite home" in Kabulonga.

17

SWAZILAND
FRONT LINE

In January 1975, four years after his return to Africa and a few months after his marriage to Zanele Dlamini, Thabo Mbeki was elected to the National Executive Committee of the African National Congress, together with his old rival and age-mate, Chris Hani. Hani was already running ANC operations out of the landlocked country of Lesotho; Mbeki was now assigned to do the same in the tiny kingdom of Swaziland, wedged between Mozambique and South Africa, a perfect launching pad for guerrilla activity into South Africa. For the first time since the early 1960s, there was political protest in South Africa; the authorities were clamping down, resulting in a significant exodus of black activists into exile, many of them students. Mbeki and Hani were to gather up the young radicals as they fled the country and channel them into the ANC.

Mbeki lodged with the family of Stanley Mabizela, the South African deputy principal of the Salesian School in the town of Manzini. The Mabizela residence became the ANC's unofficial headquarters and gathering place, the family's old VW Beetle its sole means of transportation until Mbeki rode it into the ground. Tiksie Mabizela's abiding memory of Mbeki is of an intense young man "sitting with his glass of whisky and writing, writing, writing into the night." Swaziland was completely beholden to its behemoth South African neighbor, and so Mbeki's mandate was complex: He was to sweet-talk the government into permitting aboveboard ANC activity there while also covertly running military operations across the border and persuading South African exiles to join the ANC army. The job, Mbeki's first serious fieldwork, required the kind of bifurcation of identity at which he was already adept, and for an underground operative, he adopted an unusually high profile. He was prominent on the social scene and he often had a crowd of young student admirers around him. Whether it was recklessness or strategy, the visibility brought results: Young people fleeing South Africa knew they could find the ANC in Swaziland.

One of the first people Thabo Mbeki connected with was Lindiwe Sisulu, the daughter of Walter Sisulu, the ANC leader serving a life sentence on

Robben Island with his father and Nelson Mandela. Lindiwe was studying at the university in Swaziland, and she remembers vividly her first meeting with Mbeki, who came to see her with her brother Max. Because they had gone into exile, she had not seen either of them since she was a little girl, and "they just didn't seem like the kind of people I'd imagined would liberate South Africa." Her older brother was "all scrawny and gangly," and Mbeki "the shortest man I had even seen!"

The two men were equally disappointed. Lindiwe had become a fervent adherent of the stridently anticommunist, racially exclusive Black Consciousness movement founded by Steve Biko. "What has happened to you?" Max asked. "Where were your mother and your brothers that you should turn out so badly?" But Mbeki tried a different tack: "So," he said, "you want these whites to go off into the sea and leave you?"

"Absolutely!" she replied, with all the certitude of an 18-year-old militant.

"But how will it happen?"

"They created a state for Israel and chucked the Arabs out, didn't they?" she responded. "Why can't we do the same thing? Find them a place somewhere in Europe, there must be somewhere they belong. They'll be happy there and we'll be happy here." While her older brother cringed, Mbeki saw, in the young woman's devotion, exactly what he had been sent to Swaziland to find: a route back home. He asked her to set up a meeting with her comrades and she obliged. In no time, she and her skeptical classmates were "dazzled" by Mbeki and recruited into the ANC. "He was the guru," she recalls. "He was the one giving all the answers; the one at the center."

The young radicals of the Black Consciousness generation were leaving South Africa to take up arms and free their people, and were skeptical of an older movement that seemed to have atrophied into irrelevance during its decade in exile. "We had high expectations of the struggle and our own role in it," Harry Nengwekhulu, a close associate of Biko's, said to me. "But we found we were not taken seriously, and also, it seemed to us that nothing was happening outside the country."

Black Consciousness was the latest manifestation of the original impulse in South African liberation politics; a black thread, one might say, that has always interwoven with the red one through the fabric of the South African struggle. Biko might have been riding the wave of the anticolonial movements and black identity politics of the 1960s, but he was also rearticulating a discourse that was at the very foundation of the ANC in the early twentieth century, when the movement's founder, Pixley ka Seme, had said in 1906 while an undergraduate at Columbia University: "I am an African, and I set my pride in my race over against a hostile public opinion."[1] This slogan of self-definition would provide a baseline to South African politics through the century. After Seme there were the militants of the Youth League in the

1940s who expressly hearkened back to the black nationalism of the ANC's founding fathers. A decade later, in 1957, a group of leading ANC intellectuals would leave to form the Pan Africanist Congress, declaring that Africans were "determined to wrest control of their country from alien hands."[2]

But by the Cold War years of the early 1970s, the philosophy of Africanism—seemingly touted by the United States and its surrogates, such as Nigeria—seemed more retrograde than ever. Steve Biko's vigorous independence and the Black Consciousness exiles' attempts to set up their own liberation movement were also threatening to the ANC, which believed it was preordained to lead the South African freedom struggle. For these reasons, most of Mbeki's comrades in the ANC leadership veered between dismissing Black Consciousness as irrelevant and wishing to obliterate it. Mbeki dissented from this majority opinion. He worked hard get his comrades to take the new movement seriously and work with it, if the ANC ever wished to gain a foothold in South Africa again. From the beginning, he understood the significance of Black Consciousness. "We must adopt the progressive aspects of Black Power," he said to an ANC youth gathering in 1971, given that its purpose was "to encourage a spirit of confidence among the Black oppressed masses, confidence in their own strength, an uncompromising hatred for anybody and anything that degrades the Black man."[3] And so, during the early 1970s, Mbeki spent much of his time, in student dorms and hotel rooms throughout southern Africa, wooing skeptical Black Consciousness exiles into the ANC. Mbeki would recruit the cream of these educated young people to work in his Department of Information and Publicity, and they would become his most ardent supporters.

Harry Nengwekhulu, Lindiwe Sisulu, and their comrades had the arrogance of youth. They wanted to know whether the ANC had been doing anything besides boycotting oranges. Where were the soldiers? Where were the guns? Where *was* the armed struggle? Biko had led black students out of the multiracial National Union of South African Students (NUSAS) because of the racism that he said existed even among well-meaning white liberals. Of primary concern to the Black Consciousness activists, then, was the ANC's admission of white people into the organization since 1969 and its relationship with the SACP: "A communist in South Africa," Steve Biko would later say, "will [always] be an instrument of Moscow."[4] This attitude suffused the Black Consciousness movement: Self-reliance, after all, required that Africans do it for themselves rather than expecting liberation from a foreign power with its own agenda.

When challenged with these questions, Mbeki's response was inspired. He realized that most of the Black Consciousness exiles were intellectually hungry students who had fled South Africa before finishing their studies and who had never had sight of either banned Marxist literature or any detailed history of the South African struggle. So he set them reading: They might have sought him out to "interview" him about the appropriateness of the ANC, but they found themselves unexpectedly in a study group. And they liked it.

"I got tired of just saying 'I'm black and I'm proud,'" Lindiwe Sisulu recalls. "I wanted to *do* something." And Mbeki gave her and her comrades a program, telling them, "'We *have* got a strategy. We've got people that we have to infiltrate back into the country, we are going to have an armed struggle and the armed struggle is going to bring about liberation'"—just as it had in other places. "He was talking about Guinea-Bissau," Lindiwe Sisulu remembers, "about Ghana, things I had never heard before. *Wondrous things!*"

Sisulu believes that, to the extent that Mbeki showed interest in the new movement, it was exclusively to draw his adversaries out "so that he could show us why we were wrong." But even if his interest in Black Consciousness was strategic, there was nonetheless a cross-fertilization of ideology that implanted the "self-reliance" and "self-definition" seed within him, left to germinate until his return to South Africa in 1990. Making contact with Biko's movement and bringing its adherents "home" was to be Mbeki's most important and far-reaching accomplishment during his years on the front line: An entire new generation would enter the ANC and rejuvenate it, and the Black Consciousness movement's attempts to set up its own liberation movement would come to naught. It was a task that appears to have unlocked a powerful alchemy: While the ANC absorbed the young activists into its ranks, Mbeki absorbed Black Consciousness into his—and the ANC's—own ideological bloodstream. This would find ultimate expression in Mbeki's own Africanism when became president and in his call for an "African Renaissance."

———————

It was while he was in Swaziland that Thabo Mbeki also met the man who would become his greatest ally, his deputy president, and finally his nemesis: Jacob Zuma. Zuma ran the underground out of Natal, moving recruits and intelligence out of the country, and weapons and instructions back in. With the stolid, deliberate mien of a rural Zulu man, Zuma was fearless, loyal, and affable; although he lacked any formal education, he was possessed of a canny wit that made him one of the ANC's most effective operatives. He was the son of a widowed domestic worker; as a boy in his home village near Nongoma, he had been entranced by the old people's stories of early rebellion against the British. When he went to town to look for work as a teenager, the influence of an older half-brother pulled him into liberation politics. Until he was elected to the provincial government of KwaZulu-Natal in 1994, he knew no other life. He was recruited into Umkhonto we Sizwe

(MK) in 1962 and arrested the following year, trying to leave the country to undergo training; he spent ten years on Robben Island. Released in 1973, he became responsible for reestablishing the ANC's underground in Natal.

Thabo Mbeki, the Sussex-polished gem, struck up an unlikely rapport with this rough diamond—attracted by his staunch loyalty, his innate political sensibilities, and strategic savvy. These were the attributes that would make him so indispensable to Mbeki in the 1980s and 1990s and so threatening after 1999. For his part, Zuma was hugely impressed with the son of his teacher on Robben Island. "Comrade Thabo was politically very clear on theory and strategy, and discussions with him were very invigorating," Zuma told me. "You felt you moved forward. He was a thinker, ready with ideas." Zuma learned two skills, diametrically opposed, from his new handler: On the one hand, he watched Mbeki work the room as a diplomat, while, on the other, "It was Thabo who taught me how to use a gun, what it is, the theory of it, the dismantling of it, all the rules of it."

But their relationship began, as it would finally end, with conflict: in December 1975, when Zuma had crossed into Swaziland for the first time, fleeing a swoop on the ANC's Natal underground that had netted over 50 activists. The two men had not met previously and locked immediately into a battle of wills. Zuma insisted on returning to South Africa so that he could resurrect the structure he had so painstakingly put into place, but Mbeki would not hear of it. "It smacks of adventure," he said to Zuma. "If something happens to you I'll be held responsible." Zuma chafed against this command and ultimately disobeyed it, waiting for Mbeki's next trip out of Swaziland to slip into South Africa without his superior's knowledge.

Zuma told me this story in 2003, after his relationship with Mbeki had already cooled but before he had been fired. In the retelling, he insisted that Mbeki's decision was "absolutely correct. I didn't agree with him, but you could not fault his logic." He told me that he saw, in Mbeki's operational command, what he would come to identify as the ANC leader's greatest strength: "caution in the field." If Chris Hani rather than Thabo Mbeki had been your commander, I asked, what would he have told you to do? Zuma guffawed: "To go! Of course he would have said go! Chris was an *activist*. But Thabo is a *leader*. It's decisions like that which show you that leadership's not everyone's thing."

But there was a cautionary subtext to Zuma's telling of this early conflict: Even if Mbeki had been logically correct, Zuma's strategy worked. He spent two "highly successful" weeks back in South Africa, reactivating his networks before slipping back into exile again, this time for good. Mbeki might have been right on paper, but in this seminal moment, Zuma proved the power of street smarts over formal education.

Forced into exile, Zuma continued to run the Natal underground illegally from Swaziland. In early 1976 he mistakenly recruited six undercover South

African police agents: Their intelligence led to the arrest and subsequent murder of a comrade in Natal and the kidnapping, torture, and imprisonment of two Swaziland-based ANC operatives. Having exposed the underground network, the South Africans compelled the Swazi authorities to arrest Mbeki and Zuma, who found themselves—together with Mbeki's deputy, Albert Dhlomo—in Swaziland's Mastapha maximum security prison. Mbeki and his fellow detainees were in serious trouble: The South Africans were calling for them to be deported home, which would have meant certain trial and imprisonment, netting for the authorities their biggest exile fish yet.

The Swazis tried to save face by claiming they were holding the detainees in "protective custody," to safeguard them against South African agents. But the prisoners had good reason to mistrust their capricious jailers: The Swazi police was notoriously controlled by the South African security forces. At one point the men were told they were being deported to Lusaka. According to Zuma, when they arrived at the airport "we saw that we were scheduled to fly to Johannesburg and then connect on to Lusaka. . . . We protested: 'We can't go to South Africa!' " Perhaps the plan was that they would be arrested while in transit, and the Swazis—caught between South African pressure and the rest of the continent's aspirations—would have been seen to have their hands clean. Mbeki negotiated on behalf of the trio and managed to persuade the Swazi authorities to send him and his two comrades back to prison. This, Zuma later told me, was his first experience of Mbeki's coolness: "He didn't panic."

For Thabo Mbeki, history was repeating itself. The situation was uncannily similar to his previous detention, in Bulawayo, in 1962: in jail while his enemies and his comrades haggled over whether he would be sent home to an inevitable long-term imprisonment. Eventually, a month after their arrests, Mbeki, Dhlomo, and Zuma were escorted across the border into newly independent Mozambique. They arrived there in early June 1976, just in time to join the festivities of this exuberant and still-optimistic new nation's first anniversary of independence—and just before the Soweto uprising in South Africa.

On June 16, just days after the men arrived in Mozambique, South African police attacked a massive protest by schoolchildren in Soweto against the use of Afrikaans as a medium of instruction. At least one student was killed, and several others were wounded. The students responded with a violent rampage through the township, triggering a heavy-handed response from the authorities. By December 1976, over 10,000 people had been detained, the vast majority of them children, many as young as eight. Within ten months, 575 people had died in uprisings throughout the country. Political life inside South Africa was overwhelmed with mass boycotts and treason trials.

The ANC claimed victory, but the truth is that it had very little to do with the uprising; slow to respond, it did not capitalize on the rebellion, as the Bolsheviks, for example, had during the popular uprising of 1905 in Russia. Mbeki was intensely frustrated with the ANC's inability to respond to Soweto, for he felt he had supplied the movement with both the intelligence and the contacts needed; others, however, felt strongly that he bore at least some of the blame for the ANC's lack of preparedness. Mac Maharaj, a man who was to become one of Mbeki's greatest critics (and one of the prime architects of Jacob Zuma's defeat of Mbeki in 2007) was given the task of establishing the underground that was so patently absent in 1976: He was shocked, he has said, by how little Mbeki had accomplished. This led to a public confrontation between the two men: Mbeki claimed that detailed records had been kept of activities in Swaziland during his tenure, but Maharaj countered that he was given nothing more than "an empty folder." Mbeki told Maharaj all his documents were in a trunk left with Stanley Mabizela, and Maharaj tried for months to get the trunk. Was there no trunk, was he being deliberately subverted, or were systems so bad that the left hand did not know what the right was doing? One way or the other, Maharaj was determined to wield a new broom.[5] He has also intimated that Mbeki was removed from Swaziland in 1976 because he did not have the "personality," as he put it, for front-line operational management.[6]

Maharaj is substantively correct: From his Swazi base, Mbeki did not manage to set up an underground network in South Africa to take advantage of 1976's turbulence. But even if he lost this advantage, he gained another: The vast majority of the 4,000 black South Africans who went into exile in the 18 months following Soweto joined the ANC, and many of them were processed by Mbeki. Most of these "children of Soweto" had come to political awareness through Black Consciousness, but they were not ideologically bound to it: They were militants looking for weapons rather than ideologues looking for a cause. And so, Mbeki's work in Swaziland played a significant role in the ANC becoming something of a mass movement in the late 1970s for the first time since the defiance campaigns of the 1950s. Whatever his operational failures, Mbeki was already the ANC's most effective salesman.

Being in the front-line states—in Swaziland, Lesotho, or Botswana—was acutely distressing for South African exiles, given how close and yet how inaccessible their homes and families were. Even if they slipped back into South Africa, they were unable, for security reasons, to contact their loved ones. Nonetheless, South Africans working or studying in Swaziland could cross the border at will. Thus, in April 1976, Tiksie Mabizela could stop off in Idutywa, on her way to a brother's graduation at Fort Hare, to meet Epainette Mbeki. She carried nothing from Mbeki to his mother, and nothing back, except news. When she next saw Thabo Mbeki, she told him about the visit. He had one question: "Was she alone in the shop? Was there anyone there to help her?"

At around the same time, Mbeki had, uncharacteristically, telephoned his older sister, Linda Jiba, and asked her to come and visit him in Swaziland. "Why waste money?" she responded with a lack of sentimentality typical for her family. "Rather send the money to me, and I'll give it to Mama."

A few weeks later, she received a payment for R400—a significant amount, in those days—from her cousin, Phindile Mfeti, with the coded message that it had come from her brother in Swaziland. She transferred it immediately into her mother's account. Epainette Mbeki was overjoyed: This was the very first time she had received money from her oldest son. But, shortly thereafter, Linda was visited by security policemen who told her they had intelligence that the funds were to be used for MK recruitment. Linda protested: "I got this money from my brother, to give to my mother. I know nothing about this." Nonetheless, she was arrested and taken to Pretoria, where she would be detained for ten months.

The policemen were right. Mbeki had indeed sent the money to finance the ANC's underground activities, not as a gift to his family. Before being detained in Swaziland, Mbeki had given a box of chocolates to a comrade with the message: "These are my sister's sweets." Mbeki had carefully steamed open the cellophane wrapping of the box, removed some of the candy and replaced them with R400 in notes, and then resealed the box. The "sister" was actually Lindiwe Sisulu, now back in South Africa, but through a series of misunderstandings, the money had landed with Linda Jiba, the chocolate box and its contents carefully tracked, every step along the way, by the South African security police.

Thabo Mbeki's Swazi legacy thus includes one of the most distressing episodes in the Mbeki family history during his years of exile: His innocent sister was jailed for ten months and their mother plummeted to new depths of despair. The money Linda Jiba received from her brother—the only significant money she and her mother had ever received from him— was actually the result of a broken telephone of miscommunications and had not been intended for them at all. It was a gift meant not for her but for the struggle—which must, now as always, come first.

18

GOVAN AND EPAINETTE

In May 1975, at the same time Thabo Mbeki was setting up shop in Swaziland, Epainette Mbeki received a message from her youngest son, Jama, a lawyer in Botswana: He had heard on the radio that his father had suffered a stroke on Robben Island and was contacting his mother to find out if she had any further information. It was the first that Mrs. Mbeki had heard of her 65-year-old husband's illness; distraught, she tried in vain to find out more. Finally, five months later, her daughter, Linda, received permission to visit her father. When she got to the prison, where he was serving a life sentence, he told her he had nearly died.

"Honey," Epainette Mbeki wrote to her husband on October 13, 1975, after her daughter's return, "Linda has come to see us on her return from Cape Town. We will now be able to breathe freely, we have been running round in circles ever since we collected [the news] from outside the Republic that you were ill." In the gaps between benign gossip—the only form of communication the prison censors permitted—the letter is filled with the tragedy of the empty space between husband and wife, the disintegrated family. The fact that she heard about his stroke via a radio bulletin pained her: "I have been thinking all along that you belong to the Mbeki family, what a fallacy, there have been numerous enquiries about your health, you should be proud that you belong to such a very big family, it is apparently not by blood ties alone that one can claim kinship, it was really heartening."[1] One sees the confusion between the two definitions of "family," biological and political, and senses Epainette Mbeki's ambivalence: how "heartening" it is to be in the fold of freedom fighters but how lonely too, for lurking beneath the use of the word "fallacy" is the sense of loss that she feels at having to share him, her anger at being the last to know when he is ill.

Their daughter Linda shared the anger, and was more direct in expressing it: "Tata [Father]," she wrote reproachfully after her return from Robben Island, "you must also write and tell us when you are not feeling well." A month later, she had not heard from him: "I am very worried because there's no letter coming from you.... O! Tata, don't think I will be selfish if I say that if your letters do not go to Mama, they must come to me. How else are we going to know when you are not feeling well?"[2] Certainly the authorities had acted with typical cruelty in not informing the family about Mbeki's illness, but Linda was acknowledging something else in her letter: the fact that the breakdown in relations between her parents had been exacerbated by his decade-long imprisonment to such an extent that Govan would fail to communicate with his wife even when seriously ill.

The news of Govan Mbeki's illness in the winter of 1975 came at a terrible time for Epainette. "For months on end I have been miserable," she had written to him in July.[3] The previous summer, after over two decades alone in Mbewuleni, she had finally left the village and moved to town. The distance from Mbewuleni to Ngcingwane, outside Idutywa—where she obtained a lease on a small house with a shop attached—is all of 14 miles, but for a woman who had retreated into herself after the collapse of her marriage and the imprisonment of her husband, the move down the mountain and across the floodplain of the Idutywa River was nothing short of epic.

The move was, if nothing else, a crushing admission of defeat. She felt abandoned by her husband's business associates, and she had been the repeated victim of security police harassment: "They came one, two, three o'clock....They go through everything. They take books away, even books not banned....They went round the localities, telling people to inform on Thabo and offering to pay them with tobacco." The harassment of neighbors alienated Mrs. Mbeki more, as they began to blame her for their troubles.

Unlike the wives of the other imprisoned leaders, Mrs. Mbeki received little support from the liberation movement and its benefactors: She was isolated geographically, and had neither the personality nor the connections to attract support in the way Winnie Mandela or Albertina Sisulu did. Her only regular support was from the London-based International Defence and Aid Fund (IDAF), which made irregular contributions to the study fees of Govan (who was taking correspondence courses on Robben Island) and Jama from 1966 on. According to the IDAF records, Epainette Mbeki received a £300 grant for stock in 1967, but this was the only disbursement made specifically to her; for the rest, it seems, she was a conduit. She received a £40 monthly allowance, paid to her from October 1971 onward, to assist her with the three children of Robben Island prisoner Raymond Mhlaba, for whom she had taken responsibility.[4]

In the late 1960s, she wrote occasionally to her children and to friends saying that she too was planning to go into exile or to move to town, but something deep in her personality compelled her to stay. She told me how a neighbor approached her once and suggested she move to Idutywa, where the opportunities were better. "Look," she responded, "number one, I'm a woman. And most people don't think that a woman can stand on her own. Number two, I'm surrounded by white-owned shops, and they have the same mentality that an African can't make it. I'm remaining here to prove it. And really, that's why I didn't want to go. Somehow I managed, through pure grit."

But by 1974, she told me, "It was so bad that I did not have *anything* I could call my own. The government attitude was that they could come in, any time of the day or night. They'd even go into my handbag!" To make matters worse, her business had fallen severely into debt. "The clerk of the court would come regularly. I saw I had no way out."

The closing of the shop was the end of a dream: that of a life led independent of white paymasters, acting as "civilising agents" to the *amaqaba* (traditional people) of the Transkei, as she put it to her husband in a letter at the time.[5] Govan Mbeki had sold the dream to his skeptical wife back in 1940; now, she wrote to him, "you would wish to leave there yourself. Our place looks god-forsaken." When she wrote "You have no idea how low Mbewuleni situation has deteriorated,"[6] she was of course talking about her own situation, too.

Things gradually began to get better once Epainette Mbeki moved to Ngcingwane. "The advantage of the business here is the locality," she wrote to her husband in November 1975. "It is only four miles from Idutywa. On the other hand, that is a disadvantage as I have to compete with town as far as prices are concerned and there are three supermarkets in Idutywa. Anyway, I am quite happy here, more so because I can concentrate on groceries, vegetables and fruit." At the same time, his daughter Linda reported to him that Mama was "in good health. She planted potatoes, beans, and pumpkins in the garden."[7]

Slowly, Epainette Mbeki reentered the life of the community, and by 1982 she was both secretary and treasurer of the Idutywa agricultural show. She also began a cooperative, teaching the local women to sew traditional Xhosa garments, to garden, and to raise chickens. "And, queer enough," she told me, "with my little money, I began to pull through. The people here were slightly more culturally advanced than in Mbewuleni. And about my commodities, I learnt from the community what they needed, so the support they gave me was better. And, queer enough, when the security branch came to visit me in the night, the people would come out and see what was going on, and protect me, unlike in Mbewuleni."

Her son Moeletsi sent her enough to pay for the house, and by the end of the year she could declare triumphantly to her husband, "I have bought this small homestead with the money."[8] She had, finally, her own home, which she had made herself, in a place that she had chosen for herself. She made the decision, there and then, that she would never move again, and she has stuck to it.

When I went to visit her in 2000, her family was putting immense pressure on her to move to Port Elizabeth, to be with her husband, or to Pretoria, to be looked after in the official presidential residence, but she refused. There was family conflict over this, "but one of my sons says, 'Ma, don't worry. You have always been independent. Carry on!' It's this independence, my whole family has it. It's this thing of being productive. You must not expect some- one else to do it for you. You must do it for yourself."

As we sat in the dark, damp living room of her little house in Ngcingwane, she allowed, uncharacteristically, an edge of bitterness to creep into her voice. "They can't come back now and say, 'Move in with us,' just like that. This is where I was. This is what I know. This is where I stay."

Sit with the prison archives of correspondence between ANC leaders on Robben Island and their wives and you will be struck, forcibly, by the indus- try generated by these pages of yellowing paper. Each document has a hinter- land, sometimes filling a whole box file, of analysis and commentary passed between the prison officials and the security police, as if each love letter were an insurrectionary treatise to be decoded, a land mine to be defused. The original letters themselves are defiled by the thick black of the censor's pen or even chopped up with scissors; typed copies are scarred with offi- cials' commentary. These are folded in with the most extraordinary volume of minutiae—every engagement between the prisoner and the system, from a medical visit to a request for a book, is recorded, noted, dissected. The files of information provide a suggestion of what life must have been like inside an apartheid jail: the regulation, the paranoia, the dizzying lack of perspec- tive, and the heroic efforts made by prisoners to remain human in the face of such regulated banality.

In the correspondence between Nelson and Winnie Mandela, or between Walter and Albertina Sisulu, there is something redemptive in the way the couples were able to maintain contact despite the state's interventions. They managed to conduct their affairs beneath the eyes of their oppressors with such apparent ease that they made a mockery of their small-minded eaves- droppers. But the Sisulus were firmly, incontrovertibly together when Walter was arrested; the Mandelas were still in the flush of romance when Nelson was arrested. Not so the Mbekis, whose marriage was already broken. In a free society, they might have each moved on. Instead, their relationship was frozen at a moment when there was already pain and recrimination, frac- ture and abandonment. Relationships are, of course, weakened by adversity, but are also driven by their own internal logic. Who can say, then, whether Govan and Epainette Mbeki's marriage would have been a happy one had they lived in a free society? But the system that jailed Govan Mbeki can and should be held responsible for tying him and his wife together, through his imprisonment, when they might otherwise have separated. In this way, it wrecked both their lives.

Epainette Mbeki always began letters to her husband with a term of endearment: "Honey," "My Love," "Dear Heart." And she always ended them with "lots of love" or even "lots and lots of love and kisses." But in between, they were brisk and somewhat impersonal, grim accounts of her needs or quiet reproaches for his lack of communication: "How are you and when are you writing to me, two wrongs never make one right.... I sent you R25.00. Of course official receipts were posted to me, but it would please me more to hear from you personally."[9] Matters that might have been easily resolved were he not in prison—such as the status of a license to run a drinking establishment in Mbewuleni—churned on interminably over the years.

Every now and then, she let out a little of her longing for him, and for a life lived together, or an assertion of shared values or nostalgia for their early years in the Transkei: "When are you coming back[?]" she asks plaintively in one letter, as if it were an answer he could supply.[10] From time to time, she conjures up those heated discussions about language and literature that were the signature of the Mbeki household by asking him to complete a quotation she has forgotten, or by remembering arguments about how a poem went. But even in this nostalgia she embeds a consciousness of her enforced independence: "What I really wanted to get across is, since I stay alone things are not so bad, actually more work is covered better than ever."[11]

After finding the letters that Epainette Mbeki had written to her husband in prison and her son in exile, I went to see her. I watched as she carefully read the copies I had made. "I didn't write lots," she volunteered. "Only when I had a matter that needed to be addressed or replied to." She did not hear from Thabo, she told me, "but I didn't bear a grudge": She understood that correspondence from him might endanger both of them.

In the pile of documents I had brought to her was a 1965 letter I had found in the Youth and Students Section file at Fort Hare. "Dear Thabo," it began, "you know when one has had contact with the police and the Special Branch and a host of informers, one develops a critical attitude towards overtures of friendship. I have received four Christmas Cards from different people in England.... They come from people I have never heard of.... So one is not sure whether these are genuine friends.... Please find out whether the move is genuine. Lots and lots of Love, Mom."[12] It was a classic example of how good intentions sometimes go awry in solidarity campaigns: the Anti-Apartheid Movement had begun a letter-writing campaign, asking sympathizers to write letters to prisoners and their families. But word of this solidarity campaign had clearly not yet reached Mbewuleni.

Mrs. Mbeki had enclosed part of one of the cards in the letter to her son, which has the words "happiness and prosperity in the New Year" printed on it. "Dear Mrs Govan Mbeki," the card read, "our hopes and prayers are with you this holiday season. We cannot imagine what it must be like to be imprisoned for one's beliefs. We hope the future is more [illegible] for you. The Shewburg Family."[13]

I watched her nodding quietly to herself as she read the card, and I found myself overwhelmed with emotion at the tragedy of this fine woman, so deformed by the shattering of her family and the cruelty of the state that she is unable to find solace even in the goodwill of an innocuous Christmas card from well-meaning strangers. I diverted my eyes from her and let them settle on the only adornment in her tiny front room: a plate commemorating the death of Princess Diana. "Is Princess Diana special to you, Mama?" I asked.

She looked up at the plate, and then locked me with her large-eyed stare. "I cried and cried a lot when she died," she told me. "I cried my eyes out. She really was a people's princess, like they said. She didn't have any airs of high society. She communicated with everyone equally. That was lovely about her." She went back to reading the letters, and when she was finished, she looked up at me. "Diana had her own personal problems," she said, "but she didn't allow that to get her down. She carried on."

Epainette Mbeki went to see her husband on Robben Island only twice in the 23 years he was there. The first time was in 1965, and she had come back "so sick," her daughter Linda told me, "we thought she was going to die." She was particularly disturbed by the fact that her fastidious and upright husband, like all African prisoners regardless of their age, had to wear the humiliating schoolboy uniform of short sleeves and short pants—a rule revoked only in 1979.

The next year Govan Mbeki had been transferred to Colesberg in the Northern Cape, so that he could testify in the trial of a comrade. Colesberg is only a few hours' drive from Idutywa and the prison regulations were less severe, but Epainette Mbeki was nonetheless anxious. "He is looking much better than he did at Robben Island," she wrote to her son Thabo upon her return, "and he was dressed in khaki unlike at the other place where he was dressed in Prison Garb. I can now visit him every three months and write every three months."[14] She did write, diligently, but the next time she saw him was in 1981, during her only other visit to Robben Island.

Govan Mbeki was both perplexed and hurt that his wife did not visit him more often. This hurt ossified into a permanent grievance and was among the reasons why he refused to return to the Transkei, to live with her, after his release in 1987. He might have had a sense of the difficulties his wife was going through, but he could not have known their full extent and the breakdown she had suffered after visiting him in 1965.

Epainette often wrote about visiting but never made it. It became, in fact, something of a bitter joke between Govan Mbeki and his daughter. "You can laugh until you sleep," Linda wrote to him in May 1982, "today I have received a letter from my mother saying she has changed her mind about that July trip...[because] she is going to be busy towards the end of July with the Agricultural show."[15] For Epainette Mbeki, it was work enough just to hold herself together. Her shop was her anchor; it kept her alive by a thread. She could not afford to leave it, emotionally or financially—not least for the grueling and expensive trip to Robben Island. Rather than going herself, then, she sent her children, Linda and Jama. But after Jama was denied a passport to travel to South Africa in 1966, he stopped going, and Linda also stopped after her 1975 visit, retreating into her work and never leaving the Transkei again after her release from detention in 1977. In his last years in jail, Govan's only family visits were from his grandson, Moeletsi's son Karl, whose mother brought him from Britain annually.

If Nelson Mandela was the African National Congress patriarch on the island and Walter Sisulu's role was more maternal, then Govan Mbeki was the uncle—"Oom Gov"—from whom there was much to learn, to whom one needed to prove oneself, and from whom one might elicit, if one was lucky, that wonderful deep laugh and that broad smile. Mac Maharaj has written that he has "puzzled" over the way Mbeki masked his "soft-spoken calm and gentleness" with a carapace of severity: "Perhaps the answer lies in recognising the teacher, the pedagogue in him....How many teachers mask their warmth and gentleness with a ramrod posture and a firmness which often appears as strictness?"[16]

Lionel Davis, a non–ANC prisoner, told me that while "you felt welcome immediately" with Mandela and Sisulu, "Oom Gov had to grow on you." Others recall Mbeki's inflexibility and his point-blank, even if always courteous, refusal to engage in debate with those who disagreed with him. Mbeki's ascetic nature was pronounced, and he was as uncompromising about cleanliness, order, and punctuality as he was about his communism. But there was another side to him too: Thami Mkhwanazi remembers that he "liked to strum guitar and play folk songs,"[17] and his love of the game of Monopoly was legendary.

Mbeki's fellow Rivonia trial defendant Ahmed Kathrada speculates that he "was quite content alone with his thoughts" because he "was an intellectual...perhaps it was this that drew him to spending time alone, ruminating on the struggle and on his life."[18] This reverses, perhaps, cause and effect: He was not "content alone with his thoughts" because he was an "intellectual"; rather, the intellectualism itself was a form of withdrawal, the consequence of having removed himself from the humanizing effects of the hearth and of fatherhood, a condition that was exacerbated by his wife's subsequent withdrawal from him and by his sons' enforced absence, across the waters.

Govan Mbeki had no contact with Thabo until his release in 1987. While he was in prison, Govan wrote to his oldest son only once: to instruct him to take on the role of parent to his younger brothers. Having acquitted himself of this responsibility, he did not attempt to keep in contact, with one exception: In 1982, when, after the arrest and disappearance of Jama, he wrote a letter to Moeletsi to forward to Thabo. For the rest, he told me, "It was too difficult. We were assured that the conditions [in exile] were livable, so what was there to bother about?"

Thabo Mbeki did not write to his father either: Any communication, he told me, would have constituted a security risk. This is not entirely true: Max Sisulu wrote frequently to his father and had the letters posted from South Africa (although they were ultimately withheld). Perhaps Mbeki's decision not to write to his father had as much to do with pride as with security: One could imagine him refusing the indignity of having his correspondence mediated in such a way, and one could imagine his father, even on pain of not receiving any letters, agreeing with him. But by the mid-1980s, security restrictions had relaxed enough that Walter Sisulu was receiving relatively unrestricted mail from his exiled children, and there is evidence that as early as 1975 Govan was receiving letters from Moeletsi and Jama. There would have been no problem, by 1985, if Thabo Mbeki had wished to write to his father. But letters would have had to be confined to family matters with no mention whatsoever of politics. Given the nature of Thabo Mbeki's relationship with his father and their respective consumption by the struggle, what, then, would they have written about?

And so Thabo Mbeki did not write to his father with news of his life abroad or even with the affirmation of filial pride and commitment. Instead, in 1964, age 21, he took himself off to London to a meeting of the UN Special Committee Against Apartheid and told the world how much his father meant to him: "Today we might be but weak children, spurred on by nothing other than the fear and grief of losing our fathers. In time we shall learn to die both for ourselves and for the millions."[19]

The first time that Govan Mbeki even knew that his son had written these words was when he picked up a newspaper in late 1998, 11 years after his release from Robben Island and 8 years after his son's return to South Africa. The speech had been reprinted as advance publicity for the anthology of speeches Thabo was about to publish. How, I asked the old man, had he felt reading it? He was sitting, at the time, with a copy of the anthology on his lap; it had just been released, and I had brought it down to Port Elizabeth for him. When I had given it to him earlier, he had used his long, bony fingers to trace the portrait of his son on the cover—an extreme close-up that catches all the folds of fatigue around Mbeki's dull eyes—and shaken his head with unexpectedly paternal concern: "He looks tired, Thabo. I have told him to rest more."

Now, as he contemplated his son's 1964 speech about him before the United Nations, he stroked the portrait fondly, somewhat absentmindedly, conjuring a connection from his life of absence.

"I was moved," he said. He paused for a few seconds. "Really moved."

19

THE DISAPPEARANCE
OF JAMA MBEKI

When Jama Mbeki, Thabo's youngest brother, was diagnosed with diabetes in 1979 at the age of 32, his wife, Mphu Matete, phoned all the members of his family she could find to tell them. The Mbekis and their three young girls lived in Botswana, where Jama was an attorney; Matete got through to Lusaka, and heard the familiar throaty cackle at the other end: "That one likes the sugar too much," Thabo Mbeki joked. "When he was young, he always used to steal the sugar." Three years later, in March 1982, Mphu Matete had cause to phone her brother-in-law again: Her husband had been arrested on charges of fraud and accessory to murder; he was being denied access to his medication and was very ill. Through African National Congress supporters in the United States, Thabo arranged for bail to be paid, but the day before Jama was to appear in court, he disappeared. None of his family ever saw or heard from him again.[1]

Jama Mbeki was indeed the one who stole the Mbeki family sugar; the youngest child of Govan and Epainette was the only one in the family with an effusive and outgoing personality. He had a similar rebellious streak to Moeletsi, but he could not have been more different from Thabo, as gregarious and generous as his oldest brother was restrained and prudent, a playful iconoclast who refused point blank to comb his hair or to wear anything but jeans.

Only ten years old when he was sent to the Moerane homestead in Lesotho, Jama saw himself as Sotho rather than as South African. Being brought up in Lesotho had a profound effect on his political development, as it did on Moeletsi, exposing them to a political tradition quite different from that of their parents. As Moeletsi put it to me: "We weren't institutionalized into the old Eastern Cape elite, the whole Lovedale/Fort Hare thing. Lesotho was a place with much less sense of its own importance, a place that didn't put so much stock in tradition."

The Lesotho Moeranes were stalwarts of the Basutoland Congress Party (BCP), and Aunt Mphuma, with whom the Mbeki boys lived, was one of its prevailing matriarchs. The BCP was originally an offshoot of the African

National Congress (ANC), but by the time Jama was a young man, it had developed an anticommunist Africanism that brought the party closer to the Pan Africanist Congress (PAC). Later the BCP would become the ANC's avowed enemy—a situation that may well have played a role in Jama's death.

By the time Jama Mbeki was a university student, he was a prominent BCP leader, one of those who led the charge against the incumbent Chief Leabua Jonathan's Basutoland National Party (BNP) in the country's fateful 1970 elections. When, with the support of the apartheid South African state, Jonathan refused to accept the election results and declared an emergency, Jama was one of many who fled into exile—to Botswana, where he married Matete, another Sotho in exile, and found work as a teacher. In 1973, he and Thabo met for the first time since they were children, when Jama came through Lusaka en route to Leeds, where Thabo had arranged a scholarship for him.

After Jama finished his legal studies at Leeds, he disappeared for the first time—most likely to Libya, for military training with the BCP's new army, known as the Lesotho Liberation Army (LLA), which was now mounting an insurgency against the Jonathan government under the sponsorship of the ANC's archrival, the PAC. Meanwhile, the ANC had effectively swapped sides in Lesotho and became allied with Jonathan, partly because the BCP was now firmly in the PAC camp and partly because it was clear that Jonathan was in power to stay and it was expedient to befriend him. The result of this realignment was two Faustian pacts. The Lesotho dictator would permit the ANC to work out of his country so long as it severed all ties with the BCP; meanwhile, a faction of the LLA accepted covert support from the South African regime against their common enemy: Chief Jonathan's government.

And so Thabo Mbeki found himself in a political conflict with his brother Jama far more serious than the Old Left/New Left sparring between himself and Moeletsi. And yet, perhaps because of Jama's disarming openness, a deep affection developed between them. When Jama returned to Botswana in 1975, Thabo was spending a lot of time there, trying to recruit newly arrived Black Consciousness (BC) exiles into the ANC, and it was often Jama who provided the conduit. The brothers saw each other frequently, and Mphu Matete recollects that they were "very close. The only time you would hear them arguing was over their political beliefs." Uniquely for an Mbeki, Jama was able to put family above politics. "Whatever I do for the ANC," he told his wife, "I do for Thabo." This included pro bono legal advice and representation for ANC operatives in Botswana and providing an open house for South African exiles of all political persuasions.

But the youngest Mbeki appears to have been too open, too ingenuous, to be an effective political operative, as the events that led up to his arrest and disappearance demonstrate. In late 1981 he did a deal with a group of South Africans who had arrived in Botswana supposedly looking to sell trucks.

When the local ANC underground leadership found out, they were furious: They believed the men to be South African agents and accused Jama of having compromised ANC security in Botswana. They demanded that he participate in a trap to catch the alleged agents and, in February 1982, when the South Africans contacted Jama again, an ambush was laid. One was shot through the head and burned on a bonfire; another escaped and led the Botswana authorities back to the charred remains of his accomplice. The escapee also helped identify his assailants, who were arrested. One of these was Jama, who led the authorities to the gun, which he had hidden.

Had Jama Mbeki been involved in the murder, and if so, to what extent? He told his wife that he had been given the gun after the fact and was asked to conceal it. Ultimately, that is what he was charged with: complicity in the concealment of a firearm used in a murder. But one of Jama's BCP comrades, Lebenya Chakela, says that he had personally given the gun to Jama. Out on bail, Jama said that he had been denied diabetic medication, tortured, and forced to confess; if true, it seems likely that the lesser charge was the result of a plea bargain. Either to sully his reputation or to twist his arm into further cooperation, the authorities slapped a second, unrelated charge onto his sheet: He was accused of defrauding his clients' trust funds of a few hundred dollars.

A day before his trial, Jama told his wife that he was skipping bail and leaving the country and that they would be reunited in a liberated Lesotho. His plan was to join the LLA underground and participate in the insurgency to unseat Chief Jonathan. According to his wife, he could not countenance a spell in prison, particularly given his severe medical condition, and the fraud charge meant his career in Botswana was over anyway. His BCP comrades believe that his major incentive in skipping bail was his shame at having been "turned" and that he could not bear the thought of testifying against his coaccused.

And so Jama Mbeki left Botswana on or just before March 16, 1982. By December, nine months later, Mphu Matete had not heard from her husband, so she went to Lesotho to look for him. The last person to have seen him alive was her childhood friend Fonti Miriam Mophethe, a nurse, whom he had approached in early May.

Mophethe told Matete what had happened: Jama had come to see her, heavily disguised under a traditional Lesotho blanket, because he needed medical attention. He had been smuggled into South Africa by relatives of his wife, laying low in Soweto for a few weeks, before convincing the Lesotho authorities in Johannesburg that he was a distressed migrant miner who had lost his papers. He had been in Lesotho for a while, he told Mophethe, in transit, to say good-bye to his family and was en route to his mother in the Transkei, to bid her farewell too, before leaving for Ghana to start a new life there.

Jama stayed overnight with Mophethe, and when he was ready to leave, she offered to drive him somewhere. He said he did not want to be seen in her car, so they took a taxi together.

"Where are you going?" she asked.

"*Oa ha monna ha botsoe*," he replied. Where a man goes, let nobody ask.

He alighted at a traffic circle, and she watched him meld into the sidewalk traffic of an early winter's Maseru dusk.

By the time her brother-in-law became the South African president, Mphu Matete lived alone, somewhat at peace, in the remote Namibian desert town of Gobabis. There she worked with the nomadic San people for an international healthcare nongovernmental organization. The three daughters she had with Jama became the sugar thieves of the next Mbeki generation: vivacious, intelligent, and affectionate, they were brought into the bosom of the family and were adored. But although Jama's widow remained in touch with the Mbekis, she lived at a distance from them, alienated by bitterness and hurt over the way they dealt with her after her husband's disappearance.

She had convinced herself that her husband was living underground and had not contacted her. But four years later, in 1986, she was told by a lawyer that he was no longer alive. She phoned Thabo Mbeki in Lusaka: "Did you know Jama was dead?" she asked. Her brother-in-law said that he did, but when she pressed him for details, he referred her to Moeletsi, who acknowledged he too had known Jama was dead and that he had heard about it from Thabo—who had told him that some Lesotho-based ANC operatives had seen Jama's body in a morgue. But neither surviving brother did anything to find out who killed Jama and why.

This distressed Jama's mother as much as it did his widow. In our many hours together, the disappearance of her youngest son was the only subject Epainette Mbeki was unable to broach: 20 years later, her pain was palpable, raw and unresolved. She endured it in anguished silence until the men of her family returned from prison and exile, at which point she made her feelings known: She wanted the truth, and she wanted his remains; she wanted to bury him properly. And so, in the early 1990s, the Mbekis retained a Maseru attorney to investigate. But Mphu Matete was not told about the investigation until after it had been closed. She got the name of the attorney and went to see him, and finally, more than 15 years after Jama's disappearance, she discovered what had happened to him.

Some days after Jama Mbeki left Fonti Mophethe's flat, he sought out a comrade, a doctor named Darkmore Hlaleli, as he was again in serious need of medical attention. But he was unaware that Hlaleli had been turned and was now a double agent. The doctor, since deceased, allegedly tipped off the authorities, and a notorious security policeman began to tail Jama. The Mbekis' investigation revealed that the policeman lured Jama to a taxi rank with the promise of information, and entered a taxi with him. Along the way, the taxi was stopped by a fake roadblock, and Jama and the policeman were "arrested"; the taxi continued without them, and Jama was then allegedly executed somewhere along the Leribe–Maseru highway.

The source of the Mbeki family's investigation was the policeman himself, who had demanded to be paid to show the family the exact location of the assassination. Once the Mbeki family realized that they were going to be extorted to find Jama's remains, they called a halt to the investigation; at least, however, they had confirmation of his death. Supported by his widow, Epainette Mbeki attempted to organize a memorial service, but the Mbeki men vetoed the plan. They also decided not to take the case to the police.

Remember Govan Mbeki's line to me about how he coped with the disappearances of both son and grandson: "When you go into war, if your comrade in front of you falls off his horse, you must not stop and weep. You jump over him into battle." He said something similar to Mphu Matete when she confronted him in 1996: "My child, when people have fallen in the line of war, just forget it."

Govan Mbeki was, at this point, a venerable if declining elder of the now-ruling ANC. His son Thabo was deputy president. On one level, the martial response was no longer valid. The war was over: Was there not, finally, the space to seek justice or at the very least grieve for loved ones lost during the freedom struggle? Or was it rather that, given the Mbekis' profile in postapartheid South Africa, the prospect of public grief was too threatening to contemplate? Or perhaps—in a similar vein to Thabo Mbeki's reticence about trying to find out what happened to his son Kwanda—too craven: Why should we attract media attention around our grief when so many others suffered?

For civilians like Mphu Matete—or Olive Mpahlwa, mother of Thabo's son—such behavior is inexplicable. For them, certain things must happen when a loved one dies. No matter what else is at stake, the family must come together in a ritual moment of collective grief and mark the deceased's passing. But, in Matete's view, "in the Mbeki family there is no [such] family value. They believe in politics [more] than real life."

The decision about whether to search for Jama or to seek justice was determined by a calculus of political consequences. The Lesotho operatives who killed Jama were not acting alone: They were accountable to the highest structures of the government. According to the investigation commissioned by the Mbekis, the man directly responsible for Jama's execution was a very senior member of the Lesotho defense force's military intelligence—which was, of course, working closely with the ANC. Indeed, given the close cooperation between the ANC and the Lesotho government, it should come as no surprise that ANC operatives in Lesotho knew that Jama's body was in a Maseru morgue.

When, in 1989, the ANC was finally approached for comment about Jama Mbeki's disappearance seven years earlier, it responded tersely: "As far as the ANC is concerned he never joined the ranks of the ANC after he left Botswana."[2] In fact, the ANC's man in Lesotho, Chris Hani, felt that Jama's involvement in the LLA rendered him something of an embarrassment to the movement, and several of Jama's BCP comrades actually believe that the ANC in Lesotho had a hand in his murder. There is no evidence to substantiate this, but if the investigation commissioned by the Mbekis is correct, Jama Mbeki was killed by people who were, at the very least, working closely with the ANC at the time. Perhaps this, in the end, was what Govan Mbeki meant when he told his daughter-in-law to "just forget it."

In 1982 in Lesotho, there really was a war going on. By his own admission, Jama Mbeki was back in the country as part of an insurgency: a plot to assassinate the head of state. The day after Mphu Matete returned to Lesotho, in December 1982, to look for her lost husband, a South African commando crossed into Lesotho and massacred 42 people in ANC houses—possibly assisted by members of the LLA. In such a context, it would have been untenable for an ANC leader like Thabo Mbeki to pursue his brother's disappearance or to expose his assailants—particularly to his sister-in-law, herself a strong BCP activist and a bitter opponent of the Jonathan regime. If Mbeki had pursued justice in the case of his missing brother, he might have jeopardized the fragile alliance that allowed the ANC to stay in Lesotho. Worse yet, he might have discovered that his own comrades were implicated. In the bluntest terms, he had to choose between protecting his movement and serving the honor of his brother. There was, of course, no choice.

But that was in 1982. In 1996, when the war was long over, an investigation provided the Mbekis with the names of men alleged to have killed Jama Mbeki, and the family still declined to take action. Even in peacetime, they had to subjugate their own needs to the national interest. There had been yet another convulsion in Lesotho's politics: The BCP had won an election in 1993 and, to prevent civil war, the new Lesotho government had decided not to pursue the disappearances of former anti-Jonathan activists: "There were hundreds of BCP members like my brother," Moeletsi Mbeki told me, "killed and disappeared. If we had insisted on justice for Jama, we would have opened up a whole hornets' nest for the new BCP Lesotho government."

If Lesotho had undergone a truth and reconciliation process like South Africa, Jama Mbeki's assailants might have applied for—and received—amnesty. But there was no such process, and by the time the ANC came to power in 1994, the men who had allegedly ordered Jama's assassination were still in positions of power. How could Thabo Mbeki, the deputy president of South Africa, demand that charges be laid against them?

Just as Thabo Mbeki was forced to work with his former enemies, so too were Lesotho's new rulers, relying heavily on Chief Jonathan's old military guard to remain in power. Who was Mbeki, then, to disrupt things in Lesotho? Now, as in the 1980s, personal needs had to be subordinated to the national interest. And so Jama Mbeki remained unburied and his killers unaccountable.

Remember what Mbeki said to F. W. de Klerk in 1994 when the latter criticized the establishment of a truth commission: that his family was not looking for retribution or revenge, but merely for an answer as to what had happened.[3] Two years later, as a consequence of the family's investigation, Thabo would come closer to having "that kind of truth" with respect to his brother Jama. But he would be powerless, because of his political obligations, to take it any further. He would thus be unable to bring his own closure to the process of "truth and reconciliation" that reputedly drove the South African "miracle."

20

NIGERIA

"THE REAL AFRICA"

After being deported from Swaziland in 1976, Thabo Mbeki was posted to Lagos as the African National Congress's first representative to Nigeria. When he arrived, in January 1977, the city was even more turbulent than usual: traffic-choked with the gluttony of the oil boom, frenetic with the preparations for a huge international arts festival, fired up by the Soweto uprising down south, and edgy with its own student protests following the murder of the wildly popular head of state, General Murtala Mohammed. Murtala's successor, war hero Olusegun Obasanjo, promised to return Nigeria to democracy after a decade of coups and kleptocracy. His plan was to use the country's oil dollars to transform it into the epicenter of the black world, the moral and cultural leader of the continent. A major part of this was the sponsorship of "pan-African" cultural and political activities—and foremost among these, of course, was support for the anti-apartheid struggle.

Because of Nigeria's strong connections to black America, the country had traditionally been ambivalent about the "nonracial" and Soviet-linked ANC and was more supportive of the ANC's rival, the Pan Africanist Congress (PAC). But now Obasanjo decided he would foster the fractious South African liberation movements into one united front under Nigerian patronage, so he offered to sponsor a permanent ANC representative in Lagos. Thabo Mbeki was given the job. In the beginning, some of his comrades saw Mbeki's posting as a demotion or sidelining—punishment, perhaps, for having botched Swaziland—but this was not the case at all. The prescient Oliver Tambo understood that Nigeria was potentially explosive for the ANC, given that it was both the new global hub of the anti-apartheid movement and skeptical of the movement's nonracialism; Mbeki was sent in as a fixer, and he performed magnificently.

The "worry" about the Nigerians, Mbeki told me, was that they "do their own thing. [And] they are of such importance on the African continent that they could mislead lots of people." Because of their own experiences, they did "not understand this business [of]...accommodation of the whites...."

Therefore we had to be there, to work with them." Mbeki's immediate imperative was "to influence the establishment to come over to our side."

Mbeki was pleased to discover Baba Gana Kingibe, an old Sussex classmate, working as a political aide to Obasanjo. Zanele Mbeki spent much of 1977 in Lagos with her husband, and the couple hit it off immediately with the Kingibe family; Kingibe has fond, strong memories of Zanele in his kitchen, learning the art of Nigerian cuisine, and of Thabo Mbeki disappearing enthusiastically into the turmoil of Lagos and returning, exhausted and sated, in the evening. But Kingibe warned Mbeki that the odds were against his mission: The ANC seemed "too soft" to a country aroused by the battle cries of Soweto.

Malebo Kotu-Rammopo, a South African exile from a PAC family then studying law in Lagos, was struck by the new ANC representative's gravitas: "My overwhelming impression of him was of a young person with a tremendous load on his shoulders, surrounded by older people. Expectations of him were so high." This was all the more so because of the intensity of anti-apartheid sentiment in Nigeria, which developed the only popular international solidarity movement on the continent, akin to that in Sweden and the Netherlands. Obasanjo had initiated a South African Relief Fund, to which every Nigerian was encouraged to contribute. Civil servants willingly had contributions, known popularly as the Mandela Tax, debited from their monthly paychecks, and every second song on the radio seemed to refer to Nelson or Winnie Mandela.

By the late 1970s, almost all student activism at Nigerian universities focused on the anti-apartheid movement, and much of Mbeki's work was on campuses across the country. Of course, these young Nigerians were by no means free themselves: The military regime banned all local politics. So there was an edge to anti-apartheid activism not to be found in Western Europe: Nigerians expressed their own political aspirations through the proxy of the South African struggle. As G. G. Darah, the Nigerian critic and editor, puts it, "The explosion in Soweto also exploded something in our hearts."

In August 1977 Obasanjo opened the UN Conference Against Apartheid, the largest global gathering yet of its kind. His aim was an enforced arms embargo on South Africa that, three months later, would be ratified by the UN General Assembly: Following Black Consciousness leader Steve Biko's death in detention in September 1977, even South Africa's traditional allies on the Security Council capitulated. By the role it played in the process, Nigeria reaffirmed "its total commitment to our cause," Mbeki wrote anonymously in the ANC journal *Sechaba*: "Our struggle is theirs."[1]

But the ANC told a very different story to its Soviet patrons in Moscow after the UN conference: An emissary complained about the country's "ambivalent position."[2] Here was the problem: Obasanjo's government had recently become enamored of the young revolutionaries of the Soweto Student Representatives' Council (SSRC), who had led the June 1976 uprising and were now in exile—and whose charismatic leader, Tsietsi Mashinini, had taken to slamming the ANC at every turn. Mashinini called the ANC "corrupt" and "extinct internally" and said he would even take money from the U.S. Central Intelligence Agency if it was willing to help him. The ANC responded that he was the stooge of "counter-revolutionary forces,"[3] but Mashinini, only 19, was articulate and passionate, and was "snapped up by a world eager to put a face on the now-famous Soweto uprising," as the historian Gail Gerhart puts it.[4] After Mashinini's high-profile tour of Britain and the United States, the Nigerians brought him to Lagos, which swooned.

The Nigerians gave Mashinini financial support and accommodation in the upscale Federal Guesthouse at Bar Beach on Victoria Island and opened bank accounts for him and his comrades. Then, in their attempt to bring the different South African factions together, they engaged in some social engineering: They accommodated Thabo Mbeki here, too. Malebo Kotu-Rammopo remembers the guesthouse as a place where young South Africans would gather and have "parties that always ended up in a political debate"—inevitably verbal jousting between the passionate Mashinini and the cool Mbeki.

Like so many in Lagos, Kotu-Rammopo was enthralled by the young revolutionaries around Mashinini, full of righteous fire and fresh from the front line: "They were hell-bent on maintaining their independence, on not being part of any movement. Their attitude [to both the ANC and the PAC] was 'You're trying to steal us!'" They were also "adamant that the struggle had to be a *black* struggle by *black* people." But it was at the Federal Guesthouse, listening to Mbeki's reasoning, that she first began to reappraise the precepts of her own PAC upbringing: "Although I never joined the ANC, the debates brought me round to understanding nonracialism. No more 'Africa for the Africans!'"

Although Mbeki and Mashinini had an amicable personal relationship, the ANC remained incontrovertibly opposed to any formal recognition of the SSRC. Finally, under pressure from the Nigerians, Mbeki led an ANC delegation to a "unification" meeting in mid-1978, hosted by Obasanjo, which included representatives of the PAC and the SSRC. One of the latter, Barney Mokgatle, told me how impressed he was at the way Mbeki "brought the temperature down." In a calm, respectful way, he advanced the arguments he had been honing since meeting the first generation of Black Consciousness exiles in 1974: "We are far down the line with our training and our camps. Why set up your own? Resolve your ideological problems with us from within. Come on board the moving train."

"We are already on a fast track," Mokgatle remembers retorting, with all the arrogance of youth. "Our train is moving fast while yours is halted. A lot of people don't even know about the ANC back home."

The meeting ended inconclusively, but by this point the ANC had all but won the battle. In Nigeria, Mbeki's brief was to ensure not only that his Nigerian hosts took "the correct positions," as he put it to me, but that the South African refugees pouring into the country did, too. The student leaders held out, though, even getting some military training, with the Nigerians' help, from the Palestinians—and seeing some action in Lebanon in 1980. But the group was never more than a talk shop, a marginal force eviscerated not only by the ANC but by its own internal tragedy: the collapse of Tsietsi Mashinini, around whom they had been almost cultishly organized. Increasingly unpredictable and volatile, he spent more and more time in Lagos's bars and clubs; in late 1977 he unexpectedly married a wealthy Liberian beauty queen and brought her to live with him at the Federal Guesthouse. This enraged both his comrades and his hosts; when he was ordered to leave the guesthouse, he stormed out of Nigeria and settled in Monrovia. His marriage collapsed and he ultimately moved to Guinea, suffering from an unspecified illness and declining to a lonely, unexplained death in 1990.

How could the Nigerians, eager to establish themselves as the patrons of South Africa's liberation, not but compare the juvenile volatility of Mashinini with the intense focus of Thabo Mbeki? The Soweto student leaders were smart and committed, but as the Mashinini tragedy demonstrates, they were too young, too at sea themselves, to manage both the social and the psychological challenges of exile and the expectations of a world looking for its next hero. At the time of his flight from Lagos, Mashinini was just 20 years old. Thabo Mbeki had been exactly the same age when he went into exile in 1962, but he had not fled a home in flames, and he had been transported to the nurturing atmosphere of Sussex. Mbeki's arguments were indisputable: Even with its inadequacies, only the ANC had the wherewithal to contain the Soweto generation. Tsietsi Mashinini never had a chance against Thabo Mbeki.

The year 1977 was one of the best in Thabo Mbeki's political career. He eclipsed the PAC in Nigeria and defused the Mashinini threat, and he stage-managed the tricky UN anti-apartheid conference for the ANC. He also began his term with a very challenging assignment that would bear significant fruit for both himself and the ANC: running the huge, unwieldy South African delegation at FESTAC, the Olympic-size "Second World Black and African Festival of Culture" that Obasanjo hosted in 1977 as his landmark pan-Africanist project.

There were 70,000 delegates from 59 countries at the festival; nightly performances of drama, music, and dance; boat regattas; traditional Nigerian *durbars* (horse or camel races); and a high-profile colloquium. The political debate was fierce, and Mbeki found that the very issues he had been debating with the young Black Consciousness leaders and with Nigerian officials were being performed across Lagos's urban stage: Who was an "African"? What did "black" mean?

The truth, however, was that Mbeki spent most of the festival not so much pondering the meaning of blackness as putting out fires. As leader of the South African delegation, he had to deal with problems ranging from the disappearance of the South Africans' buses (they had been stolen by the bus drivers) to the disaffection of the delegates when their subsistence money did not arrive. The South African delegation itself was an unwieldy conglomeration of people from all over the world—and different liberation movements—sorely in need of direction. There were aging veterans from the military camps with traditional Zulu dance routines and an old-fashioned choral group based in East Germany; jazzy hepcats from London and fiery young comrades just out of South Africa, lungs filled with the urgent new poetry of Black Consciousness.

The saxophonist Jonas Gwangwa, who was in the ANC delegation, proposed that all the South Africans be knitted together into one show to maximize their impact. This was contentious, given the number of artists not aligned with the ANC, but Gwangwa recruited Mbeki to his side and won the day: In a stormy meeting, Mbeki managed to persuade the delegation to accept the proposal. The result might not have been the most coherent production at FESTAC, but it represented a key moment in the branding of the South African liberation movement.

Gwangwa and Mbeki fused the ANC's understanding of international solidarity with the cultural preoccupations of the Black Consciousness movement, and the result would become an international phenomenon: culture as a vehicle for the mobilization of international solidarity unmatched by any other liberation movement. Out of it came the Amandla Cultural Ensemble, which was to play so significant a role in the ANC's international charm offensive of the 1980s. Writer Mandla Langa—who participated at FESTAC—attributes this strategy directly to Mbeki: "He understood the political purpose of using culture, which was to show the world what we Africans were capable of achieving if we were not fettered by this stupid racist ideology." This, then, was the alchemy begun at FESTAC: Not only was the ANC's own understanding of culture moved beyond the propagandistic functions of socialist revolution, but the openness of Mbeki to the cultural bias of the BC movement convinced the newly exiled intellectuals of the Soweto generation that the ANC could be a home for them.

Running the South African stall at FESTAC exposed Mbeki to two key groups of people, both of which were impressed: senior ANC mandarins and BC novices. In his work with both the SSRC activists around Mashinini and the cultural activists at FESTAC, he built on his successes with the BC movement in Swaziland and Botswana, ensuring that the ANC was now the home in exile of this new generation of struggle leaders, many of whom were self-identified artists and intellectuals. They would become his primary constituency within the ANC; he would go on to recruit and promote many to senior positions in his publicity department.

Thabo Mbeki's term in Nigeria would end with the most significant promotion of his own career: his appointment as political secretary to ANC president Oliver Tambo. Although he had been a member of the ANC's National Executive Committee for two years already, Mbeki arrived in Nigeria a young man, still needing to prove himself. He left a year later, an elder himself.

He also left, he told me, with a new understanding of Africa due to the "exposure," as he put it, to "a very different *African* society.... It doesn't have this big imprint of colonial oppression. It's something else. Very different from here. You get a sense that you are now really being exposed to the real Africa, not where *we* come from."

When I pressed him for an example of this difference, the first thing that came to his mind was the musician Fela Kuti, who invited him to visit his Afrika Shrine club in Lagos shortly after his arrival. This presented Mbeki with a dilemma, given the role Fela played in Nigerian society: that of an anarchic, countercultural critic, a lascivious and unruly demigod worshipped by thousands who flocked to his club for gatherings that were part musical spectacle, part revival meeting, part bacchanal, part protest rally. The authorities reviled him and would—soon after Mbeki arrived in Nigeria—raid his compound and burn it to the ground.

Mbeki discussed the dilemma with a Namibian comrade, an old Lagos hand, who objected strenuously: "You know, that fellow, he's going to be smoking *dagga* [marijuana].... How can we be seen in his company?"

But Mbeki decided to go, and "indeed," he told me, "when you get there, you don't really want to be seen, because there he appears onstage, Fela, he's only wearing underpants and his saxophone." Those who knew Mbeki in Nigeria say he loved Fela's music—its roots, its rhythms, and its politics. Fela took all the groovy ideas Mbeki had encountered in Europe in the 1960s and reinvented it as authentic African culture; he broke the rules, not in the permissive West but in supposedly patriarchal, conservative Africa—in a military dictatorship to boot. He was somebody spectacularly uncolonized, somebody free.

Fela's abiding obsession was with the way Africa's leaders had overturned the vision of his hero, Kwame Nkrumah. At the performance Mbeki attended at the Afrika Shrine in early 1977, he would have seen Fela perform his latest hit, "Upside Down," the message of which is ably illustrated by its Afrodelic album cover: an image of Fela as "Mr. Afrika," hanging upside down, legs tied, framed by a map of Africa and surrounded by images of the mess that has been made of it since the heady independence days of the early 1960s. Mbeki, like Fela, was obsessed with the way Africa's grand destiny, as articulated by the *uhuru* (freedom) prophecies of Nkrumah and Julius Nyerere, had been upended in the postcolonial era, and Nigeria in particular seemed to bring this out in him. Before his return to the continent in 1971, Mbeki had had no understanding of a postcolonial African dystopia; even afterward, his experiences in sleepy Zambia, laidback Swaziland, and self-satisfied Botswana could hardly have given the sense of "upside-downness" he experienced when he landed in Lagos in 1977. This was the "real Africa"—and it both attracted and repelled him.

To illustrate the way Nigeria was "a very different African society" from the one in which he had been raised, Mbeki told me not about only about his contradictory impulses toward Fela but also how a senior official in the Nigerian government had freely admitted that his colleagues promoting Tsietsi Mashinini worked for the American CIA, but could do nothing about it. Mbeki had a raft of other anecdotes, too, to make his point about the attractions—and exasperations—of this "real Africa." One was of a Nigerian woman who arrived in Lusaka to visit him in the 1980s and was appalled: "This place, why is it so clean? In the streets there's no one selling anything." Another was the story of his friend, a renowned historian, whom Obasanjo was maneuvering to get fired from his university position in 1977. The historian appealed to his uncle, a powerful emir, who then "collects all the emirs of the north and they say to Obasanjo, 'You touch our son and you're in trouble.' And yet in all these articles that [he] is writing he is denouncing the feudal system, and now this very feudal system is protecting him! So you say, 'But no, this Nigeria is very funny.'"

Listening to Mbeki talk about Nigeria, I was struck repeatedly by the complexity of his relationship with the country. Because of his time there, he portrayed himself as someone who was not an "outside observer," but who had crossed over into "real Africa" as other South Africans had not. And yet, with each example he gave, it became clearer that even though he was attracted to it, it was antithetical to everything he stood for. A "real Africa" it may have been, but it certainly was not one he would want to bring back to South Africa: dirty, hawker-filled streets, emir cronyism and intellectual hypocrisy, contradictory government policy, Afrika Shrine anarchy.

Mbeki told me that what turned him on most about Nigeria was its "openness"—as exemplified by Fela Kuti. But when I probed this, later, in a written question to him about what other "discoveries," besides Fela, he had made while posted to Lagos, he e-mailed back the following response:

> Nigeria horse & camel Durbars; Polo fraternities; cultural observations e.g. weddings & funerals; local drama & television series (Village Headmaster); rich literature; vibrant press; cultural and linguistic diversity; Education/Research excellence. Limitless entrepreneurship; (an open society under military rule) creativity; opulence and penury; material and spiritual generosity...[5]

The telegraphic style indicates that this answer was dashed off, probably late at night. Nonetheless, there is a widening lens to its structure that suggests the order of a poem; there is also the fact that the scope of the answer far exceeds the parameters of the question. This is more than a random index of memories; it is an act of creative expression that reflects, in its very form, the illogicality and uncontrollability that is its author's impression of Nigeria, and, as such, it offers a clue to Mbeki's description of the country as "the real Africa." It suggests that "openness" was not, actually, the only defining characteristic of this "real Africa" for Mbeki: Nigeria was also queer, inexplicable, contradictory, excessive, exuberant, irrational.

Nigeria's struggle for freedom is the antithesis of South Africa's, its postcolonial sequence of coups and civil wars anything but a template for South Africa's future. If this "real Africa" is exciting and provocative and liberating, it is also irrational and sometimes downright dangerous. Thabo Mbeki arrived in the country, in 1977, steeped in two European systems of reason: the secular relativism of Sussex and the dialectical materialism of Moscow. One gets the sense that, as he discovered Nigeria, he was awakened to the power of the irrational—and found it thrilling and unsettling in equal measure.

"The real Africa, not where *we* come from...": Perhaps Thabo Mbeki should not be held to account for his use of the phrase "real Africa," for it is a lazy shorthand, borrowed from travel brochure discourse to describe the difference between the cultural richness of west Africa and the comparative denudation in southern Africa. But the very fact that this word choice is carelessly dropped into an interview rather than honed into a premeditated speech opens a chink through which we can glimpse the hinterland to Thabo Mbeki's African Renaissance and the ambivalence that drove it. The "real Africa" is "not where *we* come from" but "something else," the other against which we define the self, not a real place at all. It is something to run toward and run away from all at the same time, a tropical holiday, a dream/nightmare where you find yourself wearing only underwear and a saxophone, a visit to the Afrika Shrine before tucking in safely at the Federal Guesthouse, a tropical phantasm taking hold of its dreamer in that fertile swamp of unreason that is the Lagos of the mind.

21

THE NATIONAL
INTERFERER

As Oliver Tambo's new political secretary, Thabo Mbeki moved back to the African National Congress's headquarters. This was a two-story building on Chachacha Road, the market street of Lusaka, which the movement had bought in the late 1970s, installing a sympathetic Indian clothes-seller in the shop front and clustering its office space upstairs and around the delivery yard in the back. To enter, you had to go down the service alley that runs behind the market and stop at a tall unmarked steel gate, identifiable only by the manned sentry post to its side. If you were on foot, you would exit back into the market through the shop, nodding politely to the shopkeeper behind the counter on your way out.

It was from these deliberately unassuming premises that Tambo and his team ran the state in exile that was the ANC. By 1982, the movement's military budget was at $56 million, up 60-fold over a decade; the ANC had 9,000 people on its books, 21 diplomatic missions, over 1,000 students on scholarships, a fleet of more than 100 vehicles, 2 large farms, a school in Tanzania, several military camps in Angola, and 15 buildings and 57 rented residences in Lusaka alone.[1]

Even so, the ANC was demographically tiny in comparison to the other southern African liberation movements in exile—there were an estimated 225,000 Zimbabwean exiles in southern Africa, by contrast. Why, then, does the ANC loom so large in global discourse about exiled liberation movements? The answer lies in the way the South African struggle captured the popular imagination, particularly in the 1980s; in the stark moral clarity, the clear right and wrong it presented. The ANC persuaded the world not only that it was the sole legitimate representative of oppressed black South Africans but that it was a government in exile far greater in significance than its actual size. And if the production office for this extraordinary mise-en-scène was a shabby suite of offices around a yard behind a shop on Chachacha Road—headquarters that were, in fact, appropriate to the ANC's size if not to its aspirations—the director was Thabo Mbeki.

In addition to being political secretary, Mbeki—only 36—was appointed "chief executive" of Tambo's office, as well as the ANC's chief spokesman, in his capacity as head of the Department of Information and Propaganda (DIP). Given how often Tambo was not around, Mbeki became the de facto head of the movement, superseding men much older and more experienced than he. As one Lusaka insider put it: "Thabo was not the SG [secretary-general], he was not the president, so.what was he doing there? People didn't understand. He was always 'acting on the mandate' of the president, but it was no secret that this mandate was often granted retrospectively." In some quarters Thabo Mbeki became known as the National Interferer: "He interfered in everyone else's portfolio, sometimes with permission and enthusiasm, sometimes with resentment."

Jacob Zuma puts it succinctly: "You could not fail to feel him." It was mainly because of his "drafting skills," Zuma told me, that Mbeki came to command the ANC. Mbeki had been Tambo's unofficial wordsmith since the early 1970s; now that he was political secretary, the position was formalized. His ghostwriting career had begun when he was a boy writing letters for illiterate peasants; through speechwriting, he found in adult life the perfect vehicle for his particular combination of diffidence and intellect: his desire to put his thoughts, but not his personality, into the world.

Tambo was a teacher of mathematics and a choirmaster, and the tales of his obsessive perfectionism are the stuff of ANC legend. To prepare for an address, he would get several comrades to draft speeches for him, keeping them up all night for days on end, sending an entire draft back to be retyped because of a split infinitive or a superfluous comma. No matter how many different people were set to a writing task, Josiah Jele told me, "whatever came in had to be finalized by Thabo Mbeki" even before Tambo got to look at it. This position became a source of enviable power.

Once Henry Makgothi, the ANC's education secretary, stormed out of a meeting, saying, "It's *impossible* to satisfy O. R.! The only one who can satisfy him is Comrade Thabo!" Recounting this anecdote in 2000 to me, Sipho Makana smiled when I suggested that Tambo's protégé had taken on his mentor's obsessive attention to detail, his perpetual air of dissatisfaction. Perhaps, Makana hinted delicately, "Thabo hasn't found his own 'Thabo' yet?" It was an implication I heard again and again: There was nobody in Mbeki's inner circle on whom he could rely as completely as Tambo had relied on him. Makana told me that people would complain, constantly, about how hard O. R. worked: "We get into bed, O. R. is burning the midnight oil; we wake up early the next morning, O. R. hasn't even been to bed yet. That's why he got his stroke. We have the same feeling with Thabo today. He does all the drafts himself." The comparison was made to me so many times—from Nelson Mandela himself down to cleaning staff and drivers—that I became convinced it carried a subtext: an annoyance that Mbeki's own obsessive perfectionism was an expression of his dissatisfaction with their work and an anxiety that they would never live up to his expectations.

Within the aging bureaucracy of the ANC leadership, Mbeki was often surrounded by older people who were not nearly as competent as he, and it was from this experience that he came to believe that if you wanted to get a job done properly, you had to do it yourself. He would carry this approach through to his own presidency—often to his detriment, where he stood accused of not trusting his subordinates. He was a "tough taskmaster," one of his staffers, Gill Marcus, told me, although she found this bracing: "When you go to see him, you'd better know what you're on about, because he *was* going to engage with you. I personally never found it dismissive. He would always add intellectual value." But just as some ministers in Mbeki's cabinet would later experience his perpetual skepticism as disempowering, so too did some of his comrades in exile. As one of them put it to me: "Sometimes you felt, 'He knows so much more than me, I can never live up to him.' I could walk into O. R.'s office and say, 'I don't know what to do,' and he'd advise me. With Thabo, I'd need to do a lot more homework."

The fact that Mbeki withheld opinions, emotions, and approval—and then dispensed them sparingly—may well have been a function of his character, but it also developed into a way of wielding control. When his comrades said—all the way up until his defeat by Zuma in 2007—that Mbeki did not tolerate dissent, what they often seemed to mean was that they did not know what he thought and they feared he would not like their ideas, so they refrained from proffering them.

Such resentment made the work of Tambo's young proxy very difficult indeed, and had a profound influence over the way he would come to exercise his own political power in the years to come. Whether the "mandates" he was carrying were approved only retroactively by Tambo or not, the power was Tambo's, not his own. Until he became president of the ANC in 1997, Mbeki understudied a succession of powerful older men: his father, Duma Nokwe, Oliver Tambo, and finally Nelson Mandela. Like so many clever, capable people who have spent their professional lives in the background, in the shadows of their bosses, he had to learn the art of wielding power without showing it, for he had responsibility without authority. This is one of the reasons why, over the years, he developed a reputation for being enigmatic, manipulative, and devious.

One of Mbeki's first tasks, upon returning to Lusaka in 1978, was to draft a report for Tambo looking at the strengths and weaknesses of the movement. He pulled no punches: "It is said correctly that one should judge a lion by its claws rather than its roar. We must admit among ourselves that our roar is indeed very thunderous while our claws are virtually absent."[2] Mbeki questioned the ANC's holy cow, its army, and the way the movement was focused quixotically on military conquest rather than on mobilizing the masses to rise up against the apartheid regime. From his position as head of information, he ran several publications and the movement's iconic Radio Freedom to transmit these messages back home. Many of the key phrases of the struggle—such as "make South Africa ungovernable!"—were his. But his willingness to challenge the military aroused the ire of many of his comrades, as is evidenced by a furious anonymous note to him, found in the ANC's archives, rebuking him for saying that "MK is unsuccessfull [sic]" and warning him that if he carried on "devidng [sic] our organisation," there would "always be people to take your place."[3]

Mbeki certainly *had* his place in the ANC: An Umkhonto we Sizwe (MK) commander close to Chris Hani told me about the reaction, in the camps, when the movement journal *Sechaba* published a long essay by Mbeki in 1979 called "The Historical Injustice": "Wow! It was like Marx had been reincarnated and was writing about South Africa. *Incredible!* We had immense respect for Mbeki's intellect. In fact, Chris used to say to us, 'When it comes to political analysis, the Mbeki boy has no peer.' We called him 'the ANC's Suslov' "—a reference to the Brezhnev era's chief ideologue and *eminence grise*. But, just as Mikhail Suslov was always a backroom operator and never the leader himself, the military cadres were determined that, whatever "the Mbeki boy's brilliance, they would not be led by him: 'He was not one of us.... He was a civilian. He was a softie. He had never spent a day in the camps." As the 1980s developed, word began to spread that Mbeki was "the darling of social democracy" and that he was "pursuing a negotiated settlement"; that "he doesn't want to fight."

Such suspicion was only aroused further by the other key part of Mbeki's work as head of information: his engagement with the media and with the West. This, really, was Mbeki's abiding legacy through the 1980s: to change the "P" in "DIP" from "propaganda" to "publicity." As Victor Moche, an Mbeki protégé in the department, put it, "He turned the public image of the ANC around, from a terrorist organization to a guerrilla organization. He wrested the DIP away from the conspirators and used it to project the image of a government in waiting, thus opening the ANC itself up to a democratic ethos." But paradoxically, Mbeki's very success as public relations man was to create enduring problems for him within the ANC, problems that would culminate in the political difficulties he experienced in the early 1990s on his return to South Africa, and would become the root cause of his retreat from "spin" and his almost paranoid skepticism about the media during his presidency.

Mbeki insists that he was only doing his job. He was given a clear and unambiguous brief by Tambo: "To inform people about the ANC, whoever they are. There is no way we can have a Department of Information which cuts itself off from *anybody*. And he made it clear: *anybody at all*, even those we think are suspect." This injunction was to have a momentous effect on both the ANC's route back home and Thabo Mbeki's career. The brief suited Mbeki perfectly: "He believed we had to make a transformation into being aboveground, to act like a legal organization," his friend and comrade Barbara Masekela told me. "His philosophy was that if we remained too deeply underground we would lose contact with information that might be very useful. His attitude was: 'Don't be afraid. We have a just cause. We'll convince them.' But people were very uncomfortable with this; they feared it."

For the vast majority of ANC comrades, the notion of openness—let alone of talking to one's enemies—was heresy. By the late 1970s, the ANC's ethos of secrecy had been compounded both by Soviet training and by the very real dangers facing a guerrilla movement hounded by a powerful enemy: In 1983, over 60 people were killed in cross-border raids on ANC installations by South African security forces. Within this climate of legitimate fear, the ANC's security and intelligence department ruled, its fearsome reputation expressed by the name by which it was popularly known, Mbokodo, "the grinding stone." Mbokodo's brief meant it had a supralegal status, and it became a fiefdom that used the control of information—and thus over people's destinies—to increase its power, fueling movement-wide paranoia about agents and spies.

Given his work and his background, Mbeki was bound to become a victim of this paranoia. One of the first matters of business he found on his desk when he started work in 1978 was a request from the American CBS producer Judy Crichton to make a film about the ANC. Never before had the "imperialist" Americans been allowed near the ANC, and most of Mbeki's comrades were vehemently opposed to the proposal. "I didn't want to speak to the CBS people," Josiah Jele, then the head of the International Department, told me, "because I suspected they were CIA. I didn't know if they were going to trap me into revealing things."

Mbeki had given Crichton the go-ahead before he had actually secured the cooperation of his comrades, and so—she told me—she and her crew spent three weeks hanging around the Lusaka Intercontinental. Eventually, she received a series of visits from Mbeki, each time with a companion: "I realized pretty quickly that I was being tested." One day he arrived with a woman; in the middle of the conversation, the woman suddenly interrupted: "Oh my god, Thabo! I left the sauce on top of the stove and the chicken in the oven!" The woman, it turns out, was Mbeki's wife, Zanele, and Mbeki invited Crichton back to their home in Kabulonga. Once inside, she noticed a paperback Yeats anthology on the coffee table and Matisse's dancing nudes on the wall; a Mozart concerto was on the sound system (he later explained that he always put on music when he had visitors, in case he was being bugged). "Thabo!" she cried. "I've spent nine months trying to track you 'communist terrorists' down, and I walk into your house, and I find Yeats, Matisse, Mozart!'"

It is, perhaps, ascribing too much to Thabo Mbeki's notoriously strategic mind to imagine the burned chicken episode a setup, but for Crichton, "We were friends from that moment on. I knew who he was, and he knew who I was." As the three sat together over the meal Zanele Mbeki salvaged, the CBS producer experienced the release so many would feel upon meeting Mbeki in the years to come: He is worldly, he is decent, he is one of us. Of course he could run a country.

Crichton's documentary, *The Battle for South Africa*, was a watershed for the ANC. It presented the ANC to a mainstream American audience, for the first time, as a legitimate liberation movement rather than a group of Moscow-funded terrorists. But it caused huge problems for Mbeki amongst his own comrades. "It was seen as 'flirting with the CIA,'" Ronnie Kasrils, then MK's head of intelligence, told me, "being prepared to talk to the enemy, under-mining the revolution." The film was screened to ANC members in Lusaka, and the rumors began to spread: Mbeki was a stooge of American imperi-alism. That he was an avowed intellectual who drank Scotch rather than beer and mixed easily in diplomatic circles only made him more suspect, as did his comparatively wealthy wife, who had a nice house in Kabulonga. John Nkadimeng, the veteran trade unionist and ANC leader, liked to refer to Thabo Mbeki as "the Duke of Kabulonga." It was said with respect—for Mbeki's political and intellectual mastery—but also with edge, implying Mbeki's inherited position, and also his seigneurial mien, working things from the comfort of Lusaka's leafy suburbs rather than on the battlefields of the struggle. In Xhosa culture, "going to the bush" means undergoing ritual circumcision; in ANC culture, "going to the bush" meant spending time in MK camps. In both instances, manhood is forged by endurance. Mbeki had endured neither; thus he was not a man. All of this added up to an imputa-tion of unreliability and the most terrible slur of all, *impimpi*: sellout, traitor.

In the fearful, claustrophobic, frustrated environment of the ANC com-munity, such gossip had consequences and could even be fatal: "Infiltration" was considered a "grave crime against the struggle." On the basis of no more than prima facie evidence, a tribunal could even order death by firing squad. By the ANC's own count, there 34 such cases between 1980 and 1989; most were mutineers executed in Angola in 1984.[4]

Even the son of Govan Mbeki and the protégé of Oliver Tambo was not immune: In mid-1980, Mbeki discovered that he had been classified "a CIA agent" by Mbokodo and that he was under observation. He told me that he "understood" this to be the consequence of his sensitive work and that he "didn't bother about it." But many of his friends remember that he was very angry and upset—that he threatened to leave Lusaka and even the ANC. Tambo, abroad at the time, cut short his travels to sort things out. Jackie Sedibe, a senior MK commander who was close to the Mbekis, remembers being "shocked and upset" when she saw a statement pinned onto the notice board at ANC headquarters that read something like this: "Anyone who accuses Comrade Thabo Mbeki of being an enemy agent is sabotaging the work of the movement."

I met Sedibe in November 2003, in the midst of the paroxysms caused by the revelation, by Jacob Zuma's allies, that the chief prosecutor responsible for investigating Zuma, Bulelani Ngcuka, had himself once been investigated by the ANC for allegedly being an apartheid spy. "You can see even today the deep feeling that the word 'enemy agent' evokes," Sedibe said to me. "Imagine how it was then. You have to remember the importance of trust in those days. We lived on it. If you were mistaken for an enemy agent...it could ruin your life." Clearly, the allegations against Ngcuka had opened a deep personal wound in Mbeki. He set up a commission of inquiry to investigate them, and when Ngcuka was cleared, he wrote: "None of us should ever again seek to win whatever battles we are waging by labeling others as having been apartheid spies."[5]

Many in the ANC understood the attacks on Mbeki as a way of getting at Oliver Tambo himself: "You couldn't attack Tambo," Ronnie Kasrils told me, "so you attacked Thabo instead." The canny Tambo encouraged this: He often used his de facto deputy as a kite to fly unpopular ideas; as a conductor to draw the lightning of rage and frustration away from him. This dynamic would develop through the 1980s, when Mbeki was seen to be the "sellout" talking to "the enemy" even though he was doing it entirely on Tambo's behalf.

The ANC is often lauded, by students of African liberation movements, for its ability to remain united in the face of the centrifugal forces of exile. This, really, is the legacy of Oliver Tambo, whose every decision was measured against the imperative of unity. There was unexpected mettle behind his mild, schoolmasterly exterior: He might have had "the mannerisms of an English gentleman," as the ANC dissident Mwesi Twala put it, but he was "a tough relentless leader who held the ANC together during its darkest hours."[6] Tambo's remarkable strength was his ability to straddle different camps within the ANC and to keep the peace among them. This was particularly significant in two instances: in the way he held both Africanists and communists together within the ANC, and in the way he ultimately earned the trust of both those in the military and those in the ANC's burgeoning diplomatic and propaganda sectors, whose work required them to engage more with the West and who would become more open to the notion of a negotiated settlement.

What made Tambo's leadership task all the more complex is that his every move was made in the shadow of an imprisoned—and thus infallible—martyr: Nelson Mandela. Tambo's position was explicitly to keep the seat warm for Mandela. But from about 1979, a profound shift began to take place. With Mbeki very much at his side, Tambo began to build the shattered guerrilla movement into the universally recognized custodian of South Africans' freedom and, in so doing, established an exile hegemony over the struggle. By 1987, the historian Tom Lodge could write that the ANC had actually "prospered" from "the pressures and traumas of exile," offering "to its partisans an hermetic world which has taken its moral and physical authority to heights that vastly exceed those of a political party." It was "an army, an educational system, a Department of Foreign Affairs, a mini-economy, a source of moral hegemony, in short a government...a state-in-exile."[7]

A curious and little-understood inversion thus began to take place: If "exile" becomes the "state," then are those at home not in fact exiles? They are not, of course, exiled from the land of their birth but from the liberation movement's hegemony, to which they have access only through crackly broadcasts of Radio Freedom or chance encounters with underground operatives, or notes smuggled in and out of prison. The ANC's moral power might have been bifurcated between Lusaka and Robben Island, and popular power might have been in the townships, but it was in exile that annual budgets of $50 million were raised; in exile where the anti-apartheid movement's moral capital was traded for the submachine guns, the solidarity, and the sanctions. It was in Lusaka rather than in prison, on the street, or on the shop floor that the aspirations of black South Africans were formalized into institutions and codified into hierarchies—into something approximating a state.

Thus did Tambo earn his legitimacy—and the power to choose his successor, which is how Thabo Mbeki landed up as Nelson Mandela's deputy president in 1994 and then, finally, as the South African president himself. Tambo also managed to draw almost universal respect and affection within the ANC. In his diffidence about taking the mantle of leadership, he would manage to avoid both the blindness that comes with believing one is omnipotent and the paranoia that comes with fearing one is not. He was thus able to deal calmly with his comrades' anger toward his anointed successor, particularly those in the military who were the custodians of both firearms and radical rhetoric.

According to Mbeki's friends, he understood his role perfectly. But it obviously had an effect on him. Several comrades who first encountered Thabo Mbeki during his gregarious guru-about-town Swaziland days in the mid-1970s have remarked to me how different he seemed when they met him again in Lusaka after 1978: He appeared to be more withdrawn, more preoccupied, less lively, "always moving alone," as Lindiwe Sisulu put it to me. "When there would be a whole lot of noise somewhere, Thabo would respond to it by just going into his office and closing the door. He did that quite a bit." Hence the reputation Mbeki gathered, in some quarters, for being "uppity" or a "snob," "not one of the boys," the double edge of the Duke of Kabulonga.

In many ways, Mbeki had grown up alone, at something of a distance from both his extended biological and his political families. He was thus used to keeping his own counsel, to having his own space. There was no question about his devotion to the ANC "family" and his commitment to its concerns but, from Sussex to Moscow to Swaziland to Nigeria, he had always been at something of a remove from it: a loyal and dependable but far-flung relative who could, to an extent, set his own terms of engagement. Now, upon his return to Lusaka in 1978, he was back at the kitchen sink, plunged into the familial turbulence of agendas and intrigues and emotions; an environment, as in any family, where reason is often corrupted (or leavened, as the case may be) by sentiment.

The 36-year-old who took up the post of political secretary to Oliver Tambo had daunting new responsibilities. Perhaps the exuberance of youth had been knocked out of him by the expectations placed upon him, by the lightning-rod role he was required to play for Tambo and the force of opposition against him within his own ranks. Perhaps, too, his withdrawal was a response to the subtext of the threat that "there will always be people to take your place," a retreat from the burden of patrimony, "this mantle of 'the chosen one' that created some kind of acrimony between him and his peers," as Lindiwe Sisulu put it.

It was common, another comrade told me, "for people to question whether Thabo thought he had special privileges simply because he was an Mbeki. Perhaps in response he became less inclined to share things about himself as a means to avoid the risk of his own words being used against him." In the end, Thabo Mbeki appears to have been less bothered by the patently absurd allegation that he was an enemy agent than by the insinuation that he was using his famous name to realize his ambitions—or that, conversely, he was despoiling that august name through his flirtations with imperialism. The need to carve a space for himself against dynastic expectations and resentments seems to have both empowered him politically and stunted him emotionally, and he embodies a paradox evident in many competent beneficiaries of dynasty: on the one hand, the certitude, drummed into you from birth, that the position belongs to you; on the other, the need to prove, to your peers and perhaps even to yourself, that you are deserving of it.

The house at Nyili, Govan Mbeki's birthplace, was the first western-style home built by a black man in the district. May 1999. (Elizabeth Sejake, Sunday Times, Johannesburg)

Epainette Mbeki, Thabo's mother, outside her family's home at Mangoloaneng. The collapse of the "grand country manor" during the years of apartheid had the "feel of Chekhov," says her son Moeletsi. (Joanne Bloch)

The Moerane family at Mangoloaneng, circa 1920: (left to right) Daniel, Jacane, Michael, Sofi, Renee (Saki), Fraser, Manasseh ("MT"), Epainette, Mphuma. (Courtesy of Norah and MT Moerane)

(Below left) Govan Mbeki outside Epainette's apartment on Beatrice Street in downtown Durban, circa 1937. (Courtesy of Norah and MT Moerane)

(Below right) Epainette Mbeki with Linda (18 months) and Thabo (6 months), Mbewuleni, Christmas 1942; the only existing photo of Mbeki as a child. (Courtesy of Norah and MT Moerane)

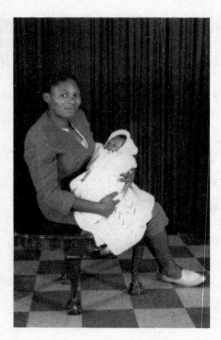

Olive Mpahlwa with Kwanda, her son with Thabo Mbeki, 1959. Because Kwanda was born out of wedlock, Olive was forced to give him to her parents to raise; he disappeared as a young man trying to find his father. (Courtesy of Olive Mpahlwa)

Thabo Mbeki with his fellow students arriving into exile at Dar-es-Salaam, late November 1962. Mbeki is at the center of the frame, looking toward the camera, in conversation with Oliver Thambo. (Courtesy of Thabo and Zanele Mbeki)

Thabo Mbeki and Essop Pahad, who would become his closest advisor, at the Pahad flat in London, mid-1960s. (Courtesy of Essop and Meg Pahad)

Thabo Mbeki with a group of South African students at his Sussex graduation, May 1966: (left to right) Donald Hawes, Kenneth Parker, Thabo Mbeki, Amina Pahad (Essop's mother), Goolam Pahad (Essop's father), Alfred Hutchinson. (Courtesy of Essop and Meg Pahad)

Thabo Mbeki with Ann Nicholson (second and third from right) at a demonstration in Hyde Park, London, 1969. Nicholson was Mbeki's girlfriend on and off through the decade. (Courtesy of Ann Nicholson)

Thabo Mbeki and Zanele Dlamini's wedding at Farnham Castle in England. Adelaide Tambo, Mbeki's surrogate mother during his exile years, is second from left. (Courtesy of Thabo and Zanele Mbeki)

Thabo Mbeki, 1970s. (Courtesy of Thabo and Zanele Mbeki)

Thabo Mbeki and Frederick Van Zyl Slabbert, leading their respective delegations to Dakar in an encounter between freedom fighters and Afrikaners, June 1987. (AVUSA Photographic Library, Johannesburg)

At the ANC's first National Conference after its unbanning, Durban, 1991: (left to right) Cyril Ramaphosa, Jacob Zuma, Chris Hani, Thabo Mbeki, Joe Slovo, Mosiuoa "Terror" Lekota. (Courtesy of Omar Badsha)

Nelson Mandela spontaneously raises the arms of F. W. de Klerk and Thabo Mbeki at his inauguration, Union Buildings, Pretoria, May 10, 1994. (Guy Stubbs)

Thabo Mbeki and Jacob Zuma at the ANC's Polokwane Conference, December 2007, where Zuma defeated Mbeki. (Muntu Vilikazu, The Times, Johannesburg)

Thabo and Zanele Mbeki (center, front) at the opening of parliament before Mbeki delivered his last State of the Nation address, February 8, 2008. To Mbeki's right is Baleka Mbete, then Speaker, who was part of the Zuma "camp" that ousted Mbeki, and who would become deputy-president. To Mbeki's left is Phumzile Mlambo-Ngcuka, then deputy president, who would resign when Mbeki was ousted. (Esa Alexander, Sunday Times, Johannesburg)

22

PARTY MAN

By the time Thabo Mbeki returned to Lusaka in 1978, a vigorous rivalry and mutual antipathy had developed between him and the man who had, a decade earlier, gone to Moscow to discipline him while he was at the Lenin School: Joe Slovo, the African National Congress's leading theorist and the dominant force of the South African Communist Party. It would be Slovo—together with Chris Hani—who would lead the charge to prevent Mbeki's rise to power in the ANC upon his return from exile and who would come very close to achieving this goal. Slovo believed Mbeki was using his brief of opening up the ANC to import Western-style democracy into the organization and had chosen this path because of ambition rather than principle; Mbeki thought that Slovo was so caught up in revolutionary theory that he had lost sight of reality.

Slovo is one of the colossi of the South African struggle, one of its largest personalities and most influential thinkers. For the apartheid regime, he was the very image of the "communist terrorist," the evil Jewish antichrist contaminating ingenuous blacks; to the millions of black South Africans who adulated him, he was the powerful embodiment of the ANC's principle of nonracialism. The SACP alliance with the ANC—and the presence of Slovo as its most visible face—probably did more than anything else to defuse the kind of racial anger that would have made a peaceful transition to democracy in South Africa impossible.

Among whites, Slovo had always been more loathed, more feared, than any black "terrorist" leader, because he had turned on his own people and because to racist South Africans, his whiteness rendered him more competent and thus more lethal. Slovo understood this demonology and worked hard to reinvent his profile: By the time he died in 1995—at 69, after a long battle with cancer—he would be universally viewed as a key agent of the transition, open and accessible, warm and friendly, a wisecracking *mensch* in red socks.

But this is not how those who worked and lived with Slovo in exile remember him. Certainly he always had a capacity for bonhomie, and was possessed of extraordinary vision and intellect and unquestionable commitment. But he was combative and could be doctrinaire, and often set aside personal loyalties in a way that was extreme even within the ANC;

ruthlessly single-minded, he had to be in charge. "I greatly respected Joe," Ronnie Kasrils, one of his closest friends, told me. "But he had his weak side too: At a theoretical level, he could not abide rivalry—even though this was something he overcame later on in life. It wasn't easy to oppose Joe, when it came to theory. He could be rough and tough in terms of defending his own position." Even his greatest protégé, Chris Hani, complained to Kasrils about Slovo's harshness. And this is where the problem arose with Mbeki, who had made it clear, as early as the 1960s, that he had his own ideas. Mbeki himself told me that it was "difficult to have an open discussion" with Slovo: "So maybe none of us challenged him strongly enough."

The main area of the contention between Slovo and Mbeki was a secret committee so hidden that most comrades did not even know both men sat on it. This was the Politburo of the SACP, instituted in April 1977, on which Slovo, Mbeki, and five others served. The notion of a Politburo was straight out of the Leninist textbook: As the body that ran the party both ideologically and operationally, it was the control room of democratic centralism. Mbeki had been a frequent contributor to the party journal, *The African Communist*, but in 1972 he quit the editorial board of the publication—never to write for it again—after Slovo excoriated him for an article he had written on China. The two men disagreed tactically over almost everything throughout the 1970s—from what the ANC's attitude should be toward Black Consciousness, to how the armed struggle should be prosecuted. But it was after a visit that Oliver Tambo led to Vietnam, in 1978, that they had their first serious run-in. It would be a battle between the movement's two leading ideologues, not just over the ANC's future direction but for the loyalty of Oliver Tambo. And it was over an issue that had fractured the movement since 1930 and would continue to do so for decades hence: whether the ANC should declare itself a socialist organization.

The ANC leaders had gone to Vietnam, in the wake of the Soweto Uprising, to look at ways the movement might kick-start mass mobilization back home. Their hosts had told them, as Tambo recorded in his notes, that the "most decisive" aspect of the Vietnamese victory was "[the Communist] Party's leadership,"[1] and Slovo went on the offensive: It was time for the ANC to declare itself "the party of socialism," he insisted. Much to the surprise of the others, Slovo found an enthusiastic supporter in the religiously devout and noncommunist Tambo—and an intractable opponent in his fellow Politburo member Mbeki.

Inspired by the Vietnamese communist experience—particularly the way religion was accommodated—Tambo now toyed with discarding one of the South African struggle's holiest cows, the two-stage theory of revolution, whereby nationalist independence precedes a "dictatorship of the proletariat." But Mbeki challenged Slovo and Tambo vigorously: The ANC could not alienate the black middle class, he said, and had to remain a "broad church."

They argued for two full days, with Mbeki finally declaring that if the ANC was indeed "the party of socialism," then the Communist Party would have to be dissolved. Slovo appeared to disarm Mbeki by assenting: why would a separate communist party be needed if the whole ANC was now socialist? But Mbeki had led his adversary into a trap: What authority had Slovo—or any of them, for that matter—to decide unilaterally to dissolve the party? Slovo had been finessed and had no choice but to retreat, taking Tambo with him. And the party remained, as ever, an underground vanguard, disseminating socialism covertly through the nationalist struggle.

The world, of course, did not even know that Thabo Mbeki was a communist, let alone a leader of the SACP. *Africa Confidential*, the influential London-based weekly newsletter, repeatedly described Mbeki as "probably not a member of the SACP," definitively exposing him only in 1989 as "a prominent member," albeit one "considered a social democrat in many quarters."[2] Everyone—even the red-baiting CIA—underestimated the number of communists in ANC leadership. There was a point in the 1970s when the only noncommunist on the National Executive Committee was Oliver Tambo himself, and of the 29 elected to the NEC in 1985, only five were not communists. Secrecy was both desirable for the party and tactically necessary for the movement, which needed to till new Western fields and attract as broad a base as possible within South Africa; it allowed the ANC to downplay the SACP's significance to anticommunist audiences while emphasizing it to socialist ones. It also gave the party a romance and a mystique—the elite cachet of a secret society—that helped establish its status as the "revolutionary vanguard" in the minds of ordinary ANC cadres.

For Thabo Mbeki in 1961, as for his parents in the 1930s, the SACP's attraction was that it was the home of the movement's intellectual elite. This remained true in the 1980s: Oyama Mabandla wrote later that he was initially "overjoyed" at having been recruited into the party, "the home of the best and brightest." But if the SACP had always been very influential in terms of strategy, there was a new element to its influence now: "I had come to realise that the Party was the seat of power, control and manipulation," Mabandla wrote, "—all else bowed to it—and I'd be damned if I was going to pass that up!"[3]

Mbeki himself wrote—anonymously, of course—in 1973 that communist parties needed to find a way to lead an "independent existence" while also wielding the "decisive influence" over the nationalist liberation movements of which they were part.[4] This is precisely what would happen with the SACP; membership remained minuscule through the 1980s but influence mushroomed. There were several reasons for this: Soviet bloc support, Slovo's seminal influence over policy, the robust socialism of newly independent countries such as Mozambique and Angola, and the sprouting of a radical socialist labor movement within South Africa. But perhaps the most important factor was something more practical: The party's control over the very dissemination of political ideas. In a paradoxical way, Steve Biko and the Black Consciousness movement were responsible for this: The only social theory compelling enough to wean the "Soweto Generation" off Black Consciousness was Marxism-Leninism. Every single cadre entering the movement had to undergo political education at the hands of commissars, and the commissariat, as the custodian of political education and theory was the exclusive domain of the party.

But something had changed since the days when party leader Moses Kotane declared himself "first a native and then a Communist"[5]; since the days of Walter Sisulu, who "saw himself as an African who could be a good Communist and a patriot" but whose "primary loyalty always lay with the ANC."[6] A 1981 Central Committee "special resolution" signaled these changes: It was not only "the right" but "the duty of all communists" within the ANC to advance the party line, to report back to their cells, and to caucus specific positions.[7] This new approach was aggressive, proselytizing, and determined to get through the nationalist phase of revolution as quickly as possible en route to the ideal socialist society. Driven largely by Slovo, it upended the logic that had governed the SACP's relationship with the ANC since the 1930s, by making the party the higher authority. "The Party is dead," said Thabo Mbeki to a comrade when Slovo was elected SACP chairman in 1984. What he meant was that the "party of Kotane" was dead. It was the "party of Slovo" now, and there would be little place in it for him.

From the beginning of the exile period in the early 1960s, Slovo had been the dominant personality in the party. But there had been a ceiling on his leadership aspirations, due to his race. Mbeki had long been a supporter of minorities being permitted to take leadership roles within the movement, yet when Slovo had made it clear in 1982 that he wanted the chairmanship, Mbeki disapproved. According to Josiah Jele, who also sat on the Politburo, Mbeki circulated his opinions on the matter in a paper, in which he argued that a newly liberated South Africa could not have a white president, as the masses would not be ready for that. The implications were clear: If no white man could lead a liberated South Africa, how could any white man—even a Joe Slovo—lead the struggle to liberate the nation?

The paper was a direct challenge to Slovo's ambitions, who responded accordingly, calling an urgent meeting at which he decried the document as dangerously racist and proposed it be shredded. Mbeki remained silent and the meeting ended inconclusively, but his paper was never seen again. And Mbeki stayed away from the next full Politburo meeting, held in the German Democratic Republic (GDR), sending a message of apology: He had family matters to take care of; his brother Jama had gone missing. Slovo found the excuse unacceptable and used it as part of a motivation for him to be dropped from the Politburo. Thabo Mbeki was no longer a member the party's highest leadership organ.

Mbeki could not recall, he told me, whether he actually put pen to paper on the matter of Slovo's candidacy, but he confirmed that he "certainly opposed" it, on the basis of race. And his explanation for why he was dropped from the Politburo was somewhat anodyne: It had become more difficult "to disappear to the GDR or someplace" for party meetings, given his growing prominence. Mbeki might imply that his expulsion was consensual and strategic, but as the news trickled down through the cells, it caused consternation. And so, two years later, he was reinstated.

Even though Mbeki was reelected onto the Politburo in 1984, he became increasingly passive as the SACP veered, under Slovo and Hani, not only away from subordination to the ANC but also toward an insurrectionism that Mbeki believed was unrealistic in light of the growing possibilities for negotiations. Through passive acquiescence, he might have walked away from "the party of Slovo" after he was dropped from the Politburo in 1981. But perhaps because of a nostalgic attachment to his father's legacy, or perhaps because he wanted to remain part of the influential "vanguard," he would not leave the party for another nine years—until remaining in it would have required him to go public about being a member, something with which he had long ceased to be comfortable.

———————

Sometime in the early 1980s, Thabo Mbeki was watching a boxing match on television at the Lusaka home of his Swedish diplomat friend Tor Sellström. Mbeki told Sellström that a group of ANC members, based in Moscow, had gone to a boxing tournament between teams from the Soviet Union and the United States. The American boxers were all black, and the Soviets, of course, all white. "Who do you think the South African comrades were cheering for?" Mbeki asked. So much for the triumph of muscular socialism over decadent imperialism: Mbeki's point was that even the most fervent African revolutionary was going to root for a brother in Stars and Stripes over a white man wearing a hammer and sickle. Mbeki, we can surmise, offered this little parable as a 1980s rendition of Kotane's mid-century observation about being an African first and only then a communist. Even while in exile, even while he sat on the SACP Politburo, Mbeki wanted it to be known where the movement's heart was.

In postapartheid South Africa, Thabo Mbeki would frequently be accused of carrying a racial chip on his shoulder. I once asked one of the very few white ANC cadres billeted in Lusaka in the early 1980s whether he had ever encountered anything like this in exile. He responded, thoughtfully, by comparing Mbeki to Hani. "Chris would go out of his way to make you feel totally comfortable"—precisely because you were white, and had made the leap into the liberation movement—"but you couldn't say the same for

Thabo." While Mbeki never expressed any kind of racial prejudice or reverse discrimination, he had an "acute sense" of unintentional or residual racism from white comrades. Mbeki once said to my informant that "in the mind of a black person, even with comrades, there is a notion that 'this white person thinks I can't do the job.' And in the mind of the black person, then, is the notion that 'I'm going to show the white person that I can do the job.'"

The story reminded me of an exchange between Mbeki and a Haitian American academic, Robert Fatton, which took place in the *Canadian Journal of African Studies* in 1984. Fatton accused the ANC of betraying its socialist principles and selling out to the bourgeoisie; he made particular mention of the movement's 1979 suspension of a far-left group of white Britain-based intellectuals, writing that this purge marked the ANC's definitive rejection of socialism and "severed the ANC's links to its most valuable and creative source of self-criticism." Mbeki's response—uncharacteristically, for those days—was drenched in sarcasm and ire. Seizing on Fatton's somewhat overblown reference to the suspended members as "the Marxist wing of the ANC," Mbeki raged that the author must view "the rest of us in the ANC ... [as] a bunch of confused, swinish lackeys of the petty bourgeoisie, unable to appreciate the pearls of wisdom offered by half-a-dozen white intellectuals based in London."[8]

In exile, Mbeki told one of his closest confidants that he believed Joe Slovo did not like him because he had refused the offer of political mentorship. Certainly Mbeki did have relationships with older white men that did not fall into this pattern of defiance—with Mick Harmel, for example. And certainly Mbeki would never have accused Slovo of being a white intellectual removed from the action. But nonetheless there appears to have been something in the dynamic between the two men that did make Mbeki feel as if he was being treated like a "confused, swinish lackey," like a black man who had to prove to the white man that he was up to the job of liberating his people.

Mbeki has always bristled when he believes he is being told what to do by people who think they know better than he; all the more so when they are not black Africans themselves. His attitude about this would be at the core of the way he pursued a "nonaligned" foreign policy for the ANC while in exile and would be the source of so much public contention once he became president: Who were his former colonial oppressors to tell him how to deal with Robert Mugabe and with HIV/AIDS? Who were white female journalists and epidemiologists to make sweeping generalizations about the sexual behavior of African men? What did Amnesty International know about the workings of Nigeria? Again and again, in the years after 1990, he would upbraid white leftists, white journalists, and white captains of industry who presumed to talk for the African or, worse yet, to tell him what to do in the cause of liberating his own people.

Mbeki's sarcastic retort to Fatton indicates that this irritation is by no means something he experienced only when he returned to South Africa. Sellström, for example, remembers how Mbeki reacted to an edition of *Sechaba* featuring illustrations of Slovo and other non-African leaders. "What is this?" he asked irritably. "Where's Nokwe? Mandela? Sisulu?" On another occasion Mbeki expressed irritation at Shawn Slovo's film about her mother, Ruth First, *A World Apart*: "Why a film on Ruth? She spent 117 days in detention, yes, but why not a film about Albertina Sisulu?"

Such anecdotal accounts of private opinions must, of course, be balanced against the record of Mbeki's professional output and personal relationships. He argued for a strategy that would bring white South Africans into the antiapartheid movement and went out of his way publicly to affirm the ANC's nonracialism as a means toward this objective. His white British Sussex classmates offer many examples of his freedom from racial resentment and remain the closest to an affective family he has ever had. Was this perhaps because they deferred to him in a way white struggle comrades did not? Or did his sensitivity about race develop, ironically, only once he left Britain, as he came up against the attitudes of white comrades and found himself both feeling the need to prove himself and resenting having to do so?

There is no empirical evidence of a direct link between Mbeki's experiences with Slovo, or any other white comrade, and his espousal of Africanist ideology, with its bedrock credo of self-determination and self-definition. But there are certainly indications of a link between Mbeki's personal experiences—particularly within the SACP—and the broad development of his political consciousness and ideological allegiance. Nowhere is this more evident than in his long, turbulent, and complicated relationship with Joe Slovo.

23

THE DIPLOMAT

"If you had told me that Thabo was a communist I would never have believed you," Carin Norberg said to me of her old friend. "He was definitely more pro-Western and pro-social democrat...he would show his suspicions against the Soviet Union." Working for SIDA (the Swedish International Development Agency) in southern Africa, Norberg recalls, "There was often this feeling you had that the South Africans in particular thought and talked the way we did. That they, like us, wanted to find a third way, a way different from the Soviet Union and the United States."

Norberg and her husband, Anders Bjurner, were posted to Zambia in 1974, and when we met in 2000, she showed me a photograph taken at their farewell party two years later: "Thabo was very flamboyant," she laughed, as we looked at the image of her husband and Mbeki caught in a moment of unmistakable affection. Mbeki must have been the grooviest cat on the diplomatic circuit: twinkling with good humor, he is kitted out in high-seventies clash—his favorite polka-dotted shirt under a broad tie decorated in oversized paisley and a striped wide-lapelled blazer. Bjurner is also beaming, albeit in more conservative dark colors. There is a gentle power play captured, as the Swede looks at the South African almost adoringly; no doubt at all who was doing the talking and who the listening as the camera flashed.

When Mbeki assumed his position at Oliver Tambo's side in 1978, the Soviet bloc was still the African National Congress's most significant funder. Following Tambo's instructions, Mbeki set about changing that. His closest friends in southern Africa were Swedish diplomats and aid workers posted there, and it was these relationships, more than any others, that led to his growing reputation within the ANC as a "social democrat." Stockholm became something of a second home for Mbeki, and it seemed to Per Westberg, the Swedish author who led that country's anti-apartheid movement, that Mbeki, like Tambo, saw Sweden as "an ideal" compared to the "necessary" Soviet Union. Mbeki would complain to Westberg about Russian demands: "One never got the feeling they had true friends in Moscow," the Swede told me, "friends they could talk to after business hours. Which they did have here [in Sweden]—friends they could be certain would not betray them to either America or Russia."

Mbeki himself has said that it was not so much not so much a preference for social democracy over communism (or capitalism) that attracted the ANC to the Swedes, but rather self-determination over clientism. He would paraphrase the Swedish premier Olof Palme: "'Sure, I do not like communists, but once you have said that you recognise the notion of people's right to self-determination you also recognise the right of the people to decide what they think.'"[1] This, then, was the formula for the "chemistry" between Mbeki and the Swedes: a shared predisposition—emotional as well as ideological—toward nonalignment; a striving for self-determination or, as Mbeki would put it, "self-definition." And thus a deep sense of trust developed between the preternaturally suspicious Mbeki and his Swedish interlocutors, who did not have their own agendas. They watched, as beaming and as solicitous as Anders Bjurner in that Lusaka party photo, as Mbeki defined himself; as he chose his polkas and paisleys and stripes and put them together the way he saw fit.

Tor Sellström, a diplomat based in Lusaka, was Thabo Mbeki's closest Swedish friend. He kept a bottle of Glenfiddich handy for any ANC visitors but quickly noted something particular about Mbeki: "Some of our friends in the southern African liberation movements could be quite heavy-handed, using our support in terms of a safety valve, but also demanding of material favours: 'Give me your best whisky!' Although he was fond of good Scotch, Thabo would never do that." For Mbeki's friends, there was never the hint of a patron-client relationship, but rather an understanding of absolute equality. There was the sense, too, of a shared worldview, rooted in the experience of coming of age in Western Europe in the 1960s. "He spoke my language, which was European," Anders Bjurner told me. "He was much more international [than many of his other comrades]; he knew about the world."

Still, his friendships were, as always, instrumentalist and expedient. Gunilla von Bahr-Tidbeck told me that she recalled how Mbeki cultivated her very deliberately once Sellström left Lusaka, because "he had to have a relationship with someone at the embassy." Mbeki would show up at her house unannounced, usually in the early evening, always accompanied by a bodyguard called Shooter. He would chat a bit with her family, good-naturedly tease her children, and then gently steer her outside for a private conversation. "I always tried to serve him a coffee," she told me. "It became a big joke, because of course I always landed up bringing him a Scotch. He'd fill it with water and take tiny sips." He also never appeared to be in a hurry, but then all of a sudden, without warning, he would be up and off. They developed a friendship, "but it was always very much on his conditions. He set the terms. When he left you had the impression he was off to another house visit. He was doing the rounds."

Mbeki's Scandinavian tilt was noticed in Moscow. The long-serving Soviet ambassador to Lusaka, Vassily Solodovnikov—understood to be the KGB's man in the region—told me that he knew "the ANC was trying to get close to the Nordic countries" and that Thabo Mbeki was the man assigned with this brief. He had heard from colleagues that Mbeki was "pro-Western, moving away from the Soviet Union," and was told that this was a sign of "divisions within the ANC." Andrei Chuzakin, then a junior Soviet official dealing with the liberation movements, also recalled his colleagues "hinting, with some regrets, that Thabo was in fact closer to the Nordic countries and Great Britain." Chuzakin, though, found Mbeki "the most pan-European, the most cosmopolitan and Westernized" of the ANC leaders—and clearly admired him for this.

In November 1986, Mbeki accompanied Tambo to Moscow for a meeting with Soviet leader Mikhail Gorbachev. It was the ANC's first-ever official encounter with a Soviet leader, and Tambo's decision to take Mbeki alone to the meeting—over several more senior comrades in the delegation—confirmed his anointment as the ANC president's chosen successor. Vladimir Shubin, the ANC's handler in Moscow, records the meeting as a marked success. At one point Gorbachev remarked that he had been surprised to see, in news footage from South Africa, that even elderly white women were taking to the streets to protest apartheid. Mbeki elicited a laugh from the Soviet leader when he responded, "Yes, we have our *babushkas* too!"[2]

An ANC leader close to Mbeki told me that at the meeting, Gorbachev slammed a balance sheet down on the table, demonstrating the costs the Soviet Union had incurred in southern Africa, and said, "We cannot continue on a collision course with the West." Shubin refutes this—and demonstrates in his own book that Soviet military assistance continued at its previous levels all the way up to 1990.[3] But even if the story is apocryphal, it signifies the understanding that had begun to take hold among those around Mbeki from 1986. Gorbachev had met Ronald Reagan just three weeks before he received Tambo, and although he complained bitterly to Tambo about his American counterpart, the writing was on the wall: A thaw in the Cold War would inevitably mean Moscow's withdrawal of support for the ANC. Nonalignment was becoming a necessity.

When, I asked Thabo Mbeki, did he actually first realize that there was a problem with the Soviet application of Marxism? I had expected him to tell me about the food lines in Moscow in the devastating winter of 1969, or his growing understanding of the imperial ambitions that lurked behind Brezhnev's rhetoric of Third World liberation. But no: He dated his disaffection to a holiday he took with his wife in the German Democratic Republic sometime in the early 1980s, when their young guide complained bitterly about the GDR's leaders. Mbeki began to wonder about the "disconnection between the leadership and the members," and this set him thinking about whether the ideals of socialism had been corrupted.

At around the same time Mbeki began visiting the United States regularly, tasked with wooing Americans into active support of the ANC. After a trip to New York, Mbeki distilled his experiences into an anecdote for his friend Sellström: He and Tambo had found themselves stuck in a taxi, in a legendary New York traffic jam, alongside an equally legendary New York construction site: "You know what?" he said to Sellström, "There was no foreman, no obvious control, and the workers actually worked! They just got on with their jobs. If a situation like that were to happen in Moscow, they'd all be sitting around waiting for instructions and drinking vodka!"

It is difficult to believe that Mbeki became aware of the alienated bureaucratism of the Soviet bloc gerontocracy or of the relationship between competitiveness and productivity only in the 1980s. The East German tour guide was saying nothing new: If Mbeki was hearing it for the first time, it was because now he was ready to listen. Perhaps, then, there were no epiphanies. These anecdotes function, rather, as route markers along a longer, more incremental and less linear journey; they point to a shift that began as Mbeki's new position as Tambo's political secretary required him to think not only about how freedom might be achieved in South Africa but what it was actually going to look like. Mbeki attempted to marry his materialist understanding of history with both the liberal notions of individual agency he had acquired in Western Europe and his heartfelt commitment to the nationalist ideal of self-determination he had experienced in postindependence Africa. And the landscape across which this journey traversed was the minefield of the Cold War.

The ANC had always considered the United States a hostile imperial power, but after Ronald Reagan came into office in 1980, it was an actual antagonist in war: It provided direct support to the National Union for the Total Independence of Angola (UNITA) insurgency in that country, while the ANC sent its guerrillas to fight on the side of the governing Popular Movement for the Liberation of Angola (MPLA). At this point, the U.S. Africa policy was dictated by the dynamic Undersecretary of State, Chester Crocker, who bequeathed to the lexicon of statecraft a new term: "constructive engagement." The U.S. plan was to put pressure on South Africa to grant independence to Namibia in exchange for the withdrawal of Soviet-funded Cuban troops from Angola, where South Africa was mired in an intractable war. Meanwhile, Crocker engaged with South Africa to achieve incremental reforms and thereby stave off a revolutionary cataclysm that might put a Soviet client in power.

Tambo told the UN Special Committee Against Apartheid in New York in June 1981 that South Africa had won "a new ally" in Washington, "more determined, more resolute than any ally that the regime has had in the past."[4] In response, a vigorous new African American anti-apartheid lobby was formed, and this gave the ANC its American trump card: the anti-apartheid struggle as the logical successor to the American civil rights movement. But if one part of the ANC's strategy in the United States was to garner popular support from black Americans, the other was to win over opinion formers and decision makers. And so Tambo's delegation, including Mbeki, also attended a large reception at the United Nations, met with the *New York Times* editorial board and also with several of the most influential foundation directors in the United States, and had a dinner with the six major American corporations invested in South Africa.[5]

Thus began Mbeki's decade-long courtship of the American liberal establishment, working in tandem with the pioneer who had set up the ANC's New York office in the 1970s and who would become the ANC's "foreign minister" and Mbeki's closest ally in the movement: Jonny Makatini. It had been Makatini who had sent the CBS producer Judy Crichton to Mbeki in 1978, writing that the United States was the new frontier for the movement: "an extremely interesting place...with fantastic possibilities" because of the way the anti-apartheid movement was replacing the anti–Vietnam War movement as a rallying point, particularly on university campuses.[6] Mbeki became a frequent visitor to the United States, usually staying at Crichton's apartment, and meeting the great and the good at the side of Peggy Dulany, the philanthropist daughter of David Rockefeller and a major patron of the anti-apartheid movement. We can measure his progress through his appearances on the opinion pages of the *New York Times*: In July 1983, when the paper published his first op-ed piece, he was identified as "a leader of the African National Congress, an exiled opposition group"; by the time he wrote his next piece in the paper, in August 1985, its opinion page editors had revised the ANC upward to "the outlawed guerrilla group fighting white rule in South Africa."[7]

Reagan's Washington would prove a tougher nut to crack: The ANC was a "terrorist" organization, Chester Crocker told a Senate subcommittee in 1982.[8] Nonetheless, Crocker understood that the ANC was a significant regional player and had the power to influence the region against U.S. plans. And so, in mid-1982, he sent a special envoy to Lusaka on a mission so secret that not even Reagan and the White House knew about it. The envoy was Robert Cabelly, and his brief was to make contact with the ANC, through the young man whom the Central Intelligence Agency had identified as most open to the West: Thabo Mbeki.

Given ANC suspicions, it would take over a year before Mbeki and Cabelly finally got together at the U.S. Information Service office in Lusaka, on September 7, 1983. Sipho Makana—an ANC leader who was also present—recalled that the encounter was "very blunt," and that he and Mbeki read it as "South Africa trying to get a message to us: 'Drop the South

African Communist Party and the Soviet Union, and we can do business.'" Mbeki refused to make any such commitment, but Cabelly nonetheless found him—he told me—to be "very diplomatic, very well traveled, without a lot of rhetoric."

In late 1986 Mbeki met Crocker himself, and recalls that the American said, "Well, to tell you the truth, we are meeting you because you are beginning to be effective in killing people in South Africa."[9] So powerful had the grassroots anti-apartheid movement become in the United States by this point that even Reagan's own Republican party had turned against him, overriding his veto of the Comprehensive Anti-Apartheid Act in the Senate; American sanctions would be among the toughest ever imposed on South Africa and would play a definitive role in forcing the South African government to the table.

Finally, in January 1987, Tambo would go to Washington, D.C.—again with Mbeki at his side—as an official guest of the United States. His meeting with the secretary of state, George Schultz, would yield little substance but would confer on the ANC the status of a legitimate liberation movement. Nearly 20 years later, it would be shocking, for anyone who had lived through the public invective against the ANC during the Reagan years, to see Mbeki standing to attention at Reagan's funeral and saying that the former president's administration had been the first in the United States "to recognise the ANC as a liberation movement and work with the ANC."[10]

After his first meeting with Thabo Mbeki in 1983, Robert Cabelly told me, he went back to Washington with three primary impressions: "Firstly, that the ANC was in no way a military threat to South Africa; secondly, that behind the united front of the front-line states, they were all very iffy about the ANC; and thirdly, that Thabo Mbeki was a very sharp guy."

The second of these three impressions turned out to be the most significant, one that Chester Crocker exploited to the hilt. On March 16, 1984, the ANC suffered its most crushing setback since it had been banned 24 years earlier when Mozambique and South Africa signed the Nkomati Accord. Brokered by the United States, this nonaggression pact effectively banished the ANC from its most important "forward area" in return for the South Africans' agreement to cease funding and training an insurgency that had plunged Mozambique into an infernal civil war. The ANC had to withdraw its military leadership and hundreds of cadres from Mozambique, but the loss was psychological, too: the country's leader, Samora Machel, had been the movement's most stalwart local ally, and the image of him shaking hands with a smug South African prime minister P. W. Botha seemed an incontrovertible victory for the latter.

Mbeki read the Nkomati Accord as the consequence of what happened when the region became victim to the play of superpowers. There was thus only one solution available to the ANC: to extricate the South African conflict from the Cold War. In his public response to the accord, Mbeki emphasized self-reliance: "If in the past we have overestimated the extent to which we could get outside support," he told the *Washington Post*, "we need to take a more realistic, objective position and know that we are to depend a great deal on our own ingenuity."[11]

The Nkomati Accord would force the ANC to begin thinking seriously about the possibility of negotiations. But Mbeki, who drove that process, told me that he began considering the prospect several years earlier, in the late 1970s, when the UN passed Resolution 435, setting the terms for Namibia's independence from South Africa. The set him and a few others in the ANC thinking about how unsatisfying it was to have Namibia's independence be defined through "some consensus developed between the United States and the Soviet Union" rather than by the Namibian people themselves; a feeling that grew even stronger when Britain brokered the Zimbabwean independence at the Lancaster House talks of 1979.

Penuell Maduna—who would become one of Mbeki's protégés in the negotiations process—remembers meeting him for the first time in Mozambique in May 1983, nearly a year prior to the Nkomati Accord. He was struck by Mbeki's insistence on the concept of self-determination as a basis for negotiations: "'You don't want to be herded by a stranger, a foreigner, into a room and be told to negotiate.' [Mbeki] was saying: 'Look at the instructive experience of the Namibians. Look at the instructive experience of the Zimbabweans. In fact, everybody talks outside them or above their heads about them, and you don't want this to happen to us.'"

Mbeki's coming to consciousness about the need for a negotiated settlement has its roots not simply in pragmatism or prophetic foresight but in an ideological commitment to self-determination and self-definition. The Nkomati Accord reinforced this commitment with an understanding that the ANC had to extricate itself from being a Cold War pawn, from the enervating and seemingly interminable status of statelessness. This meant going home. Which meant talking to the only people on the planet who had the power to permit that: the South African government.

In 1985 an initiative by the Commonwealth (of former British colonies, from which South Africa had been expelled) seemed to create the possibilities for this. It appointed an Eminent Persons Group (EPG), led by former Nigerian and Australian presidents Olusegun Obasanjo and Malcolm Fraser, to "encourage political dialogue in South Africa."[12] Mbeki and Makatini worked closely with the EPG to develop terms: Talks could begin if Pretoria would agree to unban the ANC, release Nelson Mandela, and allow free political activity—and if the ANC would agree to a suspension of armed struggle. But when Mbeki presented this idea to his comrades in the ANC leadership in May 1986, they attacked it viciously. Joe Slovo would later claim that his major disagreement with Mbeki was not over the principle of negotiations but over timing, and in this instance he was probably correct. In 1986 there was, for the first time, full-blown popular insurrection on the streets of South African townships. Several areas had become "ungovernable." Had the ANC proven itself unable to enforce a moratorium on violence, it would have lost its growing authority, both on the ground and internationally. Even Tambo was opposed to the EPG proposals, and shot the idea down.

In the end, it was P. W. Botha—and not the ANC—who shredded the proposal, by raiding three neighboring Commonwealth countries and by deciding that a suspension of armed struggle from the ANC would not be sufficient: The ANC would have to renounce violence entirely. Botha declared a state of emergency and began a new round of the most intense repression yet, detaining and torturing thousands of people. The initiative was off, and Botha's belligerence spared the ANC the international embarrassment of having to reject the EPG proposals itself. Mbeki and a few others in the ANC had long accepted that negotiated settlement was the only solution, but Pretoria's preconditions for talking, not to mention its behavior, remained untenable for the ANC. And so Mbeki doubled his efforts on what was arguably the most important mission of his political career, an extension of the work he had already begun with diplomats, journalists, and businesspeople: the isolation of the South African government from its own constituency, the wooing of white South Africans away from apartheid.

24

THE SEDUCER

Negotiating with a political adversary is not unlike dating, Thabo Mbeki told Richard Rosenthal—a Cape Town human rights lawyer who was trying to set himself up as a mediator—when they met in Lusaka in mid-1988. First, "you must agree on the principle of going out together. Only then can you discuss precisely what you're going to do together.... Later on we can talk about whether we go to the circus or listen to Beethoven's *Fidelio*!"[1] The metaphor is revealing, not only because it exposes Mbeki's understanding of romance as something negotiated and premeditated rather than organic and spontaneous, but because it demonstrates a certain self-consciousness about his own work as a political Don Juan. As Willie Esterhuyse—the Afrikaner intellectual who served as an intermediary between the African National Congress and the South African government—put it to me: "He set out to seduce me—and he succeeded."

Mbeki's charm, wrote Patti Waldmeir, the *Financial Times* correspondent in Lusaka in the mid-1980s, was "not the easy openness of character that is sometimes denoted by that term, but a personality tool wielded sharply to advantage." It was his "greatest weapon...a form of self-discipline; it masks his feelings, and ensures that he never gives anything away. It was the perfect weapon for the battle to hand. Mbeki wielded it skilfully."[2] Charm was both shield and sword to Mbeki, and he would deploy it to mount the most important propaganda offensive of both his and the ANC's existence. His genius was not only that he managed to win the West into accepting the ANC's legitimacy but that he was able to woo so many white South Africans, particularly Afrikaners, out of the arms of the apartheid government.

Using his pipe, his whiskey decanter, and his intellect to maximum effect, Mbeki exuded bonhomie and reason in equal measure. "I liked him immediately," the veteran South African journalist Allister Sparks has written of his first meeting with Mbeki. "We talked for two hours in the lounge of a hotel, he in a tweed jacket puffing on a curved pipe, looking every inch an English gentleman and speaking in tones of understanding and moderation that dispelled all the alarming images of radical revolutionaries that I had listened to back home. He was, quite simply, wonderful."[3] Sparks's colleague, Max Du Preez, agreed: "After every contact I had with him, I would return to South Africa and tell everybody who would listen: Thabo Mbeki is going to play a major part in our future, and a better man you can't get."[4]

Mbeki's portrayal of the reasonable revolutionary was flawless: It was pitched perfectly to the strategic imperatives of the time, it was visionary and courageous, and it was heartfelt too. But it was, in the final analysis, an act of seduction rather than a marriage proposal, governed always by the calculus of power and driven by expediency: Your conquests do not fall in love with you, they succumb—or perhaps they, too, are calculating the odds and have taken a decision driven by rational self-interest. Mbeki understood charm as a game of strategy: He may well have liked the people he was meeting, he may have had empathy for them and come to understand them, but they were ultimately instruments toward resolving the impasse in which South Africa had found itself, and thus toward getting home.

Which is not to say that he was insincere. Clearly, his success at the role of the ANC's public relations man is evidence of the fact that he enjoyed it and that he got something out of it—an elevation, perhaps, out of the claustrophobia of exile politics. There was a quality to his relationships with people outside the ANC—well-traveled people from the West in particular—that was lacking from those with his own single-minded comrades, many of whom, after all, mistrusted him precisely because of his own worldly appetites. But he was nonetheless playing a part, even if from the heart; a felicitous fusion of his personal needs at the time and the job that needed to be done.

Seduction is without affect, unclouded by sentiment, creative; it can be a compelling political craft. Like Nelson Mandela's negotiations inside prison, Mbeki's assiduous 1980s spadework brought South Africa to the threshold of democracy. But seduction is also often followed by misunderstanding and betrayal. For Mbeki and his conquests, particularly the white South Africans who fell for him in the 1980s, this bitter morning after would come in the early 1990s and would influence his public profile all the way through his presidency.

The notion of attracting whites to the ANC's cause was not new: It was headlined as early as 1979[5] and reinforced repeatedly from then on. But Mbeki's insight was that there was a fundamental contradiction between armed attack and wooing whites. He had said as much at the beginning of 1984, in an American interview: "There is nothing to stop us from placing a bomb in a cinema of 300 white people. But we don't do it.... With a white population of almost five million, it makes political common sense to win over as many of them as possible, to neutralize as many as possible, and not drive them into the arms of [P. W.] Botha."[6]

For those who still believed armed defeat of the enemy was both desirable and possible, the politics of force was the paradigm. For those, like Mbeki, who were coming to understand that a negotiated settlement was the only solution, the politics of seduction prevailed. And there was, of course, only one possible outcome to this latter option, as Mbeki revealed in a key 1986 *Observer* interview: "We are not talking of overthrowing the government, but of turning so many people against it that it will be forced to do what [Rhodesia's] Ian Smith had to do." Which had been, of course, to negotiate himself out of power. Mbeki actually said it: "To talk."[7]

Mbeki did not initiate the talking himself, but—as per his brief—he simply kept his door open. As early as 1984, white South Africans started trickling in, desperately seeking a solution to the increasingly intractable situation back home that was leading the country into bloody civil war. In 1985 Mbeki persuaded a skeptical Oliver Tambo to meet a delegation of South African businessmen and editors led by Gavin Relly, head of Anglo American, South Africa's largest corporation, and hosted by the Zambian president Kenneth Kaunda. On the morning of September 13, 1985, seven white South Africans descended from a plane into the tropical heat of the South Luangwa National Park, dressed in khakis as if off on a safari. The six black men awaiting them—Tambo, Mbeki, Chris Hani, Pallo Jordan, Mac Maharaj, and James Stuart—were dressed in dark suits and ties, as if off to a bankers' meeting.

One of the businessmen, liberal food magnate Tony Bloom, admitted to being "surprised (almost overwhelmed) by the cordiality of the meeting. A more attractive and congenial group would be hard to imagine. There was a total lack of aggression, animosity or hostility towards us." There were certainly some blunt exchanges, but it was difficult, Bloom concluded, "to view the group as hardline Marxists, bloodthirsty terrorists who were interested in reducing South Africa to anarchy and seizing power, with a hatred of whites.... Without in any way wishing to be seduced or hypnotised by the occasion, I believe they are people with whom serious negotiation can be undertaken."[8]

For the participants, Mbeki's persona, more than anything in particular that was said at Mfuwe, was the revelation. Publisher Hugh Murray, who organized the business delegation, remembers Mbeki as "young, vigorous, far less reserved than now. He had a forceful way about him; very direct, very funny, puffing on his pipe. A natural savoir faire. Very comforting." Relly himself told Murray, "I'd gladly have that man as my president!" But this does not mean that they experienced Mbeki as conciliatory or "dovish"; rather, they saw him as "reasonable"—an adjective used repeatedly about Mbeki by those who met him in the 1980s. In fact, Murray discerned a division of labor in the ANC camp: "Thabo didn't have Tambo's incredibly human touch. Tambo was the guy who created the warmth; Thabo was the guy who kept things on track.... Where Tambo was soft, Thabo would lay down the line." Mbeki bifurcated his approach: In the formal environment, he would forcefully articulate ANC positions, even if unpalatable; later, over the reassuring clink of ice, he would soften things with a personal connection.

This is what happened a few months later when Frederik Van Zyl Slabbert, the leader of the liberal opposition Progressive Federal Party, led a group of parliamentarians to meet the ANC in Lusaka. Slabbert thought he was coming to sell the solution of a "national convention" to a group of out-of-touch exiles, but found out very quickly that he was the student: "To say that I was overwhelmed was putting it mildly," he later wrote. "With hindsight one realises how infinitely more accomplished they were as politicians; to what extent it was part of their daily existence to charm a wide variety of people from all over the world and to make them a part of the struggle.... We were novices and like putty in their hands."[9]

In a tough seven-hour session, the ANC team—driven by Mbeki and Mac Maharaj—stripped its visitors bare. But once more the seduction happened after hours. At the end of the day, Mbeki pulled Slabbert aside and asked if they could drive alone to the airport. In the meeting, Slabbert had been most animated on the question of violence; now, as they bumped over Lusaka's potholes, Mbeki offered Slabbert his private opinion on the matter: If there were going to be "two approaches" within the ANC to ending apartheid, he had no doubt whatsoever about which would succeed: "Talking is always better than killing."

The moment of connection was made. Six months later, when Slabbert walked out of the "grotesque ritual in irrelevance" that was parliament to form his Institute for a Democratic Alternative for South Africa (IDASA), Mbeki took this as a personal victory and wrote, in a misty-eyed press release for the ANC, that while Slabbert "might have turned his back on many of his own people...millions of our people, of all races, will acclaim [him] as a new Voortrekker" (The Voortrekkers were the Afrikaner "pioneers" who trekked into the interior in the nineteenth century to escape British domination).[10]

Shortly after he quit parliament, Slabbert used the cover of a Ford Foundation conference on Long Island to arrange for Mbeki to meet one of P. W. Botha's closest advisors, Pieter De Lange, an academic and the chairman of the Afrikaner Broederbond—the secret society that was the ideological custodian of Afrikaner nationalism. The event threatened to go horribly awry, though, when one of the ANC delegates publicly threatened de Lange: "I'll shoot you, you Broederbonder!"[11] This was the primal undertow to Mbeki's charm offensive of sweet reason; after a hurried consultation with Mbeki, Mac Maharaj leapt into damage control, deftly reinterpreting the episode as a piece of live theater demonstrating the terrible anger of black South Africans. Later that day, the ANC antagonist himself went over to apologize and startled De Lange by enfolding him in a warm embrace. Two steps behind was Mbeki, who pulled De Lange aside: "Prof, let's talk."

And so later that week, as Botha was preparing to launch his second state of emergency back home, Mbeki and De Lange hunkered down for a five-hour session in the latter's Fifth Avenue hotel room, both smoking their pipes and laughing over the moment when the professor's twinkly gold Dunhill lighter failed him and Mbeki leaned over to offer his North Korean one, the gift of a recent visit.

"What message should I give my leader?" Mbeki asked, trying to draw his interlocutor into setting "an Afrikaner bottom line." When De Lange spoke about how Afrikaners were more anxious about losing their cultural identity than their economic or political power in a democratic South Africa, Mbeki seemed to understand. Certainly he set down the ANC's bottom line too, returning repeatedly to the release of Nelson Mandela as a precondition for any talks, but his message was more affective than subjective. It was, as De Lange read it, "that I am a reasonable man and therefore there are other reasonable men where I come from. You can do business with us."

By his own admission, something was activated in Mbeki by his encounter with Pieter De Lange. It was this meeting, he told me, that most prepared him for his subsequent dealings with the National Party government—for he understood for the first time how threatened Afrikaners were and how they needed to be reassured. In 1984 Mbeki had articulated the imperative of seducing whites into the struggle as simply strategic. But now a shift could be discerned in his public utterances: The imperatives were moral as well as strategic. Listen, for example, to his comments on American television in 1986: targeting white civilians would "corrupt our own struggle" by transforming freedom fighters "into killers, into murderers."[12]

Mbeki certainly did not renounce violence philosophically—in January 1987 he told the *New York Times* that violence was "a very important element to achieve change"[13]—but by this point he had met the oppressor; had lit a pipe for him and drained a glass with him. Characteristically, he converted the experience into political insight and strategy: Among his comrades in ANC leadership, writes Patti Waldmeir, Mbeki alone realized "that petting, coddling, and cajoling the Afrikaner would pay enormous dividends" and that "the ANC alone had the power to restore to Afrikaners what they most desired—the right to be proud South Africans, proud members of the human race." The initial intention of Mbeki's charm offensive was "wooing merely to weaken" rather than the seeking of "true converts." But, by listening to his interlocutors, Mbeki understood "that behind the facade of the Afrikaner bully dwelt an almost pitiful yearning to be understood, loved, and accepted by Africa."[14]

The apex of Mbeki's seduction campaign came in July 1987, when he led a high-profile delegation of 16 ANC exiles to an "encounter" meeting with 61 South Africans—most of them Afrikaners—in Dakar, Senegal, organized by

Slabbert's IDASA. The mutual affection between Slabbert and Mbeki was palpable. In all the footage and photographs, the camera invariably finds them in a huddle—the dashingly handsome ex-rugby player towering over his fastidious friend—and catches, in the glint of their eyes, the meeting of their minds. Dakar would be the first of several encounters with the ANC that IDASA would organize over the next two years, and throughout these encounters the friendship between the two men appeared to blossom. To many, its affection and creativity seemed to hold an answer to South Africa's problems.

Most of the Afrikaners at the Dakar encounter had never before traveled to black Africa: They had arrived, disoriented and anxious, these international pariahs, to be fêted in a huge public celebration of music and dance and hailed as "New Voortrekkers" by the Senegalese president, Abdou Diouf.[15] Then, in the introductions, the ANC leader's coup de grâce: "My name is Thabo Mbeki. I am an Afrikaner." "Afrikaner" is a Dutch derivative of "African": Mbeki abstracted his origins into a double entendre to harness the mood of the moment, collapsing his own identity into those of his tense and anxious interlocutors—just as he would, at another pivotal moment nine years later, build his identity out of theirs in his landmark speech at the ratification of the South African Constitution.[16] In a way, these two assertions—"I am an Afrikaner" in 1987 and "I am an African" in 1996—book-ended Mbeki's own mission to knead South Africa's two dominant and adversarial nationalist traditions into one common civic identity.

Mbeki's assertion that he was an Afrikaner "broke the ice," theologian Theuns Eloff told me. "Everybody just cracked up. It was him saying 'I'm part of South Africa. We are the same people.' It worked." Later Mbeki spoke extemporaneously about the ANC, and his mode of delivery—that effortless projection of sweet reason—was perhaps as impressive as any particular thing he said. "It was probably the most honest, direct and comprehensive explanation of the ANC's positions ever given to people outside the organisation," reported Max Du Preez in the following week's Johannesburg *Sunday Star*.[17]

The IDASA delegates' assessment of Mbeki's performance over the next few days is fascinating, particularly given his later reputation for a lack of empathy. All who participated remember that he provided the event with its emotional pulse, from the moment he ostentatiously embraced Slabbert and Breyten Breytenbach (the exiled Afrikaner poet who had hatched the plan of the encounter and helped set it up) at the airport upon their midnight arrival, to the moment he waved the delegates good-bye as they boarded a plane to return to South Africa, beseeching them to "kiss the land when you get there." In the ten days between, Mbeki said in a video interview, "We have lived together, we have eaten together. . . . In the course of that I think there is an understanding that has developed. . . . It has been a very important experience for all of us. None of us has had an experience like this before."[18]

The power of this shared experience became manifest on the field trip to Ghana the group took after the conference. "Do you really trust these whites?" Mbeki was asked by a Ghanaian journalist as they arrived. "Yes," he responded without hesitation, adding that there were whites in the ANC's guerrilla army: "There is nothing in a person's colour that defines his politics." Reporting this in the *Observer*, Allister Sparks noted that Slabbert and Mbeki "found themselves repeatedly on the same side of the argument, defending their shared commitment to non-racialism in the face of criticism from radical black nationalists."[19]

The South Africans were invited to a public forum at Freedom House on Accra's Black Star Square. Once more, speaker after speaker questioned the white South Africans' bona fides and attacked Slabbert. But Mbeki backed his compatriot up: "We appreciate that he came. We trust them. We have got on well." Barbara Masekela, one of Mbeki's closest comrades, elaborated: "Our struggle for liberation is not predicated upon race. We are not fighting white people. We are not fighting individuals. But, as South Africans together, we would like to come together to destroy the apartheid system."[20]

It was a moment of commendable courage, and it drew sustained applause from the Ghanaians. "It turned the whole thing round," Slabbert told me; not just for the Ghanaians, but for the white South Africans themselves. Until Accra, "many of the whites had remained sceptical" about the ANC's commitment to nonracialism, wrote Sparks. "However, the scepticism began to dissolve as the whites heard the ANC delegates defend the same position again and again before critical black audiences."[21] For his part, Slabbert came back besotted with Mbeki: "Shit, I'd die for that bugger!" he told anyone who would listen.

But a decade later, Van Zyl Slabbert would write that Mbeki had won the "bitter struggle for the control of the ANC...by means of patronage, favouritism, cunning and manipulation."[22] And in his own memoir, published in 2003, Max Du Preez—one of the great crusaders of South African journalism—asks "one big unanswered question": "What on earth happened to the charming, smiling, generous, warm, straightforward Thabo Mbeki we got to know in Dakar? The man who is today the president of South Africa does not possess one of the above attributes."[23] There would be, in the recollections of these two men—and of many other "New Voortrekkers" besides—the common theme of disappointment and disaffection with, and even betrayal by, the man who charmed them so in the 1980s.

What happened? To answer this, we need to return to the metaphor of seduction. Du Preez's weekly columns, written throughout the Mbeki presidency, are littered with nostalgia for an earlier incarnation of Thabo Mbeki.

"For the first time since his return from exile," he wrote during the 2004 election campaign, "I'm seeing the old Thabo: smiling, joking, charming, self-assured."[24] The previous year, Du Preez had described South Africa as a nation "desperate to love [Mbeki] and respect him and follow him. We so badly want him to be a unifying figure in our still polarised society; we so badly want him to inspire all South Africans to tackle our formidable problems together; to bring that old magic and pride back we had during the first few years after liberation. We feel a bit rudderless and confused. We are demoralised and pessimistic." Once again Du Preez holds the South African president to the image he remembers from Dakar: "The sad reality is that I know Mbeki has it in him to do all that. I have seen him doing that several times before he became deputy president and then president. He is a very charming man who had inspired many an audience. He is a very likeable man when he drops his guard and shows the human being behind the facade."[25]

Du Preez is not incorrect in his critique of Mbeki's inabilities to connect, as president, the way he did when he was still in exile. But there is an intensity to the columnist's emotion—"We as a nation are desperate to love him and respect him and follow him"—that begs a question: Are these appropriate needs for the citizenry of a functional democracy, or is Du Preez projecting, onto the nation, his own unrequited, perhaps even jilted, love?

By the third day of the Dakar talks in July 1987, writes Du Preez, "the favourite social activity of many of the delegates was both drinking a lot and making a lot of noise." The journalist had smuggled in a few bottles of South African brandy, and "there were many early morning moments of tears, nostalgia, singing, burning patriotism and eternal brotherhood. Alcohol, as was proved over and over in the next few years in South Africa, was an excellent political lubricant."[26] Every narrative of an Mbeki seduction from this era features three elements: the bottle, the briar, and the early hours of the morning. But if Mbeki was the Don Juan of the piece, then he—like any consummate seducer—was always in control. Those who managed to hold on to a modicum of self-control themselves noticed his extraordinary capacity to hold his liquor—or, perhaps more accurately, the seducer's ploy of sipping slowly at a much-diluted Scotch while perpetually replenishing the glass of one's potential conquest.

Nonetheless, by the time Mbeki went back to South Africa in 1990, the chattering classes were full of stories not only of the man's extraordinary political abilities and open personality but also of his bibulous and sexual excesses. Follow these rumors back to their sources and you will find that they begin, almost without exception, with the people whom he met in the "safaris" of the 1980s; his conquests, if you like. And to one encounter in particular: the November 1989 IDASA meeting at Marly-le-Roi, outside Paris, hosted by Danielle Mitterrand, the wife of the French president, at which potential economic models for a postapartheid South Africa were discussed. Here, for the first time, Mbeki lost control. And 60 South Africans, not all of them friends—and some of them journalists—watched it happen.

Mbeki was scheduled to deliver the keynote address at the public showpiece of the gathering: a commemoration of the French Revolution at the National Assembly. But, writes Du Preez, "when the bus was about to leave our speaker still hadn't arrived. Some of us went to look for him—and found him, with a companion, not willing to rise and shine."[27] The Mbeki-skeptics had their skepticism confirmed, and the devotees—or some of them, at least—caught their first glimpse of their idol's feet of clay. "By the time we hit Marly-le-Roi," Slabbert told me, "I was slightly disillusioned. I'd still have gone to war for the bugger. But, on a personal note, something had changed for me."

And so, in the fertile ground of confusion that was South Africa in the early 1990s, the stories of Thabo Mbeki the smooth, brilliant heir apparent would vie for primacy with the stories that he was another sodden casualty of exile. The latter was manifestly untrue. But the rumors spread, and the image of the heroic local "homeboy" Cyril Ramaphosa began to trump that of Mbeki the unreliable exile. Mbeki himself would begin to feel betrayed by the very people he had spent the better part of a decade reassuring and would decide that Ramaphosa was being deliberately set up against him by the white establishment because it felt he was someone it could better control.

Van Zyl Slabbert would play a key role in settling Mbeki in, upon his return to South Africa. But in the madness of those years, the violence and the uncertainty, the two friends would lose touch. Finally, in 1993, as the ANC was preparing for power, they would meet, in Mbeki's Johannesburg apartment, and Slabbert would offer his assistance.

"If you were in my position," Mbeki asked, "what would you do?"

"Thabo," Slabbert responded, in his habitually candid way, "I would appoint five or six expert committees in key areas to tell me every day how stupid I am."[28]

This was the time during which Mbeki was beginning to develop his own African Renaissance ideology. Perhaps he had just reread Steve Biko: "So immersed are [whites] in prejudice that they do not believe that blacks can formulate their thoughts without white guidance or trusteeship."[29] Perhaps, then, he heard in Slabbert's suggestion an acute articulation of that problem he had mentioned to his white comrade so many years previously: "This white person thinks I can't do the job." Slabbert insists he did not mean this, but it was too late: He tried repeatedly to get another appointment, if only to explain himself, but he was stonewalled and eventually gave up.

I asked Slabbert whether he agreed with my definition of Mbeki's political craft in the 1980s as seduction. "Thabo creates a level of intimacy," he responded. "He puts across the signal, 'We know what we're doing, even if the others don't understand it.' You assume the solidarity's there. It creates friendship. He is hospitable, urbane, friendly, but he uses his friendliness and urbanity to get close to the enemy." At this revelation, Slabbert gave a grunt, almost as if in some kind of awesome appreciation: "Pretty ruthless, isn't it? He's the only 'friend' I've ever had who demonstrated to me, person-ally, that friendship is expendable."

But Mbeki sees things another way. He freely admits to the instrumental-ist nature of his affections. It was always "uppermost" in his mind, he told me, "that we must understand the fact that these people are scared of us and they have educated themselves to know us as ogres.... You need contin-uously to be saying 'No, no need to fear, we are perfectly OK...South Africa is not going to break apart or start slaughtering you and all that.'" But the by-product was that out of this, a "particular definition" of national reconcil-iation emerged: "Things stay the same" for whites. Mandela would become the champion of this perspective, but when Mbeki started questioning it, he says, some white people began saying "Now this is a departure from the national reconciliation of Mandela. What is this talk about transformation? This is now a different Mbeki. He never said these things to us!"

And, concedes Mbeki, admitting to his complicity in the seduction and its bitter morning-after, "we probably never did."

25

PARALLEL PATHS
TO POWER

In July 1988 Thabo Mbeki and Chris Hani both traveled, with their respective families, to the Black Sea resort of Sochi for a ten-day summer holiday. On their way, they passed through Moscow and saw Vladimir Shubin—the ANC's Soviet handler—who asked them, separately, "When do you think you will win?" The way they answered Shubin's next question underscored the very different worlds they occupied: "Ten years more," replied Hani. "We shall be home in 1990," said Mbeki.[1]

It is not surprising, then, that on February 2, 1990, when F. W. de Klerk announced the release of Nelson Mandela and the unbanning of the liberation movements, Mbeki and Hani were literally worlds apart. Mbeki was in Europe, en route to a secret meeting with senior South African intelligence officials in Switzerland; Hani was in dusty Lusaka, taking part in an ANC leadership meeting. The meeting was interrupted by the report of de Klerk's speech just in over the wires; Vusi Mavimbela, also at the meeting, recalls that Hani was the first to respond. "Nothing has changed," he said. "We need to infiltrate *more* cadres and arms into the country!"

In England, Mbeki could not have disagreed more: "Now there really *is* no other option but to talk," he said to Van Zyl Slabbert in London. A week later, he was in the bucolic environs of Mells Park, a late-Victorian manor house outside Bath in the English countryside, at the latest in a series of secret meetings with leaders of the Afrikaner establishment. De Klerk's speech, he told the men present, was a "genuine and positive move forward."[2]

The difference in Mbeki's and Hani's perspectives reflects the profound disjuncture in the ANC through the 1980s. The schizophrenia of the times is perhaps best characterized by Mbeki's own actions in early 1989, when he embarked on a trip to the Caribbean. His first stop was Bermuda, where he attended an Aspen Institute conference alongside the National Party's information director, Piet Coetzer. "All parties now accept that the conflict will be resolved through negotiation," a source at the conference told the South African *Weekly Mail*.[3] But when Mbeki left the conference, he flew over a veritable Bermuda Triangle of parallel realities to disembark, ultimately, in Cuba. There—still a member of the South African Communist

Party Politburo—he chaired the seventh party congress, which was to adopt a strategy entitled "the Path to Power." Mbeki was actually on the drafting committee of this document, which—in sharp contrast to his message in Bermuda—called for nothing less than a "seizure of power" through "mass insurrection."[4]

"The Path to Power" was Joe Slovo's brainchild; all the talk about talk, it asserted, was nothing but an enemy strategy to disarm the liberation movement. But Mbeki knew, from his interactions with South African leaders and their proxies, that this was not true. He had been speaking to caravans of white South Africans almost continuously for over four years. How, I asked him, could he in good faith have chaired a congress that was to adopt a policy as out of step with reality as "the Path to Power"?

Mbeki's answer explains his strategy for managing dissonance within the movement through the late 1980s: "There were some people who were not only skeptical but hostile to the idea [of negotiations]. They saw it as selling out, treachery . . . you couldn't convince them about the fact that in reality the struggle was evolving away from an insurrectionary path. . . . The only thing I thought you could do was [to] run these parallel paths, and one of them would lose, inevitably. And I knew the insurrectionary one would lose."

An SACP delegate recalls being pulled aside by his Cuban hosts at the congress: "Are you speaking to your comrade Thabo?" he was asked. "While you are going on about insurrection, he's been briefing us all about negotiations!" Once it all came out, the delegate—like many others—was distressed by what he believed to be Mbeki's cynicism: "He came to Cuba to hear what we were saying. He didn't want to be marginalized, so even though he didn't believe in what we were saying, he didn't intervene. Perhaps he wanted us to play a certain role, to be the tough guy. So he kept certain things from us so that we would play this role—even though he knew we would discredit ourselves by being out of step with what was actually happening."

Mbeki's life had become an almost-impossible layering of covert encounters and high public profile, a shuttle between contexts and across time zones that would have left even the most seasoned diplomat giddy. In the ten days before he went to Bermuda, he had publicly attended a high-profile African National Congress conference in Norway and returned to Lusaka to meet with a group of Afrikaners. Immediately after the SACP congress in Cuba, he swung back through southern Africa for another safari photo op before going off to Britain to continue his secret discussions with members of the Afrikaner establishment. There, barely a month after approving the insurrectionist agenda of the Path to Power, he would hear the prominent Afrikaner academic and editor Wimpie De Klerk say that his younger brother, F. W., the newly elected leader of the National Party, was ready to talk to the ANC "without preconditions." Mbeki would respond positively: "In principle, let's say have talks about talks, which have to be unconditional."[5]

Mbeki told me that the thinking of people like Chris Hani "*would* revolve around the military struggle," because that was all they were involved in, whereas "some of us would have been exposed to broader [things], to the entire scope, really, of the struggle." Because of his interactions with white South Africans, he was already beginning to understand—as he believed his comrades could not—just how discredited apartheid was becoming in the eyes of the very people allegedly buttressing it. And because of his position at Tambo's side, he also saw, long before his comrades were able to, that the Cold War—and thus the armed struggle—was over.

If Tambo and Mbeki had been looking for influential Afrikaners to provide them with a conduit to Pretoria, so had key players in the South African government been looking for covert ways to communicate with the ANC in exile—and particularly with Mbeki. Niël Barnard, the intelligence chief driving the process, was already talking to Nelson Mandela in jail, but he was determined to prevail in the exile arena too, where the high-profile "safaris" trekking northward to Lusaka seemed to be taking the initiative out of the hands of the government. From informants at the Dakar encounter, Barnard understood that Mbeki was serious about making contact with Pretoria, but he also knew that dissidents such as Slabbert were the last people able to effect such a meeting: "I had to make sure Thabo Mbeki was approached by someone on behalf of the government," he told me, "and this someone had to be the real McCoy."

Barnard quickly found his man: Professor Willie Esterhuyse, a reformist academic from Stellenbosch University, close to P. W. Botha. Esterhuyse had been approached to participate in an encounter with the ANC organized by Michael Young, a British executive of the mining company Consgold. Barnard's agents told Esterhuyse to accept the invitation, and the professor set about recruiting other Afrikaner intellectuals to participate: Men who would not know, until it was all over, that their meeting with the ANC was a shield for Esterhuyse's covert engagement with Mbeki on behalf of the South African government. At their first encounter, at Mells Park in February 1988, Mbeki and Esterhuyse went for a walk. "I told him that I had no official mandate," recalls Esterhuyse, "and he said he had no official mandate either from the ANC. So we agreed that it should be private and confidential, then no one can complain. That's the reason why it worked: We both kept our words."

The Mells Park meetings would continue all the way through 1990, until after the ANC had been unbanned and Mandela released. As in all his other seductions, Mbeki's approach was to persuade his interlocutors (and thus Pretoria) of the ANC's reasonableness, and to get them to come round to the

ANC's way of thinking on the preconditions to negotiation: that the movement had to be unbanned and all political prisoners had to be released. The key turning point had come at the third meeting, in August 1988. When Wimpie de Klerk had spoken of "white fears regarding the unitary majoritarian state," Mbeki had responded by suggesting a "transitional period." Once South Africa got there, he said, "white fears of today will not exist, and a transformation can be negotiated."[6] A classic Mbekian solution: Let us just find a way to get to the table; all the rest can be discussed there.

Back in South Africa, Niël Barnard was reassured to learn "that there were South Africans on the other side who were interested in finding a solution" and resolved: "We had to bring them home." And so, in May 1989, Barnard's agents gave Esterhuyse his brief: He was to travel to England and tell Mbeki that the South African government was ready to meet secretly with him. For the next three months, covert calls took place between "John Campbell" in Pretoria—actually Maritz Spaarwater, the National Intelligence Service's chief director of operations—and "John and Jack Simelane" (Mbeki and Jacob Zuma) in Lusaka and Dar-es-Salaam.[7]

Meanwhile, in his ongoing conversations with Nelson Mandela, Barnard told the imprisoned ANC leader that contact had been made with Thabo Mbeki and that a face-to-face meeting was imminent. According to Barnard, Mandela was furious: "What are you trying to do? Trying to drive a wedge between me and the external wing?" The way Barnard remembers it, Mandela tried several different arguments to prevent the meeting with Mbeki from taking place. One of these was that the exiled ANC leader was a "gifted youngster" with a great future and that the South African government would compromise him by bringing him into the secret process. Another was a dare: "I'm told you have a good intelligence service. If you're so good, fly Thabo Mbeki [here]…and talk to him in front of me!" After several attempts to persuade Mandela, Barnard told me, "We decided, the hell with it, we're going ahead with it anyway."

It is hard, now, to imagine the extreme trepidation that both sides felt as they made their way on September 12, 1989, to the Palace Hotel in Lucerne, Switzerland, for the first-ever formal meeting between the exiled ANC and the South African government. The South African intelligence services trailed Mbeki and Zuma as they flew into Zurich via Brussels and were then driven by an ANC sympathizer to Lucerne; the South African agents—Spaarwater and his boss, Mike Louw—left the door of their hotel suite open so that the ANC men would not suspect a trap. Spaarwater recalls that Mbeki masked his anxiety with uncharacteristic bravado as he entered the hotel suite: "Yes, here we are, the terrorists," he announced. "And for all you know, the fucking communists as well!"

Thus did the ice—accreted over three decades—break. The NIS agents returned to South Africa with the message that the ANC was ready to talk, but two weeks later a media leak—clearly planted by a government source wishing to sink the process—threatened to undo everything: "Broeders to Meet ANC" read the banner headline of the *Sunday Times*, revealing a "secret meeting between top members of the Broederbond and an official delegation of the ANC...at an undisclosed venue in England."[8] F. W. De Klerk publicly excoriated his brother and the others for playing "into the hands of forces...intent on...destroying good order"[9] but nonetheless authorized Barnard to continue talks with both Mandela and Mbeki. Two weeks later, he began to write himself into history by relaxing restrictions on political organizations, releasing Walter Sisulu and the other remaining Rivonia accused, and letting it be known that Mandela's release would follow shortly.

Parallel to these talks with agents of the South African government, the ANC had been going through its own process of policy reform. "We've got to win the battle of ideas," Mbeki would say, according to the ANC lawyer Penuell Maduna. "It's not enough to pull down the flag fluttering outside the Union Buildings. We've got to convince everyone that there is a future after apartheid, and that it looks good."

The movement would have to develop a vision to convince white South Africans that it was safe for them, too, to lay down their arms. The first part of this process involved the development of liberal constitutional principles, and by 1987, constitutional guidelines had been set: freedom of association and expression, a multiparty system, a free press, individual rights: all the freedoms of liberal democracy, albeit within a still hazily defined mixed economy.[10] This last was the stickler, according to Maduna: "The most difficult issue was the economy. The other ones were not so hard. Not even multiparty democracy,...[as] the ANC never wanted a one-party state....But the economy! That was another story."

Mbeki's thinking about a negotiated settlement and about economic policy were already interconnected. By continuing to wage armed struggle toward the goal of conquest, the ANC would be laying the grounds for its own future failure: Not only would it inherit a wasteland, but it would not have the wherewithal to manage whatever part of the economy remained functional. The only possible solution was to work with the capitalists in South Africa. Doing so entailed both a negotiated settlement and a far more liberal approach to economic policy than the ANC followed at the time. At a key ANC meeting in 1988, Mbeki addressed the issue directly: Certainly the Freedom Charter—the ANC's foundation policy document, drafted in 1955—might be "correct" in its calls for nationalization, but "suppose that happened on day one of the revolution?" The answer, of course, was "that the democratic state would be faced with an immediate problem of how to manage that wealth." Because the ANC did not have the resources to run a modern economy, the consequence would be "counterrevolution."

Mbeki went through the Freedom Charter, deflating its clauses one by one. Land redistribution was a "correct objective, no doubt about it." But had anyone thought of the "million houses" that would need to be built to accommodate all those taking up their newly reinstituted land rights, "the schools that are necessary, the piped water, the health services, the roads, the cinemas"? And so, said Mbeki, he needed to ask a "rather heretical" question: "What to nationalize? How to do it?" He offered a couple of detailed case studies of how nationalized industries would fall apart without the involvement of foreign investors and gave the example of Kenneth Kaunda's disastrous nationalization of Zambia's mines, which had—as they all knew by having lived through it—wrecked the economy of the very country in which they now were meeting.[11]

"It took a long time for us to sell our strategy to our people," Mbeki's close comrade Sipho Makana told me. "The soldiers accused us of betraying them. Their attitude was that you could not reform the system, you had to crush it. But things were changing. We found ourselves alone. The frontline states were tired, they'd had enough of a hammering from the South Africans. If there was a chance, we had to exploit it." By 1988 the chance had presented itself. The Soviet Union and the United States signed an accord, along with South Africa, Cuba, and Angola, that ended the Angolan and Namibian wars and paved the way for Namibia's independence. It also effectively ended the ANC's own armed struggle: One of the terms was that all Umkhonto we Sizwe (MK) operatives had to leave Angola, and in early 1989 the Soviets airlifted the ANC's thousands of combatants to camps in Uganda, half a continent away from the front line. This, the MK leader Joe Modise later told me, was the moment he realized that South Africa's only solution would be a negotiated one.

Africa's global political identity had been predicated, for so long, on the relentlessly southward motion of liberating black Africans from colonial oppression. But now this seemed stalled at the Limpopo River, and, for African states, the normalization of relations with Pretoria had become economically imperative. If the ANC itself—South Africa's moral voice— were to propose a workable accommodation with the racist regime, how could anyone refuse to accept it? The strategy, as designed by Mbeki, was for the ANC to draft a document that would be endorsed first by the front-line states and then by the Organization of African Unity (OAU), and then in ever-increasing concentric circles up to the United Nations as a global position.

Mbeki's obsessive drafting of the final text of the document and then his persistent marketing of it was a preview for his later use of continental bloc politics to lead the process of African regeneration once he was president. It became known as the Harare Declaration, and within the ANC the mythology around it was intense—not least because it allegedly resulted in the stroke that Tambo suffered after accompanying Mbeki and others on a punishing tour of the front-line states in Kaunda's plane and then participating in the all-night drafting session in front of Mbeki's laptop. The clinching advice, Mbeki told me, had been given by Tanzania's elder statesman, Julius Nyerere: "You haven't defeated these people," Nyerere told the ANC delegation. "That's why you are negotiating with them! And therefore you need to create a necessary space which recognizes that this is not a defeated force."

The Harare Declaration was accepted by the OAU on August 21, 1989, and by the UN General Assembly before the end of the year. It "committed the ANC to intensify the struggle against apartheid," but it also urged South Africans "to get together to negotiate an end to the apartheid system."[12] The ANC had reclaimed the high ground, but despite its public victory, there was turmoil behind the scenes.

What angered Thabo Mbeki's detractors most was not so much that he was talking to the "Boers" but that he was not talking to *them*. Precisely because of the ANC antagonism toward any kind of engagement with the enemy, Mbeki—with Tambo's approval—kept the talks secret: Beyond the carefully chosen circle of trusted confidants who attended the meetings (including Jacob Zuma), few in the ANC knew about them. Chris Hani was furious when he found out, at an ANC leadership meeting on February 22, 1988, that Mbeki was absent because he was meeting with Afrikaners in the English countryside. "Let the minutes record," he fumed, "that we register our extreme displeasure that Cde [Comrade] Thabo has unilaterally gone to London without any...consultation and without a mandate from the NEC [National Executive Committee]."[13] Hani warned his comrades that the people on the ground were beginning to suspect them of "selling out," and seemed to represent the majority opinion when he said that the ANC needed to strengthen its leverage through continued armed struggle before it could even begin thinking about talking to the enemy.

But both the Berlin Wall and P. W. Botha had fallen. It was the end of the world as the ANC knew it. And now, at the very moment he was most needed to hold it together, Oliver Tambo was incapacitated. On August 9, the day the ANC approved the Harare Declaration, Tambo collapsed in his office in Lusaka. He was airlifted to London and then moved to a hospital outside Stockholm, where he was offered free treatment. Mbeki might have been Tambo's anointed "heir," but the ANC was not a monarchy. According to the movement's constitution, the secretary-general, Alfred Nzo, was now its acting leader. But Nzo was ineffectual, and while Mbeki himself might have been the custodian of Tambo's legacy—and running the ANC's most urgent process—he was junior in age and in status to several other members of the NEC. He was also deeply unpopular. Because they knew so little about what had been happening in the talks, most ANC leaders were unduly suspicious of them. And thus, more so than ever, of its prime proponent.

By January 1990, the South African media was describing Mbeki as the ANC's "Crown Prince Charming" and as one of a caretaker triumvirate heading the ANC, together with two older-generation figures (Nzo and Thomas Nkobi).[14] Such media coverage bothered some of his comrades, who—unfairly—blamed Mbeki himself for it. In the months following Tambo's stroke, Mbeki manifested the best and worst of his political acumen in the way he tried to take control of the ANC in order to keep negotiations afloat. As he would do once he became president, he found technical and bureaucratic solutions to his political problems, working within already existing rules and structures to achieve his goals. But as would also happen during his presidency, he was tripped up by his high-handed inability to bring others along with him.

The bureaucratic vehicle Mbeki used was the ANC President's Committee (PC)—which Tambo had convened as an oversight body over negotiations, allowing him to canvass opinions away from the heat and the contention of the NEC. It was essential, of course, to keep the delicate negotiations process afloat, but now, without Tambo around, some in the NEC came to see the work of the PC as the usurpation of their own authority. In October 1989, when De Klerk released all the remaining Rivonia prisoners except for Mandela, and relaxed restrictions on political parties—in effect, allowing the ANC to organize within the country—the confusion within the ANC leadership deepened and found a lightning rod in Mbeki: When Hani said that "individualism should be combated," he was referring directly to Mbeki. Hani's words seemed to unlock the floodgates, and even Mbeki's supposed allies got caught up in the condemnation: Sipho Makana complained that "globe-trotting may be necessary, but...you can't govern if you are ungovernable yourself." Jackie Selebi—another supposed Mbeki loyalist—agreed: "Accountability to the membership is important. In Lusaka we are considered not to be a 'leadership' but a 'readership.'"[15]

At the same meeting, Ronnie Kasrils urged the ANC to use the "legal space" that had arisen from De Klerk's relaxation of restrictions to "develop [a] people's militia" that would work toward a "seizure of power." Even Joe Modise, one of Mbeki's strongest supporters on negotiations, said that "the situation inside demands bigger blows," and Slovo concurred: "We still have to continue to hit the enemy." It would take Mbeki loyalist Aziz Pahad to bring things back to reality: How, he asked, could the ANC not "take into account changes in the political situation...?"[16]

The disorientation and even panic among the ANC leaders is distressing to read. At one point Slovo spoke about how, "at a time when we are called upon to grapple with one of the most exciting and promising moments in our history, and probably one of the most dangerous,...my impression is that there is no leadership coming from us."[17] Later, he cried: "We have a gaping hole with the President not being with us."[18] The ANC leaders inevitably turned upon themselves: Dan Tloome spoke of how "the morale of the people is low....There is no unity between leaders and the rank and file....All the time orders come from the top and they are rejected." And throughout all of this the veteran trade union leader Stephen Dlamini repeated a refrain, as if reciting an imprecation against the unknowable tomorrow: "The only thing to do is armed struggle....The tiger doesn't change his spots....We must move directly in with our AK[-47]s."[19]

There are, in the minutes of the ANC leadership's meetings from the time, some other bizarre non sequiturs that speak to the comrades' confusion. One can discern, for example, their discomfort at being in the limelight after having lived underground for so long. "I often get dismayed at the amount of what is known about ourselves as individuals," Makana said. "There is also the question of what we do [under influence of] women and wine." They also were concerned with the comparative ease with which one of their number appeared to be making the transition: "I am concerned that the media are harping on the issue of the Crown Prince," said Joe Nhlanhla at one point. "We can treat such matters as nonsense but people ask us about them....We need to be careful what we say."[20]

Meanwhile, the "crown prince" himself was conspicuous by his absence from these Lusaka chronicles of despair. He was in Kuala Lumpur, successfully persuading the Commonwealth to endorse the Harare Declaration. He was in Washington, D.C., meeting President George H. W. Bush's new Africa man, Herman Cohen, and charming policy wonks at a Carnegie Institute breakfast. He was "John Simelane," on the phone to Pretoria, planning the next meeting between the ANC and the South African government. He was packing his bags, preparing to go home.

26

REUNIONS

On January 15, 1990, two weeks before F. W. De Klerk would lift all restrictions on the African National Congress and announce the release of Nelson Mandela, Govan and Epainette Mbeki flew to Lusaka, along with Walter and Albertina Sisulu and five other recently released ANC leaders. Here they were to meet, for the first time in nearly three decades, those comrades and family members who were in exile. As they stumbled, blinking, off the Zambia Airways twin prop plane and into the soft tropical midafternoon rain, they were tracked by dozens of television cameras, jostling with uniformed young cadres for a seemingly impossible moment of intimacy with these fragile icons of struggle. When the Sisulus stepped off the plane, their son Max rushed forward with his three-year-old son and embraced his father emotionally. A few moments later, as Govan and Epainette Mbeki appeared, Thabo was urged to do the same, but he refused forcefully to break protocol and chose instead to wait patiently in the reception line and shake hands with his father before hugging him later, off-camera.

Max Sisulu had been "furious," his wife Elinor writes, "that no provision had been made for the members of the delegation to spend time with their families. After all, a few words of greeting and a hug at the airport did not constitute a sufficient reunion for people who had been separated for nearly thirty years." A Zimbabwean, Elinor Sisulu "found it ironic that the ANC, which had always deplored the break-up of family life under apartheid, should place such little importance on the reunion of families. One had the sense that the political objectives were so overwhelmingly important that emotional needs had to take a back seat."[1]

Unlike the Sisulus, the Mbeki family did not chafe against this hierarchy. Asked upon departure from Johannesburg about how he felt about seeing his oldest son again, Govan Mbeki had replied: "Not much finer than seeing the others. You must remember that Thabo Mbeki is no longer my son. He is my comrade!"[2] It is unthinkable that Thabo Mbeki, having been raised within this ethos, might have broken protocol the way Max Sisulu did. With Tambo ill, Mbeki was more than ever a contender for the highest ANC leadership: He needed to project an air of presidential dignity, but in a way that would elicit no suggestion whatsoever that he might be using the arrival of his famous father to further his own campaign.

A step behind Govan Mbeki as he disembarked was his wife, Epainette. It was the only journey Epainette had ever made outside South Africa, but, she told me, it was "the worst trip I ever traveled." Unlike the other Rivonia accused on the trip to Lusaka, who had just been reunited with their wives, Govan Mbeki had been free for over two years already, released in November 1987 as part of Nelson Mandela's secret negotiations with P. W. Botha. But these two years of freedom and had only underscored the failure of their marriage and exacerbated their alienation from each other.

Things had gone wrong for the couple from the moment of Govan's release, not least because of the authorities' callous indifference—or, worse yet, their manipulative machinations. Epainette had found out that her husband was a free man via the radio news. Later that day, she had received a visit from the district police commander, who confirmed that Govan had been released but could give her no further details. She had spent a confused, anxious night before being woken with the news that her husband was in Port Elizabeth and that she was to meet him there. He had been dumped at the Holiday Inn without even his lawyer's knowledge, and he had been forced to hold a press conference before even meeting family and consulting with comrades. Physically frail and 77 years old, he had stated defiantly that he was still a communist and a revolutionary, words that would earn him a highly restrictive banning order preventing him from public life for the next two years. It was hard not to believe that the state had set him up for this, just to show the world how unreconstructed the "terrorists" were and how wrong it would be to release Mandela.

If the first footage of Govan Mbeki as a free man is distressing to look at, caught as he is in the headlights of a media frenzy after 23 years in jail, how much more so is his reunion with his wife, also enacted in the full glare of cameras. The two appeared disoriented and confused, and in the ensuing week her disorientation only grew. With evident discomfort Epainette stood, in the public eye, at her husband's side on a visit to Johannesburg and then on a triumphant tour of Port Elizabeth. When, privately, she spoke of needing to return to her business in the Transkei, he appeared to be relieved, and made it clear he would not be joining her—even if his banning order were to be rescinded: "Port Elizabeth is my home. I am staying here."

Epainette Mbeki was back in the Transkei within a week of her husband's release. This was the moment, she told me—rather than his departure from the Transkei in 1953 or his arrest and imprisonment in 1964—when the marriage finally collapsed. The possibility of divorce was raised and rejected because of their son's high profile: "For the sake of Thabo I thought, 'Let's suffer through it.'" Which they did, separately: he in an apartment found for him in the Port Elizabeth township of New Brighton, she behind the shop in Ngcingwane.

But then, in October 1989, when the other prisoners were released and a trip was planned for them and their wives to reunite with their children and comrades in exile, the couple was forced together again. Given their family's stature, they would have to go along—and would have to perform, to their children and comrades and to the world, the illusion of reunion. Perhaps too, although she does not say it, Epainette Mbeki harbored her own fantasies of reconciliation.

Whenever the camera of the ANC film unit documenting the visit to Lusaka catches Walter and Albertina Sisulu together, they are engaged with each other or with other comrades; Govan and Epainette Mbeki, however, turn away from each other even when seated side by side. Both Mbekis seem awkward and uncomfortable, as much with each other as with the limelight, and often seem lost in their own thoughts. Particularly with the Sisulus in the foreground, the grand story of the trip was the rekindling of late-life romance and the triumph of families torn asunder by apartheid and now brought back together again. But Epainette Mbeki has never been one to dissemble, and the pretense was almost too much to bear.

If, at the Lusaka reunion, Thabo and Moeletsi noticed what was going on between their parents, they chose not to say anything. For Moeletsi—who had come up from Harare, where he now lived—it was "bizarre" that "we all [still] spoke the same language." Politics provided the continuity: "Immediately, we got into political discussion." Elinor Sisulu was one of several to note the immediate rapport between Moeletsi and his father, and she writes about the "envy" she felt, watching the two at a party she and Max threw for the reunited families and comrades: They were "engaged in deep conversation, completely oblivious to those around them."[3]

Not so with Govan and Thabo Mbeki. On the evidence of the ANC's footage of the events, one might conclude that father and son were avoiding each other. There is, however, an arresting image of them from the official reception held by Kenneth Kaunda at Lusaka's State House. The father sits on a couch next to his old comrade, Joe Slovo, as the respectful son squats beside them, his back to the camera. With a broad smile Slovo holds the floor, and as the Mbekis listen, the father clasps his son's extended hand in his own and looks on at him with an expression that could only be described as pride.

Two weeks later, on February 2, 1990, while Mbeki was with his parents and the other released leaders were visiting Tambo at his Stockholm sanatorium, F. W. De Klerk opened the South African parliament with his announcement that the ANC would be unbanned and Mandela released. "Thabo was white" with shock, recalls Van Zyl Slabbert, who dined with him the next day in Britain. "Well, as white as Thabo can be." Aziz Pahad, who was with them, "kept on repeating, 'What do we do now?'" To Slabbert, the shock seemed "understandable. You get what you wish for, but then what? Suddenly, it was a whole new ball game."

In the next few days, Mbeki shuttled between London and Switzerland, where he held two more meetings with his South African government counterparts, working toward setting up a formal meeting between the ANC and the South African government in South Africa. On February 8, he participated via satellite in a special edition of ABC's *Nightline* television news show with Ted Koppel, broadcast out of Cape Town, with the South African foreign minister Pik Botha and the Zulu nationalist leader Mangosuthu Buthelezi. It was the first time a leader of the ANC had appeared publicly with a South African government official in decades. In a harbinger of the new era, the program was broadcast to South Africans too, who watched, in astonishment, the televised love-in between Mbeki and Botha. Botha praised the ANC leader for his "reasonable attitude": South Africa had made a "mistake" in not talking to the ANC "years ago," he said, before concluding with an emotional reference to both his fellow participants as "my black brothers."

Koppel could not resist. How did it feel, he asked Mbeki, to be called a "brother" by a representative of a government that had branded him a terrorist for decades? Mbeki responded by carefully itemizing all the ANC's conditions that still needed to be met before real negotiations could begin, but concluded that "we must all accept, as Pik Botha was just saying now, that we are all of us, black and white, brothers and sisters. And if we see ourselves as South Africans, with one nationhood and one destiny, I think a solution then becomes possible."[4] It was startling, in 1990, to hear these blood rivals talk like this, and thus began one of the odder friendships of the transition: the surprisingly friendly relationship between South Africa's two "foreign ministers," the former bullish and labile, the latter diffident and contained. By the time Mbeki returned to South Africa about six weeks later, he had already spoken to Botha on the phone several times, and their joshing banter would be the yeast of the first meeting between the government and the ANC in Cape Town in early May.

In the tumultuous weeks that followed, the world changed. Nelson Mandela, unseen for three decades, began to fill in his own picture: a saintly lack of bitterness, a grandfatherly admixture of severity and warmth, a seemingly fluent grasp of the complex national and global politics into which he had emerged. Within days he was on the road, and he would spend the better part of the year abroad, greeted everywhere with adulation.

Two weeks after his release he too touched down in Lusaka and immediately filled the power vacuum left by Tambo's illness: "Everyone fell into line behind his view of how to deal with Pretoria and spoke glowingly of his political acumen and sense of strategy," wrote Allister Sparks.[5] Even Chris Hani was won over: "I think we're going to learn from him...to forgive and forget and to look forward to building a new South Africa."[6] Mandela was elected the ANC's deputy president, beneath acting president Alfred Nzo, and it was agreed that Mbeki—assisted by Zuma—would remain responsible for communicating with the South African government and for setting up plans to return. The era of Mbeki's "unmandated" status was over; he was now firmly accountable to the leadership of the ANC under Mandela. By late March, Jacob Zuma and five others had been smuggled into South Africa to arrange for the return of the ANC's exiles. This was a deep secret: Neither side had nearly enough of a mandate from its constituency to be talking directly yet, and on the government side there were still many who were deeply opposed to De Klerk's actions.

For Mbeki and his comrades in exile—particularly those under his direct supervision in its diplomatic corps—the unleashing of Mandela on the world was both exhilarating and nerve-racking. For decades they had been preparing for this: Every door to every palace—every state house, every presidency—was suddenly open to them and their cause. But Mbeki and his team soon discovered that what made Mandela so extraordinary a communicator also made him difficult to manage: It was not only that he was often more intuitive than logical but that he—a member of the Thembu aristocracy—worked the world in a regal rather than a revolutionary manner. It took significant effort, for example, to dissuade him from accepting an invitation to meet the reviled prime minister Margaret Thatcher when he went to London in April 1990 and to spend his time instead with the loyal friends of the anti-apartheid movement.

With Mandela, Mbeki slipped into what appeared to be a mirror of his relationship with Tambo. Since 1989, his de facto position as the ANC's "foreign minister" had been confirmed. The fact that he was both the ANC's ranking diplomat and its leading mind on negotiations now made him indispensable to Mandela. No one could navigate the byzantine corridors of international diplomacy as well as Mbeki; neither could anyone rustle up an eloquent speech so efficiently in the hours before dawn. At first, Cyril Ramaphosa had appeared to be Mandela's primary aide, but he was quickly replaced by Mbeki, who wrote almost all the ANC leader's speeches in 1990 and early 1991. Some of Mbeki's detractors suggest that he was responsible for getting Ramaphosa "iced." More likely, he simply outpaced the trade unionist: No one else had Mbeki's stamina for—and experience with—the hotel-room life that Mandela's grand global circuit required.

But the relationship between Mandela and Mbeki remained formal, without intimacy. "It wasn't Thabo's way to promote himself," one ANC insider told me. "He is naturally reserved and respectful with elders. Even with O. R. [Tambo], he was deferential. But somehow, with O. R., he overcame this. With Madiba [Mandela's clan name], however, they never really moved beyond it. Mutual respect was there, yes, but friendship, no."

Often, in the years of negotiation to come, Mbeki could not help himself comparing Mandela with Tambo: "This is not the way O. R. would have done it," he would complain to his confidants, or "Where is the wisdom of O. R. when we need it?" In addition, there was the complexity of paternal relationships in the "family" that was the ANC: in the figure of Tambo, Mbeki had merged the political father with the emotional one. But at the very moment of Mbeki's homecoming, when he perhaps needed him most, this father figure was no longer available to him and was replaced, instead, by two others: Govan Mbeki, his biological father, and Nelson Mandela, his new political one. Neither, however, could provide the emotional and political ballast that Tambo had. Both had forsaken their families and had never really experienced fatherhood; both had spent decades in prison; both could be severe and recriminating and somewhat cold, despite their outward warmth.

And both brought the baggage of their own long history with each other into the newly reunited family, for Nelson Mandela and Govan Mbeki loathed each other: They had disagreed on strategy while in MK underground and had feuded for years on Robben Island. Mbeki had challenged Mandela's leadership in jail and then, after his release, spread the word that Mandela had "sold out" to his captors. Mandela would also have heard, for years, about the intense relationship between Tambo and Thabo Mbeki. In the shadows of such histories, could the newly released patriarch have expected the filial loyalty due to him from the "son" of Govan Mbeki and Oliver Tambo? The year 1990 was one of family reunions for the ANC. But with all the turmoil and excitement that was South Africa at the time, one gets the sense that Nelson Mandela and Thabo Mbeki failed to find in each other the father and son—the mentor and protégé—both may well have been looking for.

27

COMING HOME

"At one o'clock I was in Lusaka and at three o'clock I was in Cape Town," Thabo Mbeki said to me with calculated blandness when I asked him to recount the experience of returning to South Africa after 27 years in exile. His narrative of homecoming is one of seamlessness. Unlike his three-month overland ordeal when he went into exile, "there wasn't any abruptness" to his return, no kind of "revolutionary jump" over the border. And this was not only because of the wonder of air travel; it was because he was "not meeting strangers" in the upcoming negotiations. "We had a good sense of who they were and how they thought"; it was "a kind of continuum."

Mbeki was on a Zambian plane with four comrades: Alfred Nzo, Joe Slovo, Joe Modise, and Ruth Mompati. Their return had been delayed for weeks because of intense violence on the ground. After police had opened fire on demonstrators in Sebokeng, south of Johannesburg, killing 12 and wounding hundreds, Nelson Mandela had withdrawn from talks, asking how President F. W. De Klerk could "talk about negotiations on the one hand and murder our people on the other."[1] In Lusaka, Mbeki and one or two others had argued passionately that Mandela should reinstate the meeting: The violence, they had argued, was being orchestrated by reactionaries in the armed forces determined to undermine De Klerk, and any retreat would be a victory for them.

Eventually, De Klerk had agreed to appoint an independent commission of inquiry into the violence and the talks were scheduled for May 2 at Groote Schuur, the Cape Town presidential estate; now, on April 28, 400 ANC supporters came to Cape Town's airport to greet the returnees, Govan Mbeki among them. This time Thabo Mbeki stood beside his father and wept. But, like Odysseus and his father, Laertes, when the Greek warrior returned to Ithaca after 20 years of wandering, these were tears of sadness rather than triumph, Mbeki told me later; tears about "why people had to wait for so many years, and so many people dead just to do something which is as easy as what we are doing. . . . It actually proved so easy to come back. We come, we arrive, we land, they put us in a bus and drive us to a hotel and that is it."

The hotel to which Mbeki and his comrades were driven was the opulent Lord Charles overlooking the vineyards of Somerset West above False Bay. Nearby was Vergelegen, one of South Africa's grandest and oldest wine estates, established by the first Dutch rulers of the Cape. It was now owned by mining and industrial giant Anglo American, which offered it to the ANC for its preparatory meeting before the talks. Thus Mbeki's first days home were spent in the very heart of the white South African settler culture he had dedicated his life to uprooting.

A room in Vergelegen's main house charts its history, and here one finds a photo of Mbeki, flanked by Aziz Pahad and Joe Nhlanhla, on the lawns of the estate during a break at the ANC meeting. Mbeki seems slightly uncomfortable, in a too-tight suit coat over a pullover, an outfit conjuring the threadbare revolutionary rather than the urbane statesman in waiting. He is no longer in the broad paisley ties and floral shirts of the fashionable young Sussex-trained freedom fighter. Nor has he yet appropriated the stockbroker style of broad-striped shirts or the comfy middle age of black cardigan over a golf shirt. Rather, the photo captures its subject in some interregnum of style—Gramsci's old-not-yet-dead-and-new-struggling-to-be-born rendered sartorially—as he negotiates the space between exile and home, the transition between being in opposition and being in power.

Now home and unbanned—he and the others were granted temporary indemnity from prosecution—Thabo Mbeki could finally have a face, a voice, and he remained a firm favorite with the media he had been wooing for the past decade from exile. His address to the Cape Town Press Club at the end of the second day of the Groote Schuur talks was described in one paper as "a diplomatic *tour de force* from the man who is regarded as the ANC's crown prince: the audience was visibly impressed by his sophisticated and conciliatory approach."[2] Speaking to the assembled journalists, Mbeki provided the defining sound bite to this first open encounter between the ANC and the government: "Within a matter of minutes," he said, "everyone understood that there was no-one in the room who had horns...."[3]

The meeting ended with the Groote Schuur Minute, an agreement which stipulated that political prisoners would be released, exiles could return, and security legislation would be amended so that ANC members could work freely. At the opening of the meeting, Mbeki had reportedly introduced himself with a self-deprecating joke: "I'm Thabo Mbeki. I carry the bags of my leaders."[4] The "bag-carrier" metaphor, a favorite of his, was something of a pun. On one hand it conjured the apprentice, the subordinate, the one who does all the schlepping while his *bwana* swans ahead. But it also connoted transit, a journey, dislocation, the reality that the ANC was not home yet. When you reach home, the first thing you do is put your bags down. His return might have seemed seamless, but such relief would elude him for many years.

———————————

Thabo Mbeki might have been the head of the ANC's Department of International Affairs, but his primary posting was as ambassador to white South Africa. He understood that democracy was not going to be wrung solely out of bilateral discussions with the Nationalist Party government: If the ANC was to prevail, other bastions of white privilege would have to be won over, too. One of his first tasks back home was to help set up an encounter between the ANC and white captains of industry at the Carlton Hotel in downtown Johannesburg. There Mandela read the speech, written by Mbeki, that would lay out for the first time the ANC's approach to the postapartheid economy, allaying fears of wholesale nationalization. When it became clear that Mbeki had nowhere to stay, a group of businessmen, largely connected to Anglo American, offered to put him up in an executive suite at the Carlton Court, the hotel's annex. This would be his home for the next few weeks, and perhaps it was living in the nowhereland of a hotel suite that softened Mbeki's landing: It was, after all, precisely the kind of transient existence he was used to.

But the ease of his arrival came at a price: His reputation for aloofness, already well established in Lusaka, accompanied him. In Lusaka, he had tended to stay away from headquarters, particularly if he was writing. Now, in Johannesburg, he kept his distance from the ANC's new offices on Sauer Street—offices as plush and frenetic as Chachacha Road was shabby and torpid. He thus had little contact with the rank-and-file and remained at some distance from the messy process of merging the three strands of the movement—exile, prison, and internal—into one.

And so the ANC gossip mill spun. Whereas Chris Hani made a point of going home to the Transkei and establishing a constituency among his own people, Mbeki checked into the Carlton Court. The grist: Mbeki was a "capitalist crony" who might sell the movement out. But as one of his staffers from the time put it to me, "It's unfair to accuse Thabo of not being close to the grassroots. He wasn't assigned to the grassroots. He was given other crucial things to do." One could argue, too, that through no fault of his own, Mbeki—unlike Chris Hani or Jacob Zuma—did not have a home base to return to. But the impression remained, even if unfair: Mbeki's "home" appeared to be the high-flying corporate world.

The perception was shared equally by Mbeki's comrades and the corporate world itself, which spoke habitually of Mbeki as "our man in the ANC." A profile of Mbeki, written at the time he was appointed deputy president in 1994, describes him as "the favoured son of the business community. His urbane manner, his sartorial elegance and his pragmatism commend him to South Africa's wealthy classes."[5]

Mbeki's mission was twofold: to win the corporate sector over to the ANC's vision for a future South Africa and, equally important, to hit it for much-needed financial support for the movement. Fundraising was not, of course, Mbeki's portfolio, but because of his connections, he became one of the ANC's prime rainmakers. Inevitably, this exposed him—from the very moment of his return to South Africa—to the murky territory of corporate patronage.

Van Zyl Slabbert recalls raising the issue of Mbeki's tenancy at the Carlton Court in the winter of 1990: "Thabo, you can't carry on living off Anglo like this. It must be costing a fortune!" Slabbert had the solution: His own business partner, Jürgen Kögl, owned an unoccupied furnished apartment in Hillbrow and would be glad to host Mbeki for as long as necessary. Slabbert introduced the two men, and shortly thereafter the Mbekis moved to 1401 Park Mansions on Van der Merwe Street, up above the mayhem of this rapidly deracializing and increasingly edgy inner-city neighborhood. Kögl would become one of Thabo Mbeki's most important confidants, politically providing the key bridge to the saber-rattling Afrikaner right wing just before the 1994 elections and personally advising the Mbekis on their finances.

Subtle, sophisticated, and obsessively discreet, Kögl was in a class of his own. But, inevitably, Mbeki attracted the attentions of brasher benefactors, some of whom underwent dramatic Damascene conversions. They were outsider entrepreneurs, like the hotel magnate Sol Kerzner, previously generous supporters of the apartheid government but now willing to voice contrition backed up with material support: Kerzner, for example, is alleged to have contributed a total of R2 million to the ANC's electoral efforts.[6] Such new friends inevitably did some damage to Mbeki's reputation, particularly among those looking for evidence that he was a sellout. Perhaps the low point was an ill-considered surprise fiftieth birthday party in June 1992, allegedly funded by Kerzner. The bash generated some of the little negative publicity Mbeki received in the early 1990s, the result of a murderous coincidence and a bad judgment call. On June 17, the day before the party, armed Inkatha Zulu nationalist residents of the migrant labor hostel in Boipatong, south of Johannesburg, went on the rampage and massacred 46 people. This was the worst—and most blatant—occurrence of the "third force" violence that seemed calculated to disrupt the transition, and would precipitate the ANC's withdrawal from negotiations. The birthday party was scheduled for the evening of June 18, Mbeki's actual birthday, but it was not canceled. And so the Johannesburg *Sunday Times* could write that weekend: "Fresh from the killing fields of Boipatong, ANC leaders turned out to celebrate Thabo Mbeki's 50th birthday this week...hosted by close friend and top businessman Paul Ekon at his double-storey home in Johannesburg's plush Lower Houghton."[7]

This was at a time when Mbeki was being most severely criticized by his comrades for being out of touch with the masses and too close to business.

It might have been unfair to hold the surprise party against him—he did not know it was being planned, after all, and two of his major detractors, Joe Slovo and Cyril Ramaphosa, were among the revelers—but to many it came across as an act of supreme callousness. Given Kerzner's allegedly corrupt relationships with the leaders of the black homelands, Mbeki's relationship with the "Casino King" was particularly offensive. The net effect of such incidents made Mbeki realize "that dealing with white businessmen was a minefield," one of his closest advisors told me, and so he withdrew. "I think it is not unfair to say that we were naive in those early days and that we got a little burned."

Mbeki always personally made much of propriety. His ideology of self-determination was both personal and political: Neither he nor the movement should be beholden to anyone but the masses. Once in power, he would not always appear to have the will to rein in subordinates and would become implicated in patronage allegations himself, but his own lack of interest in material things is legendary. "The good things in life" were books, music, briars, and—of course—fine single malts. During his presidency, cameras and golf clubs were added to the shopping list; his "sartorial elegance," as the media would have it, was largely his wife's doing. Everyone close to Mbeki has a story about his almost ingenuous relationship with things, his lack of interest in acquisition. "Chief," he would say to an acolyte at the airport, "Zanele forgot to give me money this morning. Won't you go get me some Rum and Maple?"—his rather plebeian taste in pipe tobacco.

Mbeki's wife had always taken care of his finances, and it was she who, upon return to South Africa, insisted that they buy property: a comfortable but modest apartment, in the predominantly Jewish northern Johannesburg suburb of Riviera, which she acquired in 1993. And yet Mbeki was by no means ascetic. From his Sussex years onward, he grew accustomed to being around great wealth. During his first Christmas holidays back home in December 1990, he and Zanele visited Kerzner in his beachfront estate at Sandy Bay in Cape Town. He also made a Christmas visit, sometime in his first years back, to his friend Tony Bloom's home on "Millionaire's Mile" in Plettenberg Bay. "Do you mean to tell me," Mbeki said, in a walk along Robberg Beach, "that all these mansions are only used for a few weeks a year and the rest of the time they stand empty?" Was this mock ingenuousness, a way of drawing his hosts out on the subject of redistribution? Or was Mbeki really just coming to terms with the immense disparities in wealth he was encountering now that he was back home?

Mbeki had been drifting for years from his original political home in exile, the South African Communist Party. In 1990, the drift became a schism. Joe

Slovo and Chris Hani—the party's two most senior leaders—argued that it was time for communists to come out into the open now that that the liberation movements were unbanned. Thabo Mbeki and Jacob Zuma and their faction disagreed fervently: Given the sensitive work they were doing, particularly among skeptical whites, some leaders at least should remain "underground." Slovo accused Mbeki of wanting to destroy the party and issued a fiat: Come out, or forfeit your membership. Mbeki and his faction refused to go public and thus were dropped from leadership positions. Their ideological adversaries believe that this was their game plan from the start, but when I asked Mbeki whether the events of 1990 had finally given him the excuse to leave a party he had long wanted to quit, he denied it: "This was post collapse of the Soviet Union… [the Soviet] experiment had failed. So you would have needed a lot of discussion. A kind of redesigning of the socialist perspective." Of course, no announcement was ever made—how can you put out a press release saying you have resigned when your membership is secret in the first place?—and many comrades believed he was indeed still "deep underground." This led to a bitterness that rankled throughout the Mbeki presidency: that he betrayed his roots with his neo-liberal policies and his increasingly strident attacks on the left.

But even though he would protest to the contrary in various ideological tracts drafted subsequently, the truth was that Mbeki finally abandoned the traditional "left" in 1990 and found another political home: that of Africanism, the redoubt of the black middle class whose identity he now actively embraced. Even though the bulk of his work at the time was with white South Africans, the prevailing impression—both among his own comrades and in the media—that it became his social milieu too was altogether incorrect. An entirely different world was opening up to him, and it was through his engagement with a new social network of black professionals and businesspeople that his African Renaissance ideology, which would drive much of the policy of his presidency, was born. In these new relationships, he appears to have found if not quite a home, then at least a solution to the exile's predicament of feeling like a stranger in the land of one's birth.

The ties began in the mid-1980s, when delegations of black South African businessmen—tarred as "collaborators" by the militant youth of the townships—had embarked on their own "safaris" up to Lusaka to engage with the ANC in exile. In 1978, a still-militant Mbeki had written that "black capitalism has no redeeming features whatsoever"[8]; now, however, he found himself moved by the accounts his interlocutors gave of their difficulties as black entrepreneurs, up against not just apartheid but white monopoly capital too. The businessmen were skeptical about the ANC because of its socialist ideology, but Mbeki managed to convince them that the movement was on their side because it aimed to destroy the monopoly capitalism that stifled them. In the process, he became very close personally to some of these businessmen, and they opened doors for him back in South Africa.

Prior to its banning, the ANC's natural home had been precisely this middle class; it was this world, of course, that had spawned Govan and Epainette Mbeki. But three decades of armed struggle and communist influence had estranged the ANC from its original constituency. For the most part, the tiny but influential African elite aligned itself more with the Black Consciousness tradition and particularly its African American permutation of personal advancement and the attainment of excellence. Now Mbeki, seeking to reconnect the ANC to these roots, enthusiastically embraced the idea of "black economic empowerment" (BEE), which borrowed heavily from Malaysia's indigenization program and was designed to transfer control of the economy from white South Africans to black ones.

BEE would become the driving tool for socioeconomic change of the Mbeki era and would find ultimate expression in his administration's charters, whereby each industry had to commit to transformation targets. The charters aimed, on average, for 25 percent direct ownership of equity by blacks by 2014, but by 2006 these targets were still way off: Black ownership hovered at around 8 percent.[9] By the end of Mbeki's presidency there would be a major debate over the effectiveness of BEE, with critics from the left arguing that it was "empowerment of the few" and Mbeki himself agreeing that it had failed in significant ways.

Mbeki by no means invented the idea of finding ways to catapult black players into the mainstream economy through affirmative action. But he became a passionate and engaged advocate for the agenda from the moment of his return to South Africa, at a time when the ANC—with its anticapitalist ideology—remained deeply skeptical about the notion. The truth is that Mbeki's engagement with the issue had little effect on ANC policy at the time, and the ANC's lack of initiative in the area created the space for the private sector to appropriate the concept for its own ends. Moeletsi Mbeki, one of the most fervent critics of the project, has written that the private sector offered up BEE during the negotiations process as a way of avoiding the more radical option of nationalization; BEE would thus became a sop to the new political elite, a "voluntary wealth redistribution" resulting in "the emergence of a new class of unproductive, rich black politicians and ex-politicians who have become the key political allies of the economic oligarchy in preserving the [status quo]."[10]

In the early 1990s, Thabo Mbeki tried—and failed—several times to sneak BEE policy into the ANC lexicon. Many times he seemed to be the only ANC leader addressing the issues of the black professional class, often at fundraising events. In 1992 he and Zanele attended a Sunday afternoon barbecue at the Pretoria home of the youthful Pan Africanist Congress deputy president, Dikgang Moseneke, one of South Africa's only black advocates, soon to be a pioneer black industrialist and, eventually, deputy chief justice. The event was a social gathering, organized by the host and a few others to welcome the Mbekis "home" and to introduce them to black professionals across sectarian lines. Mbeki urged those gathered to take on the commanding heights of capital; at a subsequent meeting in a game reserve, attended by about 50 of the very cream of black professionals and ANC politicians, he gave the event they were attending, and the process they were initiating, a name: the African Renaissance.

The men and women who engaged with Mbeki at these events were not merely participants in a bilateral discussion between politicians and businessmen. They came to form the nucleus of Mbeki's social world, far more so than the white businessmen, intellectuals, and journalists who had been his drinking buddies in previous years. It was out of the Moseneke gathering and others like it that Mbeki would develop his black kitchen cabinet, known as the Consultative Council—a group of black leaders in politics, business, the professions, and academia, who would meet regularly at the presidential guesthouse in Pretoria throughout Mbeki's years in office. With the exception of the Pahad brothers, they were black Africans; here, among like minds, Mbeki would develop his ideas about African Renaissance and hone the instruments he would use in his attempt to attain it: BEE and the New Partnership for Africa's Development (NEPAD), a policy that sought to liberate the continent from its dependence on the West.

The African Renaissance would become Mbeki's foundation ideology, its clarion call seemingly lifted straight out of Black Consciousness ideology: "The beginning of our rebirth as a Continent must be our own rediscovery of our soul...a journey of self-discovery and the restoration of our own self-esteem"[11]; "the self-definition of Africans by Africans themselves."[12] Over and over through his presidency, Mbeki would use such language; indeed, his second anthology of speeches is entitled *Africa: Define Yourself,* and is peppered with citations drawn from the Africanist canon: W. E. B. Du Bois, Frantz Fanon, Amilcar Cabral, Ngugi wa Thiong'o, Walter Rodney, Malcolm X, Kwame Nkrumah, and (albeit only once) Steve Biko.

When I asked him what prompted this ideological shift, he responded that what had shocked him most upon return to South Africa in 1990 was the deculturation of black people: "It was very clear that something [unique] had happened in South African society, something that didn't happen in any other African society," he told me. "The repeated observation [among returned exiles] is that 'These South Africans are not quite African, they're European.' And the reason was that the culture in other parts of Africa had not been as destroyed or as destabilized as had been the case here." The bleak picture he painted of a decultured South African society was one not only of dislocation, but of amorality, too. Urban Africans had had their "cultural base" destroyed, "and there was no value system which in fact replaced it, except Christianity"—and even that was about "going to church on Sunday" rather than ascribing to a moral code. To illustrate this, he spoke about how South Africans would try to "cook up a set of clothing, which they think makes them African." He noticed, too, how "scared" the black intelligentsia was, "afraid to stand up and speak out" in comparison to other parts of Africa: "There's a sense of inadequacy . . . a 'slave mentality,' perhaps not quite as bad." (This is something he said publicly and repeatedly; it was disingenuous, given that opinion pages of South African newspapers were replete with black voices, throughout his presidency, many of whom were very critical of him and the government.)

Observing all these indicators of "slave mentality," Mbeki told me, he realized "that we had to do something here which would address recovery." Using the Africanist apothecary of self-definition and self-reliance, he prescribed the African Renaissance. His critics say this treatment was not curative but palliative, calculated to distract South Africans from what really ailed them: grinding poverty, increasing unemployment, crumbling social services, an ever-increasing gap between rich and poor. He countered that it was a long-term treatment, and the only one possible, for it would lead to an erasure of the culture of dependency that prevents Africa from moving forward.

On one level, Thabo Mbeki's engagement with the black professional class was strategic, Mbeki at his instrumentalist best: an extension of his earlier work with the Black Consciousness activists in the early 1970s. As Saki Macozoma, an activist turned businessman who became one of his closest allies, put it to me: "At a time when black professionals were feeling they did not have access to politicians, Thabo found a way of engaging with them, socially and intellectually." He understood that this class could not but grow. He also understood the lesson of social upheavals the world over: The first dissidents of a revolution are not the peasants or the workers but a restive bourgeoisie. It was thus critical not only to grow a black middle class but to find a way to bring it into the ruling elite and to hold it there with a set of policies (BEE) and an ideological frame (Africanism) that resonated with its own aspirations. Mbeki would go on to use the African Renaissance to bring on board articulate black journalists, lawyers, and academics who might otherwise have become the ANC's most damaging critics. (His defeat at the hands of Zuma in 2007 would demonstrate the limits of his strategy of co-opting a black middle class: many of the beneficiaries of BEE would become his harshest critics—either because they had been forced out of politics by him and were seeking revenge, or because it was in *their* interests, now, to shift their allegiances to the new political elite.)

But on another level, the project was profoundly personal, arising from Mbeki's own need—no matter how seamless his arrival might have appeared—to find a home base within the anxious and uncertain landscape of a return from exile. Remember Mbeki's unnerving experience, in 1992, of going to his father's birthplace for the first time to participate in his uncle's burial, and realizing how little he knew about where he came from, because of the ideology of his parents and the exigencies of struggle and exile. Here he was, the perpetual outsider now inside: back home. How was he going to negotiate this predicament?

To become, all of a sudden, a "traditional African," or a Transkei or Eastern Cape homeboy, was not yet an option. He was not Jacob Zuma, nor was he Chris Hani. He could not set himself up as a rural patriarch the way Zuma did; neither could he return to the Transkei the way Hani did. In fact, he insisted on staying away—to avoid any imputations that he might be trying to develop himself into a regional strongman. Perhaps unwittingly, he was mimicking his father, who had refused to return to the rural Transkei after being released from jail. But, on another level, the younger Mbeki was also defining himself against his father. Govan Mbeki was, after all, the archetypal Eastern Cape homeboy; as much as it was an article of political faith for the father to draw power from a regional base, it was one, for the son, to be unshackled from local politics and expectations, to be able to move, freely, on the national and global stage: "I don't need to build a constituency," he said, rather arrogantly, in a 1995 interview. "I was born in that area [the Eastern Cape] but I took a decision that I'm not going [back] there."[13]

This would change after 2005, when Mbeki would activate his Xhosa heritage—or allow it to be activated for him—to establish an Eastern Cape beachhead against the challenge of Jacob Zuma. But in the early 1990s, Mbeki believed that having no particular constituency was "a fortunate thing...once you are identified as being [the] candidate of one bloc then it means you are not a candidate of another bloc."[14] The comment was disingenuous: While being a free-floating "national interferer" worked, to a point, in exile, it was impossible to advance a leadership career, in the newly constituted mass-based movement, without significant popular or bloc support. And Mbeki grasped this: He would become Mandela's successor because he understood the party machine far better than his rivals. Never comfortable as a populist, and acutely aware of his disconnection from the rural peasantry of the Transkei, he knew he would not make it as a local hero, particularly in the backyard he shared with Chris Hani. He would thus have to find other "homes": political, emotional, and physical.

Vusi Mavimbela, Mbeki's political counselor from 1994 on, told me how exasperating his boss's refusal to go to the Eastern Cape was: "I belong to South Africa and not the Eastern Cape alone!" Mbeki would say. Because of his upbringing and background, Mavimbela told me, Mbeki was "obviously more attracted to a continental self-definition than an ethnic one."

His response to his alienation from the entanglement of roots was not so much to dive into them but to abstract his way out of them, into pan-African identity. Alongside the strategic considerations already explored, this impulse is clearly what triggered his thinking about Africanism, the African Renaissance, NEPAD, and the African Union.

Given all this, Mbeki's new social world—the people he associated with at get-togethers like the Moseneke barbecue—offered him a solution, both politically and personally, with their African American–style fusion of roots pride and personal aspiration. Mbeki, the sophisticated cosmopolitan, appeared to like the way that "African" signified a contemporary and geographically indeterminate identity for them rather than an atavistic, local, or ethnic one. He also seemed inspired by their determination to be the very best within their professions, to make their millions and yet to be unashamedly African. These were people with whom you could talk about complex financial instruments—and listen to township jazz or slaughter an ox.

Mbeki never wore traditional garb or contemporary "African" couture, and could be quite contemptuous of such superficial drapery. He was far more interested in the way his new friends attempted to find meaningful applications of "black consciousness" within contemporary South African society, in their belief in an aggressive and confident black middle class. Certainly, these new friends provided key mobilizing networks for Mbeki. But something else was happening too. He was moving away from the claustrophobic, byzantine world of the ANC-in-exile now come home, a world he could no longer trust ideologically or politically: he was done now with organized communism and with armed struggle, and the knives were out for him, sharper than ever. He had just left the South African Communist Party but remained a vanguardist, an intellectual elitist. He needed a new inner circle, a new "politburo," with a new credo, to drive his political goals. He seems to have found it among the black professionals and entrepreneurs he met in his first months back in South Africa and in the ideology he developed with them, of an African Renaissance.

28

SIDELINING

The African National Congress's 1991 National Conference—its first one back home—was an extraordinary event: exuberant and edgy; part American-style jamboree, part struggle symposium. There were over 4,000 people in attendance at the University of Durban-Westville in the hills above the Indian Ocean port, and if the ANC had a moment of home-coming—and of awkward reintegration—this was it: Many of the delegates, just indemnified from prosecution, were in fact home for the very first time. Rambling, disorganized, and contentious, the five-day event was nonetheless a triumph, heralding the ANC's transformation from underground liberation movement to government in waiting. It also lifted the shroud of myth and mystery—the absent presence of imprisonment and exile—from the ANC's heroes and required them to compete for leadership positions in the light of day. It launched, into the South African public imagination, the generation of leaders who would prevail over the next two decades.

And even though it rather brutally thwarted (at least for a while) Thabo Mbeki's leadership aspirations, the conference provided one of the finest moments of his career: when he managed to convince a hostile floor, at 3 a.m., that it was time for the ANC to call for an end to sanctions against the South African regime. Mbeki's argument was that change was irreversible: Most of the world had dropped its embargoes on South Africa already anyway, and unless the ANC adapted to the new environment, it was going to lose the advantage. "You could have heard a pin drop," one delegate told the media. "He was electrifying."[1]

Nelson Mandela, exhausted, had failed to win the floor on the subject himself, and was on his way out of the hall for a break, but turned around to listen, rapt, to Mbeki's argument. "Already Thabo was beginning to have this reputation of being moderate," recalls Sydney Mufamadi, the trade unionist who would become one of his closest allies. "But that did not deter him. He stood up, had the courage of his convictions, argued convincingly, and when he was finished, he got a standing ovation." Mufamadi was seated next to Joe Slovo and Ronnie Kasrils. "What do you think?" he asked them. They were convinced. Given their militant profiles, however, they drew the line at applause. "They were still afraid to associate themselves with this moderate—they did not stand up."

Even if the militants were willing, grudgingly, to accept Mbeki's arguments, they were certainly not willing to have him lead them. When it became clear that Mbeki was the only candidate running to be Mandela's new deputy, Chris Hani decided to compete. More than one ANC leader recounted Hani's exact words to me: "If Thabo stands I will stand against him. I will not serve under him. He will sell the ANC down the river."

The substantive allegation against Mbeki was that, as head of the ANC negotiations team, he had failed to bring the talks about talks with the South African government to a head. There had indeed been very little forward movement in the 18 months since the ANC's unbanning. The ANC team had found itself locked in a series of squabbles with F. W. De Klerk's government: about the definition of "armed struggle," about who qualified for indemnity as a returning exile, and about which political prisoners should be released. To be sure, much of this was not Mbeki's fault. The seemingly-random "third force" violence had precipitated a vicious cycle: Murderous political destabilization eroded trust between the parties, which prevented them from moving toward agreement, which engendered more political violence. And De Klerk seemed genuinely to believe that, by buying time and showing Mandela to be ineffectual in the face of political destabilization, he could stay in power by cobbling together a majority of "moderate" South Africans of all races against the ANC. In the face of all this, Mbeki was criticized for not being combative enough to force De Klerk to face reality. So determined was Mbeki to keep talking at all costs that he did not seem able—or willing—to bring things to a boil, to threaten a return to the battlefield and risk plunging the country into crisis if the government failed . to meet the ANC's preconditions for negotiation.

And so Mbeki had become a determined opponent of the militant agenda of "rolling mass action" proposed by Hani and his comrades, who still believed that a mass uprising could bring the government down relatively peacefully, much as had happened in East Germany. Mandela led the majority in the middle, who wanted to use mass action to leverage the ANC's positions in negotiations, but Mbeki spoke out consistently against such strategy, adamant that mass action would shatter the delicate agreements that had already been made and would undermine the whole process. Mbhazima Shilowa, the trade unionist who had initially opposed Mbeki's approach but would eventually quit the ANC in 2008 to set up his own party once Mbeki was fired, put it to me thus: "I don't think Thabo was any less mistrustful [of the other side] than we were. He just understood that we had no choice but to reach an agreement with them. No matter how little we trusted them."

Mbeki insists that the anger of the masses was overstated by those in favor of militant action so as to advance their own agendas. To make his point, he likes to tell the story of how, after a meeting in Pretoria, he was being driven out of a parking garage basement by Jacob Zuma when the parking attendant refused to take their money: "The fellow there sees me, leans over, and his face lights up. 'Go away!' he says. 'I don't want you to pay!' And this is an ordinary worker! So where the idea comes from that these people are so angry that we must take this step [of stopping negotiations], I don't know!"

Mbeki recounted this story to his comrades in leadership when arguing against suspending negotiations. But while his instinct about general popular sentiment might have been correct, could he not see how such evidence could hardly advance his cause—and could only damn him further in the eyes of his detractors? While the likes of Hani and Winnie Mandela, Nelson's wife, were on the battlefields, in the squatter camps following a massacre or at the barricades of the newly formed Self-Defence Units, giving succor to the wounded and arms to the aggrieved, Mbeki's signal exposure to "the ordinary worker" was a brief encounter, from the back of a luxury vehicle, coming out of the secure underground parking of a luxury hotel in downtown Pretoria!

Many of the leaders of the United Democratic Front (UDF), the internal wing of the ANC, who had been at the barricades during the tumultuous 1980s were shocked at how deep the tensions from exile ran, between the Slovo/Hani faction on one side and the Mbeki/Zuma faction on the other. "It seemed like there was a hearts-and-minds campaign to win the support of the internal people," one of them told me. That UDF comrades became suspicious of Mbeki had perhaps less to do with ideology than with style. Anxious themselves about the fate of their exhilarating, edgy experiment in popular democracy that had arisen out of the 1980s, they saw in Mbeki's elusiveness the embodiment of the hierarchical and authoritarian ANC in exile. In contrast, Slovo and Hani's new, aboveground South African Communist Party became a vehicle for mass-based militancy, and Hani, in particular, appeared to find himself more at home on the streets of South Africa's townships than he had ever been among the ANC oligarchs in Lusaka. "The sense we got from Thabo," one of the UDF leaders told me, "was that he was a corridors-of-power person. And because of his contempt for mass action, he didn't use it to leverage the ANC position. Therefore, he gave up too much and alienated his support base." Another told me that "Thabo misread us as rejectionist, but he didn't understand our two-tier strategy: to talk with a big stick. He didn't really know how to use it [the big stick], so he wanted to throw it away."

In this context, Hani's candidacy at Durban was a gambit, and it worked: Chary of a public scrap between doves and hawks at so delicate a moment, the movement's grandees persuaded both Mbeki and Hani to stand down in favor of the elderly Walter Sisulu, and the crisis appeared to be averted. The battle was displaced, in effect, to another election: that for the powerful post of secretary-general. There was widespread agreement that the ANC's ineffectual incumbent, Alfred Nzo, needed to be replaced by someone younger and more dynamic, so Jacob Zuma decided to contest him. Zuma was effectively Mbeki's deputy in the negotiations team and had left the SACP with him in 1990. He would later style himself as the darling of the left, but in 1991, the militants were as skeptical about him as they were about Mbeki. And so Hani, Slovo, and their SACP comrades looked for a suitable candidate to oppose him—and came up with Cyril Ramaphosa.

It was a masterstroke. Ramaphosa, a lawyer by training, had been a UDF leader and was arguably the most successful trade unionist South Africa had ever seen, having built the behemoth National Union of Mineworkers from scratch. Although the ANC was still governed by the Lusaka clique of returned exiles, most delegates on the floor would be "internal" people keen to break the Lusaka stranglehold and among whom the militant Ramaphosa was immensely popular. The move paid off: Ramaphosa trounced both Zuma and Nzo. In an effort to balance "internal" and "exile," Zuma was appointed his deputy.

Ramaphosa was a decade younger than Mbeki, Zuma, and Hani; of these three, the one he most closely resembled was undoubtedly Mbeki. Both were blessed with a formidable intellect and a preternatural strategic common sense; both, too, were adored by the media and respected by the establishment. Both masked ruthlessness with charm. But whereas Mbeki shied away from conflict, Ramaphosa—never losing this charm for a moment—seemed to relish putting the knife in. He was not much taller than Mbeki but significantly stouter, and something about his bigness of personality—his large, easy laugh and backslapping affability—made him fill whatever space he entered. You would be aware of Mbeki in the corner of a room and would be drawn to him for an intense one-on-one encounter; Ramaphosa, however, would be the first person you would see upon entering, usually surrounded by admirers, easy to greet but hard to pin down. Ramaphosa came across as voracious and welcoming, Mbeki as ascetic and skeptical. And whereas you often felt you had to prove your worth to Mbeki, Ramaphosa instantly made you feel you were the most important person in the room. In their different ways, though, neither man encouraged intimacy; both were notoriously inscrutable.

Ramaphosa had not been a member of the ANC underground before its unbanning and thus had had little relationship with the movement in exile. Unlike Mbeki, for whom the ANC was a cathedral, the trade unionist understood it as a means toward an end: that of liberation and, his detractors would say, his own advancement. Ramaphosa was not from the ANC elite: he was an outsider, a township operator, the Soweto-born son of a policeman, a member of the minority Venda tribe, creative and iconoclastic, always looking for the advantage. He could be brashly ambitious and arrogant, but you could not fail to be won over by him; Mandela, for example, developed an affectionate paternal relationship with him that was very different from his respectful but distant way with Mbeki.

Mbeki vigorously denies that he has ever been in competition with Ramaphosa and makes much of the mentorship he offered the younger man: "When he was elected I took him to my hotel room to discuss this post of S-G [secretary-general] and how to handle it." Sydney Mufamadi, close to both at the time, was the third man at this encounter. He remembers that they sat up, drinking and talking, until around 4 a.m., and that Ramaphosa appeared to be "very appreciative," but in the following months, the attitude of ANC's new secretary-general toward Mbeki hardened. At one point, when relations between Mbeki on the one side and Slovo and Mac Maharaj on the other were at an all-time low, Mufamadi approached Ramaphosa: "Shouldn't we take it upon ourselves to mediate?" he asked.

Ramaphosa's response shocked him. "No," he said. "I know that people like Mac, Joe, and Thabo are senior to me politically. But now I'm the secretary-general. Mac and Joe accord me due respect. Thabo has not shown me that respect at all!" From that moment, Mufamadi told me, it was clear to him that Ramaphosa "had made up his mind that...there was a side to take. And in so doing, he squandered the opportunity we had to mediate between the two sides."

If Mbeki's comrades and colleagues had always been ambivalent about him—had always laced their fear, and even dislike, of him with avowed admiration—then this was clearly expressed in the polls at the Durban conference. While they were not yet prepared to anoint Mbeki Mandela's deputy, they nonetheless accepted the absolute necessity for him to be in leadership. In the vote for the new National Executive Committee (NEC), each of the voting delegates was required to vote for the 50 people of their choice, and 1,824 of them—93 percent—put Mbeki on their list. This put him just behind Chris Hani—who came first with 94.7 percent.[2] Immediately after the conference, the new leadership gathered to select its National Working Committee (NWC), responsible for the day-to-day running of the organization. This time, in the election by their leadership peers, Mbeki came first with 66 votes and Hani second with 65.[3] For Mufamadi, "It was as if the conference delegates and then the NEC were saying to Chris and Thabo, 'We want both of you equally. It's not like we're choosing one or the other.'"

But what happened next is best described as a palace coup. It took place in the first week of August, while Mandela was away on a visit to Cuba, as were both Mbeki and Zuma, attending a conference at Cambridge. Zuma heard about the event on the BBC and went rushing over to tell Mbeki: Ramaphosa had convened the leadership while they were away and had sidelined them!

Zuma had been relieved of his position as head of ANC intelligence and replaced by the UDF leader Mosiuoa "Terror" Lekota, a man with no previous intelligence experience. And Mbeki had been replaced, as head of negotiations, by Ramaphosa himself. Slovo in particular had lobbied intensively to replace Mbeki with Ramaphosa. For most of the ANC leadership, it was not so much about the deficiency of Mbeki as the promise of Ramaphosa. The reading of the situation by the state intelligence services was not incorrect: "They thought Thabo Mbeki was too subtle," Niël Barnard told me. "They thought, 'Perhaps the way to tackle these Boers is through an abrasive labor man.'"

Was Mandela party, even in his absence, to the decision? Mbeki insists that the ANC president was more upset than he was, and Ramaphosa confirmed to me that Mandela was indeed "the only one who expressed unhappiness" about the decision. But, Ramaphosa said, Mandela's complaint was "procedural, not substantive. He believed the secretary-general should have his hands free to build the organization; that's what he would have preferred. But in the end he accepted it. He was convinced by the others: the task at hand was negotiations."

This acceptance did not come easily, though. Shortly before multiparty talks were finally set to begin, in late 1991, Mandela and Oliver Tambo—still very ill after his stroke but now back in South Africa—called the ANC's negotiations commission to an emergency meeting. The commission consisted of Mbeki's old team together with Ramaphosa's new appointments. Still bothered by the decision to replace Mbeki with Ramaphosa, Mandela pulled one of his favorite stunts: No one would leave the room, he said, without stating his preference for who should lead the commission. One by one, the comrades nervously proposed one or other of the men, until it came to Tambo who, frail and unable to speak clearly, simply lifted his cane, pointing it in Solomonic fashion, to a third man: Zuma. No one felt comfortable disagreeing with Tambo, and Zuma got the job of chairing the negotiations commission. But the commission remained a back room, from which Zuma and Mbeki would wield their influence behind the scenes. Ramaphosa carried on running the actual process from the front line. It was his show.

One senior ANC official chose to describe the difference between Mbeki and Ramaphosa as that between "architect" and "builder." This is accurate, to a point. Certainly, Mbeki designed the foundations, and many of his fundamental concepts—often developed out of "sketches" provided first by Tambo, Mandela, and Julius Nyerere—prevailed. These included the multiparty process, the two-phase interim government, and the compromise ultimately embodied in the "sunset clauses" (proposed by Slovo but first suggested by Mbeki), which prescribed a Government of National Unity (GNU) and guaranteed ancien régime officials their jobs. But the job description "builder" does not begin to describe the creativity with which

Ramaphosa undertook his role; if he was not quite the architect, he was, in effect, the engineer and site manager and interior decorator all rolled into one.

By the time CODESA (Congress for a Democratic South Africa) was convened in December 1991, some sort of equilibrium between the two men had been established. Mbeki took responsibility for leading the ANC in a working group responsible for designing the interim government while Ramaphosa led the working group set up to develop the new constitution. Around Mbeki's table, the Nationalist Party (NP) did not concede much, but agreement and compromise were reached with minimal conflict. Around Ramaphosa's table, several issues were irreconcilable, finally resulting in the collapse of CODESA in May 1992. Certainly the issues faced by Ramaphosa were more contentious, but by comparing what happened in the two groups, one can begin to understand the fundamental differences in negotiating style between the men. Mbeki kept people talking at all costs, while Ramaphosa brought matters to a head through brinksmanship. Mbeki worked with what was possible to establish a beachhead for further advances, while Ramaphosa forced a deadlock to shift the balance of power in his direction.

By the time the reconstituted CODESA 2 plenary opened on May 15, 1992, the only outstanding issue was in Ramaphosa's group, where the sides remained deadlocked over the NP's insistence on what would amount to a minority veto over the constitution. Ramaphosa made a final offer that he knew his opponents would refuse, because it would remove the NP's ability to veto a constitutional amendment.[4] Mbeki was horrified; he would have found a way of framing an offer with language vague enough to take the process to another level, and he argued forcefully against Ramaphosa's approach. But he found himself alone: All his comrades now supported Ramaphosa's game plan, which was, as the journalist Patti Waldmeir wrote, not about doing a deal but about forcing a breakdown: "The government felt too strong to settle and its rivals too weak. The ANC set out to reverse that equation, forever."[5]

It worked. CODESA 2 collapsed and was superseded by a "rolling mass action" campaign. And then, as if on cue, the day after the new campaign began, the Boipatong massacre took place on June 17, 1992: 46 innocent people were slaughtered by marauding Zulu nationalists, reportedly under the watchful eye of the security police. Mandela declared that South Africa was "back in the days of Sharpeville" and that "the chasm between oppressor and oppressed" remained "unbridgeable."[6] The darkest period of the negotiations era began, dubbed by the South African media the "winter of discontent."[7] What good, muttered Mbeki to his closest confidants, did it do to speak like that when the two sides would inevitably have to come back to the table? In early September, the ANC led a reckless march into Bisho, capital of Ciskei, an "independent" black homeland in the Eastern Cape. Soldiers fired on the demonstrators, killing 29. Just as the Boipatong massacre had forced a breakdown in talks, the Bisho massacre shocked both sides into realizing the inevitable consequences of not talking. Within two weeks—largely owing to the extraordinary relationship between Ramaphosa and his National Party counterpart, Roelf Meyer—the two sides were back at the table. Finally, on September 26, 1992, a "Record of Understanding" was signed between the two sides, clearing the way for the next—and final—round of multiparty negotiations.

At an angry ANC leadership meeting in the aftermath of Boipatong massacre, Thabo Mbeki had argued passionately that the ANC should not withdraw from negotiations under any circumstance. "If you stop these negotiations now, we'll have to come back to them [later]," he said. "But what has happened is that the forces responsible for this violence consolidate. You give them space and it is quite wrong." But not one comrade, not even his closest allies, offered support this time, he told me: "I said 'No, it's not right.' But I was alone. I was alone."

At roughly the same time as this meeting, Ann Page—one of Mbeki's English connections from the British Anti-Apartheid Movement—found herself in Johannesburg and called her old friend. "Can I take you out to dinner?" she asked. "No, no, I don't have time to eat," came the response. "Meet me at Shell House. Let's go for a drink."

Shell House was the skyscraper the ANC had bought, suspended above Joubert Park and the frenetic Noord Street taxi ranks. Page and Mbeki wandered out onto Jeppe Street and landed up at the Johannesburg Sun Hotel, a favorite watering hole for the ANC comrades who worked across the road. "Is this all right?" she asked, and he laughed sourly: "If I can't set foot in my own city, what's it all been for?" The meaning of Mbeki's sardonic comment would only become clear as the evening wore on.

Page remembered vividly how every head turned when they entered the bar. She remembered how Mbeki uncharacteristically seated them "in the line of fire, whereas in the past he'd put himself somewhere where he wouldn't be disturbed"; how the evening was punctuated with visits to their table by "supplicants" with whom Mbeki was "graceful but a bit distant"; how, without ever being called, Mbeki's "watchfully discreet" flunkies would arrive and replenish their glasses so that their "chief" never had to get up; how, despite Mbeki's earlier plea that he did not have time for dinner, they sat in the bar drinking until around midnight. And how, late in the evening, "at some point Thabo lowered his guard and stopped talking in grand theoretical great-visionary terms, and said to me: 'It can't be so bad if I'm sitting here like this, can it? I can't be *that* unpopular, can I?'"

The way Page remembers it, Mbeki explained his comment to her thus: "I've been out of the country for so long [that] I've supposedly got no profile. I lived abroad, but they must be able to see that I was there—I am here— sweating for them." Page understood this to be the dislocation—the alien- ation—of the returned exile, and, in this context, Mbeki's earlier comment made sense: "If I can't set foot in my own city, what's it all been for?" She felt a terrible sadness. Her friend was not home yet.

Several of Mbeki's friends have told me that this fastidious man was depressed to the point of not caring about his appearance in 1991 and 1992. He turned, one said, to "fleshpot things; wine, women and song...he took his eyes off the prize for a brief while and decided to have a good time." According to another, while he most certainly "did not curl up into a ball and become dysfunctional," he was definitely "dejected and a bit despon- dent. He did not understand why he had been dropped in this way." By all accounts, the two years in which he was sidelined, between mid-1991 (when he was forced to withdraw his candidacy for deputy president of the ANC and was dumped as the movement's chief negotiator) and mid-1993 (when he was elected to replace Tambo as the movement's national chairman) were among the most difficult of his life—at least until his ousting from power fifteen years later.

29

INTO POWER

On April 10, 1993, Chris Hani was assassinated in his driveway, in a suburb outside Johannesburg. It was later discovered that his assailants, right-wing extremists, were acting independently, but at the time it seemed to most South Africans that the murder was part of a plot to derail the negotiations and plunge the country into civil war. F. W. De Klerk's government was paralyzed; in the midst of the terror and fear, the state-owned broadcasting service gave Nelson Mandela the opportunity to address the nation. It was during his successful appeal for calm—rather than at his election a year later—that Mandela effectively became South Africa's ruler. Hani's massive funeral seemed barely able to contain the rage and the emotion that swept through the country. Oliver Tambo attended and developed a chill; he died five days later.

According to Adelaide Tambo, Thabo Mbeki spent three hours with her husband on his deathbed and was the last person to talk to him. Mrs. Tambo believed that there was a passing of the torch in those hours, which her husband spent with his political son rather than with his flesh and blood. As the shock of Hani's murder forced both sides to resolve their outstanding issues and set an election date, Mbeki withdrew completely, refusing to see anyone. It was, for many of his friends, the first time they had ever seen him unhinged.

It could not have been easy for Mbeki. Whatever his dying mentor might have told him, Tambo did not have the power to anoint a successor: There was Mandela, and there was Cyril Ramaphosa. If Thabo Mbeki was going to carry Tambo's torch, he was going to need to develop a constituency. With Hani's murder, the threat of a right-wing destabilization suddenly became palpable. Not only would Mbeki have to act on his unfashionable conviction that the extremist spoilers had to be brought to the table at all costs, but he would simultaneously have to engage himself in the struggle for leadership of the ANC in a way he never had before. Such a balancing act would be far tougher than the simple rite of passage following the death of a beloved parent.

A short while later, Mbeki was dining with the Pahad brothers at their home in Mayfair, the Indian neighborhood to the west of Johannesburg. Present, too, in this innermost circle was Umkhonto we Sizwe (MK) head

Joe Modise. When the conversation turned to the state of the ANC's leadership in the wake of Tambo's death, Modise suggested that Mbeki should replace his old mentor as national chairman, and his close confidants set out to engineer this.

Just as Mbeki had been sidelined by a small group of people rather than by the masses themselves, he would be elected to ANC high office by power-brokering political elites within the movement. The limits of this approach would become clear from 2005 onwards, during his battle with Jacob Zuma. But in the early 1990s, in the wake of Tambo's death, Mbeki played such politics to greatest effect with two people in particular: Peter Mokaba and Winnie Mandela, both of whom had formidable constituencies. Mokaba was the overbearing presence in the ANC Youth League, with which Mbeki had an organic relationship because of his own history as a youth leader. Mandela was not yet president of the Women's League—she would become so, with Mbeki's tacit support, by the end of the year—but was by far the dominant personality in it, and in the townships and squatter camps around Johannesburg.

On the surface, the two seemed unnatural allies for Mbeki: They were precisely the kind of populist demagogues he usually steered clear of, and they had, in fact, formed something of a militant populist troika with Hani before his murder. But they shared two things with Mbeki: a growing ideological affinity around Africanism and a mutual commitment to halt the ascendancy of Cyril Ramaphosa, whom they both loathed. There was also another, darker bond at work: While Mokaba and Mandela could both boast massive grassroots support, both were vulnerable within the ANC leadership because of troublesome histories. Mbeki's understanding of power often led him to seek out strong but vulnerable people who might need his patronage, and both Mokaba and Mandela had become dependent on him to give them access to—and protection from—the old Lusaka exile elite.

Mbeki got to know Winnie during the international trips he took with the Mandelas in 1990, and she had singled him out as a confidant during her ongoing troubles with the law and within the ANC. As the Mandela marriage collapsed, Mbeki became the primary intermediary between husband and wife. Mbeki frequently defended Winnie in the early 1990s, even insisting, against her estranged husband's strenuous objections, that she be included in the first ANC government. Later they would fall out, but while Mbeki "has always been aware of Winnie's weaknesses," as one of his advisors put it to me, he also appreciated her power—and was also the beneficiary of it: She stood squarely with Mokaba, her close comrade, in the 1993 campaign to ensure that Mbeki became her ex-husband's deputy.

The debt of the charismatic and flashy Mokaba to Mbeki was even greater than that of Winnie Mandela, for Mbeki had saved him from the humiliation of exposure as a suspected double agent. In 1989 ANC intelligence under

Jacob Zuma had launched an investigation into Mokaba and tried to detain him in Lusaka; on Mbeki's urging, Tambo had intervened and arranged instead for the youth leader to be "rehabilitated." The deal was that he would be allowed to return, untarnished, to South Africa, but would be kept out of any leadership positions until his name was fully cleared. Mbeki's patronage overturned this ruling, however, and it was not long before Mokaba was elected to the presidency of the ANC Youth League once it was unbanned.[1] At Mbeki's insistence, Mokaba too—like Winnie Mandela—would later be given a junior deputy ministership in Nelson Mandela's government. Mbeki would drop him from his cabinet in 1999, in part because his illness had incapacitated him (he would die of AIDS in 2002.) But until his death he would remain one of the president's most loyal troubleshooters, floating contentious ideas on subjects Mbeki himself could not be seen to support too actively—most notably, the position that HIV might not cause AIDS and that antiretroviral medication was toxic.

In June 1993, Mokaba said publicly that Mbeki should be Mandela's deputy and successor, and the ANC Youth League launched a campaign to make this happen. The first step was—as had been discussed at the meeting at the Pahads' home—to get Mbeki elected into the senior leadership as national chairman. But Mandela had already decided on his own candidate for the post: Kader Asmal, a fluent, hyperactive, and highly intelligent law professor who was one of the drafters of South Africa's new constitution. Mandela's mission was not so much to stymie Mbeki's ambitions—although this might have played a part—as to promote an ethnic heterogeneity in the upper echelons of the ANC. He was acutely aware of the allegations that the ANC was Xhosa-dominated: Electing a non-African (Asmal is of Indian descent) would demonstrate, he believed, the movement's nonracial bona fides. But Peter Mokaba objected strenuously and lobbied effectively. In the end, Mbeki trounced Asmal in a vote put to secret ballot.

There is something of the victor's bravura in Mbeki's tone in interviews he gave after his election, an uncharacteristic immodesty that suggests that he had, at last, decided to play the power politics needed to assure his ascendancy. In one interview, he made it clear that he was now "the custodian of all policy," responsible for formulating the ANC election manifesto.[2] In another, he insisted that he also should remain on as head of international affairs, as no one else had his connections: "It is easy for me to phone almost any foreign minister in the world and get access," he boasted.[3] Mbeki has always been a master at finding advantage within the prescribed regulations and thus making the rules work for him. As national chairman, he took a shell that was created for Tambo but never really exploited and used it to become a figure of at least equal stature to Ramaphosa in the final months of negotiations, and thus a true contender for the position of

Mandela's deputy. The National Interferer was back—but this time with a previously unarticulated hunger for high office.

Bolstered by his new confidence in a senior elected position, Mbeki would flourish once more, in the conditions of secrecy required, away from the klieg lights of the negotiations at the World Trade Center outside Johannesburg, where the multiparty talks were taking place. If consensus had been reached inside the tent of negotiations, there were still major problems in the wilderness beyond, and Mbeki was now tasked to deal with them. He became the movement's outrider: While Ramaphosa kept things going within the tent, Mbeki patrolled its perimeters with Zuma at his side, corralling in the spoilers and the go-it-aloners: primarily the Afrikaner secessionists and Chief Mangosuthu Buthelezi's Zulu nationalists. Ramaphosa did not take the spoilers' Armageddon threats seriously and believed that by remaining outside, they would marginalize themselves into oblivion; Mbeki, however, was of the firm conviction—as his friend Jürgen Kögl told me—that "you never isolate the radicals. You always keep them talking." And so, "while Cyril [Ramaphosa] and Roelf [Meyer] were dancing at the World Trade Center"—a reference to the famous shimmy the two men took once final agreement was reached on November 21, 1993—"the Zulus and the Boers were preparing for war! And it was Thabo who went out and disarmed them."

In the wake of the Hani assassination, an Afrikaner secessionist movement had solidified around the charismatic figure of General Constand Viljoen, a military hero and former head of the South African army. Like an Old Testament prophet, Viljoen had come out of retirement to lead his people to freedom: He formed a movement, which he called the Afrikaner Freedom Front (AVF), to fight for the ideal of a *volkstaat*—an independent Afrikaner state. Although the general was no longer in the formal leadership of the South African Defence Force, he still commanded the authority to raise a secessionist army that could tear the country's armed forces in two, and Mbeki understood this. He realized that F. W. De Klerk had lost control of the military, which now needed to be negotiated with separately, and that the retired general was its most legitimate representative.

And so, beginning in August 1993, with Mandela's knowledge, Mbeki and Zuma began meeting secretly with the general and his lieutenants, in encounters brokered by Jürgen Kögl, who was connected by marriage to the Afrikaner military establishment. "Tell us honestly what you think of the ANC," Mbeki asked at the first of these meetings, which took place in a pigeon-racing club east of Pretoria. Viljoen responded that while he did not like communists, there were a lot of similarities between Afrikaners and blacks: "We believe we can do a deal with black people."

Between August and December, Mbeki and Viljoen led their respective sides to eight meetings in total—most of which were conducted around the dining room table in Kögl's art deco apartment in downtown Johannesburg. At one meeting, Mbeki played his trump card: "Define for us the *volkstaat*. What sort of an animal is it? Is it a zebra or is it a warthog?" The idea of an independent Afrikaner state was, of course, simply not viable: Mbeki's strategy was to ask questions to get his counterparts to visualize their *volkstaat*—and thus to come to the same conclusion themselves. Where would this *volkstaat* be? Who would live there? Would it be a democracy? How would it survive?

Viljoen was encouraged that Mbeki and his team were at least willing to listen to him—unlike their comrades in the negotiations, who had dismissed him out of hand. By early December 1993, however, the general snapped. "Look!" he responded, when Mbeki tried once more to convince his counterparts that they had nothing to fear from an ANC government, "it's not a matter of fear! It's a matter of our perception of freedom. We want to govern ourselves." The way Viljoen tells it, Mbeki threw his hands up in the air in exasperation: "Then we're miles apart." Finally Mbeki abandoned his habitual tendency to insist on common ground where there was none and agreed that the ANC would have to look at Afrikaner self-determination.

Was Mbeki really willing to consider Afrikaner self-government? Or had he just changed tack in order to keep his adversary talking? One way or the other, Mbeki's team—much to the astonishment and even the outrage of many of their comrades—admitted the idea of a *volkstaat* into the negotiations process. On December 21, 1993, Mbeki and Viljoen reached accord: The AVF agreed "to the development of a non-racial democracy"—an extraordinary breakthrough—while the ANC accepted that the Afrikaner "ideal of self-determination" needed to be addressed. The agreement was taken to Mandela, who approved it, and a press conference was called. But at the eleventh hour, Ferdi Hartzenberg—Viljoen's coleader—said he was unable to sign, thus forcing Viljoen to withdraw. Mbeki had some trouble on his own side, too: The general sentiment in the ANC, and particularly from Ramaphosa, was that he had gone too far. Mandela, swayed, declared that there would never be a *volkstaat*. Viljoen's supporters openly called for war. The line between the two sides went dead.

Eventually, in late January 1994, the two teams met again at Mbeki's initiative, and it was here that Mbeki had his brainwave: "Let us use the April elections themselves as a referendum for the *volkstaat*." The genius of the idea was that it would compel the secessionists to participate in the democratic elections. They would show their strength not with fire but in the way the Afrikaner had first won power in South Africa: through the ballot. All votes for Viljoen's party would be counted as votes in favor of a *volkstaat*, which would be investigated further by a statutory body that was compelled to marry Afrikaner aspirations to the self-determination principle of the interim constitution.

Viljoen jumped at the proposal. But while the general's decision to participate in the April 1994 elections might have been encouraged by Mbeki's creative and persistent efforts, his final shove into the democratic process came not through his meeting with the ANC but rather from the extraordinary set of events that took place in the black homeland of Bophuthatswana ("Bop") in early March. When the homeland leader Lucas Mangope—another recalcitrant—called for help against ANC mass action in favor of reincorporation, Viljoen raced over to organize the Bop army into resistance. Meanwhile, the cavalier cowboys of Eugène Terre'Blanche's neo-Nazi Afrikaner Resistance Movement (AWB) came riding into town, lobbing hand grenades and shooting indiscriminately at black people. The Bop soldiers responded with mutiny; in the signal event, three AWB men were executed in cold blood in front of a TV camera. The image, beamed into the living rooms of white South Africa that evening, transmitted a warning not only of the fatal dangers of resisting the inevitable but of the bloody mess that would accompany any civil war. Viljoen later said that it was at this moment that he realized the tide of blood he would release if he went to war,[4] and registered his party to contest the elections.

In their dealings with Viljoen and his *volkstaaters*, Mbeki and his team—foremost among them Jacob Zuma—understood the basic conservatism of humanity: its instinct toward inertia. They worked off the premise that, once safely inside the system, the Afrikaner separatists would lose their hunger for the uncertainties of a *volkstaat*. They were proven right. Viljoen's party would win over 400,000 votes in the elections and send nine people, led by the general himself, to parliament. The Volkstaat Council would be duly convened, but it—and with it, the idea of the *volkstaat*—would die a quiet and unheralded death. Fifteen years later, the Freedom Front +, as it was now known, remained in parliament, albeit with vastly diminished numbers: In a trenchant indication of the failure of the movement, the bulk of its support defected to the Democratic Alliance (DA)—led by an English-speaking Jew, Tony Leon. The National Party, meanwhile, first formed an alliance with the DA and then dissolved into the ANC. A century of Afrikaner nationalist politics was over. Asked, in 2001, whether he was naive to believe the ANC might ever contemplate a *volkstaat*, Viljoen conceded that Mbeki had outwitted him—and also that the hunger for a *volkstaat* had abated: "The ANC realized, especially after 1996, that most Afrikaners didn't experience the new South Africa that negatively. So they started thinking they could take chances and ignore these agreements."[5]

But Viljoen did not doubt Mbeki's personal bona fides. Mbeki, he told me, "realized the importance of the Afrikaners and the need to get some form of agreement between us and the ANC." If the basis of this understanding came from Mbeki's genteel sessions with Willie Esterhuyse and other members of the Afrikaner intelligentsia at Mells Park, then it was deepened by his encounters with the farmers and soldiers around Viljoen: the *volkstaat* frontiersmen. One of the greatest achievements of the postapartheid South African state is the way it managed to shift the "minority rights" discourse from "self-determination" to "cultural autonomy." Part of Mbeki's strategy for achieving this was the valorization of Afrikaner identity and the embrace of it as an indigenous culture. Kögl remembers Zuma saying, as they drove back from that first meeting at the pigeon-racing club, "These are our people, they are the people of the soil. We must work with them." Mbeki would not have expressed himself so emotionally. But he would have agreed, entirely, with the sentiment.

Thabo Mbeki's talking cure worked a charm with General Viljoen and his Afrikaner secessionists. But in the case of the other major recalcitrant, Chief Mangosuthu Buthelezi and his Zulu nationalist Inkatha Freedom Party (IFP), the evidence of Mbeki's success is a little less clear, and the relationship a lot more complicated.

Buthelezi was originally an ANC man, a comrade and close friend of Nelson Mandela and Oliver Tambo. In 1969, however, he had decided to accept the position of chief minister of KwaZulu, the black homeland established for the Zulu people by the apartheid authorities, as part of their policy of "separate development." The ANC was virulently opposed to this policy, but Buthelezi managed to persuade his old friend that he was incontrovertibly an ANC man and that his new position could be used as a beachhead for mobilizing insurrection. Tambo tasked Mbeki to help Buthelezi set up a political organization, and Inkatha was thus formed as an ANC proxy. But Buthelezi refused to play ball, repeatedly rebuking the ANC publicly, specifically for its sanctions policy and its commitment to armed struggle, and becoming increasingly intimate with his apartheid paymasters. By 1979, when the relationship between Buthelezi and the ANC finally collapsed after a failed peace meeting in London, Mbeki was one of the strongest proponents within the ANC for severing ties with the chief. When, eight months later, Inkatha sent men armed with sticks to intimidate striking students back into school, Mbeki drafted a statement that Buthelezi had assumed "the mantle of collaborator [and] ... the vile role of a police agent."[6] Even Tambo was forced to declare that his old friend had "emerged on the side of the enemy against the people."[7]

Thus began a brutal and bloody turf war between Inkatha and ANC supporters in the province of Natal; by the time the ANC was unbanned, thousands of people had been killed and many more displaced. The violence was exacerbated after the ANC's unbanning in 1990, seemingly fanned by "third force" agents of the state using armed Zulu migrant workers to perpetrate random acts of violence so as to destabilize the negotiations process. Meanwhile, Buthelezi was outraged that he seemed to be excluded from the cozy relationship developing between the ANC and the Nationalist Party (NP), his erstwhile allies. And so he led the IFP into a band of malcontents known as the Concerned South Africans Group (COSAG), which also included Viljoen's AVF. Buthelezi's main grievance was the ANC's insistence on a unitary state: In a free South Africa, he insisted, Natal should be an autonomous constitutional monarchy under the Zulu king. It was, of course, a power play, and it was rejected out of hand by both the ANC and the NP; in response, Buthelezi stormed out of the negotiations process and threatened war. After months of escalating political violence on the ground in Natal and a violent confrontation with the ANC that left 53 dead in downtown Johannesburg just a month before the April 1994 elections, both the ANC and the NP resigned themselves to a forceful removal of Buthelezi from his bantustan fiefdom.[8]

One ANC leader who strongly opposed this approach was Jacob Zuma. A Zulu himself, Zuma believed passionately that the schism among his people had to be healed and that the wayward Inkatha had to be returned, at all costs, to its mother movement. Although he was a commoner, Zuma was a staunch traditionalist and was as well schooled in the byzantine rituals of Zulu politesse as he was street smart. Zuma managed to persuade Mbeki—as skeptical as anyone about Buthelezi's bona fides—that the Zulu chief needed to be engaged with, and also had Mandela's ear on this score. Eventually, Mandela and Buthelezi made a deal: the IFP agreed to register provisionally for the elections, pending "international mediation" on Buthelezi's constitutional disputes with the ANC. Thus began the cliffhanger brinksmanship that would take South Africa to the edge before the elections—and the final conflict between Mbeki and Ramaphosa in the weeks before Mandela would choose one of them to be his successor.

The ANC and the IFP quickly agreed on a group of mediators—led by Henry Kissinger and Lord Peter Carrington, former U.S. secretary of state and British foreign minister respectively—but they could not agree on the terms. When Mbeki led the ANC to a final crisis meeting on Sunday, April 10, 1994—just two weeks before the election—he appeared to break the deadlock. Buthelezi had wanted the election date to be negotiable, and Mbeki conceded this, having been given absolute verbal assurance from Buthelezi, he told me, that the IFP would accept the election date if all other matters were resolved. But the deal was not acceptable to Ramaphosa, who exploded when he found out about it and successfully petitioned Mandela to reject it: "If we fell into the trap of mediating the election date, the entire process could have been scuttled," Ramaphosa would later say. "Millions of people were geared up for their liberation, and if there had been any attempt to postpone the election I think the country would have blown up."[9]

The collapse of the international mediation initiative was the lowest ebb yet in South Africa's slide into chaos in the weeks before the elections. Kissinger and Carrington packed their bags, but one of their advisors remained behind: the Kenyan Washington Okumu, who made one last attempt to talk to the IFP leader alone. Now, at the eleventh hour, Buthelezi bought Okumu's argument: The elections were going to go ahead anyway, and if he did not participate he would be left out. There were now barely ten days to go, and a frantic weekend of shuttle diplomacy ensued. Finally, on Tuesday, April 19, Mandela, Buthelezi, and F. W. De Klerk met at the Union Buildings in Pretoria and signed the deal: The IFP was in. Just ten days before the polls, Buthelezi's electioneering machinery was ready to roll, with huge numbers of posters warehoused and waiting to be put up. It all confirmed Ramaphosa's view rather than Mbeki's: that, as Ramaphosa later said, the IFP's "intention was to hold the country to ransom and extract the maximum possible concessions."[10]

Nonetheless, Mbeki's keep-'em-talking principle, used so effectively just a few weeks earlier with Viljoen and the Afrikaner right wing, played a key role in sealing the deal with Buthelezi, too. Accord could not be reached on the constitutional status of the Zulu monarch, and so Mbeki's precedent from the Afrikaner secessionist talks kicked in: As with the *volkstaat* issue, it was agreed that this tricky issue too would be deferred until after the elections, when international mediation would once more attempt to solve it. As with the Afrikaner secessionists, the Mbeki logic triumphed with Buthelezi: Bring him in, promise to see to his grievances once the country has made it to the other side of the rainbow, and hope that the grievances recede as he busies himself with the authority and status accorded him in the new democracy.

It would work, for a while at least. In what many believe was a peacemaking rig of the results, the IFP conveniently won 51 percent of the province of KwaZulu-Natal in the elections and, with that, enough votes to qualify it to form a Government of National Unity with the ANC and the NP. Mandela and Mbeki agreed that Buthelezi be given the senior cabinet portfolio of home affairs; two years later, when De Klerk pulled out of government, it was Mbeki's idea to give Buthelezi the cabinet committee chairmanships that De Klerk had previously held and to have him appointed acting president when both the president and his deputy were out of the country.

But it did not take Buthelezi long to realize that, like Viljoen, he had been conned. The ANC had no intention of submitting to international mediation, and the substantive issue had become obsolete anyway: The Zulu king, Goodwill Zwelethini, had decided that he was, after all, content with his lot in the new South Africa. Enraged, Buthelezi refused to participate in the constitution-making process. But still, he and his IFP colleagues remained in the ANC cabinet on the national level and continued to rule in coalition with the ANC in KwaZulu-Natal. Zuma, who forged ever-closer relations with his IFP counterparts in the province, described to me how astute Mbeki was in using African solidarity to bring Buthelezi "home," by urging the Zulu leader that South Africa needed to run against the continent's stereotype of factionalism; to show the world that blacks could "come together and run this country." When the IFP looked set to follow De Klerk's NP out of the government in 1996, Mbeki played this winning card again: "De Klerk hopes to prove that without the National Party, no government will ever stand," Mbeki said to Buthelezi. This, of course, was a race thing: Blacks cannot do it alone. "So we need to prove that we can run a government, being black." The way to prove this was "to work together. We can't repeat the bad stories of the past in Africa."

Later, the relationship would fall apart completely, and Mbeki would drop Buthelezi from his cabinet in 2004. But even if Ramaphosa had been right in 1994, and Mbeki had misread Buthelezi's commitment to respecting the election date, the odds he had gambled on when he insisted on keeping Buthelezi within the process had paid off: just as his strategy had neutralized the Afrikaner far-right, it ultimately declawed the old belligerent, rendering him anachronistic and dispensable.

Thabo Mbeki was not one of those millions of South Africans who stood, for hours, in the great leveler of a long, snaking line on April 27, 1994. He, like the other leaders of the political parties, was denied the experience of the good-natured shuffle toward the voting booth, chatting with fellow voters across race and class lines, which would become the archetypal experience of that magnificent day. Assigned to monitor Pretoria, Mbeki was not even able to vote on April 27, as he was pulled into urgent talks regarding the late opening of voting stations in the city. Instead, he voted on the second polling day, in an almost deserted school in the Indian township of Laudium—another conscious assertion by Mbeki that he was "above" ethnic or regional constituencies.

The interim constitution mandated that the head of the winning party appoint at least two deputy presidents and stipulated that one of them would come from an opposition party. There was little doubt that F. W. De Klerk would be the latter, but it would take the better part of a week for Mandela to make up his mind about who from the ANC would fill the other post. The reason for the delay was that Mandela was at odds with the senior leadership of his party: He wanted Ramaphosa while they wanted Mbeki. Mandela claimed, once more, that his preference was motivated solely by his wish to broaden the ethnic base of the ANC leadership, and he stressed to me that when the senior ANC officials (including Walter Sisulu and Jacob Zuma) insisted on Mbeki, he assented "because I really do have confidence in Thabo and in his leadership ability."

But it seems that the ethnic argument was once more Mandela's polite way of articulating his ambivalence about Mbeki, and he actually consulted far more widely than he admits—including to the ANC's alliance partners, the South African Communist Party and the Congress of South African Trade Unions (COSATU), who were fervently behind Ramaphosa, and other African leaders, particularly Kenneth Kaunda, who gave their support to Mbeki. Only four days before the inauguration, he called Mbeki in and told him he would be deputy president. The younger man was "very surprised," one of his confidants told me. "He had become resigned to losing out to Cyril, and was expecting finance or foreign affairs." Mandela, the maverick, had initially selected another rebel, another maverick, to replace himself: someone with a history on the shop floor and in the streets rather than in the corridors of ANC power; someone who might have remade the movement as radically as Mandela himself did in the 1950s. It would have been a high-risk gamble. But the ANC grandees vetoed this and went for the safe insider. In the end, then, Mandela acquiesced to the wishes of his recently deceased predecessor and to the hegemony that had developed in exile.

Two years later, after overseeing the process of writing the new South African constitution, Ramaphosa would quit politics and go into business as one of the pioneer black executives—in large part because he felt edged out of the ANC by Mbeki. But many around Mbeki believed that his old rival's move into the business world was shrewdly calculated; they suspected that—despite Ramaphosa's public profile as a political radical—he had been earmarked early on by big business as its candidate, aggressively promoted through a fawning media. Ramaphosa, the logic went, would be parachuted back into politics a few years later, his hands apparently clean but utterly beholden to the business establishment and captive to the racial supremacy of white liberals.

These suspicions would finally come to a head with preposterous allegations in 2002 of a coup plot involving Ramaphosa and two other men, Matthews Phosa and Tokyo Sexwale, both of whom had been charismatic provincial premiers and were now also businessmen after having been edged out of politics by Mbeki. Mbeki's police minister, Steve Tshwete, publicly aired details of the alleged conspiracy on television: According to a rather dubious source, the three men were plotting to exact their revenge on Mbeki by accusing him of being behind Chris Hani's murder, and Mbeki's own life was now allegedly in danger. Mbeki's intelligence advisors were astonished that he seemed convinced of the report's truth—or was, at least, determined to use the allegation as a canard to suppress potential rivals. The incident also marked the beginning of the chill between Mbeki and Jacob Zuma, for Mbeki accused his deputy of passing confidential information on to the alleged plotters. In the years thereafter, Zuma himself would allege that he was the victim of a political conspiracy orchestrated by Mbeki—and Ramaphosa, Phosa, and Sexwale would lead the successful charge to get Mbeki dismissed from office once a judge seemed to affirm these allegations in 2008.

In 1994 Mbeki might have won the leadership battle against Ramaphosa but he still was anxious about taking power in the fraught and unpredictable environment that was South Africa in the mid-1990s: He still believed that the forces of counterrevolution were ranged against him. His worldview was deeply conspiratorial: Throughout his years in office, he habitually accused his critics of being ultraleftist conspirators or counterrevolutionaries; if they were white, of being racist too. Any appreciation of how Thabo Mbeki came to power and how he would leave it—and of how he wielded it for the 15 years in between—must take into account his conviction that there have always been conspiracies deeply set against his ascendancy, reaching not only to the early 1990s and his struggles with Joe Slovo and Cyril Ramaphosa but into exile too, back to 1978 and the allegations that he was an enemy agent. Mbeki might have modernized the ANC with extraordinary vigor when it came to ideology and economic policy, but he would hold to the exile's understanding of politics—and the outlawed freedom fighter's experience of intrigue—throughout his years of power.

At his best, in his years in office, he would overcome this anxiety; at his worst, he would succumb to it and find himself drawn into intrigues more appropriate to an underground guerrilla movement fighting for its freedom than for a government now in control of Africa's largest economy. His lived understanding of power was that it was both gained and conceded through conspiracy. And so, unlike Nelson Mandela, who came to power riding a wave of extraordinarily positive sentiment and went into office utterly sure that he had the good wishes of his own supporters and political opponents alike, Mbeki's moment of liberation, in 1994, was far muddier, more compromised. On one hand, there was the shadow of Mandela himself to contend with; on the other, the worry that—even having been appointed the deputy president by Mandela—his position was by no means secure. He carried that anxiety, that heaviness, with him into power—a hunched, skeptical counterweight to the reconciliatory optimism of Mandela—and would never really be able to release it.

30

TRANSITION
THE BATTLE OVER
THE ECONOMY

On May 10, 1994, Thabo Mbeki stood beside Nelson Mandela and F. W. de Klerk in the amphitheater of the Union Buildings, taking the pledge of office with the world's eyes upon him. How could he not have felt triumphant as the might of the apartheid military machine saluted him? How could he not have felt vindicated, in his vision for South Africa, as Nelson Mandela grasped his hand and that of De Klerk and lifted them up into a double-V of victory before a wildly cheering crowd of tens of thousands gathered in the gardens below?

On a superficial level, the dream of liberation had been redeemed. "Let there be justice for all," Mandela could say in his inaugural address. "Let there be work, bread, water and salt for all. Let each know that for each the body, the mind and the soul have been freed to fulfill themselves. Never, never and never again shall it be that this beautiful land will again experience the oppression of one by another and suffer the indignity of being the skunk of the world. Let freedom reign. The sun shall never set on so glorious a human achievement! God bless Africa!"[1]

These were Mandela's finest words since his speech from the witness stand at the Rivonia trial in 1964. They were written by Thabo Mbeki. Seldom has Mbeki written as beautifully for himself as he has for others—and particularly for Mandela. One feels his own liberation from the constraints of struggle, his own embrace of the possibilities of freedom. And yet Mbeki's own public voice would become increasingly anxious once he gained office, and a strange dualism would emerge, as he scripted both roles in a complex call-and-response of rainbow-nation optimism and jeremiad anxiety. "We are free!" Mandela sang out loud. "Well, no, not yet..." responded a voice at the back of the room, laden with skepticism and doubt. It was Mbeki's task, self-assigned, to remind South Africans of the difficulties of the transition: the centuries of racism and white supremacy to be overcome; the recalcitrant civil service inherited; the severe skills deficit among those now in power; the constraints that the global economy imposed on South Africa. "What happens to a dream deferred?" he would ask, citing Langston Hughes, to make the point that "the repressed, hidden, disguised and barely recognised conflicts of our society" would erupt to the surface and "explode" if the expectations of the masses were not met.[2]

Mbeki was, in effect, South Africa's new prime minister. Mandela, the president, was remarkably hands-off, and saw himself as having one role alone: reconciliation. He paid little attention to matters of state beyond the maintenance of peace and security. The result, Mbeki told me, was that "the running of the government shifted to the deputy president's office.... Madiba [Mandela] didn't pay any attention to what government was doing. *We* had to, because *somebody* has to."

While the Mandela era was inspirational, it was also scattershot, as is evident in the statistics: In its first four years in office, the African National Congress government rolled over an average of about R11 billion a year—simply because it did not have the capacity to spend.[3] There was significant progress in the rollout of electricity, water, and roads, but land restitution and housing remained snagged, for years, in red tape. And the provision of key services—particularly education, health, policing, and justice—remained woefully behind the needs of the population. This was a consequence of the budget rollovers combined with the traumas of integrating the many disjointed apartheid services into an equitable whole, and the severe skills shortage in the new bureaucracy, exacerbated by the ill-advised decision—supported by Mbeki—to pay out any ancien régime personnel who wished leave.

Mbeki acknowledged many of these problems, and attempted to explain them. "We discovered many things we didn't know,..." he said in a *TIME* magazine interview in 1996, "and as a result some of our expectations about the pace of change had to be moderated. . . ."[4] The strain of this inability to deliver, for a new political elite whose entire identity was set on liberating their people and rectifying the injustices of the past, was enormous. It brought out, in Mbeki, a prickliness and defensiveness that took everyone—not least his previous admirers in the media—by surprise. Attending the Cape Press Club in August 1994, he accused the media of "harbouring a tendency to look for crises and to look for faults and mistakes"[5]—an allegation he would repeat and hone in the next few years. Such criticism was "quite normal when you are treating an apartheid government," he later said, but entirely inappropriate when dealing with a democratic one.[6]

Mbeki was soon branding any media criticism of the ANC as racist and any black journalists critical of the ANC as Uncle Toms. Thus began a vicious cycle of accusation and recrimination that spun, almost out of control at times, all the way through the Mbeki presidency. Mbeki felt stung by a media that had adulated him for so long, now that it took a critical approach to his own executive office. "Mr Fix-it turns to Mr Fluff it,"[7] blared the pro-ANC *Mail & Guardian* headline after a particularly bad run of political management by Mbeki in early 1995. At around the same time, Mbeki fell out with the organized business sector, his primary constituency in previous years: he blamed South African corporate executives for bad-mouthing the new government internationally, suggesting that this too was driven by racism.

How had the media darling turned, so quickly, into a media villain; the "favoured son" of the business community become its greatest antagonist? We have looked at the role that Mbeki's persona of "seducer" played in this: the morning-after hangover of betrayal and disappointment to which both Mbeki and his "conquests" awoke in the early 1990s, following their steamy safari sessions. Mbeki himself believes that the fallout was largely because his profile as "conciliator" changed abruptly. The reason why this happened, he told me, was that he and his comrades were required to make such an effort to reassure whites of their place in South Africa that they of necessity underplayed the inevitable changes that would have to happen. Mbeki became the bad cop who had to remind South Africans about the difficulties on the other side of the rainbow.

But it also had to do with Mbeki's insecurity—would he be able to do the job the world expected of him?—and his certainty that there were forces ranged against him, just waiting for him to trip up. It was an open secret, for example, that he had penned a paranoid anonymous ANC discussion document in mid-1994 that outlined an unholy alliance ranged against the new government, made up of ultraleftists, the old right wing, and liberals— particularly the white-owned media.[8] The document did not need to spell out that the beneficiary of such a conspiracy would be Cyril Ramaphosa— even more popular than ever as the head of the Constitutional Assembly and still a possible threat to Mbeki.

Fueling this paranoia was a profound change in the naturally diffident Mbeki's status. For 30 years, in exile, he had been the embodiment of a cause and the spokesman for a movement; he had laid claim to no subjectivity and was thus never personally accountable. Now, however, he was the elected representative of the people, accountable to them, and held up to a new kind of scrutiny by a robust and often-skeptical media. This put his personal life, and his personality, in the public eye as it never had been before—and, particularly in the chaotic way he ran his schedule and his office, he was often found wanting: he was often late, or did not show up for meetings. Always one who preferred to work, undetected, in the background, he struggled profoundly with the spotlight now trained on him; one that seemed to pick out all his flaws, even as it airbrushed out Mandela's.

When Mbeki and I spoke, in 2004, about his nightmares of "the dream deferred" during his first years in office, he reminded me of a statement that the then premier of Gauteng province, Tokyo Sexwale, had made in the mid-1990s: "We are in government, but we are not in power." Although Sexwale had been "quite unwise" to articulate this publicly, Mbeki said, "there is a sense in which it is true." Certainly "there was a sense of disempowerment" during those first years in office—and the primary example he gave of this was the way he and his government handled economic policy.

———————

Nelson Mandela came out of jail in 1990 an ardent supporter of nationalization. But by the time he became president four years later, he insisted that the ANC had been "cleansed" of any "single slogan that will connect us to any Marxist ideology."[9] Mbeki had been the key player in an intense effort—not only by members of the ANC's Department of Economic Policy (DEP) but also by old international friends of the anti-apartheid movement—to educate the released prisoner on the realities of the new global economy.

Mbeki, a trained economist, played no formal part in the development of ANC economic policy prior to 1994, although his international affairs portfolio and his relationship with the business world meant that he was usually the first contact for foreign bankers and global bureaucrats alike. With connections nurtured through years of diplomatic work, he was also the young DEP crew's entrée into the world of the international financial institutions. In this capacity, he led an ANC delegation to Washington to meet the World Bank and the International Monetary Fund (IMF) in 1992; he also arranged for many DEP staffers to be trained at Goldman Sachs in New York.

The DEP head, a young Coloured activist named Trevor Manuel, quickly became Mbeki's protégé; under Mbeki's tutorship, Manuel wrested ANC economic policy away from a group of illustrious left-wing London academics who advocated for a strong state role and inevitable deficit spending, and quietly set about writing a policy in accordance with the conventional wisdoms of the World Bank and the IMF—emphasizing a limited state and the encouragement of private sector growth. The DEP's approach was by no means secret, but its briefings were ill attended, and the only senior leader with the intellectual background to be able to follow the complex macroeconomic debates presented was Mbeki himself. Characteristically, Mbeki seemed to relish, and at times even safeguard, the DEP's obscurity: he too, after all, was somewhat marginalized during these years, and he worked quietly with Manuel and his team below the radar. Manuel was both an extraordinarily quick study and a powerfully persuasive politician: It did not take him long to win over his comrades in the DEP and to earn for them a kind of rogue pioneering status within the ANC. They were a Camelot, comrades brave enough to take on the high ground of international capital, trailblazing cowboys of reason and modernity. And their quiet guru was Thabo Mbeki.

By 1993 the ANC's attraction to market-friendly economic policies was manifest: Five months before it came to power, it signed a letter of intent with the IMF committing itself as the future government to a program of fiscal austerity in return for a $850 million loan for South Africa. But there was a fundamental incoherence to ANC policy: At the same time that this was happening, the movement unveiled its Reconstruction and Development Plan (RDP)—in effect, its election manifesto. Led by trade unionists and former United Democratic Front activists, the RDP attracted the iconic status of an updated and fleshed-out Freedom Charter, but its virtue was its failing: The product of popular consultative process, it was more the wish list of the "broad church" that was the ANC than the workable policy of a new government coming to power with enormous expectations on one hand and crippling debt on the other.

The perception of this incoherence, together with unfounded rumors that Mandela was dying, caused a currency crash in early 1996; one exacerbated by Trevor Manuel's appointment as finance minister following the resignation of Chris Liebenberg, a nonpartisan banker. Despite Manuel's conservative approach to economics, the market saw a black man, a former revolutionary, and it panicked. Manuel's solution was an emergency plan, called GEAR—the Growth, Employment and Redistribution program—developed in conjunction with academics and World Bank consultants. GEAR called for precisely the kind of fiscal discipline and investment-friendly tax incentives the international financial institutions believed in, but was in stark contrast to the redistributive RDP, which was soon rendered obsolete.

Mbeki was GEAR's godfather, and he and Manuel—supported by Mandela—advocated it with steely determination. One of the messages the new ANC government needed to get across was that, in an environment of heightened contestation, it was firmly in charge and that the communist tail no longer wagged the ANC dog. And so the policy was presented as a fait accompli; it was nonnegotiable. Knowing that GEAR would be unpopular, particularly to the ANC's left-wing allies, Mbeki made a point of giving Manuel political cover, introducing it in parliament and then goading critics at the press briefing afterward with the line, "Call me a Thatcherite!"[10] Mbeki insisted that there was no other way, and his defense of GEAR would bring out a belligerence in him never seen before: He would dismiss the policy's critics as ideological, puerile, irrational, mendacious, racist, and politically expedient. His identification with Thatcher was revealing: as with the Iron Lady—and as would be evidenced later by his determination to review the science of AIDS—he was willing to be a prophet in the wilderness, totally alone if he was convinced of the correctness of his position. By 1998 both he and Mandela were threatening to eject the Congress of South African Trade Unions (COSATU) from the ruling alliance if it continued to challenge GEAR.

Meanwhile, behind the scenes, Mbeki worked to bring key leaders of both COSATU and the South African Communist Party on board in a series of encounters that became known as the Under the Tree meetings—so named not just because they took place in the deputy president's leafy garden but because they invoked the style of traditional African consultative leadership to which Mbeki aspired but which had been so disregarded in the implementation of GEAR. The strategy was to identify key leftist leaders unhappy with GEAR and to bring them into personal and informal contact with Mbeki. Away from their constituencies and the need to project militancy, they might be swayed by his sweet reason. One of the participants, Kgalema Motlanthe, recalls that "Mbeki did the sums for us, he used logic to convince us, and it worked. Once I listened to him, my position changed. And I was not the only one."

Powerful new alliances were forged "Under the Tree": with Mbeki's patronage, Motlanthe would be elected ANC secretary-general. (But then, having become estranged from Mbeki, he would be elected deputy president on the "Zuma ticket" that defeated Mbeki in 2007, and would become South Africa's third democratic president once Mbeki was fired.) But on the whole, Mbeki's strategy backfired. By co-opting sympathetic individuals rather than engaging with their constituencies, he alienated these men from their mass base; and by excluding the more radical critics from his inner sanctum, he made lifelong enemies who would play the key role in his later downfall. And so, for example, while Mbeki won over Mbhazima Shilowa, the union leader, he ignored Zwelinzima Vavi, Shilowa's deputy, who had already carved a niche for himself as the radical counterpoint to his superior and who would replace Shilowa in 1999 on an anti-GEAR ticket.

Similarly in the SACP, where Mbeki formed a close bond with the general secretary, Charles Nqakula, the power shifted to a formation around the deputy chairman, Blade Nzimande, who ascended to the highest office, the position of general secretary, at the party's July 1998 congress. Like Vavi, Nzimande also rose on the wings of a more assertive identity for the SACP: GEAR, he said was "the most serious strategic threat to the National Democratic Revolution."[11] This enraged Mbeki, who let loose a public irascibility that would become one of his trademarks once in power, using carefully selected quotes from party discussion documents to accuse his critics of collusion with racist counterrevolutionaries determined to see African governments fail.[12] Rather than bringing angry young men like Nzimande and Vavi into the tent, he left them outside to freeze; this was in a strong counterpoint to the traditions of both Tambo and Mandela.

With Mandela's imprimatur, Mbeki would be elected, unopposed, as ANC president in 1997. But the damage was done: Vavi and Nzimande would become Mbeki's most persistent critics within the ANC alliance leadership and the architects of Jacob Zuma's victory against him in 2007. In the years to come, the left would come to see the government's embrace of GEAR as the turning point in the ANC's destiny, the final betrayal, by Mbeki and the middle-class values he represented, of its core constituency and its allegedly socialist legacy. GEAR would engender far more internal dissent than either Mbeki's AIDS skepticism or his "quiet diplomacy" in Zimbabwe. It would lead directly to the most serious schism the party had experienced in its century of existence—and would fuel the rebellion against Mbeki after he fired Zuma in 2005.

How was GEAR a primary example of the "disempowerment" the new ANC government felt upon coming to power? In 2004, Thabo Mbeki admitted to me that, in retrospect, the government's response to GEAR's leftist critics had been "pretty weak": "It would be easy to deal with it now, but then at that time, because of that sense of disempowerment—there were these forces that were buffeting you and all of this talk of foreign investors, there were certain things you had to do to place the economy on a particular footing...it was dictated [that] if you don't do them you are going to fail."

One of GEAR's most notorious failed promises was that South Africa would rapidly achieve a growth rate of 6 percent per annum, which would solve the country's unemployment crisis. In fact, the growth rate never exceeded 5 percent, and it was accompanied by increasing unemployment, well over 30 percent. "We repeated that statement," Mbeki said, "...because you sort of felt hemmed in by a world that demanded that certain things must be done." Now, in 2004, Mbeki felt he could say that the promise had been "incorrect": "You can have a 10 percent growth rate and it is not going to solve the problem of unemployment, because we have people who are unemployable.... You can say that now and nobody is going to say 'There they go, talking rubbish again.'... The government has greater confidence in its capacity to convince these people. It is not afraid of a confrontation now."

But it did seem, in the late 1990s, that the ANC government actually wanted a confrontation; that it was taking a hard line over GEAR so as to project a confidence it did not really possess and thus demonstrate that it was up to the job of governing. In that era, the ghost of Latin America loomed large, specifically the "macroeconomic populism" of rulers who had spent their economies into ruin in an effort to make good on their election promises. Even though they would never say it, Mbeki and Manuel saw the RDP as the thin edge of the wedge of this kind of populism, and they used the economic crisis of 1996 as a form of exogenous shock, perhaps even exaggerating the dangers of the crisis so as to force the fiscal austerity and macroeconomic balance they believed essential for maintaining South Africa's sovereignty. Viewed this way, GEAR and the heat it generated were the consequences not only of the economic crisis of 1996 but also of the deep divisions within the

ANC itself and the party's inability to reach consensus regarding economic policy; divisions that remain unresolved.

Seen this way, the conflict was inevitable, a fracture not just between "leftists" and "centrists" or—as the left would have it—between the workers and the new bosses, but between those whose job it now was to run the state and those whose job it remained to represent the people. GEAR heralded the end to the experiment of participatory democracy with which Mandela came to power, and its replacement by a new hegemony—the grabbing hold of the reins of state by an ANC now in government rather than fighting for freedom.

Out of this conflict grew two competing narratives, both emanating from within the ANC alliance itself. The first of these pitted an elite vanguard of forward-thinking modernizers against the appetites of global capital, the recalcitrance of an inherited public service, and the easy populism of rabble-rousers who did not understand the complexity of the global economy. It was the kind of story by which Thabo Mbeki defined himself, a story that claimed to redeem the lost legacies of Africa's *uhuru* generation. The opposing narrative saw the ANC government as the betrayal, rather than the redemption, of such legacies; it was a tale of weakness and cowardice at best and venality at worst. This is the *impimpi* [sellout] story we know from the ANC's days of exile. The purveyors of this story were convinced that the ANC leadership had betrayed its own constituency through a Faustian neocolonial pact with the private sector, and justified their pessimism with often credible indicators of social dysfunction and increasing human distress. Its punch line, usually implied but increasingly explicit, was that the South African majority was worse off, under an Mbeki-led ANC government, than it had been before.

The hero and the *impimpi* are the two archetypes by which the freedom fighter defines an identity. And so, while these two competing narratives of the South African transition might have had recourse to the empirical data of social research, they were also rooted in the soil of myth; they were thus impossible to adjudicate as they pitted indicators of progress and regress against each other. One side would trumpet the two million houses that the government built in its first ten years; the other would counter with the backlog of housing needs that still exists. One side would praise the achievements of social welfare grants introduced by the ANC government upon which 12 million people would depend by 2008; the other would decry the absence of a basic income grant. Statistics became chimerical, and the subjects of all this contention—the people of South Africa themselves—tended to get lost in the haze. For every fired worker that COSATU dug up, the government would parade a proud new homeowner who no longer had to walk 12 miles a day to fetch clean water; for every distressed shack-dweller the social movements claimed to represent, the ANC would exhibit a passionate comrade, enthusiastically going to the polls to return Mbeki with an ever-increasing majority.

The conundrum of the South African politics of the transition was that these two subjects were usually the same person, increasingly disaffected and increasingly loyal to the ANC at the same time. The Mbeki government broadcast polls showing high approval ratings and seemingly limitless patience with the slowness of social transformation; the left warned that even the most patient subject had his limits, and that—as Mbeki himself once had warned—the dream deferred would inevitably explode. There cannot be many places in the world where a bottom line was so contested—by people, no less, who shared the same struggle mythology and were in the same party. How did the apparent consensus of the moment of liberation evaporate so quickly? Perhaps it was a function of the fungible 1990s, where everything seemed possible yet nothing was certain. The ANC government could come to power with its expansionary RDP in 1994 and dump it two years later in favor of GEAR. It could put into place labor market regulations to rival the most socialist of economies and, at the same time, tariff reform in line with the most capitalist: The impossible goal of "national reconciliation" was, precisely, to be all things to all people. But this meant a perpetual balancing of constituencies, a crisis-driven administration that moved from day to day by staving off challenges—now of investment strikes from the right, now of labor strikes from the left—that threatened to bring the whole fragile edifice of the new democracy tumbling down. And so, because of the illegitimacy of the previous regime on one hand and the allure of popular democracy on the other, the Mandela government, lacking confidence anyway, found itself at the center of a hegemonic struggle for influence, one it struggled to withstand.

If the leftist critique of Mbeki and the ANC is to be believed, what was going on was nothing less than a "battle for the soul of the ANC," waged by the agents of global capital: seducing party leaders with snazzy "scenario planning" exercises and an endless round of Washington freebies and glamorous cocktail parties while at the same time warning them direly of the consequences if the ANC did not reform. Seen this way, GEAR was "a culmination" of the liberation movement's "moral surrender" to the market: The party's neophyte economists had been "force-fed a neoliberal agenda" by the World Bank and the IMF, and the multiparty talks were, in the end, less significant than the offstage negotiations happening between the ANC and agents of global capital.[13]

To counter this, Joel Netshitenzhe—Mbeki's head of policy—wrote in 2004 that "the art and science of governance is essentially about weighing trade-offs and making choices. With a budget deficit close to ten per cent and the country a debt trap, the choice was either to borrow more and end up, begging bowl in hand, at the IMF and World Bank, or to reduce the budget deficit while reprioritizing expenditure in order to ensure sustainable development. The government chose the latter." GEAR was thus "a structural adjustment policy, self-imposed, to stabilise the macro-economic situation."[14] There is more than a little revisionist spin to this, but the sentiment is clear: For its architects and political managers, GEAR was a means toward self-reliance rather than a capitulation to old colonial masters. It was driven by the ANC's fear that it would land up pawning South Africa's independence by borrowing from the IMF and the World Bank to service its debt.

As much as his other flagship policies, such as black economic empowerment and the New Partnership for Africa's Development, then, GEAR is a product of Mbeki's New Africanism. Its wellspring is the ethos of self-reliance and autonomy we have tracked in him since his youth: the need to redeem the dream, the promises made by the generation of Nyerere and Nkrumah but shattered by three decades of neocolonialism, that Africans would do it by themselves. And yet the left saw GEAR as exactly the opposite. As Mbhazima Shilowa put it, before he was converted to the cause: "We are in danger of relinquishing our national sovereignty in the sphere of economic decision-making and sacrificing it on the altar of profit."[15]

Here, then, is the irony of GEAR: The left might have accused Mbeki of selling out to the agendas of international capital, but the reason why he embraced the policy with such fervor in the first place was precisely because he was following his lodestar of self-reliance—an amulet, perhaps, against the pain and disempowerment, the paradoxical relinquishing of agency, that characterized the transition. Third World basket cases slide, as if programmed, into neocolonial debt; Mbeki was determined to prove to the mandarins of global capitalism that Africans could play them at their own game and compete within a modern, global economy without becoming indebted to them. Weaned on Marxist theory and raised by a movement that believed it could shape the destiny of its people, he was never entirely comfortable with the underpinnings of GEAR; this is evidenced by the way he did not pursue structural reform, such as privatization, as vigorously as he might have. But—the son of struggling black traders—he was determined to survive independent of white creditors or paymasters. He would do anything to avoid hocking the shop.

31

THE ARMS DEAL
SOUTH AFRICA'S POISONED WELL

While Thabo Mbeki was strong-arming the South African economy away from state spending and toward fiscal austerity, he presided over a parallel process that did exactly the opposite. From 1996 to 1999, he chaired a cabinet subcommittee that commissioned the purchase of R30 billion worth of armaments—specifically, submarines and frigates—from a French-German consortium and fighter-jets from a British-Swedish one. The "arms deal," as it became known, eventually cost the South African taxpayers almost double that figure.[1] It also mired the African National Congress government, just when it was reestablishing moral rule in South Africa, in an interminable bog of messy corruption scandals and investigations. This would result in Mbeki's firing of Jacob Zuma in 2005, in charges of fraud and corruption laid against Zuma that same year, and in a savage judicial indictment of Mbeki himself, when a judge ruled that Zuma had been unfairly treated and suggested that the president had criminally impeded justice by tampering with the investigation. Although this judgment would be later overturned on appeal, it led to Mbeki's own ignominious forced resignation in September 2008.

But the irony is that if the arms deal became the poisoned well of post-apartheid South African politics, then it was Mbeki himself who initially contaminated the water—even if this was done with the best of intentions. He championed the deal from the outset, with an ardor quite remarkable in one so skeptical of military expansionism during his own time as a freedom fighter. And as the allegations multiplied, he became increasingly strident in his defense of it. He repeatedly said that while there might have been impropriety in secondary contracts arising out of the arms deal, his government should shoulder no blame for that, as it was not responsible for those contracts. He also insisted, on the basis of an investigation commissioned by parliament, that there was no evidence of misdemeanor in the primary contracts for which the government was responsible.[2]

But according to the senior ANC parliamentarian involved in commissioning this investigation, it was a shameful whitewash. In his 2007 memoir, Andrew Feinstein makes two explosive claims: that a senior cabinet minister told him to drop his call for the investigation because the ANC itself had benefited directly from the arms deal, and that investigators found proof that the defense minister, Joe Modise, was corrupt, but were instructed to bury it. Feinstein also rebuts, convincingly, Mbeki's claim that the government had nothing to do with secondary contracts.[3]

Feinstein's own story exemplifies the political turbulence generated by the arms deal. The ranking ANC member on the parliamentary Select Committee on Public Accounts (SCOPA), he had played a key role in the committee's efforts to unravel the allegations of corruption related to the deal. But when he tried to appoint the crusading anticorruption judge, Willem Heath, to a multiagency investigation of the deal, he found himself up against Mbeki, who refused to accept Heath, claiming the judge had an antigovernment bias. The ANC effectively declawed SCOPA, forcing Feinstein to quit parliament in 2001 in a move that was a death knell for parliamentary oversight and rendered the legislature little more than a rubber stamp for Mbeki's executive office.

Mbeki's response to the sustained criticism of the arms deal has been to allege a conspiracy, powered by the media, "determined to prove everything in the anti-African stereotype"—"that Africans, who now govern our country, are naturally prone to corruption, venality and mismanagement."[4] Was he protesting too much? Fueled by the political rivalry between himself and Zuma, the allegations surrounding the arms deal did not go away. When Mbeki fired Zuma after the latter's financial advisor was found guilty of bribing him to secure a secondary contract related to the deal, Zuma's response was that people wishing to know about corruption in the arms deal needed to ask Mbeki himself, since he had run the process.[5] It was certainly true that Mbeki was at the center of the deal: He had played the key role, for example, in overturning a prior deal to buy Spanish ships—a deal the navy wanted—in favor of far more expensive German ships. By despite several allegations of impropriety against him, there was never any hard evidence that Mbeki himself had been involved in corruption.

But even if he was not corrupt himself, and even if he was right that there was no evidence of any government corruption in the deal, the political wisdom of embarking upon it remains questionable: first, because it cast "long shadows,"[6] as Mbeki himself put it, over a new and idealistic government, given the very nature of arms procurement; second, because in an era with such high expectations for socioeconomic transformation and the simultaneous need to tighten belts, it was bound to attract scrutiny and opprobrium. Did Mbeki really believe that a righteous ANC would be able to do clean business in so notoriously insalubrious a marketplace as the arms trade?

Those close to him say that he understood the risks but decided that they needed to be taken anyway.

In the beginning, the ANC government seemed ill disposed to spending money on arms: Mandela projected himself as a "butter" president rather than a "guns" one. And, particularly given his own nonmilitary profile, there was no reason to believe that Mbeki himself would be any different.

Yet the reality of the ANC's inheritance countered such righteous aspiration. Suddenly the Mandela government found itself responsible not only for a voracious defense force suffering from serious fatigue—in terms of both morale and hardware—but for integrating the demobilized liberation movement armies into it. Even before 1994, the generals had made it clear to their political masters that their ongoing quiescence was dependent on the upgrading of the force. While Joe Slovo—the old hawk—argued that "South Africa's greatest defence will be a satisfied population" and that the budget would be better spent on social services,[7] Mbeki—the old dove—insisted that the South African military would be obsolete in a decade if action was not taken immediately. In the end, Mbeki led his cabinet subcommittee toward inflating the defense acquisition budget from R8 billion (a figure to which the military brass themselves had willingly assented in 1995) up to the R30 billion announced in 2000.

What had happened to convince Mbeki to do this, at the very time he was leading the government's austerity campaign? One compelling argument was around "offsets," a form of legal bribery: The bidders offered to invest in the economy to the tune of R104 billion if their bids were successful. Particularly in the context of South Africa's inability to attract any other direct investment, the trade and industry minister Alec Erwin persuaded Mbeki that this was one way out of South Africa's economic crisis. But the government was forced to admit in 2006 that only 13,000 of the promised 65,000 thousand jobs had materialized.[8] In the end, arms companies seemed to find it cheaper to be fined for noncompliance than to deliver on their promises.

Mbeki and his committee were fully apprised of these risks. When Mbeki was presented with an economic affordability report in 1999, he shrugged off its pessimistic scenarios and told his officials that government had no choice but to risk it, given South Africa's continental obligations. To make his point, he quoted the French president Jacques Chirac, whom he had recently seen and who had sneered, "Why can't you [Africans] sort out your own problems?" It was in this context, Mbeki said, that South Africa needed a modern, state-of-the-art military.

The offsets argument might have tipped the scales toward the more expensive German and British deals for Mbeki, but it was not the clincher.

Far more significant was his ideological commitment to African self-determination and his promotion of South Africa as a continental powerhouse influential enough to keep the peace in a restive neighborhood. South Africa had to prove to a skeptical world that it was a big enough player to do the kind of high-level trade implied by the arms deal and that it was a reliable friend to the North Atlantic Treaty Organization countries from which it planned to make the purchases. It also had to amass the firepower to warrant being respected, as the region's giant, by both its neighbors and the global community. This was the cornerstone argument of Mbeki's African Renaissance: South Africa's own growth and development was not possible on a decaying, conflict-ridden continent, and so investment in the neighborhood must be an essential component of the country's own growth strategy.

But the "regional peacekeeper" argument has clear holes: What good would frigates do, after all, keeping the peace in landlocked Darfur? And the fighter-jets South Africa bought were far better suited to conventional military activity than to peacekeeping functions. The very nature of the hardware acquired by South Africa in the arms deal suggests that forces other than the country's desire to keep the regional peace were at play in Mbeki's cabinet subcommittee on defense acquisition.

To understand the pull of upgrading the defense force among the ANC's leaders, we need to return to May 10, 1994, the day of the inauguration of Nelson Mandela and Thabo Mbeki, with its signal moment heralding the transfer of power: the old apartheid army saluting its new commanders in chief as the Impala fighter-jets swooped low over the Union Buildings, literally raising the hair on the backs of the necks of South Africa's new leaders with the revelation, "Oh my Lord, those are ours now!" The sovereignty of the modern nation-state resides as much in its ability to defend itself against aggressors, real or perceived, as in its monetary currency, its heraldry, or its national language. How much more so this must have been for the ANC, given both its own martial history and the sheer weight of the hardware it was inheriting—not to mention the expectations of the men who operated it.

Mbeki's own particular history in the martial ANC must figure in this equation. Despite his Soviet military training, he was never fully accepted as a military man, and he was always skeptical about the possibilities of armed struggle. He was, instead, the "black Englishman," the softie. His insistence on a negotiated settlement was viewed by many ANC soldiers as a function of cowardice rather than of savvy.

But one could not lead the ANC in exile if one did not have the support of the military. And in this respect, the patronage of one man played an indispensable role in Mbeki's ascendancy: Joe Modise, the head of Umkhonto we Sizwe (MK), the ANC army. Modise had long been an ardent defender of Mbeki and was key to his rise to power. Now, in his role as the ANC government's first defense minister, Modise became the most passionate advocate for upgrading the defense force, and he found a willing patron in Mbeki. Was this a function of Mbeki's debt to a corrupt man, or his own insecurity with the hard men of war? He knew he would one day be commanding the generals himself: Could he be certain of their loyalty, or would it have to be earned, by showing his commitment to their defense force in the way that military heroes such as Slovo might not have needed to?

Modise told me that the vulnerability Mbeki was concerned with was not so much his own as that of the fragile new democracy: "Thabo and I understood something that maybe others didn't, because of our dealings with the generals [during negotiations]. We could not be sure in those first years of their absolute loyalty." Mbeki himself is adamant that such considerations had nothing at all to do with the decisions of his cabinet subcommittee, but Alec Erwin told me about a meeting at the deputy president's Cape Town residence, where Mbeki said—as Erwin recollects it—that "a discontented, uninspired military is dangerous. If you don't reequip this defence force then it starts disintegrating, and...you've got a lot of discontented soldiers who feel they are not part and parcel of the future, and that they are being ignored."

Mbeki claims that his commitment to arms procurement was motivated primarily by the government's constitutional obligation to maintain the integrity of the country's defense force. Certainly, too, it was driven by his sense of continental responsibility (or aspiration) and by his anxieties about the lack of investment in South Africa. But it was also driven by Mbeki's assessment that the security Mbeki was buying South Africa with a R30 billion price tag was not from external aggressors but against the internal threat of a disaffected military, still skeptical—on both sides—about the negotiated settlement and still carrying, in its increasingly obsolete arsenal, the serious threat of destabilization. On top of all this there was the emotional pressure of the transition. If, indeed, the ANC was "in government but not in power" through the 1990s, what better remedy to the feeling of disempowerment than by the oldest means available to a state: might? Thus did the ANC government come to make a decision that would haunt it for years to come, the consequences of which would be described, by the judge who threw the Zuma case out of court in 2008, as "a cancer that is devouring the body politic and the reputation for integrity built up so assiduously after the fall of apartheid."[9]

32

MANDELA AND MBEKI

"ONE GOOD NATIVE"

"**M**adiba," Thabo Mbeki said as he stepped up to the podium to accept the mantle of African National Congress president from Nelson Mandela at the party's conference in Mafikeng in December 1997, "members of the press have been asking me how it feels to step into your shoes. I've been saying I would never be seen dead in such shoes. You wear such ugly shoes!"[1] At that moment of gravity—a moment on which Mbeki's entire career had been focused—he was betrayed, momentarily, by the schoolboy in him, by the awkward braggadocio of someone whose performance is measured, perpetually, against the stature of a father figure and who now needs to make his own way.

Mandela had just praised his "brilliant" successor but offered him a public warning too: "One of the temptations of a leader who has been elected unopposed is that he may use his powerful position to settle scores with his detractors, marginalise them, and in certain cases, get rid of them and surround himself with yes-men and -women." You could not "keep the forces together" if you did not "allow dissent," Mandela counseled. "[P]eople should even be able to criticise the leader without fear or favour." The comment was vintage Mandela: By assuring the delegates that he knew Mbeki was not "going to sideline anyone," he was simultaneously calming fears and warning his successor publicly that these fears existed and needed to be addressed.[2] Mandela knew, of course, that many of Mbeki's comrades remained troubled by the high-handed way in which he had managed the debate over economic policy, and in what they perceived to be the underhanded way he had dispatched potential opponents.

Mandela's decision to step down was unparalleled on the African continent and signaled his determination to counter that blight on postcolonial Africa, the ruler-for-life syndrome. By retiring in this way, Mandela entrenched the overriding legacy of his presidency as a country that not only beat the odds on racial and ethnic conflict but that entrenched the rule of law in an unassailable bill of rights. These feats alone guarantee Nelson Mandela his sanctity: He goes down in history as the man who, like Martin Luther King before him, gave the world a dream. But he was a far better liberator and nation-builder than he was a governor, and so in contrast, Mbeki marketed himself as the technocratic, truth-telling antidote to the madness and the magic—the scattershot celebrity—of the Mandela era.

A key difference between the two was Mbeki's eschewal of a kind of African paternalism that prevailed in the ANC despite its progressive political traditions. "O. R. [Tambo] was a daddy," a prominent member of the ANC said to me. "It's like that with Madiba too. He makes it his business to know the names of your wife and children and to ask after them, even if he has never met them. Thabo doesn't do that. And so, among some comrades, there might be complaints that he doesn't invite people to sit and talk, 'under the tree,' like the old African patriarch." People obeyed Mandela because they loved him, because he was their benevolent father; Mbeki could never command allegiance from such a wellspring, so he needed to earn it elsewhere: People had to respect him, even fear him. If Mandela, the patriarch, loved his people despite their many flaws, Mbeki required them to prove themselves to him. If Mandela had been a passionate player, Mbeki would take on the role of skeptical and rather aloof observer.

And so if, during his presidency, Mbeki lacked the noblesse oblige of a chief, of a Mandela, it was because he was *not* a chief. He was of the nose-to-the-grindstone middle class. Whereas the aristocratic Mandela had grace, the bourgeois Mbeki deployed charm. Mandela was the chief whom everyone called "Tata" (father); Mbeki the commoner whom everyone called "chief." Mbeki demonstrated that peculiarly middle-class ego: the prove-yourself impulse. As with Mandela, leadership was expected of Mbeki, but it was understood that such destiny would come about only through application and service. Perhaps this explains Mbeki's youthful diligence as opposed to Mandela's own hotheaded rebellion (he fled his destiny and an arranged marriage for the delights of the big city and a career in law). "Xhosa custom, ritual and taboo were the alpha and omega of our existence, and they went unquestioned," Mandela has written[3]; even when rebelled against, they were a touchstone. Mbeki, raised to question everything, landed with the critical identity of the perennial exile: that "disconnect" from his roots. His was a deficit-driven leadership, insofar as it sought to make whole that which was incomplete, both in himself and in the world.

But even if Nelson Mandela and Thabo Mbeki did not find, in each other, some imagined political father and son—or even, more simply, a comfortable intimacy—they developed an effective working relationship in office together. This is evident in the way Mandela handed over so much of the detail of governance to his deputy and in their agreement on the key issues: most notably on economic policy. Mbeki, however, often felt that Mandela treated him like an apprentice, even as he delegated the actual management of the state to him. He expressed particular annoyance, for example, at the way Mandela deemed it necessary to take him abroad and introduce him to the world's leaders following the Mafikeng conference: "I don't need *him* to expose me to the world," he complained. It was he, after all, who had first introduced Mandela globally after the latter's release from Robben Island. Mbeki, intensely private, also sometimes bristled at Mandela's paternalism: his belief that, as the elder of his political family, it was his duty to intervene in the personal lives of his subordinates. This was not the mere meddling of an old busybody; it was the practice of a political art, and many younger comrades adored him for it. But Mbeki did not like the overweening interest Mandela showed in his personal affairs in the early 1990s, particularly regarding his marriage. "Thabo felt he was being patronized," one friend told me. "He felt he could handle his own affairs."

Mbeki wished to be nobody's father, and nobody's son either. And yet here was the paradox. Despite all his bucking against the paternal style of leadership that Nelson Mandela represented, one cannot dismiss the effects of his own upbringing within the ANC: the replacement of his biological family with a political one, and thus the way he vacillated between the understanding of the ANC as a family on one hand and the ruling party of a modern economy on the other. If competence is the driving characteristic of a modern economy, then loyalty is the defining characteristic of a family, and Mbeki often appeared to value the latter over the former. This internal conflict between atavistic patriarch and rational manager would be manifest in the way he kept some spectacularly inept people in office, such as health minister Manto Tshabalala-Msimang, and in the way he handled the firing of Jacob Zuma in 2005.

At the core of the difficulty between Mandela and Mbeki was—unsurprisingly, given the "ugly shoes" dynamic—the issue of reputation. Given that Mbeki had been the ANC's ranking diplomat for so many years, it was perhaps inevitable too that this difficulty would begin to play itself out in the field of foreign affairs. The first major clash came in late 1995, when Nigerian dictator Sani Abacha arrested writer Ken Saro-Wiwa and eight other environmental activists. A global campaign was launched to save them, on a scale reminiscent of the "free Mandela" campaigns of a previous era, and it seemed that the South African president was the only person with the authority to shame Abacha into changing course. The pressure on Mandela was intense, but Mbeki had sold him on a "softly-softly" approach, convincing his boss that he had an inside track to the dictator and that, whatever might be said in private, it was imperative to demonstrate African solidarity in public. Through Mbeki's back channels (set up via the contacts he had made when he was posted to Nigeria), Abacha promised not to execute Saro-Wiwa and his codefendants.

But in November 1995 Abacha went back on his word, and had the man killed. Mandela, livid, called a press conference to say that South Africa would lead the world in isolating Nigeria from all international organizations. By doing so he might have redeemed his reputation as the world's moral icon, but Mbeki, who had pleaded with him not to take a stand, was extremely irritated by what he saw as his boss's impetuousness: It shut down the line to Abacha and any further influence the South Africans might have had. Mbeki argued for realpolitik against Mandela's idealism and won—Mandela backed down—but many within the ANC and internationally were distressed by what they saw as Mbeki's hypocrisy. He seemed to be advocating precisely the kind of "constructive engagement" with tyranny that he had once so effectively slammed with respect to apartheid South Africa. (In the end, South African influence made little difference: The Nigerian nightmare would end only with Abacha's suspicious death, allegedly by poison, two and a half years later.)

The Abacha debacle provides a blueprint for Mbeki's later approach to Robert Mugabe. In Nigeria in 1995, as in Zimbabwe five years later, Mbeki worked off the belief that the West's condemnation of African tyranny was driven by we-told-you-so racism and neocolonial meddling rather than any real concern for the subjects of such tyranny. He also seemed to believe that any public criticism of an Abacha or a Mugabe would play into the racist belief that Africans were unfit to rule themselves. He said as much publicly, in the midst of the Abacha controversy: "Many in our society genuinely believe that as black people we have no capacity to govern successfully, much less manage a modern and sophisticated economy. These are very quick to repeat the nauseating refrain—look what has happened in the rest of Africa!"[4]

At around this time, one of Mbeki's white staffers remembers referring, in passing, to Abacha as a dictator. Mbeki exploded: "How do you know he's a dictator? Do you know him? Have you ever met him? Well, I have, and I don't think he is a dictator." What Mbeki seemed to be taking exception to, Mbeki's interlocutor told me, "was a white man calling a black leader a dictator. If a white calls a black a dictator, he's saying that blacks can't rule...and by extension that he, Mbeki, is not up to the job of taking over from Mandela."

Mbeki called this attitude "Mandela exceptionalism" when he was being polite; the "one good native" syndrome when he was not. The argument went like this: Africa was irredeemable, and Mandela was the only good leader ever to come out of it; once he left office, South Africa would sink like the rest of the continent into the mire of corruption and decay, as Nigeria had. It seemed to Mbeki that Mandela was actually colluding in the world's impression that he was the "one good native," the consequence of which was the perception that all other black leaders—Mbeki foremost—were incompetent. Mbeki believed that Mandela's complicity in this syndrome came from the way he sent the message to white South Africans that nothing was going to change: Mandela's mantra of "national reconciliation" had become debased into meaning nothing more than "maintaining the status quo." This accommodation had its roots in Mbeki's own analysis that reassuring white South Africans was the key to assuming power. But now, on the other side of freedom, Mbeki felt it was necessary to begin articulating the truth that reconciliation was "unrealizable" unless it was "accompanied by the fundamental transformation of the entire social-economic fabric of our society."[5] This line, which he repeated in one way or another almost every time he spoke, began to be seen as a deviation from Mandela-style "national reconciliation."

Mandela had set the tone for his presidency with two extraordinary lines, delivered spontaneously in Afrikaans to the crowds at his 1994 inauguration: *"Laat ons die verlede vergeet! Wat verby is verby!"* (Let us forget the past! What's done is done!)[6] There was no reason to believe, at the time, that his new deputy thought any differently. In fact, when asked for comment at the voting booth a few days earlier, Mbeki had said: "Something new and good is being born, and it makes it possible to forget all those bad things that happened to us in the past."[7] But, five years later, Mbeki's rhetoric was very different: "When one walks around this country, one finds that the legacy of apartheid still sits on our shoulders," he said on the campaign trail in 1999. "The memory of apartheid is fading and perhaps there is too much forgiveness. I think we *should* be angry about our history of enslavement of our people, about colonisation, and angry about apartheid."[8]

Mbeki's change in tone was understandable: Five years into freedom, inequality had not evaporated, and he felt hamstrung in his ability to do anything about it. But his hardened language—his belief that South Africans should face into the legacy of their difficult history and not bury their heads in the sand—was also a function of his own battle to grow a discrete political identity within the deep shade of Mandela's profile as the universal icon of forgiveness and reconciliation. When I asked Mbeki about his differences with Mandela while in office, he conceded only one real problem: conflicting approaches to racial reconciliation. Mbeki felt that Mandela's approach to the issue negatively affected his own acceptability as his successor and thus his ability to effect real transformation. South Africa just could not "sustain a view of national reconciliation of the kind of which the media approved" and with which "Madiba cooperated," he told me. I have seldom seen Mbeki as exercised, or as impassioned, as when he spoke about this: "You just couldn't do it! It was wrong! Just wrong!"

Mandela's staff—all of whom were handpicked by Mbeki—felt strongly that they needed to use the personage of Mandela "to consolidate national unity," as his director-general (chief of staff) Jakes Gerwel put it to me. Mbeki argued fervently with them that by so doing they were perpetuating the "one good native" syndrome, but "they wouldn't listen to me, until the matter came to a head" in February 1996, just a few weeks after the Saro-Wiwa affair, when the rand crashed on the back of an unfounded rumor that Mandela was dying. The South African *Sunday Times*, the country's largest paper, wrote that the collapse of the rand was "a reminder" that Mandela's "extraordinary stature as a peacemaker and conciliator remains the pivot of international confidence in our future," and that Thabo Mbeki was not up to the job of maintaining Mandela's legacy: "He simply does not inspire confidence.... Where Mr Mandela projects warmth of spirit and generosity, Mr Mbeki appears manipulative and calculating.... Where Mr Mandela inspires affection, even love, Mr Mbeki evokes uncertainty and fear." Certainly, "these perceptions may not be fair," but "markets are as ruthless in passing judgement as they are swift, and the idea that Mr Mandela may be replaced by Mr Mbeki inspires great nervousness."[9] There it was, in black and white, in newspapers being opened up across South Africa on the morning of February 18, 1996: Thabo Mbeki was personally responsible for the fact that the South African currency had gone into free fall. And the reason was simple: He was a black man who was not Nelson Mandela.

Mbeki insisted that Mandela himself respond, and the following week a piece was published under Mandela's name, entitled "Don't praise me to damn the rest," which demanded of the world to cease its duet of "hero-worshipping" him and "denigrating" Mbeki.[10] Referring to the issue a few years later, Mbeki wrote about how "the cynics and the sceptics...tried to scare the people about their future...pretending that President Mandela, with his 'magic,' was the only person capable of guaranteeing the better future for our country."[11] In reaction, Mbeki fixed his political psyche on two things: first, that, despite national reconciliation, whites were still racist in that they did not believe that blacks were equal to the task of running South Africa; second, that he would prove them wrong.

The differences between Mandela and Mbeki over how to deal with the past finally erupted over the report of Archbishop Desmond Tutu's Truth and Reconciliation Commission (TRC) in late 1998. As president of the country, Mandela accepted the report when it was submitted to him. But as the new head of the ANC, Mbeki decided to challenge it legally, his primary objection being the way the report had found the ANC guilty of gross violations of human rights for its treatment of detainees in its Angolan camps in the mid-1980s: It was "scurrilous," Mbeki said, to equate the ANC's excesses with those of the apartheid oppressor. But Mbeki's appeal failed, and Tutu responded angrily: "Yesterday's oppressed can quite easily become today's oppressors," he said in a radio interview.[12] Mbeki retaliated by accusing Tutu himself of the crime of Mandela exceptionalism; of being full of "dark foreboding about a future without President Mandela," in which "national reconciliation, tolerance and liberty" would be in "grave danger" now that "tyrants-in-waiting" were poised to take over.[13]

Mbeki had initially been a great proponent of the TRC and of its fundamental principle of even-handedness. In 1993 he had even said that if "the ANC was responsible for violations of human rights," then "we need to air the truth."[14] There were two reasons for his change of heart: his growing conviction that South Africa was using "reconciliation" to bypass the "truth" of its deep-seated economic inequality and his feeling that the principle of even-handedness, once applied, demeaned the righteousness of those who had fought for freedom. But why, then, did he simply not say that he disagreed with some aspects of the report and leave it at that? Why did he go so far as to try to prevent its publication with a legal suit? Joel Netshitenzhe, one of Mbeki's closest aides, is convinced that Mbeki "fully understood the impact" of the decision to go to court, "but decided that he wanted to fight the battle anyway," seeking controversy over the TRC report because he felt he needed to put his own, post-Mandela imprimatur on an ANC that would be driven by the imperatives of transformation rather than reconciliation. Mbeki needed, most of all, to show the constituency that was about to elect him in the 1999 polls that he was no longer the "black Englishman," the moderate, the softie. Even if he was not a fighting man himself, he more than anyone would defend the honor of those who carried arms in struggle, of those who had had to cross difficult moral territory to deliver their people from bondage.

Mbeki was elected unopposed as ANC president in 1997 for several reasons: his skill at playing the party machine; the fact that Cyril Ramaphosa backed off at the last minute; and in large part because Mandela decided that he needed to be supported at all costs, in the interests of a stable transition—this despite Mbeki's concern that Mandela was undermining him. Mbeki was the "de facto ruler" of South Africa, Mandela said in London in July 1997: "I am shifting everything to him."[15]

In 1999, Mbeki led the ANC in a well-funded and efficient general election campaign, in which he adhered to one of his favorite dicta, Amilcar Cabral's "tell no lies, claim no easy victories." Mbeki offered up a cool, non-triumphalist appreciation of the successes and failures of the first five years of democracy, and the electorate seemed to respond. The contrast with Mandela was profound, and instructive. When Mandela had entered a room while on the stump, people had swooned; they wept and sang. So bathed in the patriarch's sanctity and love had they been that they were often rendered speechless. Mandela's encounters with ordinary people had been passionate, moving—and often incoherent. Now Mbeki seemed to have the opposite effect: A slight man, he entered quietly and spoke softly. His presence might not have been charged with emotion, but it encouraged speech and demanded reason.

Mbeki was rewarded with a landslide—and increased the ANC share of the poll from the 62.6 percent Mandela earned in 1994, to 66.4 percent. But at the party's victory celebrations, he was almost willfully out of tune with his jubilant supporters: there was no wife at his side, no rah-rah, no triumphalism, just a clear recapitulation of his policies and a sober, authoritative confidence. The message, once more, was clear: The emotional era of "Madiba magic" was over, to be superseded by workmanlike technocracy. Mbeki's final lines were carefully chosen: "Go back to work."

From 1994 to 1999, a dynamic had developed between the image of Mandela and that of Mbeki. The impression of ease and openness that Mandela projected, coupled with his willingness to reconcile and the love that he inspired, came to be seen as evidence of his commitment to democracy; an impression underscored, of course, by his decision not to run for a second term. And so the converse was assumed to be true: Mbeki's backroom ways, coupled with his unwillingness to absolve white South Africans of their guilt, became evidence not just of his racism but of his Stalinism too. This was unfair to Mbeki, who nonetheless allowed it to become a self-fulfilling prophecy, through the prickly way he responded, either directly or through the party machine, to criticism, and consequently in the mounting feeling of many in the "broad church" of the former liberation movement that their advancement was limited if they did not toe the line.

Now, having won power, Mbeki himself quickly withdrew from the expansiveness of his election campaign, relying on formal set-pieces for public engagement: *imbizos,* or "village meetings," where he would go out and meet the people for a day or two; and his weekly letter on the ANC Web site, which would become notorious for the intemperate broadsides fired against foes, real and perceived. The presidency certainly became more substantive and hands-on, but it also became introverted and mistrusting—all the more so when Mbeki was stung, just a year into his tenure, by the two most contentious issues of his career, his positions on AIDS and Zimbabwe.

The notion developed that, in contrast to Mandela, the insecure Mbeki became power-hungry and developed what became known as an imperial presidency. As the battle lines would be drawn between him and Jacob Zuma, Mbeki's alleged imperiousness would become the primary allegation against him by Zuma's allies: both the ANC and South Africa were "drifting towards dictatorship," Zwelinzima Vavi of the Congress of South African Trade Unions would say; the South African democracy was "excessively presidential," the South African Communist Party's Blade Nzimande would add, hinting that the ANC under Mbeki was becoming more and more like the Zimbabwe's ruling party under Robert Mugabe.[16] Most strongly, Archbishop Tutu—by no means a supporter of Jacob Zuma—would use the platform of the annual Nelson Mandela Lecture in 2004 to describe the ANC's elected representatives as "unthinking, uncritical, kowtowing...voting cattle," more accountable to the party leadership than to their constituents and "browbeaten with pontificating decrees from on high." Tutu would urge Mbeki to be more like the "moral colossus" of Mandela, "an icon of forgiveness, compassion and unanimity and reconciliation."[17] In Mbeki's sharp response to Tutu—he accused the archbishop, in almost as many words, of being a self-serving liar[18]—he seemed to confirm the concerns about his intolerance of dissent, voiced by Mandela at Mafikeng in 1997.

What irritated Mbeki most about the discourse of "Mandela exceptionalism," from the beginning is that it cast Mandela as the great democrat and him as the "tyrant in waiting" (or, more mildly, as the imperial president), whereas he experienced the reality as exactly the opposite: Mbeki felt that *he* was the modernizer who believed in the supremacy of the rule of law; that he was the one who worked always within the rules of democracy, perpetually having to rein in the somewhat autocratic tendencies of his superior, who ruled with more than a little imperial caprice. Mbeki told me, for example, that Mandela's chief of staff, Jakes Gerwel, complained that he was unable to do his governmental work because "all he had time to do was to organize the personal programs" of the icon that was Mandela. Gerwel denies ever having said this to Mbeki or that he had anything to do with Mandela's personal diary, but the anecdote speaks to Mbeki's perception: that Mandela's status precluded good government and that his executive style privileged personality over process. It sometimes seemed to Mbeki that Mandela believed that certain privileges were due to him merely by virtue of his status. He was, after all, the embodiment of the nation.

Mbeki's response was to increase the institutional power of the office substantially. He established a newly rebranded presidency as the central node of all policy formulation and coordination, and made the most senior civil servants contractually accountable to himself rather than to their individual ministers. The SACP's Jeremy Cronin has suggested that the ANC government was pushed into a strong, centralized presidency by pressure from its new allies in the private sector, as part of a capitalist project to counter bottom-up influence from the ANC's unionist and leftist alliance partners; the result, he writes, was an alienation of ordinary people from the project of governance—and thus the outpouring of popular support for Zuma after 2005.[19] But whatever the political fallout—and however high-handedly he managed it—Mbeki's restructuring of the executive presidency was driven by the need to provide efficient and coherent leadership from the top, which is not necessarily a euphemism for autocracy. Whether he was successful in this endeavor is another matter.

The tightening of the reins at the center of government was mirrored by a similar process within the party; "a certain 'presidentialising' of the ANC itself," as the SACP would put it.[20] From 1997, Mbeki centrally appointed the governments of municipalities and provinces won by the ANC, and a committee chaired by Zuma (at that point still a firm Mbeki ally) vetted all senior bureaucratic appointments. In an environment of such severe unemployment that the state was often the largest (or sole) employer, local and provincial governments became vital dispensaries of jobs and tenders, and were thus intensely contested; this situation was exacerbated, rather than ameliorated, by the centralized appointments, and even more so by the top-down way Mbeki's ANC managed conflict, usually by sending in a posse of leadership heavies to lay down the law. This was the exile approach to conflict resolution, germinated in a military, hierarchical context, and was in sharp contrast with the consultative ethos of the United Democratic Front and the bottom-up approach that was experimented with during the Mandela era. This centralization would be reversed in the wake of the rebellion against Mbeki: At the 2007 conference that elected Zuma over Mbeki, delegates would reassert the party's authority and reclaim the right for its structures to appoint mayors and provincial premiers—and even to vet cabinet appointments.

Ironically, given his central role in the "presidentializing process," Zuma would become the ultimate beneficiary of the ill will it engendered: In province after province, grassroots ANC members became alienated because of the top-down way the ANC now imposed appointments upon them. Mbeki's insistence that he needed to keep a tight rein over appointments to ensure efficiency and prevent patronage was taken as evidence of his high-handedness—his unwillingness to trust popular will—and was perceived as a source of patronage itself, the putting into place of mandarins loyal to the center rather than to the people they served. Thus did the impression develop—strengthened by some of Mbeki's later cabinet appointments— that while Mandela, a "strong" leader, was willing to surround himself with competent independent voices, Mbeki sought out vulnerable nonentities who would defer to him and depend on his patronage. The truth is more complicated: Despite some spectacularly bad appointments, there were many strong, competent people in Mbeki's administration and cabinet. Concurrently, there was a rapidly shrinking pool from which to choose as many of the most competent people fled to the private sector, only in some cases because they felt sidelined by Mbeki. Nonetheless, the fact that this impression remained, and fueled the negative impression of Mbeki's legacy, was a consequence of his inability to obtain popular support for his appointments; to marry his technocratic approach with democratic process.

Perhaps the greatest sacrifice made in the interests of alleged technocracy was of parliament, which had been—like so much of the era of Madiba magic—colorful, critical, and rambunctious for the first five years of democracy. Mbeki used the party to rein it in: within the ANC caucus, loyalists, often those who lacked the necessary skills, were promoted, while freethinkers were marginalized. The key threshold was crossed in December 2002, when—as discussed in the previous chapter—the ANC took control of the powerful

Standing Committee of Public Accounts (SCOPA), traditionally chaired by a member of the opposition, and removed Andrew Feinstein, the senior ANC member of parliament on the committee, because of his dogged investigation of the arms deal. Feinstein, who quit politics shortly thereafter, would later write that the whole episode was "the beginning of the loss of accountability, humility and integrity that had characterised the early years of the ANC in government."[21]

On July 19, 1998, seven months after his "ugly shoes" misstep at Mafikeng and just under a year before he told the country to "go back to work" after winning the 1999 elections, Thabo Mbeki found himself on stage with Nelson Mandela again, this time as part of a live-for-TV celebration of his predecessor's eightieth birthday. On the previous day, Mandela's actual birthday, the South African president had married Graça Machel, in a private ceremony at his home; now, the newlyweds were fêted by a variety concert, televised globally, featuring international superstars such as Michael Jackson and Stevie Wonder. Perhaps it was inevitable that Mbeki's demons would get the better of him again, given how extreme a rendition the event was of the Mandela-as-living-icon phenomenon, and that it took place in that strange interregnum of a lame-duck presidency following Mbeki's election as ANC president. When it was time for him to toast Mandela, Mbeki chose King Lear's tragic words to his daughter Cordelia—his double-edged fantasy of the prison of retirement—just before their deaths: "Come let's away to prison./ We two alone will sing like birds i' th' cage./ ...So we'll live,/ And pray, and sing, and tell old tales, and laugh/ At gilded butterflies, and hear poor rogues/ Talk of court news; and we'll talk with them too—/ Who loses and who wins, who's in, who's out."[22]

"Come let's away to *prison*," to a man who had already spent 27 years behind bars? Why, asked the South African critic Darryl Accone, did Mbeki choose to use such "curiously inappropriate excerpts from a play about an unwise ruler over the edge of senile dementia," words that signify "the retreat from the world of an autocratic and splenetic ex-ruler [into] the decrepitude of his dotage"?[23] Although the rest of the short toast drips with overwrought acclamation, Mbeki made sure to underline, to those who cared to listen carefully, what he meant by his use of the quote: "As Lear wished for himself and his offspring," he said to Mandela, "we too urge you to live, and pray, and sing, and tell old tales, and laugh at the gilded butterflies which will continue to come to you to tell you all manner of idle gossip."[24] In other words: Go away. Retreat into the dotage of idle chitchat, with the wife young enough to be your daughter, and leave us alone to carry on with the real work. "Typical Thabo!" exclaimed a senior ANC leader to me at the time. "The thing is, Madiba *was* flattered. And that's Thabo's subtle brilliance. He was saying 'Yes, you are just like Lear. You fall for flattery too, and here is the proof of it!'"

"Come, let's away!" In the beginning, Mandela played along with the script, insisting that he wanted nothing more than a quiet retirement to his bucolic Transkei. But, as one of Mbeki's closest aides put it to me: "It's not like [Mandela] stopped being an icon" once he stopped being president, "and that was a difficult thing to manage." Mbeki was now the president of South Africa, but it was almost as if the world did not notice: Mandela remained the global symbol not only of South Africa's freedom but of some kind of universal redemption. And he did not, in the end, retreat to his home village of Qunu in the Transkei for a twilight of prayer, song, gossip, and lepidoptery. No; he had been removed from society for too long to want to leave it again. He set up three powerful new philanthropic institutions in his name, and he was not at all shy to use his little black book to fund-raise for and publicize the issues he held dear: world peace, the fight against poverty, the rights of children, and—inevitably—the fight against AIDS.

Until the AIDS confrontation, described in the following chapter, Mandela was scrupulous about staying out of Mbeki's terrain. But there was bound to be friction. There were a series of slights that were generally petty (Mbeki's failure to return a phone call for three months) but that culminated, says one senior ANC figure who is close to them both, "in the perception, on the part of Madiba, that the president doesn't take him seriously." It was a complex denouement to a relationship that had been taut since the beginning. Not only did Mandela have to deal with the realities of being a private citizen once more, but he was aging too, with all the attendant implications of a loss of power. How could he not have felt, on top of this, the global pressure to continue acting publicly in a manner appropriate for a living icon? Perhaps Mbeki "didn't fully appreciate" Mandela's vulnerability, one of his closest comrades acknowledged, and "did not nurse his ego the way he might have." Perhaps, too, after three decades of being a deferential bag-carrier, Mbeki was just too busy with matters of state to worry about such vulnerability.

In May 2000, when Mbeki controversially embraced Robert Mugabe at the opening of a trade fair in Zimbabwe at the height of that country's land-invasion crisis, Mandela started warming up for the role he would play in the upcoming years: South Africa's moral conscience. Although he under-stood his successor's diplomatic approach toward Mugabe, he said, "the masses don't have to follow the same route." Unlike Mbeki, who refused to criticize Mugabe, Mandela made it clear that "we have to be ruthless in denouncing such leaders."[25]

Three weeks after his Zimbabwe comments, Mandela jetted off to the United States for an unscheduled meeting with Bill Clinton at the White House, allegedly to discuss Burundi, where he was mediating the process to end that country's civil war. Was it coincidental that the visit took place just days before Mbeki was to meet Clinton himself in his first state visit to Washington—the express purpose of which was to establish himself, in the American mind, as the new South African president? It is hard to believe that this was a deliberate Mandela ploy; more likely, it was simply bad planning. But the net effect was that, in the media glut that greeted Mandela, Mbeki was barely noticed.

Perhaps it was Mandela's closeness with Clinton that triggered an unexpected stop on Mbeki's American trip: a visit to Texas to meet with the Republican front-runner for that year's elections, George W. Bush. The two men hit it off immediately: Mbeki has told several people that, when he first met Al Gore, the vice president and Democratic Party candidate had arrogantly told him what needed to be done in Africa, while Bush now said, in his good-ol'-boy way, that he knew nothing about Africa, so *"you* tell *me* what you think I should do."* Now, as Mandela and Clinton's friendship grew stronger—cemented over their shared commitment to the fight against AIDS—so too did their successors bond. At different points, Bush publicly affirmed both Mbeki's AIDS line and his Zimbabwe policy. Extraordinarily, given South Africa's highly vocal opposition to the Iraq invasion, Mbeki had unparalleled access, for an African leader, to the White House.

At one point, Bush allegedly complained to Mbeki that he felt awkward being phoned by Mandela when it was now Mbeki who was his South African counterpart. Meanwhile, Mandela would complain that in the course of the day he could call all the world's leaders and the only one who would not return his call immediately was "my own president." Mandela began to send signals that he disapproved of Mbeki's leadership style: "The proper thing to do is have free and vigorous debate on every issue and to criticise everybody, including the President," he would say in 2001.[26] The turning point would come with coup plot allegations leveled against Cyril Ramaphosa, Tokyo Sexwale, and Matthews Phosa: This is when Mandela would begin engaging actively again in ANC politics, and attending National Executive Committee meetings, of which he was an ex-officio member. He became more and more convinced that his warnings, issued at Mafikeng, had not been heard; inevitably, Mbeki's dissident position on AIDS—and the extraordinary lack of any disagreement with him on the subject by other ANC leaders—became a lightning rod for Mandela's concerns. This is examined in detail in the following chapter.

By early 2003, relations between the two men were so bad that a BBC crew, filming a feature-length documentary of Mandela, captured an extraordinary exchange at a wedding banquet to which both had been invited. We watch Mandela becoming increasingly angry as Mbeki's late arrival delays the proceedings. When the presidential entourage finally arrives, the microphone picks up Mandela snapping irritably at his successor, "We are hungry!" Mbeki adds insult to injury by refraining from apologizing, blandly responding, instead, "I'm sure you are." Mandela claims his revenge from the podium: "In the late thirties," he says, "there used to be a president of the ANC who used to say 'I am the black prime minister. I cannot come early to meetings. I must come late, and all of you must see what a black prime minister in this country looks like.' I think my president here has taken after that president." The camera cuts to Mbeki and catches him in one of his characteristic gestures, his fingers steepled, looking heavenward with unveiled exasperation.[27]

A few months later, in July 2003, Mbeki made peace by agreeing to draft an eighty-fifth birthday message to Mandela, in which he lauded his predecessor—seemingly without sarcasm—as "God's gift to the world" and a "monument to the triumph of the human spirit." He also cogitated on the meaning of home: "In 1988, the imprisoned Mandela asked a local lawyer to find his family's kraal [homestead]. It was no longer there. No matter. The place Nelson Mandela has carved in the hearts of all the people of South Africa is his true and abiding home. It will remain there forever."[28]

In the shadow of Mandela, Mbeki often made it clear that he had no need to be loved, so long as he was respected. And yet we can read the definition of Mandela's home—a place "carved in the hearts" of his people—as Mbeki's own fantasy of the hearth. It is hard to imagine a more beautiful definition of home; hard, too, to read it without noting that at the time of its writing, Mbeki himself had never been back—or even expressed any interest in going back—to his own birthplace at Mbewuleni. Unlike for the deeply rooted Mandela, "home" is defined for Mbeki not by where one comes from but by what one does. It is something one forms oneself—something a person literally carves into (or out of) society—rather than something that forms the person. It is profoundly implicated with power—not necessarily naked power, power for power's sake, but the power to change the lives of the people one were raised to lead. It has to do with being the president and having an effect, with being respected and accepted as a true leader. With casting one's own shadow; carving one's own mark.

Shaun Johnson, who edited the publication in which the birthday message would appear, recalls taking the copy through to show Mandela: "He reads it twice and his eyes tear up. He calls Zelda [la Grange, his assistant] in, and asks her to get 'my president' on the phone."

By 2005 there would be some rapprochement—a function, in large part, of Mandela's decision to stop criticizing Mbeki publicly, partly because of increasing frailty and partly because he had, as the next chapter will show, succeeded in pressuring the South African government to dispense antiretroviral medication. As the ANC imploded over the battle between Mbeki and Zuma in 2007, Mandela would fulminate to confidants about the former's mistreatment of the latter. But there would be no public rancor.

33

MBEKI AND AIDS
"YES, WE ARE DISEASED!"

When, in 2001, journalist Debra Patta asked Thabo Mbeki whether he would be willing to take an AIDS test, he fudged: "It might be dramatic and make newspaper headlines," but it would be "irrelevant to the matter." Patta pushed him: "Would it not set an example?" "No," Mbeki responded firmly. "It would be setting an example within the context of a particular paradigm."[1]

Mbeki said something similar to me in 2000, when I asked him if he would ever consider taking antiretroviral medication, were he to become ill with AIDS. "I wouldn't," he responded, because if he was told that he was HIV positive, he would wonder what was being tested: "Maybe there is something, I don't know what it might be, which is compromising my immune system, but I [would] have no reason to believe that it is [HIV]."

In 1999, in the year Thabo Mbeki became president, an estimated 25 percent of all pregnant women in South Africa were already HIV positive. By the time he began his second term, five years later, these figures had risen to nearly 30 percent, and the death rate among women between the ages of 25 and 34 had more than quadrupled. By 2005, a government national household survey estimated that 10.8 percent of all South Africans—about 5 million people—were living with HIV. International health agencies estimated that, in that year alone, 320,000 South Africans died of HIV-related illness—about 800 a day.[2]

Unlike some of the more radical AIDS dissidents, Mbeki never denied there was an AIDS epidemic, although he did believed its scale was over-exaggerated. Rather, he questioned the origins of the epidemic, repeating the dissident line that no causal link had ever been established between HIV and AIDS. He also questioned the efficacy of antiretroviral medication, which he came to believe was highly toxic and was being dumped onto unsuspecting Africans by the profiteering pharmaceutical industry. Mbeki saw, in the discourse of the AIDS epidemic, an assault on Africa, and in particular on black male sexuality, and he set out doggedly to challenge it.

In his first year in office, Mbeki would open the global AIDS conference in Durban, the world's eyes upon him, with the message that poverty, rather than a virus, caused the epidemic. He would send a letter to the leaders of the world claiming that the suppression of the AIDS dissidents' ideas was tantamount to apartheid oppression. He would appoint a presidential advisory commission, comprised equally of orthodox scientists and dissidents, to adjudicate on whether HIV caused AIDS. He would question the science of AIDS repeatedly, and he would stall the rollout of an effective treatment program until compelled to do so in 2002 by a court order and a rising tide of opinion against him led by Nelson Mandela. A credible Harvard study would later claim that this delay directly caused the deaths of 330,000 people.[3]

Mbeki's obsession with questioning the "paradigm" of AIDS scratches the deepest mark against his legacy. The roots of his AIDS dissident position are complex: They emerge out of his political personality and his particular reading of the politics of race, sexuality, and global inequality in the shadow of AIDS, as well as the specific political circumstances facing him in 1999, when he stepped up to the presidential podium, out of the shadow of his predecessor's glory. Mbeki was expected to perform the alchemy of transmogrifying the "Mandela miracle" of a peaceful transition into something durable and tangible, at the very moment when plague and death were being predicted on an unprecedented scale.

From the beginning, much of the African National Congress's inability to respond adequately to AIDS has had to do with timing. The epidemic struck at the very moment the ANC was preparing for power. In 1990, Chris Hani had been the first ANC leader to urge the movement to deal with AIDS, but his comrades were not able to hear him: They were too busy trying to reel South Africa back from the brink of civil war and to establish themselves as the new government to grapple with the advent of a plague.

What made AIDS even more difficult to deal with was the particular way that stigma around it had rooted in South Africa, where the first cases had been among gay men and where there was thus a perception—nonexistent in the rest of sub-Saharan Africa—that AIDS was a function not just of promiscuity but of "deviancy," too. As black people began to get ill and die, the "gay plague" quickly mutated into "black death" in the South African media, prompting a stern and punitive public awareness program from the dying apartheid regime's health authorities. In the townships, alarm calls about the epidemic thus seemed to be yet another way of controlling not only population growth but pleasure and free will too, while in the suburbs it became the latest receptacle for white South Africa's endemic *swartgevaar* (black danger) anxiety. Popular magazines and newspapers carried articles about "Maids with AIDS": *They* were coming to get you, if not with their

AK47s, then with their virus.[4] And into this cesspit of stigma the ANC's heroes returned—from countries, such as Zambia and Uganda, where there was already a severe epidemic. Right-wingers demanded that all exiles be tested for HIV before being allowed to return; such attitudes "definitely put us on the defensive," an ANC spokesman said in 2000. "We...understood that this was a disease that we needed to deal with. But we also resented the National Party's demonization of us as promiscuous...terrorists bringing death and disease home to our people."[5]

The ANC leaders were faced with a profound psychic quandary: Even if they were not vectors of infection themselves, how was it possible that, at the very moment they assumed their victorious place as the leaders of a democracy they had struggled for decades to bring about, they were presented with a dying populace, with a plague to which there were no answers? This was the era of birth of democracy, of the emergence of a life-force out of the cadaver of apartheid, and yet here were portents that the fear of death—rather than the celebration of life—would drive the country into the future, and that the carrier of this morbidity was sex. It was one bridge too far, certainly, for Nelson Mandela himself, who was awkward talking about such matters and passed responsibility for AIDS onto his deputy: Mbeki was given an interministerial committee on the issue to chair.

In the Mandela cabinet there was one minister passionate about the fight against AIDS, Nkosazana Dlamini-Zuma, then health minister and Jacob Zuma's wife (they would divorce in the late 1990s). An ANC medic in exile and a close Mbeki confidante, she had played a key role in the adoption of an exemplary National AIDS Plan in the early 1990s; once in office, however, she had come up against bureaucracy, the lack of political will of her colleagues, and, of course, the funding strictures imposed by the Growth, Employment and Redistribution (GEAR) program of fiscal austerity. Rather than bringing into being a significant, serious program, she became caught in one nasty squall after another. The first was around the improper funding of an AIDS awareness play, *Sarafina 2*, and the second around an attempt to fast-track a dubious homegrown antiretroviral called Virodene.

Both *Sarafina 2* and Virodene were rash, ill informed, and ultimately illegal. But both arose from a sense of desperation about the encroaching epidemic and the state's seeming inability to do anything to stop it. And into the squall of the second scandal—the advocacy of Virodene—Dlamini-Zuma swept Mbeki himself, who became a patron of the drug's development and even allegedly secured a share of its profits for the ANC. In a moment of false redemption, Mbeki paraded 11 apparent beneficiaries of the therapy before cabinet, gushing about the drug's possibilities. He could only have been deeply embarrassed when evidence emerged that active ingredient in Virodene, an industrial solvent, could actually activate AIDS in HIV-positive patients.[6]

Shortly thereafter, Dlamini-Zuma launched her final attempt, as health minister, to kick-start high-level political support for the fight against AIDS: a government AIDS campaign that Mandela was due to launch at a made-for-TV live broadcast from an orphanage in October 1998. But at the last minute Mandela pulled out, and the job was given to Mbeki, who read an exemplary prepared speech stating that if the epidemic was not faced squarely, "South Africa's dreams will be shattered."[7] The event, however, had been prepared for Mandela, who is easy with children in front of the camera; the way Mbeki dealt with the HIV-positive children around him seemed to undercut his own message about caring and nondiscrimination and to exacerbate the fears about his impending succession and his ability to connect policy, no matter how good it was, to his constituents' flesh and blood.[8]

This was the last time Mbeki espoused the standard line on AIDS. In mid-1999, just after entering office, he received papers from two South Africans who had come to believe that AIDS was a hoax: a sometime science journalist named Anita Allen, and a lawyer named Anthony Brink. The papers led him into the arcane and conspiratorial world of dissident literature, specifically a Web site, virusmyth.net, and into communication with the AIDS dissidents who would shape his opinions. He felt deeply betrayed by Dlamini-Zuma: Why, he asked her, had she not told him that there was a dispute among scientists about the etiology of AIDS? When she answered that she did not think it necessary to inform him as science had long ago resolved the matter, his suspicions were confirmed. As he put it to me later: "One of the things we make a mistake about is thinking a medical doctor is a scientist. They're not. They're craftsmen and craftswomen. So you make an assumption about their capacity to think out of the box."

One of Mbeki's great weaknesses, even some of his most loyal comrades have told me, was that he often does not trust others to filter data for him: He liked to hear it himself directly from the source and make his own decisions. This informed the way he set up direct relationships with key underground operatives during the 1980s, bypassing the structures set up to do the job; it was also a frequently heard criticism of him, during his presidency, by both ANC officials and his cabinet ministers. It played no small part in his downfall. And it informed his thinking about AIDS.

Mbeki perceived himself as a prophet in the wilderness. This is what got him up in the morning and got him through the day. He was the one who said, when no one else believed it, that the ANC had to embrace the market and the West if it was to survive. He was deeply unpopular for it, but he was proven right. He was the one who said, at the height of the South African conflict, "Lay down your guns and talk to the enemy." He was called a traitor, an *impimpi*, a black Englishman in tweeds. But he was right again. Now, in the difficult transition, he found himself once more in a tiny minority of free-thinking dissidents. Once more he might be overwhelmed by conventional thinking. But once more, in the long run, he believed, with absolute conviction, that he would be proven correct.

———————————

Plaintiffs of all types, cranks and savants alike, dispatch their briefs to heads of state every day and are rarely engaged with. Why, then, did a busy man just beginning his presidency choose in mid-1999 to pick up and engage with the papers sent to him by two passionate amateurs? And why, in the months to come—the first months of his new presidency, the foundation time of his own legacy—did Mbeki embark on a quest to overturn the long-established conventions of scientific inquiry and the seemingly inviolate wall that had long been set up between science and politics?

On October 28, 1999, shortly after reading the Allen and Brink papers, Mbeki surprised everyone by concluding an address to the National Council of Provinces—the upper chamber of the legislature—with a non sequitur lecture on the importance of not accepting conventional wisdom. He used two seemingly disconnected examples to make his point: the incidence of rape, which he claimed was being deliberately exaggerated, and the use of azidothymidine (AZT), which the South African government was being urged to make available in short-term doses to rape victims and HIV-positive pregnant mothers, but which—Mbeki now said—"a large volume of scientific literature" alleged was "in fact a danger to health."[9]

Mbeki was indirectly answering an article that had been written six months earlier by the journalist Charlene Smith. Smith published a graphic account of her own rape, claiming that there was a rape "every 26 seconds" in South Africa and describing how the authorities had given her a battery of medications—except AZT, the one that might actually save her life: "The rapist bestows a death sentence and the state, by refusing to give cheap medication that could save many women, becomes executioner. I thought the death sentence was outlawed."[10]

A few months earlier, the Treatment Action Campaign (TAC) had been formed, and its inaugural campaign focused on making AZT available to HIV-positive pregnant mothers. The state had made it clear that it was unable to provide the treatment purely on the basis of cost. This was one reason why the AIDS treatment issue became interesting to those on the left: It was an object lesson in the consequences of fiscal austerity and sharpened the issues raised by the dispute over economic policy. Was the state really willing to condemn society's most vulnerable to death in the name of a balanced budget? In the face of Smith's accusations and the TAC's highly effective lobby, the AIDS dissident literature was nothing less than a godsend. Now Mbeki could claim there was another reason to withhold AZT: It was itself a possible death sentence—and it was being peddled by those very agents of globalization against which the South African left had avowedly set itself.

Since it had come into office, the ANC government had been attempting to lower the cost of medicines through "parallel importation": the purchasing of brand-name drugs from third parties at the cheapest rates possible. But with the active support of the U.S. government, Big Pharma (the pharmaceutical industry) claimed that this violated international copyright agreements. From 1997 onward the matter had bedeviled the binational commission Mbeki ran with Al Gore, then the U.S. vice president. In mid-1999 Gore proposed a deal: He would use his leverage with the pharmaceutical companies to get them to make a cost-reduction deal for antiretroviral drugs with South Africa, if in return that country dropped its campaign for intellectual property rights. Mbeki believed that Gore was trying to buy him off, and refused.

The whole experience confirmed Mbeki's suspicions: The state of the world's health was in the hands of corporations that were accountable to shareholders, not the sick; enterprises that were, by definition, more interested in profit maximization than in solving the world's illnesses. And so, he told me, "When these matters are raised by Anita [Allen] and then Anthony Brink, by this time I say, 'These pharmaceutical companies are dangerous! It's possible that they could be handling these things in a way that is suggested [by the dissidents].'" In other words, that Big Pharma was deliberately overstating the evidence that HIV causes AIDS—or at least ignoring any evidence to the contrary—so that it could recoup its investment on the costly research it had put into the drugs.

There is another aspect to Mbeki's decision to take on Big Pharma. Following the Asian crash of 1998, when the forces of globalization threatened to swamp and destabilize developing economies, the rand had gone into free fall once more, losing 14 percent against the dollar. In this context, Mbeki radically revised his take on South Africa's place in the world economy. Globalization might be an unavoidable reality, he said, but its process "ineluctably results in the reduction of the sovereignty of states, with the weakest, being ourselves, being the biggest losers."[11] The Asian crash and its consequences had brought to the fore the primal global iniquity, what Mbeki would later call "the globalisation of apartheid."[12] This realization would power his stewardship of the New Partnership for Africa's Development (NEPAD), designed to make the continent self-sufficient, and his frantic years of high-powered negotiations for a new deal for Africa with the leaders of the Group of Eight (G8) countries. It is not a coincidence that this burst of action took place at precisely the moment at which Mbeki was developing his thinking about AIDS and about the way the pharmaceutical industry—using the instruments of globalization, such as the World Trade Organization—exploited such global iniquities.

Mbeki was a man who trained in development economics at Sussex in the 1960s; who, from the time he sat in his father's study at Mbewuleni as a boy, interpreted the world as a place through the binary opposition of exploiter and exploited. But since the 1980s, his pragmatism meant that he accepted the necessity of working within the strictures imposed by the institutions of globalization, and of putting into place a system which accepted the logic that capitalists, rather than the state, would drive growth. In the eyes of many of his comrades to the left—in the eyes of his old Sussex comrades, not to mention his own father—he had "rolled over," and it is not difficult to imagine that he internalized some of this criticism.

Where, during the years of contention over GEAR, was Thabo Mbeki to put his history of struggle against capitalist imperialism? Where his honor? What was he to do with the ideology on which he was spawned? It was not discarded. Rather, it found its place, as he was developing his ideas about the "globalization of apartheid," into an all-consuming battle with the multinational pharmaceutical industry, warping into a belief that Big Pharma was so evil that it could control not only the government of the world's largest country and left-wing activists, but the production of scientific knowledge itself.

Mbeki read voraciously about AIDS through November and December 1999. During the year-end holiday with his Sussex friends in the Eastern Cape, he showed them the AIDS-dissident Web sites. Early in the new year, Malegapuru Makgoba—a prominent immunologist—received a midnight call from him on the matter and then, a few days later, a couriered volume of about 1,500 pages of dissident material. A few years earlier, Makgoba had waged a bruising "dissident" battle against the white liberal elite that ran Wits University, and it was clear that Mbeki was seeking common cause with him on AIDS. But Makgoba demurred, writing back that the evidence that HIV existed was "beyond dispute today" and that the dissident view was "based on flawed arguments that distort, misrepresent and misinterpret scientific facts."[13] Later Makgoba would take Mbeki on publicly, accusing him of having "collaborated in one of the greatest crimes of our time" by denying the rollout of antiretrovirals.[14]

At around the same time Mbeki wrote to Makgoba in January 2000, he decided to contact the dissidents directly. He sent a list of eight questions about AIDS, together with the answers provided by his own health minister, now Manto Tshabalala-Msimang, to the biochemist David Rasnick, a leading dissident.[15] At this point, Tshabalala-Msimang's answers still followed orthodox science, but Rasnick's response demonstrates the way the dissidents began to influence public policy in South Africa. What, he asked was "the justification for lumping together the well-known diseases and conditions of poverty...that Africans have been suffering from for generations, and renaming them as AIDS?"[16]

Mbeki, at this point, had not yet spoken publicly about poverty as a cause of AIDS. So far his public questioning had been limited to the toxicity of antiretrovirals. Two weeks after he received Rasnick's response to his questions, he aired the poverty thesis for the first time: Safer-sex campaigns were not enough to combat AIDS, and interventions had to look at "the challenges of poverty," too.[17] Then, a few weeks later, in the invitation he issued to prominent scientists to participate in his Expert Advisory Panel on HIV/AIDS, he made it clear that he was willing to take on the question of whether HIV existed too.[18] The initiative would ultimately collapse because the orthodox scientists wisely withdrew, but it nonetheless achieved one of Mbeki's objectives, which was to portray the science of AIDS—as the South African scholar Nicoli Nattrass has noted—"as deeply contested, and contestable."[19]

In the beginning, playing the role of patron to the AIDS dissidents appealed to Mbeki: Not just that he could convene the planet's greatest minds to solve one of the world's greatest mysteries, but the very notion of the dissidents as Galileos, which was how they saw themselves. In a letter written to the world's leaders—and leaked, by an astonished White House, to the media—Mbeki wrote that the dissidents were treated as "heretics" who in earlier times would have been "burned at the stake" and who had been subjected to a "campaign of intellectual intimidation and terrorism," a "holy crusade," "borne by a degree of fanaticism, which is truly frightening." He even likened their predicament to South African freedom fighters who were "killed, tortured, imprisoned and prohibited from being quoted."[20] Such was the passion lit within him by the dissidents' cause that he had actually come to identify with them. This was not lost on the dissident Charles Geshekter, who described Mbeki as "a person who challenges received wisdom" even within the ANC, offering as an example the way he had advocated "opening up talks with the rulers of the apartheid state."[21] Geshekter understood his man well: In an age of attrition and concession that was the transition, Mbeki had indeed found his cause.

When I asked Thabo Mbeki, in 2000, why he had allowed AIDS to absorb him so, he responded with animation: "It's the way it was presented! You see, the presentation of the matter, which is actually quite wrong, is that the major killer disease on the African continent is HIV/AIDS, this is really going to decimate the African population! So your biggest threat is not unemployment or racism or globalization, your biggest threat which will really destroy South Africa is this one!" He told me how even the World Health Organization (WHO) had said in 1999 that AIDS constituted only 16 percent of "the burden of disease" in sub-Saharan Africa: so "what about the other 84 percent? Why are we not talking about that? And these are killer diseases."

Mbeki is not the only one to have argued that the effect of AIDS has been exaggerated.[22] But if this has been the case, it has been merely by a margin: South Africa's own official statistics demonstrate that the effects of the epidemic are catastrophic. Mbeki, however, did not accept the margin-of-error argument. Rather, he believed it to be a self-serving attempt by the "AIDS industry" to justify its continued growth, in concert with Big Pharma's preoccupation with its profit margins. He also saw it as the latest agent of Afro-pessimism; yet another stick to bludgeon the continent into its reputation as irredeemable. Reverting to a racist image of Africans as being unable to control their sexuality, the world wanted to dump expensive and toxic medications on unsuspecting Africans while ignoring the real causes of AIDS: Africa's ongoing poverty and underdevelopment.

Mbeki emphasized repeatedly that Africans had to find African solutions to African problems. But his thinking derived, almost exclusively, from American dissidents—particularly the ideas of Geshekter, a historian. Geshekter had tracked the way that colonial medicine had traditionally pathologized Africans; once AIDS exploded across Africa, he applied this understanding to the way scientists spoke about it. When, at the 1994 World AIDS Conference, a Japanese delegate said that AIDS would only be stemmed "once Africans controlled their sexual cravings," Geshekter responded angrily in an article in *The New African*, which Mbeki would later read on AIDS dissident Web site virusmyth.net: "It is the political economy of underdevelopment, not sexual intercourse, that is killing Africans. African poverty, not some extraordinary sexual behaviour, is the best predictor of AIDS-defining diseases."[23]

There are two axioms to the dissident argument as articulated here by Geshekter. The first is that poverty is a cause of AIDS. The second is that if poverty causes AIDS, then HIV does not and that AIDS therefore is not transmitted sexually. The first axiom is generally accepted by all scientists in the field: malnutrition, lack of access to medical treatment, and dirty water all affect the immune system, and poverty also forces women into risky transactive sex. Some critical scholars go further, saying that Mbeki was entirely correct to raise poverty as a cause of AIDS, as the conventional approach does not pay enough attention to it and concentrates to a fault on safer-sex programs—in no small part because of racist preoccupations with excessive African sexuality.[24]

In the beginning, at least, Mbeki focused primarily on the "poverty causes AIDS" axiom, developing it most famously at the opening address of the Durban World AIDS Conference in July 2000. There he insisted that AIDS could not be blamed "on a single virus," that it thrived in an environment of "poverty, suffering, social disadvantage and inequity," and that, even according to the WHO, "extreme poverty" was "the world's biggest killer."[25] Prior to the conference, 5,000 people, including many prominent scientists, signed the Durban Declaration, affirming that the evidence of HIV causing AIDS was "clear-cut, exhaustive and unambiguous."[26] During Mbeki's speech, many delegates walked out in protest. Mbeki read the furious reaction against him as a "sustained attempt to hide the truth about diseases of poverty," as he would later put it.[27] But what the Durban delegates were really protesting against was the way Mbeki was using a political standard—the protection of the right to free speech and open debate—to adjudicate a scientific dispute, which had already been settled according to the methods of scientific proof. More important, they were worried that if Mbeki believed the first axiom of the dissident argument (that poverty caused AIDS), then he might also accept the second, more pernicious one, too: that HIV did not.

Certainly Mbeki questioned the link between HIV and AIDS. But did he actually believe that AIDS was not sexually transmitted and that South Africa and the world were thus wasting billions on behavior-modification programming? While he made a point of always mentioning safer-sex campaigns whenever he spoke about AIDS, his questioning effectively minimized the significance of sexual intercourse in the spread of the epidemic, something to which he admits. He conceded, to me, that his position might have had the "unintended consequence" of undermining his own government's safer-sex campaign, but, he insisted, "I wouldn't agree that because you might get that result, [you should] stop raising these questions."

In fact, Mbeki had come to share Geshekter's analysis that safer-sex campaigns provoked "inordinate anxieties and moral panics" across Africa and that public health programming had become obsessed with controlling sexual behavior rather than focusing on real, treatable illnesses, such as malaria and tuberculosis. The effect was to ignore the real cause of African illness, which was poverty, and to seek to control—as sterilization programs had in the past—a rampant and primitive African sexuality.[28] When, in 2000, the *Washington Post* published an article by Charlene Smith that claimed that rape was "endemic" and had become "a prime means of transmitting the disease,"[29] Mbeki believed he saw Geshekter's analysis writ large. Smith was "blinded by racist rage," he wrote, and this had driven her to reproduce "hysterical" claims about AIDS incidence in South Africa.[30] In an ongoing correspondence war with the leader of the opposition, Tony Leon, Mbeki referred more than once to "the desperate attempt made by some scientists in the past to blame HIV/AIDS on Africans, even at a time when the USA was the epicentre of reported deaths from AIDS."[31]

Much of Mbeki's correspondence on the matter seemed to nurse the sharp spike of grievance about being lectured to, about his own backyard, by people who were not Africans themselves but thought they knew better. In response, questioning AIDS became a political act, the latest battle in the war for African self-determination: "Critical to the success of the historic African transformation project is our courage to stand up for what we think and feel is correct," he wrote. "We must have confidence in ourselves to say and do what we believe is right." This meant "free[ing] ourselves of the 'friends' who populate our ranks, originating from the world of the rich," who, "perhaps dressed in jeans and T-shirts," take "advantage of an admission that perhaps we are not sufficiently educated."[32]

Mbeki would return to this theme repeatedly in the next few years, alleging in October 2001 that Africans were being forced to adopt the "strange opinions" of AIDS orthodoxy "to save a depraved and diseased people from perishing from self-inflicted disease." Even black doctors were trained to feel inferior "by being reminded of their role as germ carriers... [and] as human beings of the lower order, unable to subject passion to reason," by a racist medical discourse "convinced that we are but natural-born, promiscuous carriers of germs, unique in the world...doomed to an inevitable mortal end because of our unconquerable devotion to the sin of lust."[33]

This argument was taken to its logical conclusion in a document anonymously written by Mbeki and distributed in 2002, which spoke about how "the HIV/AIDS thesis" entrenched "centuries-old white racist beliefs and concepts about Africans and black people," and which parodied the kind of response Mbeki believed Western donors wished to hear from Africans:

> Yes, we are sex crazy! Yes, we are diseased! Yes, we spread the deadly HI virus through our uncontrolled heterosexual sex! In this regard, yes, we are different from the US and Western Europe! Yes, we, the men, abuse women and the girl-child with gay abandon! Yes, among us rape is endemic because of our culture! Yes, we do believe that sleeping with young virgins will cure us of AIDS! Yes, as a result of this, we are threatened with destruction by the HIV/AIDS pandemic! Yes, what we need, and cannot afford because we are poor, are condoms and antiretroviral drugs! Help![34]

The 100-page "monograph," dubbed the "Castro Hlongwane" document, caused a furor because of the way it added an African nationalist strain to the AIDS dissident argument, describing AIDS doctors as latter-day Mengeles and the black people who subscribed to the orthodox scientific approach as "self-repressed" victims of a slave mentality. Among its strongest claims was that Mbeki's recently deceased spokesman, Parks Mankahlana, had been "vanquished by the antiretroviral drugs he was wrongly persuaded to consume," killed by doctors who "remain free to feed others the same drugs."[35]

Later in 2002 Mbeki wrote that "we will not be intimidated, terrorised, bludgeoned, manipulated, stampeded, or in any other way forced to adopt policies and programmes inimical to the health of our people. That we are poor and black does not mean that we cannot think for ourselves and determine what is good for us. Neither does it mean that we are available to be bought, whatever the price."[36] Over the course of two years, what had begun as a quest for scientific truth, arising out of a genuine concern for the welfare of his people, had morphed, via a polemic against orthodoxy and a call to open inquiry, into an impassioned cry for self-determination and for the rights of the South, of black people, to make their own decisions and to resist a new wave of slavery—"we are not available to be bought, whatever the price"—from the North.

The great social battle of Mbeki's first term in office was that between his administration and the increasingly fervent, highly organized AIDS activists of the TAC, led by Zackie Achmat. And the terrible irony of the public contention about AIDS in South Africa is that both Mbeki and the TAC had their roots in the same politics: not just the South African liberation movement, but the North American AIDS-activist movement that emerged out of the epidemic in the 1980s. This movement is characterized by the direct action group ACT-UP and its subsidiary, the Treatment Action Group, which shook the establishment with a vital principle to which both sides in the South African AIDS debate religiously adhered: In the face of the mystery of AIDS, laypeople have the right to take control of their own health and to hold experts and authorities to account. If the TAC activists were beneficiaries of this legacy—in the way they became self-educated experts in treatment and empowered themselves to engage, directly, with scientists and pharmaceutical manufacturers and regulators—then so too was Thabo Mbeki, in the way he insisted on interrogating scientific "truths" and understanding the reasoning behind them.[37]

And even though Mbeki would not accept it, they shared a common enemy: the extortionate practices of the pharmaceutical industry. Why, then, such terrible conflict? Why do both sides believe, so passionately, that the other has blood on its hands? The anthropologist Didier Fassin explains it as a clash of two different types of denial. If Mbeki and those around him refused to accept the severity of the epidemic because they experienced the discourse around it as racist, then the treatment activists put too much faith in treatment, seeing antiretroviral drugs as magic bullets, some kind of deus ex machina that would not only cure people with AIDS but solve the AIDS crisis too.[38]

The AIDS activists would counter, correctly, that their fixation on treatment was only because they were up against an authority that had pushed them into that corner by questioning the efficacy of treatment every step of the way and thus denying them the opportunity to live long, relatively healthy lives, as HIV-positive people in the West now did. Certainly the intensity of the protest against Mbeki might have been fueled, in part—as some ANC leaders understood it—from a raging against hopelessness and mortality, by the need to apportion blame, somewhere, for the injustice of an early, sexually transmitted death. Certainly, too, the AIDS activists's seeming unwillingness to understand the compromises that a resource-strapped government has to make might have sometimes hampered their own cause. But perhaps, in the end, the answer as to why two sides with such similar political lineages diverged is that nationalist ideology intervened on one of the sides: For Mbeki, the quest for self-determination over health—the legacy of the AIDS epidemic in the West—became confused with the quest for political self-determination. The result, for South Africa, was catastrophic.

In 1996, at the height of the era of Mandela Exceptionalism, the South African *Mail & Guardian* had enraged Mbeki by asking, in a banner headline, whether he was "Fit to Rule?" The fact that the newspaper asked the question again specifically with respect to AIDS in 2001[39] fed the analysis, by Mbeki and those around him, that criticism of his approach to AIDS was no more than an extension of the "one good native" syndrome: The racists would find any excuse to justify their belief that all African leaders, save the saintly Mandela, were incapable of governing their people. This grievance became even more acute once more adulation than ever was heaped on Mandela when he stepped into the AIDS fray to challenge Mbeki.

Why, I asked Thabo Mbeki, did he think that Nelson Mandela had taken on the AIDS issue with such fervor? He responded obliquely, by telling a story to explain to me how he believed Mandela had "strayed" into the issue. Since the days of his presidency, Mandela had been strong-arming corporate executives to invest in rural schools and clinics; now, shortly after Mbeki took office, he told me, Mandela had brokered the building of a rural prenatal clinic by the German pharmaceutical company Boehringer Ingelheim, the manufacturers of nevirapine. Mbeki and his cabinet members vetoed it, he told me, because they thought it was being built to test drugs rather than to provide services—in other words, that an ingenuous Mandela had allowed himself to become the instrument of Big Pharma.[40] This, Mbeki believed, provoked some kind of resentment in Mandela: "It came up close to him as a conscious effort on my part to disempower him." The implication of the story is clear, and shocking: Mandela had "strayed" into AIDS advocacy not just out of heartfelt conviction but also as a response to the disempowerment he had felt at the hands of his successor; a disempowerment typified by his inability even to deliver a clinic to his Big Pharma benefactors.

Many of Mbeki's inner circle also believe that Mandela took up AIDS as a way of going into combat with his successor. Certainly Mandela was concerned by the effect Mbeki's position was having on South Africa's international reputation and was deeply distressed by the inability of other ANC leaders to take Mbeki on. He was determined to set an example to them—or at the very least to provide some cover for them so that they could take action themselves. But the core of Mandela's late-life activism, insists his advisor Jakes Gerwel, was his "genuine devastation at the way people were dying through AIDS." He also wanted to make amends for having failed to champion an AIDS agenda at a time when his voice might have made a real difference. Most of all, Mandela believed that Mbeki was wrong, morally and politically, to question conventional science and that the South African government was making a fatal mistake by prevaricating over the provision of antiretroviral therapy rather than following international best practice.

And so Mandela used the 2000 Durban AIDS conference to launch his own campaign. In striking counterpoint to the skepticism with which Mbeki had opened the event, Mandela said that the dispute over the cause of AIDS was "distracting from the real life-and-death issues we are confronted with."[41] A year later, he said that he found it "difficult to reject or repudiate" some of the criticism of Mbeki, and slammed the government for dragging its heels on the distribution of antiretrovirals: "We must not continue to be debating, to be arguing, when people are dying."[42]

Not least because of Mandela's intervention in Durban, Mbeki's international profile came to be dominated by his alleged denialism. "AIDS, AIDS, AIDS!" a member of one of his international delegations at the time said to me upon return from a trip. "That's all anyone wanted to know about. Did he or didn't he believe that HIV caused AIDS? It was as if some kind of crazy Africans had come to town. As if we were Mobotu, Bokassa, and Idi Amin rolled into one! That's when we realized this thing was killing us!" There was not a mention of Mbeki in the international media without the tag "AIDS denialist" attached; not a press conference not commandeered by the issue, which even made a cameo appearance on the television series *The West Wing*. Even when it was not explicitly mentioned, South Africans accompanying Mbeki abroad saw, on the face of almost every one of his interlocutors, that raised colonial eyebrow, as if Mbeki were confirming the world's worst expectations about the capacity of African leadership.

Some of Mbeki's closest advisors actually believed that his very life was at risk. It was not unusual, in the parallel universe that was the presidency between 2000 and 2002, to hear otherwise-reasonable people saying, in absolute seriousness, that the Americans were planning to engineer regime change to get rid of a president whose actions were causing the pharmaceutical industry to lose billions a year. Everyone, from the ANC's tripartite allies to Mandela himself, seemed to have been "bought" by Big Pharma; never had the tendency of the Mbeki presidency toward paranoia been more acute.

In October 2000 Mbeki told the ANC parliamentary caucus that he was the target of a massive counterintelligence campaign by Big Pharma because his questioning was threatening its profit margins. Astonished members of parliament heard that the pharmaceutical industry was acting in concert with the Central Intelligence Agency against him, and that even the activists of the TAC were on its payroll.[43] Mbeki later denied making these allegations, but the notes of a parliamentarian present confirms them, and more than one of his most senior advisors made similar allegations to me off the record.

In April 2001 there was the brief optimism of common purpose in the fight against AIDS with the decision by Big Pharma to settle with the South African government over parallel importation. But this evaporated quickly: The health minister, Manto Tshabalala-Msimang, made it clear that she would not expand the state's administration of nevirapine beyond its pilot programs, and the TAC responded that it would take the state to court over the matter. When Tshabalala-Msimang lost the appeal, she responded angrily that she would rather defy the law of the land than feed "poison" to her people[44]—a statement the government would be forced to retract. With the nevirapine judgment, Mbeki's campaign against antiretrovirals had been lost. Most ANC leaders understood this, and more than a few heaved a sigh of relief.

Meanwhile, Mandela had been trying for over a year to get an appointment with Mbeki to discuss AIDS. When they finally met in early 2002, Mandela felt he was treated dismissively—say those close to him—as a "quarrelsome old man." And so he took his most provocative action yet: At the very moment the South African government was appealing a court judgement compelling it to provide nevirapine to pregnant HIV-positive mothers, he approved the awarding of a prize in his name to the two pioneering South African doctors of the treatment. The ceremony took place the night before Mbeki was to give his annual state of the nation address, and seemed calculated to embarrass the South African president: After losing his place in his speech and stumbling for a minute, Mandela looked up and said, "At least I am willing to admit when I have made a mistake."[45]

Edwin Cameron, the HIV-positive judge who is one of the leaders of the AIDS movement in South Africa, has written that that "Mandela's intervening moral voice" played a significant role in shifting the government away from its resistance to antiretrovirals.[46] If nothing else, it gave some in Mbeki's cabinet the courage to take their chief on. But it also led to Mandela's humiliation at an ANC leadership meeting in March 2002 to discuss the AIDS issue. Mandela was devastated as speaker after speaker stood up to admonish him having been "undisciplined" by raising his concerns outside the formal structures of the ANC; he left the meeting despondent about how the culture of debate and dissent had been stifled within the party.

Nonetheless, the meeting was something of a turning point: Several participants told me that by remaining silent, the majority were signaling their agreement with Mandela, and that this represented a real breakthrough on AIDS. The groundwork had already been laid by Nkosazana Dlamini-Zuma, now foreign minister, who at an earlier meeting had spoken about the damage the perception of Mbeki as an AIDS denialist was doing to his and South Africa's reputation. Now officials forcefully countered the argument that the state did not have the resources to roll out universal antiretroviral treatment and demonstrated convincingly that such therapy ultimately would be cheaper than looking after sick people in hospitals. And then Joel Netshitenzhe, one of Mbeki's closest advisors, spoke about how the government had allowed itself to be hijacked into being the scapegoat for South Africans' feelings of helplessness in the face of the epidemic—by its contradictory messages and by its failure to connect the scientific debates to the actual human misery of the epidemic. These critiques won the day, in no small part because of Mandela's backing. Mbeki promised to withdraw from the debate and leave it to the scientists and the bureaucrats, and the cabinet announced the government's intention to roll out universal antiretroviral therapy.

What had happened was not quite a rebellion. Only one elected ANC representative, Pregs Govender, the chair of a parliamentary committee on the status of women, resigned and publicly criticized Mbeki. And even behind closed doors, only one or two people actually had the courage to tell Mbeki that they thought he was wrong. Indeed, many of those who played key roles in convincing him to withdraw actually supported his position but had come to conclude that the forces waged against him were simply too great to conquer: He needed to concede this battle to win the war, they believed.

The way Mbeki put it to me, he finally acquiesced to a "general appeal" from his colleagues and officials, because they felt it was hampering their effectiveness in implementing the government's AIDS program. "So I said okay, fine...let's stop this public debate." But this did not mean, in any way, that he had changed his mind. Five years later, in 2007, he told me how "very unfortunate" it was that his initiative had been "drowned" by a vicious campaign, one that claimed "that I've said that HIV does not cause AIDS, which I never did,...all these charges about genocide, and so on. The consequence of which was to stop the scientific inquiry, and I'm afraid that doesn't solve the problem! Very, very regrettable."

Mbeki's decision to withdraw from the AIDS debate was, according to his close comrades, one of the most difficult of his long political career: nothing less than a fall from innocence. Mbeki saw himself having to make one of those terrible calculations of power: to sacrifice the lives of those who, he was convinced, would die from taking antiretrovirals in order to safeguard his government, his country, the ANC's project of transformation, and—some of his advisors believed—his own life too. His advisors persuaded him to make the decision to withdraw by suggesting that even if the government permitted the roll-out of antiretrovirals, it should offer them as a choice, and make the dangers known. "The message we need to give," a senior presidency official told me, "is 'There is no cure for you. Careful about what you take. It could kill you.'"

Effectively, the actions and statements of Manto Tshabalala-Msimang, the health minister, gave voice to this policy from 2002 onward. More impressionable and politically vulnerable than her predecessor, she had become a fervent believer in Mbeki's positions on AIDS and particularly in his doubts about antiretrovirals. And so now she repeatedly articulated the notion of choice, by aggressively promoting nutritional therapies (such as beetroot and garlic, or olive oil and lemon juice, or multivitamins) or traditional remedies (such as the *ubhejane* potion marketed by an untrained herbalist in Durban) as an alternative rather than a complement to antiretrovirals.[47] In so doing, she allowed public health policy to give expression to Mbeki's own continuing concerns about antiretrovirals—and, presumably, to his conscience.

It was a most unsatisfying compromise: a difficult public health campaign that required forceful leadership but that had the support neither of the president or the health minister. How, in such a context, could the implementation not be ambivalent and fraught? Mbeki's silence was at times more ominous than his previous speech. It was as if he were standing back, with his arms folded and his eyebrows raised in habitual skepticism, waiting for everyone else to come to their senses.

At times, he could not resist being baited. In 2003, for example, he had told the *New York Times* that "personally, I don't know anyone who has died of AIDS."[48] And yet, only a few months earlier, he had buried one of his oldest comrades from Lusaka; the previous year, his friend and comrade Peter Mokaba; two years before that, his spokesman, Parks Mankahlana. All three had died of AIDS-related illness, as had many others in his broader world. By 2006 AIDS would strike Mbeki's immediate family, with the death of a close relative. And so, when he said that he did not know anyone who had died of AIDS, he was playing with words, because he had agreed that he would no longer say, directly, what he continued to believe: that it was the antiretrovirals rather than AIDS that had killed them and that if they had followed alternative therapies they might have lived longer.

Toward the end of his tenure, Mbeki mellowed on the subject of AIDS, one of his confidants told me. This was largely because he believed that his interventions had had a significant effect: The international agencies did now admit poverty as a critical cofactor to the spread of the epidemic; it was common cause that malaria and tuberculosis had to be fought too, alongside AIDS; the role of nutritional therapy had become more accepted as an essential part of the treatment of immune deficiency. Mbeki also thought that many of his concerns about antiretrovirals have been proven correct, in particular the problems of resistance that had arisen with respect to nevirapine in pregnant

HIV-positive mothers. ("Orthodox" medics respond that nutrition has always been as central a tenet to healthcare as hygiene has and that while healthy diet and food security are essential, the nutritional supplements his health minister and others promoted could actually be detrimental to immune-suppressed people. They also say that while resistance to nevirapine has been observed and that treatment is being adjusted accordingly, science always works with "best available knowledge" and that this principle is particularly relevant in a situation of crisis: It was thus appropriate to prescribe AZT at first and then nevirapine, and now more sophisticated treatments were developed.)

Mbeki's own political problems, following his firing of Jacob Zuma in 2005, created space for the kind of aggressive, public leadership around AIDS lacking before then. This was evident in the way Zuma's successor, Phumzile Mlambo-Ngcuka, took control of coordinating AIDS policy and garnered universal praise for a new strategic plan on AIDS. When Tshabalala-Msimang took ill in late 2006, her deputy, Nozizwe Madlala-Routledge, stepped into the breach, making it known that she had been forbidden by her superior to talk about AIDS to date, and took on the issue in a refreshingly straightforward and non-defensive way. She spoke publicly about the relatives she had lost to AIDS, she publicly took an HIV test, she praised the treatment activists, and she was highly critical of her own government's policy, speaking openly about how Tshabalala-Msimang's focus on alternative therapies had created confusion and even unnecessary death. Mbeki was livid: Madlala-Routledge had publicly slammed the policies of the government of which she was part and had flouted time-honored ANC protocol by criticizing a comrade and a superior. But for a while, common sense prevailed: The junior deputy minister might have been talking out of turn, but she had done South Africa's public profile the world of good. She stayed in the job, but by June 2007 Tshabalala-Msimang was back at work. While Madlala-Routledge remained a voice of conscience, she had little real authority. Then, in August 2007, Mbeki finally found reason to fire her on the basis of two alleged misdemeanors. She would, however, be elected into the ANC leadership at the conference that rejected Mbeki as ANC president in December of that year. And when Mbeki was fired in September 2008, Tshabalala-Msimang would finally be sidelined, and replaced with Barbara Hogan, who had been one of the very few ANC parliamentarians to challenge Mbeki on AIDS, and who was an active supporter of the TAC.

Hogan's appointment of Fatima Hassan, a prominent AIDS activist, as her special advisor was a calculated move to demonstrate that the Mbeki era of AIDS dissidence was well and truly over.

As the South African edition of this book was going to print in 2007, I received a phone call from Thabo Mbeki, asking whether I had seen the "Castro

Hlongwane" document, the AIDS dissident tract that he was alleged to have written. Of course I had: It had been placed in the public domain five years previously. When I asked whether he was its author, he said that it had been written by a "collective" but agreed that it was an accurate reflection of his views. The following day, his driver delivered a hard copy almost twice as long as the one circulated in 2002, with citations from publications as recent as August 2006. Mbeki had never previously contacted me unsolicited, and my reading of this unusual interaction was that he wished the record to reflect that—despite his near silence since the initial distribution of the document—he still held to the views expressed in "Castro Hlongwane."

Some of the new language in the document was stronger than ever. There was an epigraph, at the top, from George Bernard Shaw—"All great truths begin as blasphemies"—and a quote from a Canadian AIDS dissident: "Is there really much difference, then, between a medieval peasant being told that sinners will spend eternity burning in Hell, and an ordinary citizen of this country being told that if he or she has sex without a condom they risk contracting a fatal virus?"[49] There is no question as to the message Thabo Mbeki was delivering to me along with this document: He was now, as he had been since 1999, an AIDS dissident.

I only had one in-depth conversation with Mbeki about AIDS, in August 2000, in the white heat of the controversy. The two-hour-long discussion offered me deep insight into his thinking; thinking that did not change in any significant way in the years following. I tried to engage him on the question of stigma, in an attempt to ascertain whether he was in some kind of denial about the epidemic. Why, I had asked him, did he think that prominent people living with AIDS—including ANC leaders—did not talk openly about it?

His answer revealed the extent to which he had come to read AIDS personally through the prism of sexual shame. Given the conventional wisdom that "people's immune systems collapse because of sexual promiscuity," he told me, "if I stood up tomorrow and said, 'I am HIV positive,' the assumption would be that the president has been sleeping around with prostitutes! And I suppose that nobody would want themselves to be identified like that!" He extrapolated this into a critique of the conventional approach to fighting AIDS: Talking about sex as a vector for the disease was actually counterproductive, he believed, as it increased the stigma and drove people underground. Talking about poverty as a vector for the disease, however, would have the opposite effect and would thus make public health programming more effective. If people could come to see that their illness was a consequence of the conditions of poverty—such as no clean source of water—and not just of sexual promiscuity, they would be much more open to acknowledging that they had AIDS: Poverty was nothing to be ashamed of.

There is a clear problem with such reasoning, even beyond the moral judgment it implies: What about Peter Mokaba, and other middle-class Africans with AIDS? Mbeki had an answer, and it was rooted in two interconnected dissident theories. The first is that one of the main causes of immune deficiency is repeated exposure to common bacterial sexually transmitted diseases, such as syphilis. The second is that AIDS is a "lifestyle" syndrome: If Africans get it because they are poor, then middle-class gay men get it because of their decadent ways—their use of recreational drugs, which weaken their immune systems, and their rampant sexual activity, which exposes them repeatedly to sexually transmitted diseases.

Mbeki did not mention the latter "lifestyle" theory specifically, but it was clear, from the story he told me about a recent conversation he had had with the former Zambian president Kenneth Kaunda, that his thinking was influenced by it. Kaunda had set up an AIDS foundation after the death of his son and was critical of Mbeki's stance: "How can AIDS be a disease of poverty if my son died of it?" he asked his old protégé. Mbeki responded by telling Kaunda about the Lusaka he had encountered when he arrived in the early 1970s, only a few years after independence. "You suddenly had young people with a lot of money," and this led to a rash of decadence: Young members of the new elite, for example, "took pride in smashing cars," for example, because they had never really had cars before; they were also "in and out of bed with prostitutes." Mbeki told Kaunda that his son must have been part of this culture, leading "a lifestyle which was very dangerous to health."

Here was Mbeki's point: Postapartheid South Africa was going through exactly what Zambia had undergone in the 1970s: "You see it among our DGs [directors-general] here....They are suddenly landed with lots of money. Well, they think it's lots of money. And the Mercedes, and the BMW, and the particular lifestyle develops." Several of his senior bureaucrats, for example, had become addicted to gambling. "It's a particular lifestyle. It's bound to be a consequence. They haven't settled down. They're not accustomed to it."

The implications of this analysis are profound. First, it suggests that, in spite of himself, Mbeki had internalized more than a little of the voice of the stern, censorious Western public health official he decried elsewhere. What are his descriptions if not those of a people—or at the very least a class—"doomed to an inevitable mortal end because of our unconquerable devotion to the sin of lust," as he would put it? This is the Mbeki of the hedge; the Mbeki who grew up on the very frontier between *qaba* (traditional Xhosa) and *gqoboka* (Christian convert) and who had a mission, like his mother, not only to educate but to clothe the "red" people whom she found when she arrived in Mbewuleni, to make them conscious of the shame of the nakedness. This is Mbeki the missionary, the vanguardist. Even if he did grow up poor, he was the child of an elite, and he was exposed to great wealth while exiled in Europe. He is "accustomed to it"; his people are not, mortally so.

But what is also so striking about Mbeki's analysis of the "lifestyle" causes of middle-class African AIDS is that it constitutes a purely materialist reading of sexuality. In the spirit of Marxist notions of bourgeois decadence, it sees AIDS as a function of rapid class change that has alienated a new elite from its worker and peasant roots to the point of morbid pathology. This makes the epidemic a lot easier to imagine: Poor people get AIDS because they are poor; rich people get AIDS because they became rich too quickly. In the first case, poverty can be addressed—indeed, it is the very mission of the ANC to address it—and in the second, things will "settle down" as the new elite gets used to its new wealth. This is far safer ground than having to wonder about the dark workings of sexuality and the reasons why people cannot change their sexual behavior, even if they know that they could save their lives by doing so. If we are dying because we have too little (or too much, too quickly), then Mbeki's mission—the ANC's raison d'être—prevails. If, however, we are dying because we cannot control our primal urges, Mbeki's own liberatory paradigm is shattered. We are the Africans whom our colonial oppressors said that we were, and we have not been able to liberate ourselves from their definition of us.

There is also something visceral rather than cerebral in Mbeki's nightmarish descriptions of the decadence of a newly liberated elite, consumed by avarice and lust. They recall something he said in 2006, when he delivered the annual Nelson Mandela Lecture: "Every day, and during every hour...the demons embedded in our society, that stalk us at every minute, seem always to beckon each one of us towards a realisable dream and nightmare. With every passing second, they advise, with rhythmic and hypnotic regularity—Get rich! Get rich! Get rich!"[50] Such language suggests a revulsion for having unleashed a curse upon the society he was meant to have liberated. He sees those around him—his own comrades, members of the same political elite—filling the loneliness with morbid addictions to prostitution and gambling; with the willful smashing of the fruits of their victory; and with the consequent eruption, across the body of a newborn South Africa, of the lesions and ulcers, the stigmata, of an epidemic whose roots he felt compelled to deny.

34

MBEKI AND ZIMBABWE

"RED-TELEPHONE DIPLOMACY"

In the first months of 2000, at the very time Thabo Mbeki was most exercised about AIDS, he found himself on the wrong side of global opinion on another issue: how to deal with Zimbabwe's Robert Mugabe. In this instance, the dilemma was tougher—or, at the very least—not self-inflicted in the way the AIDS controversy was. Mugabe, always edgy and already with the blood of a 1982 ethnic genocide on his hands, seemed to descend into brutal tyranny after he lost a referendum in February 2000 to a new civil society coalition named the Movement for Democratic Change (MDC), now the first serious opposition to his rule under the leadership of the trade unionist Morgan Tsvangirai. The white farming community bore the brunt of Mugabe's rage, and he actively supported a savage offensive against the farmers by land invaders masquerading as liberation war veterans. The motivation was two-pronged: to punish the white minority for having broken a silent pact and become involved in politics (they provided much of the backing and the organizational support for the MDC) and to show his own restive supporters that he was serious about giving them back their land. By the beginning of April, nearly 1,000 white farms had been confiscated; in the next few months, over 20 farmers were killed, many more were brutally beaten, and thousands were dispossessed. The economy—based on commercial agriculture—collapsed, and a spate of exiles fled the country: Over the next five years, this would rise to around 4 million, nearly a quarter of the population. Those who were unable to leave faced starvation and increasingly severe state oppression.

Mbeki was in a predicament: Mugabe had already accused Nelson Mandela of being a colonial stooge; he would not balk at doing the same thing if Mbeki took any steps against him, and unless he used force, Mbeki had little way of influencing him. The South African president was determined to minimize the fallout and maintain regional stability. And so he worked off the template he had developed during the Nigerian crisis five years earlier: keep your oar in, maintain your influence so that you can work the eventual solution to your advantage; try not to leave things in the hands of the unpredictable masses. In both Nigeria and Zimbabwe, Mbeki exhibited an unshakable faith in backdoor and behind-the-scenes maneuvering; a hatred of confrontation, particularly with allies; a distaste for the dramatics of activist opposition politics; the instinctive recoil from public criticism of a sitting African head of state; and, most of all, a sense that Africans needed to solve their own problems. Mbeki called it "quiet diplomacy," but it is perhaps better termed "red-telephone diplomacy": the belief in the back channel, along which people in power could resolve problems solely by talking to each other, away from the mess of public contention.

In Nigeria in 1995, as in Zimbabwe from 2000, Mbeki seemed certain that the line from his red telephone in Pretoria across to General Sani Abacha's in Abuja (or Mugabe's in Harare) would carry logic far more compelling than the threats of what his officials disparaged as "megaphone diplomacy." A symptom of this logic, in both cases, was a marked aversion to meeting with those who did not have red telephones—with those activists and leaders in opposition. This significantly compromised his ability to be an honest broker, particularly in Zimbabwe, where MDC leaders often turned on the news to hear Mbeki announcing that peace talks between themselves and Mugabe were imminent, even though he had—they claimed—never communicated this directly with them.[1]

At an emergency regional summit to deal with the matter at Victoria Falls in Zimbabwe in April 2000, Mbeki extracted an undertaking from Mugabe to cease the violence in return for a promise to intercede with the United Kingdom, which Mugabe blamed for reneging on promises made at Zimbabwean independence in 1980 to fund land reform. Implicit in the deal was that Mbeki would not condemn Mugabe. The Zimbabwean president broke one agreement after another in the next eight years. But still, Mbeki stuck doggedly to his side of the contract, insisting that the only way to bring about a solution in Zimbabwe was to coax Mugabe into stepping down rather than to force him out of office and trigger a civil war even more brutal than the state terror and famine already enveloping the country. And so South African election observers rubber-stamped a patently rigged election in 2002, and fought against the isolation of Zimbabwe internationally, or of the imposition of any form of sanctions against the Mugabe regime. Public criticism of Mbeki's appeasement of Mugabe would become most intense in 2008, when he refused to denounce Mugabe after the ruling Zimbabwe African National Union–Patriotic Front (ZANU–PF) staged an effective coup. Mbeki even declared—preposterously—that there was "no crisis" in the country, while a delighted Mugabe looked on.[2] Such apparent appeasement provoked an international furor. Zimbabwean author Peter Godwin described Mbeki as "vacillating, dithering [and] morally compromised"[3]; others drew attention to the alleged hypocrisy of Mbeki, who had played such a prominent role in calling for sanctions against the apartheid regime.

Mbeki's apparent dismissal of the MDC in Zimbabwe seemed to make a mockery of his own calls for an "African Renaissance": Here, across the border, was precisely the regeneration he was calling for, in the form of a robust civil society initiative that crossed race, class, and ethnic boundaries to fight for constitutional reform. And yet the South African government seemed to be running away from it, preferring the older, more comfortable conventions of ZANU–PF, no matter how direly it had atrophied into kleptocracy and corruption. Despite Mbeki's own earlier modernization of the ANC, he clung to the anachronistic belief that the MDC was an agent of the old colonial powers—specifically Britain and the United States—rather than of the aspirations of the Zimbabwean people themselves. Perhaps Mbeki was running away from a similar scenario in his own country, too: a mass movement, led by the trade unions, rising up against the country's liberators. The South African Congress of South African Trade Unions (COSATU) had become Mbeki's most bitter foe—and would later become a fervent supporter of both the MDC and of Jacob Zuma in his battle against the South African president. This no doubt played a significant role in Mbeki's attitude toward the MDC.

One of Mbeki's harshest critics on Zimbabwe was his brother Moeletsi, who had lived in Zimbabwe for ten years and was an active supporter of the MDC. Like many others, Moeletsi believed that South Africa should engineer Mugabe's removal by pulling the plug on Zimbabwe's power, given that it had not paid its bills to South Africa, which supplied its electricity, for years.[4] This, after all, was the strategy that the apartheid prime minister John Vorster had used to force Ian Smith to the negotiating table with Mugabe and other freedom fighters in the late 1970s, when he threatened to strangle the Rhodesian state by stopping all cross-border traffic. But Thabo Mbeki believed that such action would only harm ordinary people and would quicken Mugabe's descent into dangerous self-delusion. "Mugabe's critics tell us to turn off the power," one of Mbeki's Zimbabwe negotiators told me. "Well, you know what Mugabe says? 'Go ahead! Do it! Turn off the power! We'll sit in the dark! We didn't need electricity during the *chimurenga* [independence war]. Why should we need it now?'"

Mbeki himself continued to insist that there was no alternative to "quiet diplomacy": Had Iraq not taught the world a lesson? he asked me. "You can come with everything you've got, with the great huge power, with billions of dollars, but if...the local population doesn't agree, you are not going to produce a solution." Even if many of them were victims of brainwashing and intimidation, well over 40 percent of the voters in the 2008 election supported Mugabe: he was not universally reviled in his own country. More pertinently, Zimbabwe's significant armed forces remained firmly behind him.

Mbeki had many practical, logical reasons for his strategy: not only his wish to prevent a bloody civil war and an even greater flood of refugees across the South African border, but a not-unfounded skepticism about the skittish leadership of the opposition. He also understood that South Africa already had a reputation as an arrogant upstart—and that Mugabe still commanded much allegiance on the continent. But whatever the logic behind Mbeki's position regarding Mugabe, there was emotion too, and history. And at its root was the little-understood relationship between the two men, going back to 1980, when Thabo Mbeki seemed to be the only man who expected—and even approved of—Robert Mugabe's victory in Zimbabwe's first democratic election.

In 1980, for most in the ANC, Mugabe's party, then called simply the Zimbabwe African National Union (ZANU), was the enemy; Oliver Tambo himself had once called it the "spurious stooge [of] the imperialists."[5] ZANU was aligned to China and the Pan Africanist Congress, while the ANC's ally was Joshua Nkomo's Zimbabwe African People's Union (ZAPU), part of the same Moscow-aligned cluster of liberation movements, also headquartered in Lusaka. In the Zambian capital, Nkomo's decisive defeat in the 1980 election felt like one for the ANC itself: Zimbabwe now threatened to become a bulwark against—rather than the anticipated bridge toward—the ANC's own passage home. "My God, we were depressed," one midlevel ANC comrade then living in Lusaka told me. "I remember a group of us—all [Communist] Party—drinking miserably through the night as if at a wake. I think we even said we would rather have had [Ian] Smith [the white Rhodesian leader] than Mugabe."

Mugabe's support was from the majority Shona ethnic group, while Nkomo's was from the minority Ndebele. The Ndebele are the descendants of Mzilikazi, the Zulu King Shaka's breakaway general, and the link between ZAPU and the ANC was thus affective as well as ideological: Comrades from the two organizations shared the same language and culture, trained together in the Soviet Union, fought together in the bush, and lived together in Lusaka. But by the late 1970s Thabo Mbeki had accepted—as few of his comrades were able to—the ethnopolitical arithmetic of Zimbabwe: Mugabe, and not Nkomo, would ultimately gain control of the country and thus of South Africa's route home. Mbeki thus believed that, whatever the ideological and cultural barriers, the ANC had to mend the relationship. He was, he told me, among a tiny minority of ANC leaders who felt this way and who "maintained some kind of informal contact" with the ZANU leadership before 1980. This view was apostasy in the South African Communist Party and Umkhonto we Sizwe (MK), and certainly contributed to the branding of Mbeki as "unreliable" at the time.

But Mbeki told me that Oliver Tambo agreed with him and tasked him to make the peace with Mugabe's ZANU. Mbeki's main contact was the man he would attempt to maneuver two decades later into Mugabe's shoes: Emmerson Mnangagwa, Zimbabwe's prime "securocrat." Mbeki's approach to the ZANU grandees then, as during his presidency, was supplicatory, and—then, at least—it appeared to work. Twenty years later, Mbeki told me that the deal he made was the finest one the ANC had ever been offered by an African country, and that he made a solid peace with his movement's former foes.

But the records of the Swedish foreign ministry—which supported both the ANC and ZANU—tell a different story. They are littered with complaints from the Zimbabwean officials about the ANC, in effect accusing the South Africans of opportunism and expediency for showing interest in ZANU only after it won the election. It is hard not to feel, reading these records, that the Zimbabwean government has had a long track record duping its ANC comrades: When the Swedes anxiously conveyed the complaints to Mbeki in Lusaka in October 1980, he breezily responded that the strains between ZANU and the ANC "were history" and that the ANC expected official approval by the Zimbabwe government within the month.[6]

Two years later, the relationship seemed dead, caught in the wake of ZANU's assault on ZAPU and the four-year genocide in Matabeleland, which saw over 20,000 Ndebeles killed by Mnangagwa's murderous Fifth Brigade. The ANC military was still very involved with ZAPU, and MK's entire command—20 to 30 people—was rounded up and imprisoned, many of them tortured. The ANC's infrastructure in Zimbabwe was destroyed; only in 1985 was an office set up that brokered enough of a truce for the ANC to start working properly from Zimbabwe again.

Still, Mbeki insisted to me that such "historical tensions" had disappeared among "those of us who were dealing with the Zimbabwe government fairly regularly." And to make this point, he told me an anecdote, somewhat at his own expense, about how he had caused an international incident sometime in the late 1980s by failing to come home one night. The way he tells it, he had stayed up till the early hours of the morning with a visiting Swedish delegation and had then rushed to the airport at dawn to greet a group of visiting white South Africans. When Zanele Mbeki awoke and found her husband not there, she reported him missing; in a panic, Kenneth Kaunda threw roadblocks up all around Lusaka and called Mugabe to tell him Mbeki had been kidnapped. Mbeki was, of course, in Lusaka at the time, sleeping off a hangover—he did not tell me this himself—at a Swedish diplomat's residence. And like the sheepish son who knows he is in for a reprimand, he told me with a wry smile, he did his best to avoid both Kaunda and Mugabe for a while. But he finally found himself cornered by the Zimbabwean leader at a conference. "Young man," Mugabe said, wagging a finger at him, "you must tell us next time you don't sleep at home." The point of the story, the way Mbeki told it, was that by this stage he and Mugabe (and thus the ANC and ZANU) were kinfolk; that Mugabe cared about him as if he were his own son.

———————

Thabo Mbeki has often told the story of how Zimbabwe voluntarily put its own land reform process on hold, because the year it was to begin—1990— was the year of the South African breakthrough, and Mugabe had been persuaded to defer land reform so as not to scare white South Africans from agreeing to majority rule. Mbeki's conclusion was that because Zimbabweans sacrificed their own rights to land to help liberate their neighbors, South Africans now had to support them in their endeavors to get their land back.[7] Where many Zimbabweans might take issue with Mbeki, of course, was in his insistence on backing Mugabe as the legitimate bearer of these aspirations. Mbeki's argument would be that if he had listened to the "people" of Zimbabwe, the result would have been disastrous for them. His leverage was his special relationship with Mugabe, going back to 1980, and the best chance for Zimbabwe was for him to exploit that: The fact that he failed, until 2008, was beyond his control. There may well be truth to this argument. But the failure of Mbeki's Zimbabwe policy was that he could not find a way to keep the red telephone line open to Mugabe while simultaneously telegraphing his disapproval of the Zimbabwean president's actions to the world—and to suffering Zimbabweans themselves.

This was a difficult job, to be sure. But why did African's most skillful statesman seem so ill-equipped to handle it? Mbeki struggled to articulate his Zimbabwe policy clearly because Mugabe's defiance spoke to his own inflamed nationalism at the time, manifested—we have already seen—by his response to the AIDS epidemic and his reading of the racism behind the adulation of Nelson Mandela as the "one good native." Mbeki might have found a way of distancing himself from Mugabe in an attempt to disprove the one good native theory; instead, he allowed himself to feel that he, like Mugabe, was the victim of Mandela exceptionalism, and this threw him into a defensive posture. The more critics implied that his "quiet diplomacy" was a policy of appeasement that made him a Mugabe in training himself, the more determined he was to prove that his way was correct.

Mbeki took particular exception to the patronizing attitude of the British government, whom he blasted for telling him how to run his own neighborhood, and the Zimbabwe dispute came to tarnish his otherwise excellent relationship with Tony Blair. Blair and his government had become the greatest supporters of Mbeki's New Partnership for Africa's Development (NEPAD), leading the Group of Eight (G8) nations toward a grant of R620 billion for strategic funding for Africa that would begin to lessen its dependency on aid and strengthen the democratic process on the continent; now Blair made it clear to Mbeki that NEPAD would never get real support for as long as there was no strong moral line taken, by African leaders, on Zimbabwe. By 2003, after failing in his attempts to get the Commonwealth's suspension of Zimbabwe lifted, an enraged Mbeki wrote that he accepted Mugabe's version of history: that it was Britain, in fact, that had created the problem by reneging on a commitment to fund land redistribution in Zimbabwe because it did not want to dispossess its "kith and kin." Mbeki agreed with Mugabe that this, and not alleged human rights abuse, was at the root of Zimbabwe's crisis, for it had forced Zimbabweans to take matters into their own hands.[8]

The truth is that by 2000 Britain had already given the Zimbabwean government £44 million for land reform, but because it believed that these funds were disappearing into the Mugabe kleptocracy, it refused to make a second payment of £36 million until sufficient controls were put in place. This was unacceptable to Mugabe, and Mbeki—although voicing his disapproval of the violent way the farms were being confiscated—in effect supported him, asserting that Western attacks on Mugabe were racist and hypocritical.[9] Mbeki believed with a passion that the only reason the Western world (and white South Africa) had demonized Mugabe was because his victims were white farmers rather than nameless black masses: "A million people die in Rwanda and do the white South Africans care?" he raged in an interview with Allister Sparks. "Not a bit. You talk to them about the disaster in Angola, to which the apartheid regime contributed, and they're not interested. Let's talk about Zimbabwe. Does anyone want to talk about the big disaster in Mozambique, from which it is now recovering? No. Let's talk about Zimbabwe. You say to them, Look at what is happening in the Congo. No, no, no, let's talk about Zimbabwe. Why? It's because 12 white people died!"[10]

Mbeki had a point, of course—as did he when he told Sparks that he believed white South African reactions were governed by the unjustified fear of land invasions to follow at home. But because he read any white criticism of Mugabe as racist, an attack on Africans' ability to govern themselves, he could not see the political imperative of quelling such fear, an imperative particularly pressing given that he was simultaneously attempting to sell his NEPAD investment plan for Africa to the leaders of the Western world. His racialized reading of the Zimbabwean crisis also sometimes seemed to prevent him from acknowledging that Mugabe had strident black critics too, not to mention millions of black victims.

It was hard, then, not to come to the conclusion that Mbeki himself seemed to be driven by an atavistic loyalty to Mugabe, a "father"—even if exasperating, even if dangerous—within the family of freedom fighters. Morgan Tsvangirai, the MDC leader, was treated with contempt because he was not part of this family: He had no struggle credentials, and his support came from a broad-based civic movement that directly challenged the liberation movement's hegemony. Tsvangirai's ascendancy thus signaled the struggle-family's inevitable demise—and presented, to many in the ANC, an alarming harbinger of this eventuality in South Africa too. Mbeki thought it a far better solution to manage a succession strategy within the family and to help put into place a trustworthy comrade whose familial ties with Mbeki—whose blood bonds of struggle with the ANC—would underwrite Pretoria's influence in Harare. But this strategy came up, ultimately, against the will of the Zimbabwean people, who in the first round of the presidential elections in May 2008 gave Tsvangirai the most votes, albeit not a clear majority. Tsvangirai now had the moral authority of a victory behind him: Even if Mbeki's apparent appeasement did, as his critics suggest, enable Mugabe to intimidate the MDC out of contesting the runoff election, Mbeki had no choice at this stage but to mediate an equitable settlement between the two. Mugabe understood this, too, and capitulated to a settlement that saw him remain president but with severely limited powers, and with Tsvangirai as prime minister and head of government.

Had Mbeki reverted to his usual approach, so unpopular with his South African comrades in the early 1990s, of papering over irreconcilable differences rather than forcing them into the open? And by not taking a strong moral stand earlier and cutting off Mugabe's lifeline of economic support (and political cover), had Mbeki given the tyrant leverage that enabled him to remain in office via a power-sharing deal when he should, by rights, have been long gone? Mbeki was adamant that his only capital was his special relationship with Mugabe, which he would continue to use, even if doing so enraged and infuriated the rest of the world.

In the end, the result was an unfair deal for Tsvangirai, certainly, but one that nonetheless shifted the balance of forces unmistakably away from ZANU–PF and toward the MDC—toward democracy and the reconstruction of the country. Nonetheless, by early 2009, the two sides were still fighting over the details of the settlement, and the country remained paralyzed in the face of a devastating famine. Zimbabwe would prove to be one of the graveyards of his legacy.

At ten minutes past two on the morning on Thursday, August 30, 2001, Govan Mbeki died of congestive cardiac failure, at his home in Summerstrand in Port Elizabeth. He was 91 years old. His final request to Dr. Mamisa Chabula—his doctor and companion in the years since his release from prison—had been to be wrapped in his favorite African National Congress blanket and cap. When we met after Govan Mbeki's funeral, she told me that in all of her years with him, she had never heard him say he missed anyone: "But a few days before he died, he said to me, 'Misa, I miss Thabo.' It was at that point I knew that he was finally going."

The timing was terrible for Thabo Mbeki. In its ongoing battle with the ANC over macroeconomic policy, the Congress of South African Trade Unions (COSATU) had called for a national antiprivatization strike to coincide exactly with the UN World Conference Against Racism, which Mbeki was hosting in Durban. Never had public acrimony between the governing ANC and its alliance partners to the left been so severe: The dispute over Mbeki's controversial economic policies had come to a head in the week his father was dying. Mbeki left Durban for the day and spent the afternoon with his father. When I asked him what they spoke about, his answer was "practical things," nothing "spectacular." He then reminded me, unsolicited, of the distance in his family: The Mbeki children had been raised "to be used to being without [our parents]." Still, Dr. Chabula remembers that Mbeki left his father's home filled with sadness, wanting to move Govan to Pretoria, to the comforts—and, presumably, final resting-place status—of his son's official residence.

But Govan Mbeki demurred: he would die in Port Elizabeth and be buried there, rather than in ceremonial pomp in Pretoria or Cape Town, or in the Transkei, from whence he came and where his wife still lived. He was very specific: He wanted to be laid to rest among the graves of ordinary working folk in the dilapidated cemetery at Zwide, one of the city's more abject townships. The iconoclasm of this final wish was profound, a disavowal not only of his marriage but of the traditions of clan and kinship too, an active and final assertion that he belonged more to the urban proletariat of Port Elizabeth than to the amaZizi of Mpukane or the Mbeki household of Idutywa. It was also a willfully political act; "Oom Gov's last revenge," as one of the family put it to me. The canny old man must have known that he would be granted a state funeral and that a burial in Zwide would force all the apparatus of state into a direct encounter with the poverty of the township and thus compel the new black elite to confront it.

When I arrived to pay my respects at Govan Mbeki's residence the day before the funeral, I found Epainette Mbeki sitting alone in her late husband's bedroom. She had always filled her universe with the weight of her purpose, despite her tiny frame; now, however, she seemed smaller than usual, perched on the edge of her husband's large bed as if she did not belong in this place of strangers. Her face was set in a rictus of perseverance; she seemed to be reliving the vulnerability she experienced in those years after her husband's arrest. "When he was imprisoned," she said to me, unprompted, after a long silence, "his friends abandoned me like rats from a sinking ship. Like rats. They would see me on the street and expect me to ask for help, but I didn't. I didn't ask for help then, and I won't now."

Mrs. Mbeki would spend the following day, in the glare of the media, quietly set between her two sons, one step behind the coffin. Did she find a way to say a personal good-bye? "No. The whole thing was not planned with consideration for me. It was for the public. And actually, that's how Oom Gov wanted it. And so I said, 'Well, let it go.'" Here she was, then, this careful woman who cannot abide pretense and show, unable to mourn privately for the end of a long and difficult marriage, required by the apparatus of state and the expectations of the world to perform public grief for a man who had long since forsaken her.

The day belonged to the movement: tributes by Nelson Mandela and Jacob Zuma; interminable struggle songs, prayers, praise songs, and sermons. The president stayed close to his mother, silent and stricken, acknowledging condolences with the kind of curt but respectful nod that disinvites further engagement, then weeping quietly at the graveside. But even in silence, Mbeki was of course the focus of the day. He was not allowed to forget that he was to be held responsible for redeeming his father's dreams of freedom. Almost every one of the multiplicity of praise singers who blessed the event mentioned it. "Govan!" yelled one, in Xhosa. "You have done your life's work well. Thabo! Now the world is looking at you!"

Jacob Zuma addressed Mbeki directly. "My brother, Comrade President," he said, "you, as an individual have shown an extraordinary fortitude to rise within the ranks of the ANC to become its president and that of this country despite the difficulty of having a father imprisoned, of growing up without him. You took a decision that a permanent solution would be to put all efforts into the struggle for liberation."[1] Zuma was perceptively acknowledging that Mbeki's condition of disconnect—his attenuated familial relationships—had been to sublimate all emotions, all relationships, all desires, into the struggle for liberation, a revolutionary impulse that stems not just from the oppression of his people but from his own early wounds. Although it was not public knowledge, the relationship between Mbeki and Zuma had already begun to sour, and Zuma's speech was an olive branch, an address from one brother to another given that "in many ways our father Oom Gov represented a father to me too."[2]

Inevitably, the funeral became an enactment of the very issues the left was protesting about in its antiprivatization strikes. Just two weeks before he died, the COSATU general secretary Zwelinzima Vavi had declared that if privatization threatened to enlarge the gap between rich and poor, then "the worst gap is the one among blacks themselves," some of whom had become an "arrogant" new elite.[3] Now this very elite was forced to bump its way, in a miles-long cortege of luxury German vehicles, through a tight human avenue of very poor people waving Govan Mbeki good-bye. There was something festive and celebratory in the air—not just that Govan Mbeki truly was a local hero in these neglected quarters, but that the carnival of power had come to town—and most onlookers cheered for the dignitaries they recognized. Some, however, made no bones about their feelings. "Look at your fancy cars!" one woman yelled to a prominent black businessman as he alighted from his BMW. "We don't even have the money to take a taxi!" Her companion took up the cry: "Go back to Pretoria, and only return when you have some houses to give us!"[4]

There was, in the end, something extraordinary in the presence in their hardscrabble landscape of all the official pomp that comes with a state funeral: the military brass, the ceremonial guard trumpeting the Last Post, the coffin draped in a South African flag. But there was also an ostentation that is part of any grand township funeral, all the more uncomfortable in this environment: the Mercedes hearse, the undertaker's branded bunting, the fashion parade of mourning garb, the tombstone itself—a gleaming marble affair that seemed to swagger unnecessarily over the tin notices stuck onto metal staves that are its modest neighbors. Govan Mbeki's grave itself was thus rendered a symbol: not only of his (and his family's) status, but of the rareness of that status, and of the fact that the vast majority of his people did not come anywhere nearly close enough to sharing it.

In the year following his father's death, Thabo Mbeki mounted a sustained attack on his critics to the left, accusing them of trying to hijack the ANC toward the impossible end of socialist revolution.[5] COSATU retaliated, with the kind of language that ultimately would be used to unseat Mbeki five years later: The ANC had been taken over by an "authoritarian clique" seeking to revive the "negative tendencies" of exile, such as "intolerance," "paranoia," and "personal abuse": "[A]ny dissent is seen as disloyal or even counter-revolutionary...vitriolic attacks and the deliberate spreading of malicious rumours have become commonplace, as has the use of race."[6]

It was in this highly contentious environment that the ANC gathered at Stellenbosch University in the Western Cape in December 2002 for its first national conference since Thabo Mbeki had succeeded Nelson Mandela at Mafikeng five years previously. Throughout the year there had been talk of rebellion but, extraordinarily, Mbeki was returned unopposed, as were the five other senior officials, all supposed Mbeki loyalists (including Zuma as deputy). Mbeki prevailed, not through a Tambo-style approach of building consensus but rather through a party-strongman corralling of power: the successful appeal to an atavistic sense of unity in the face of "counter-revolutionary" forces, the skillful working of the party machinery to ensure compliant delegates, and—looming unsaid in the background, in contradiction to Mbeki's powerful presidential address slamming corruption and the decline of revolutionary values[7]—the unspoken hand of patronage. The ANC was no longer a liberation movement but a party in power. Branch delegates were no longer activists, but—more often than not—implicated in the system that Mbeki controlled: councillors, bureaucrats, government contractors. In South Africa, elected officials generally do not have well-established professions or trust funds to fall back on once they leave public service, and their incomes often support ten or more people. Not only their livelihoods but the well-being of their families and their fragile new status in the middle class—with mortgages, credit cards, and children in private schools—depended on the maintenance of the status quo. Even if they were unhappy with Mbeki, they acted in their own interests and returned him to the leadership of the ANC and thus of the country with more power than ever.

The ousting of Thabo Mbeki at the next ANC conference in 2007 would demonstrate the shallow base of his Stellenbosch glory. And Mbeki's opponents had not so much capitulated as beaten a strategic retreat. Nonetheless, for about a year before and after his 2004 electoral victory, a period lasting from the Stellenbosch conference to his firing of Jacob Zuma in early 2005, Mbeki presided over an apparently united ANC, with a command over the movement unmatched even by Mandela in his heyday.

The ANC was returned to power in May 2004 with an increased majority, up from 66.4 percent to 69.7 percent, its highest margin yet, even though the inevitable runoff of democracy meant that the turnout poll decreased significantly. An image from Mbeki's campaign stump became iconic. He is in a modest living room in Khayamnandi, a desolate township in the hills outside Port Elizabeth, surrounded by elderly people dressed simply but neatly, with the kind of hard, weather-beaten faces characteristic of the region. What is unusual, even shocking, about the image is that the patrician president is splayed out on the grubby tiled floor, a knee clasped in his arms, stretched out between an avenue of the scuffed shoes of the people sitting, on chairs, to either side of him. "Mbeki's Extreme Makeover" read the *Sunday Times*: The president, the article concluded, was "successfully changing people's perceptions" that he was aloof and inaccessible.[8]

I happened to be following Mbeki that early April as he blazed through Port Elizabeth. The photograph was taken at the end of a long day even by the standards of Mbeki's campaign: He had already done walking tours in three townships, visited at six homes, held two rollicking rallies, and addressed a business luncheon. That morning, at dawn, he had stepped briskly off the presidential plane in a neatly pressed black suit over his signature yellow golf shirt and rubber-soled walking shoes. As the day progressed—as the stories of hardship and distress accumulated—he became more and more rumpled until, by the time he reached Khayamnandi, he looked more like a working man—a clerk, perhaps—coming home from a hard day at the office than the president of the country.

The light in Khayamnandi was golden, the shadows were long, the crowds lining the streets impatient: Their guest was many hours late. A twilight air of madness, festive but also desperate, erupted when the cavalcade of dark cars eventually made its way up the hillside. Visibly exhausted, Mbeki was transported through the crowds and into a series of homes. In one, an elderly man had dragged himself across the crowded sitting room and slumped himself down in the chair that had been reserved for the president. When the old man realized what he had done, he rose immediately, but Mbeki urged him to remain seated—and plunked himself down on the floor. Mbeki has often been accused—not without cause—of having succumbed to the pomposity of power, but here was another side of him. His action signified the workmanlike way his intimates know well: "Who cares where we sit? There's a job to be done." So deeply engaged was he in the tale of woe being told—as always, about official callousness—that by the time a chair arrived for him, he waved it away impatiently.

Media commentary suggested that he had taken to the stump in this way in part because the ANC did not have the funds for a high-tech media campaign and in part as an expression of his own cynicism: the ritual of descending to the street to pretend to be a "man of the people" so as to harvest votes before disappearing, once more, into the aerie of power.[9] There might have been truth to both accusations, but two other things were clear: It was working, and Mbeki was enjoying himself, more and more, with every outing. There was not that grimace, present in previous images of Mbeki, of having to fulfill an irritating and time-wasting responsibility.

The campaign was devised by Stan Greenberg, the American pollster who had played so great a role in securing Bill Clinton's victory 12 years previously. Its cleverness—it seemed to me—was that it put Mbeki into situations where he could perform, before the cameras, a core facet of his actual personality, one occluded all too often by the trappings of power. And so he was able to put up with the dancing and the kissing because he understood it as something you had to do, outside, so that you could get inside, to listen. I fancied I saw, in the diligent recorder obsessing about the detail of an electricity cut-off or an illegal tavern, that letter-writing little boy from Mbewuleni, imbued with missionary consciousness, the duty to help those less fortunate than himself. I saw, too, the unexpected ease that comes from having grown up around ordinary folk even if you are not one of them yourself.

The "makeover" was more than skin deep: As Mbeki became exposed to the electorate for the first time in five years, he appeared to undergo a striking change of rhetoric, one that signaled some kind of ideological homecoming, to the policies of social democracy and poverty alleviation that had characterized the ANC before the fiscal austerity imposed by GEAR in 1996. On one level, Mbeki was giving political expression to an empirical fact: because of the tight management of the state treasury, there was some fat in the budget for the first time since the ANC had come into office. But there was also a startling reversion to old wisdom: "Trickle-down" economics did not work in the South African context, and the only solution to poverty was state investment. By the end of 2003, he would launch a public works program; by 2005, a R372 billion state growth fund; and by 2007, a comprehensive social welfare system—one that would see South Africa spending more per capita on poverty relief than any other country and that would see 12 million South Africans (over a quarter of the country) receiving welfare, usually in the form of child support or old-age pensions. The flip side of this was that for 4 million South African families, this was the only form of income: unemployment remained astronomical, at between 29 and 40 percent during Mbeki's second term.[10]

Mbeki's own advisors volunteer that the 2004 election steered him directly toward talking about poverty in a way the ANC had not done since the heady Reconstruction and Development Plan days a decade previously: His outings forced him to take note of the huge gap between the ANC's rhetoric of service delivery and the reality on the ground. But something else had been feeding the shift, away from the "Washington Consensus" line, in Mbeki's rhetoric: He had become embittered by the way the private sector was not responding to his government's business-friendly policies with investment. As one of his senior aides put it to me: "We had done everything by the book and where was the money? Why was there not the promised increase [in foreign investment]? Thabo often voiced his frustration about this. This is where his analysis of Afropessimism comes from—his understanding that even if we did everything right, we would still be seen by the world as useless Africans. So if we were going to do anything, we needed to do it for ourselves."

When I went to see Thabo Mbeki in the afterglow of his 2004 victory, he was bullish with confidence. Did he still worry about "the dream deferred," I asked him, with all its apocalyptic premonitions? He waved the question aside as the preoccupation of another era. Now, he insisted, there was no possibility of "some big eruption"; his impression was that there was "a much greater sense of joy in South African society today. Whichever side of the street you are, [there is] a much greater sense of celebration, and I think this reflects a much greater sense of reassurance amongst everybody." On the campaign trail, he had certainly encountered grievance and complaint, but he had experienced this as constructive civic engagement rather than explosive disaffection.

As I had watched Mbeki on the campaign trail during 2004, I had kept on thinking about a speech he had made to his Sussex friends at his fifth-seventh birthday party, just days after his inauguration in 1999, when he had revealed the pledge he had given to a dying Afrikaner banker: to "walk the country" he was destined to govern so that he could finally get to know it. It seemed to me, I suggested to Mbeki, that he had done just that on the campaign trail. Did this finally constitute a homecoming, at last, ten years after his return from exile?

Mbeki took up the notion with gusto, and spoke—at length, and with considerable emotion—about the discoveries he had made while campaigning: mainly that the "sense of joy and celebration" to be found on the streets of South Africa came equally from whites as from blacks. His reading of the national zeitgeist seemed to be drawn, specifically, from the way the ordinary people he met had responded directly to him. It was, in a way, a reprise of his 1980s seduction campaign, but this time with ordinary people in working-class suburbs rather than with the Afrikaner elite on secluded English country estates. He told me, now, about some of these encounters: how he bought a pipe for one man to help him stop smoking cigarettes; how a little boy told him that "his best birthday present was to play in the street with the president"; how he was invited to a *braaivleis* [barbecue].

In the 1980s, Mbeki was somewhat transformed by his encounters with white South Africans, even if he did not always admit it. Now, nearly two decades later, Mbeki volunteered to a profound transformation from his encounters with ordinary Afrikaners. He came to see, he said, that "the sense of national cohesion and unity is actually very high" in South Africa. The shift in analysis from his position a few years earlier—where he focused obsessively on how South Africa was "two nations," one rich and white and the other black and poor—could not have been starker. At the core of this new outlook was a revelation: White people accepted him as their president, despite the fact that he was black and even though they were not going to vote for him. "They sit there, they are talking to their president, they have certain demands, they have critical comments to make like everyone else, but there is no sense of 'this is not one of us.' No sense of distance." And now, because he was being accepted, he too could finally accept them, white South Africans, as being "as African as I am."

I was taken aback. This was the great seducer, the man who managed to win the Afrikaner establishment to accept black majority rule. What did it say about his own level of disconnection—what the pundits might uncharitably call "paranoia" or "insecurity"—that it had taken him this long to realize that ordinary Afrikaners, raised in a highly authoritarian political culture, would respect a president merely by virtue of his office regardless of his color? What did it say about the depths of South Africa's racial pathologies—and the way that Mbeki had internalized them—that the most powerful man in the country would expect ordinary white folk to reject him on the basis of the color of his skin?

In the past, Mbeki told me, he had understood white people as "invalids," as having been "infected with all these ideas of racism and racist superiority. You have to coax them into this new South Africa. You have to be very tolerant and understand[ing]." White racism had been a pathology to be pitied, to be healed. But now, a decade after the end of apartheid, he had ceased, for the first time, to see white South Africans in the abstract, as a motive force of history or as a sanatorium full of patients succumbing to a dying ideology. Rather, he finally began to experience them as fellow citizens, as human beings, "as African as I am." And this revelation had come about through the way they engaged with him as president. What he heard them saying during his walking tours was "in reality, we are not invalids. We want to be part of this process of building this [country]. And you see it in their response to their president. There is no sense of alienation, there is no guilt or anything. It's just their president."

I was reminded, listening to Mbeki talking about Afrikaners, of a comment he had made in a British newspaper a few years previously, after a meet-the-people visit to a desperately poor rural area. He told his interviewer that he had been "frightened" by the "kind of devotion, attachment, level of confidence, extreme excitement" he found when he went out and engaged with ordinary people, people who were "almost verging on the fanatical, they are so enthusiastic."[11] Once more I was struck by his ingenuousness: Given the power that radiated from his office, the power that he had to change people's lives—and the utter powerlessness of the South African rural poor—how could it be otherwise? There was the sense, in this observation—as there was now in his discussion about Afrikaners—of a bookish prince discovering for the first time that his subjects were flesh and blood.

Mbeki's close aide Joel Netshitenzhe once gave me an eloquent description of the way abstract revolutionary principles had materialized into flesh and bone and landscape for people such as himself and Mbeki: "For years, you talk about 'the masses,' their aspirations, but the country itself, the people, its institutions, are almost like lifeless objects, motive forces. It takes a bit of time before all these objects become a living part of you. It takes time before you begin to appreciate the child barefooted in the beautiful rural area more than just as the receptacle of your delivery. It takes time to settle, to appreciate the child as a child, in a beautiful space. To realize that these are people, not ideals." Now Mbeki had a different, but no less powerful, way of saying the same thing. When he first came back from exile he thought, " 'We have got to fix this problem.' You look at it, analyze it and all that, and say, 'There are the problems, now how do we fix them?' But to become *of* it, now that takes something else!"

Mbeki told me that the way he had first fulfilled his promise to that dying Afrikaner to "walk this land" was by choosing different parts of South Africa to take his annual Christmas holiday. One year he found himself in the desert wilderness of the Karoo National Park. He was not particularly eager to go, he admitted to me, and when he got there, he spent a lot of time taking photographs, his new hobby. Trying to capture this vastness, this beauty, he felt something profound stirring inside him, but he could not name it. It took form only later when he came across a comment made by a group of German tourists in the Visitors' Book: "*Stille*" they had written: that is all. He knew the word, from the German Christmas hymn—"*Stille nacht, heilige nacht*," "Silent night, holy night"—and understood immediately what he had been feeling: "These Germans must be right," he thought to himself, for the word *stille* was "such an accurate description of the impact of the Karoo. Not [just] stillness, but a sense of rest and repose, of peace, of quiet, of calm, and of an integrated world"; it implied that "there is no longer any alienation of the human being from nature and nature from the human being, and there is this quiet integrated world of repose."

Two things struck me as I listened to Mbeki describe this Walden-like epiphany. The first was that an experience I take for granted even if I cannot always access it—that feeling of peace, of quiet, of calm—was something entirely new for this man who has spent most of his adult life uprooted, disconnected, exiled. And the second was that he had used the word "integrated" so forcefully to describe an internal psychic condition rather than the external postapartheid world he was responsible for governing. It seemed to me that, whatever might still be in store for him and however his legacy might be judged, Thabo Mbeki was finally home. The electorate had given him a huge vote of confidence, and he was correct in viewing it as something of a plebiscite on his presidency. There were no longer any paternal shadows: no Govan Mbeki, no Duma Nokwe, no Oliver Tambo, no Nelson Mandela. The victory was his own.

In February 2006—over four years after the death of Govan Mbeki, and two years after the death of Thabo's sister, Linda—I traveled back with Epainette Mbeki to Mbewuleni. Since my previous trip, a new tar road had been built. The presence of something as simple as well-cambered macadam meant one no longer felt that sense of a bumpy ascent into a world removed from modernity. There was electricity up in Mbewuleni too; Thabo Mbeki's home village seemed, finally, to be connected to the country that he governed. There was something else different about this particular trip back to Mbewuleni: We were with Olive Mpahlwa, the mother of Thabo Mbeki's missing son Kwanda, whom I had last encountered, in such terrible distress, in Port Elizabeth in 2000. Olive had left Port Elizabeth for good, with its memories of the fruitless search for her son and her failed encounters with his father, and had returned to Mbewuleni to take occupancy of her late father's homestead. She had been recruited to come back, it transpired, by Mrs. Mbeki herself—to work in an AIDS hospice being set up, in a big white house on the crest of the hill that was to have been the Mbeki retirement home.

The house had been built by Epainette and Govan Mbeki's daughter, Linda, and was to have been her gift to her reunited parents, after her father was released from prison. Shattered by apartheid and the struggle against it, they would have a place to grow old—a family hearth at last. But of course, it was not to be, and so Linda decided to run the place as a tavern, an outpost of the thriving business she had developed 19 miles away in Butterworth. The previous time I had visited Mbewuleni, the house had been in a state of decay, with pigs and chickens wandering freely through it and four midday drunks sprawled around an old kitchen table. It had carried something even more devastating than the rural decay I had seen in the other family seats I had visited on that trip, the Mbeki home at Nyili and the Moerane farm at Mangoloaneng. There, at least, embedded in a shattered Hammond organ or a hand-carved oak table, was a sense of paradise lost; here, however, it seemed as if the plaster fantasy of reconnection had not even dried before it had started cracking.

But in 2004, shortly after Linda's death, Epainette Mbeki had been approached by a Ugandan medic living in the Transkei who already ran an AIDS hospice in Butterworth, looking to expand his business. She offered him the white house, and when he said he needed staff, she asked Olive Mpahlwa—a trained nurse—to come back to Mbewuleni. Seed funding to refurbish the building was secured through a small self-help grant from the American embassy, and now they were looking for the wherewithal to make the place operative.

Olive Mpahlwa showed me around the Linda Mbeki Hospice, as the facility was named. There were not yet any patients, but the transformation was extraordinary. That signature tavern-smell of sweat and spilled beer had given way to disinfectant, and the bedrooms had been painted and tiled, transformed into wards with hospital cots set in fresh blue linen. "I haven't found my son," Mpahlwa said to me, "but I have found peace. It's making me to be able to beat things, now that I am back home. I look at my earlier life, I see my family, I see my son Kwanda, aged two, aged ten, and it brings out something indescribable. All these memories are pleasant memories." She credited Epainette Mbeki with her newfound well-being, even if the way she did so reinforced the centrality of her lost son to her identity: Epainette "has had such an impact on my life, because she knew Kwanda so well. I draw on her. She's very supportive. She's a role model."

The first time I had visited Mbewuleni, Epainette Mbeki had despaired at her inability to inspire the village women to get so much as a bread-baking project off the ground. Now the hospice had trained 24 unemployed locals to be caregivers. Under Olive Mpahlwa's supervision, they arranged themselves into the Linda Mbeki Hospice Choir to serenade us. Their lyrics—borrowed from the songbook of South Africa's vibrant grassroots AIDS movement—were unexpectedly frank: "Some are positive, some are negative, some don't know. Mrs. Msimang, please give us something for AIDS. People are dying."

While we were there, "the Doctor"—as the Ugandan medic was universally referred to—arrived, bounding out of his car wearing a houndstooth jacket and a zooty shirt. He seemed to think I was a prospective funder but, strangely, did not have any documentation about the hospice save a company registration certificate. When I asked him about his background, he told me that he had been in the Ugandan military, had emigrated to South Africa in 1994, and had already helped hundreds with the micronutrient solution that he had invented and patented himself. My alarm bells, already primed by his imprecision about his medical training, began to ring when he boasted of a 60 percent success rate with the solution. When I cross-questioned him later, he told me he had a master's degree in sports science from Kiev, Ukraine, and a qualification in herbal medicine from Uganda that entitled him to be called "doctor." He also told me that his micronutrient solution was made from the moringa tree, widely known for its nutritional and medicinal properties.

If, then, by 2006, the tar road and electricity brought Thabo Mbeki's South Africa to his home village, so too did the AIDS hospice named after his sister. For in the Eastern Cape—as in other parts of South Africa stricken by HIV but not yet within the net of the government's belated antiretroviral program—enterprises were popping up all over the place dealing with the reality that, suddenly and inexplicably, a large part of the economically active population was getting sick. AIDS had become an industry, and entrepreneurs were making a living off it, if not from ill consumers themselves, then from agencies willing to provide funding for AIDS services. There is nothing intrinsically wrong with this: If the state is not going to provide the services, then somebody must, and that somebody—of course—needs to feed his own family.

But there was, to at least some of the new AIDS enterprises, a dark side: not just that they preyed on the fear, panic, confusion, and funding bounty that are side effects of the AIDS epidemic, but also that they exploited an age-old ambivalence about Western medicine and doctors, rekindled by Thabo Mbeki's particular questioning of the AIDS epidemic. In this environment, home-grown solutions were often touted as alternatives to supposedly "Western" pharmacology, and fitted in with the perception—fueled by Thabo Mbeki's own AIDS skepticism—that antiretroviral drugs were some kind of toxic waste being dumped by Western pharmaceutical companies on unsuspecting Africans. During the height of the epidemic, South Africa's poor black communities seemed particularly susceptible, and were awash with alternative therapies often taken in lieu of drugs: either because sufferers had been persuaded that antiretrovirals were bad for them or, more frequently, simply because the drugs were not available to them.

This, then, was the troubled atmosphere around any attempt at alternative AIDS therapy in South Africa in the first decade of the twenty-first century, no matter how well intentioned it may have been. And it was—unavoidably—what came to mind when "the Doctor" started boasting about the 60 percent success rate of his moringa solution. When I questioned him about his product, he made it clear that he did not offer it as an alternative to antiretrovirals but as a supplement; anyway, he added, the drugs had only recently been made available through the public health system in Butterworth, and so his therapy had been the only option to date.

I drove away from Mbewuleni hoping, against my own mounting skepticism, that "the Doctor"'s enterprise was legitimate and that the Linda Mbeki Hospice would succeed. The ironies would be too great if someone with as much integrity as Epainette Mbeki had been duped into lending her family's name to quackery that had arisen in the vacuum formed by the deficiencies of her son's government's AIDS program and on the back of his own skepticism about antiretroviral drugs. And the personal consequences would be too distressing too, for Mrs. Mbeki and Olive Mpahlwa, if the big house on the hill was to revert, yet again, to dysfunction and disrepair.

But by mid-2007 the project seemed to have collapsed. The number of caregivers was reduced, and Mrs. Mbeki had created a distance from "the

Doctor." Olive Mpahlwa—whose car had broken down—had moved in to the home at Mrs. Mbeki's insistence, as it was closer to the Idutywa road and thus had access to transport. And yet neither woman—they spoke to each other daily and saw each other frequently—seemed to have lost much of her new optimism. Olive found a plot on which she hoped to build her own retirement home. And Mrs. Mbeki was caught up enough in her other projects—her women's craft group, a new secondary school named after her in Ngcingwane, and a children's home in Komga—to be able to say to me, with sanguinity, "You win some, you lose some."

It seemed that—whatever was going to transpire with the hospice—Epainette Mbeki and Olive Mpahlwa had found some kind of resolution: lives free, at last, from the pain of absent men. "Everyone wants me, left and right," Mrs. Mbeki said to me. "To some, I say, 'No, that's too much for me.' I'm so, so, busy. Actually, figuratively, it seems, my husband was just sitting on me. I couldn't move. But now that he's gone…I haven't got time I can call my own. Even locally, people come with their problems, minor problems and so on. I am far, far busier than I was when my husband was alive."

Later, though, Olive Mpahlwa would move away from Mbewuleni once more, to look after her grandchildren in East London, her life still a struggle against emotional and material hardship: she spent her days at a taxi-rank, earning her income by renting out her cell phone by the minute. And Epainette Mbeki would be drawn, by her son's political battle for survival against Jacob Zuma, to the maternal role she had eschewed for so long: writing a stirring polemic in his favor just before the 2007 ANC congress and stating that she—a member of the ANC family to her core—would leave the organization "and join a new political party, because we have suffered as a people a lot in the way Thabo has been treated."[12]

In April 2007, Thabo Mbeki used a visit to the Eastern Cape capital of Bisho to announce his ill-fated candidacy to remain ANC president for a third term. He then traveled the 60 or so miles to his mother's homestead in Idutywa, where a traditional amaZizi thanksgiving ceremony was performed for him. The ceremony was clearly calculated to activate Xhosa support for Mbeki against the Zulu Zuma, and when I met one of Mbeki's oldest comrades the following week he was appalled: "Can you believe that this is the man who once upon a time refused to pander to ethnicity to such an extent that he wouldn't even visit the Eastern Cape? Now there he is, playing the Xhosa card. J. Z. [Zuma] and the Zulus versus Thabo and the Xhosas. Isn't this what we fought against all our lives?"

Had Mbeki retreated, by force of political circumstance, into being precisely the kind of regional *caudillo* he disparaged in men like Zuma? Or had he, more simply, come home, finding at last the base, that center of gravity, every leader needs? Perhaps, for a politician—even one as high-minded as Thabo Mbeki—the two inevitably become indistinguishable.

The last time Mbeki had submitted to the rituals of his clan had been in 1999, during that year's election campaign, when he had been photographed, swathed rather uncomfortably in beads and skins before being fortified for battle with the froth of a secret herb and the armpit of a goat. He had spoken about the experience with a certain detached bemusement and presented it to me as an example of the "disconnect" he felt with his roots: the alien- ation—but also the critical distance—of the perpetual outsider. All his life, he had built his identity and his intellect on his outsider status, but he had resolved nonetheless, at the event, to attempt to explore the roots that pro- vided "the connection, the passion, the involvement" he saw in others but could not access himself.

In the eight years between these two amaZizi thanksgiving ceremo- nies—the one at the wax of his power and the other in the wane—Thabo Mbeki activated many policies based on or influenced by a reconnection with African identity, or what his critics called "nativism."[13] These ranged from his African Renaissance ideology and his foreign policy, including the establishment of the African Union, to the entrenchment of the principles of Black Economic Empowerment, to his determination to confront racism, to his insistence that cries about a crime "crisis" were driven by racism, to his approach to contentious issues such as AIDS and Zimbabwe, where African solutions were upheld as preferable by virtue of their provenance. These were clearly, for Mbeki, steps along the path to homecoming, a path that led—paradoxically—to the accusation that he had relinquished his criti- cal outsider subjectivity and succumbed instead to the baseness of being a homeboy.

"Borders and barriers which enclose us within the safety of familiar ter- ritory can also become prisons, and are often defended beyond reason or necessity." The Palestinian intellectual Edward Said wrote that the exile understands this, as the rooted man cannot; there can be no sharper defi- nition of the ossification that comes with narrow nationalism. In contrast, Said wrote, the exile's need to compensate "for disorienting loss by creating a new world to rule" affords him the immense creativity of the novelist, the chess player, the political activist, and the intellectual: "Each of these occupations requires a minimal investment in objects, and places a great premium on mobility and skill."[14] Contrast such creativity with the "prison" of chauvinism, the redoubt of nativism. But contrast such perpetual move- ment, too, with the condition of *stille* as experienced by Mbeki in the Karoo. Such is the ambiguity of coming home.

Just after Mbeki's participation in the amaZizi ritual at his mother's house, I sent him some questions: "What, in your recent visit to your mother's home, has struck you about the landscape of your childhood, and how it has changed? Have you ever been back to Mbewuleni? If so, when? And what were your impressions?" His answer suggested that it was not quite time yet to tell the story of his own homecoming and that when it was, *he* would be the one to tell it: "The place my mother stays is Ngcingwane. We didn't grow up there. We grew up in Mbewuleni. So it's a different sort of place. I haven't been to Mbewuleni since we came back. I will go there. I know the people from there are complaining about that. I will go there at some point. That's when I think we can answer the issue about the landscape of my childhood."

THABO MBEKI, JACOB ZUMA, AND THE FUTURE OF THE SOUTH AFRICAN DREAM

When Jacob Zuma took the podium after defeating Thabo Mbeki for the presidency of the African National Congress in December 2007, he made a point of referring to Mbeki as "a comrade, friend and brother."[1] This was not simply the obligatory magnanimity of a victory speech: Mbeki and Zuma had been the closest of comrades and political partners for three decades, and their fallout had torn the ANC in two, paralyzing South African politics for nearly three years. This feud between brothers—struggle heroes who had fought side by side to liberate South Africa—seemed to carry the anxieties of an entire nation. If the Mandela years had been the era of the dream and the Mbeki years that of the dream deferred, South Africa now found itself in a time beyond dreams. The political crisis triggered by the battle between Mbeki and Zuma forced South Africans to face the truth that they were no longer "the world's greatest fairy tale" but rather a messy and unpredictable democracy with a deep history of conflict and inequality to overcome, run by flawed and self-interested men rather than saints and heroes. For all the anxiety and uncertainty this provoked, it was a necessary and very healthy maturation of the South African democracy; a coming of age. There was no "final destination" to some grand transition into democracy but rather small steps taken along a road—even if this road seemed, at times, to be unendurably bumpy.

The crisis began in late 2002, when a press leak revealed that Zuma—the country's deputy president under Mbeki—was being investigated in connection with corruption charges. These charges arose from his relationship with his longtime financial advisor, Schabir Shaik. Authorities had stumbled across evidence suggesting that Shaik had solicited a bribe worth

R500,000 a year from a French arms company on Zuma's behalf. The formidable common purpose with which Mbeki and Zuma presented themselves to the South African electorate in 2004 concealed the deep rift within the ruling party precipitated by this investigation. In the years to come, Zuma would be fired by Mbeki and Mbeki himself would be ousted. South Africa would find itself in an interregnum that would move the country away from both the redemptive possibilities and the understood compromises of the postapartheid era that had been ushered in by Nelson Mandela, and into a new epoch of uncertainty.

Postapartheid South African politics had never been this rough, and Mbeki himself was deeply implicated. The South African president had, in fact, been briefed about the allegations against his deputy since at least 2001; in November 2002, he had declined to accept Zuma's offer of resignation.[2] Then, in August 2003, he had given the go-ahead for Bulelani Ngcuka, the national director of public prosecutions (the South African attorney-general), to issue a statement that Zuma would not be charged, although there was a prima facie case against him.[3] Zuma and his supporters saw this as a deliberate ploy to damn him even though there was not enough evidence to get him into court. They believed he was being victimized by Ngcuka as part of a conspiracy to dispose of him, led by Mbeki himself. They countercharged that Ngcuka had once been investigated as an apartheid spy and was exacting revenge for this; Mbeki appointed a judicial commission of inquiry that cleared Ngcuka on that charge but criticized his conduct in the prosecution of Zuma. Both Ngcuka and the justice minister, Penuell Maduna, resigned.

Mbeki asked Zuma to resign too, but by this point Zuma's attitude had hardened, and he dared his boss to fire him. Mbeki blinked and instead authorized a statement to be released declaring that no action would be taken against his deputy. This was not only because of the presumption of innocence but because of "trust...based on confidence that was so central to survival and success in the conduct of struggle."[4]

The day after this statement was issued, I happened to have an interview with a senior ANC leader intimate with both men. "This is the worst time for us to talk about the ANC," she said to me. "We have never been more depressed." This was a woman who had suffered more than most during the years of struggle. "Surely not," I countered. "You've been arrested, detained, tortured; you've had your family shattered by exile and imprisonment. You've lived without even the least flicker of possibility of return home in your lifetime. How can you even compare this to that?"

My interlocutor's response was resolute, and signaled the depth of the crisis: "No, this is worse. It's tearing us apart." Given that the ANC still understood itself, somewhat atavistically, as a family rather than a modern political party, this was conflict of a different order from that, say, between Gordon Brown and Tony Blair, or Barack Obama and Hillary Clinton. It was a blood feud rather than a power play or an ideological battle: Cain versus Abel rather than Saul versus David. Nothing could be worse.

———————————

Thabo Mbeki and Jacob Zuma met in the field in Swaziland in 1975. Exact political contemporaries, they advanced through the exile hierarchy on parallel tracks, and became a close political duo who worked together covertly to set up contact with the South African authorities and then ran negotiations together until sidelined by Cyril Ramaphosa and his supporters in 1991. Even after that, they had been a formidable combination, working together to bring recalcitrant Afrikaner secessionists and Zulu nationalists into the 1994 elections. In 1997 the ANC selected them as president and deputy president of the party respectively; no one doubted that they would rule the post-Mandela era side by side.

As political partners, they had manifested an "uncanny coordination," as someone close to both told me. If Mbeki was the head of the movement, then Zuma was its heart: The latter's easy affability and empathetic demeanor meant that he held the party and the ruling tripartite alliance together. Zuma took on the role of smoothing the feathers that Mbeki seemed unconcerned about ruffling: with the AIDS community, with slighted alliance partners, with prickly egos in the provinces. If you felt unaffirmed by the chief, you knew you could find a sympathetic ear with his deputy, and both men seemed to understand, even if tacitly, this division of labor.

But beneath the public impression of a watertight political duo, the relationship frayed, as did so many once comrades found themselves no longer in the trenches together but running a state. Mbeki began to worry that Zuma possessed a dangerous combination of unhealthy ambition and poor judgment (manifested not least by his relationship with Shaik), and Zuma began to feel that the loyalty he had long shown to Mbeki was not being reciprocated. Although Mbeki had come to believe that Zuma did not have what it took for high office, he nonetheless supported his old comrade to be the ANC deputy president in 1997 because he believed Zuma was the only person strong enough to keep out the volatile and unpredictable Winnie Mandela—by this point divorced from Nelson Mandela—who was making a play for the post.

But after the 1999 elections, Mbeki attempted to bypass Zuma by offering the deputy presidency of the country to the ANC's former foe, the Zulu nationalist Chief Buthelezi, as a gesture of reconciliation. The ANC leadership in KwaZulu-Natal, led by Zuma, scuppered the plan, by demanding the premiership of the province (where it did not have a majority) in return; something they knew Buthelezi would reject. Buthelezi declined the post, thereby clearing the way for Zuma himself to take it and thus remain in the line of succession. Now that they were in the presidency together, the relationship between the two men deteriorated rapidly. Zuma felt that he was kept out of any significant decision making, while the technocrats around Mbeki saw the deputy president as an incompetent drain on the presidency's can-do image. Things crashed in 2001, when Mbeki became convinced that there was a coup plot against him, led by Cyril Ramaphosa, Tokyo Sexwale, and Matthews Phosa, and that Zuma had been supplying them with information. He confronted his deputy; this led to Zuma's extraordinary and seemingly unprovoked press statement that he had no aspirations to become president.[5] According to comrades close to both of them, it was at this point that trust was broken irrevocably—no matter what the 2003 statement later said. But still, Zuma remained in office, and uncharged.

Finally, in April 2005, a court found Schabir Shaik guilty of a corrupt relationship with Zuma and sentenced him to 15 years in prison.[6] Now Mbeki felt compelled to take action. He fired his deputy, claiming that despite the presumption of innocence, it was his constitutional responsibility to protect the rule of law. In what seemed like a deliberate attempt to further humiliate Zuma, Mbeki chose as his new deputy the minerals and energy minister, Phumzile Mlambo-Ngcuka—who happened to be the wife of Bulelani Ngcuka. Zuma's primary antagonist would now be sleeping in the bed at the deputy president's residence that Zuma had been forced to vacate.

Immediately following the Shaik ruling, Zuma himself was finally charged. He agreed to step down from all responsibilities within the ANC (where he remained deputy president) until after his trial, but two weeks later, a party conference—the National General Council of May 2005—demanded that he resume them. At this point Mbeki's apparent hold over the party suddenly shattered, as his many detractors coalesced in support of Zuma as a way of voicing their dissatisfaction with him. This, in effect, was the moment that the Zuma presidential campaign began: He was packaged as something of an "anti-Mbeki," effusive, empathetic, and responsive. The ANC had always been led by people from Mbeki's elite, educated class; Zuma, by contrast, was the unschooled son of a rural Zulu domestic worker, a traditionalist and polygamist with many wives and allegedly about 20 children. His obvious flaws—his insolvency, his choice of friends, his patriarchal attitude toward women—only seemed to make him more attractive to ANC members: He was generous, a man with human appetites, in touch with the people. And he was, most important, a victim, deserving of sympathy and support.

Certainly, Zuma was a "homeboy" as Mbeki was not: While Mbeki was self-consciously dislocated from his roots because of the lives of his intellectual activist parents, Zuma was deeply enmeshed with his clan and family. But much of the way Zuma characterized himself—"the herdboy from Inkandla"—was spin: He was as much part of the ANC elite as Mbeki was; indeed, he had been the ANC's head of intelligence and security in exile, and he was shaped far more by his experiences as an intelligence operative than by his goat-herding as a boy in rural KwaZulu. The spin nonetheless took hold. Unlike Mbeki, who presented himself as irreproachable and thus was continually found wanting, Zuma presented himself as a South African everyman with all-too-understandable flaws who symbolized the alienation of the ordinary person from the machinations of the new black business class and technocratic elite; who had, in fact, been ejected from the banquet of victory for not being sophisticated enough. In this way, he came to reflect the aspirations of so many South Africans who felt their lives had not improved since the advent of democracy, in sharp contrast to the immense wealth—now black as well as white—they saw all around them.

Later in 2005, the HIV-positive daughter of a close comrade of Zuma's laid rape charges against the man she described as a father figure: Zuma, she alleged, had taken advantage of her while she was staying in his home. In his 2006 trial, Zuma was ultimately acquitted, but not without being forced to concede that he had had unprotected sex with the woman even though he knew she was HIV positive—and that he, the man responsible for the government's anti-AIDS effort, had sought to inoculate himself against infection with a postcoital shower. In a society that claimed to lead the way in the field of gender equality, he also manifested a retrograde attitude toward women: The accused had been asking for it because of her suggestive clothing, he said, and it had been his duty, as a Zulu man, to satisfy her. Equally troubling was Zuma's inability—or unwillingness—to control the unruly mob outside his court appearances, who maintained with fervor that his accuser was an Mbeki stooge and that the entire case was another plot by Mbeki to bring down their man. Even if this was correct, the fact that he fell for it displayed an astonishing lack of judgement. Meanwhile, images of Mbeki were burned and insulting songs sung against him; so severe were the threats leveled at Zuma's accuser herself that she was forced into exile.[7]

The Zuma campaign was driven from three places. The first was Zuma's own KwaZulu-Natal home base. People there believed that the ANC had been dominated for too long by Xhosa-speakers from the Eastern Cape (whence both Mandela and Mbeki hailed) and relished the possibility of a Zulu ascendancy. The second was the firebrand ANC Youth League, which was inspired by Zuma's charismatic populism and which was thrilled with the power of being king-maker: to propel Zuma into office just as, a generation before, it had made Thabo Mbeki by promoting him over Cyril Ramaphosa.

The third base, and perhaps the most prominent in terms of influence, was the leadership of the ANC's left-wing alliance partners, the South African Communist Party (SACP) and Congress of South African Trade Unions (COSATU), which felt that Mbeki's economic policies were a betrayal of the movement's roots, not just in their "neoliberal" content but in the way they had been imposed top-down. Zuma had, in fact, always been on Mbeki's side in the economic debate, but the leaders of the SACP and COSATU, Blade Nzimande and Zwelinzima Vavi respectively, had come to believe that he was more amenable to their ideology. In their determination to rid the ANC of Mbeki and his financial managers, they became, more than anyone, the architects of the Zuma ascendancy. Both men loathed Mbeki, whom they believed had demeaned and marginalized them. Given the reality that since 2004 Mbeki had presided over a significant shift to the left in government policy, the powerful support they brought to Zuma was ultimately more personal than it was ideological. In 2005 Vavi predicted that the Zuma movement was a "tsunami" that no one would be able to contain; later, in a bilateral meeting with the ANC, he aptly described the Zuma support base as a coalition of "the walking wounded"[8]: people with axes to grind because they felt that they, too, were victims of Mbeki's machinations—or perhaps (Vavi, of course, did not say this himself) because they felt they had been denied access to the patronage that inevitably trickles down from high office.

Mbeki had indeed made many enemies over the course of his tenure, because of his aloof and high-handed leadership style, his tendency toward intrigue and conspiracy theory, and what was perceived to be his centralizing and authoritarian approach to power. This management from the center manifested itself in many different ways, but nowhere more controversially so than in the "deployment" policy of Mbeki's ANC, which attempted to assert control over the state through an approach learned from the democratic centralism of Marxist-Leninist vanguardism in which both Mbeki and Zuma were steeped. One consequence was to politicize the bureaucracy by rendering all appointments susceptible to patronage; another was to alienate the party's grassroots from access to power by imposing all provincial and local appointments, such as premiers and mayors, from the center, rather than permitting them to be elected from the ground up, according to the precepts of electoral democracy. Although Mbeki insisted this was a way of inoculating local politics from patronage, it profoundly alienated ordinary members from the power of the state and laid the president open to charges that he was instituting his own systems of patronage, charges seemingly substantiated by some spectacularly inappropriate appointments. It is ironic that Zuma has been the beneficiary of dissatisfaction with this process, for he was the head of the ANC's deployment committee and thus its central enforcer. The Zuma-led ANC would reverse Mbeki's controversial centralized appointment of premiers and mayors, but the deployment of political cadres into the bureaucracy would remain firmly in place—although the ANC promised, in its 2009 election manifesto, that it would "implement corrective measures" to make government more efficient.[9]

In Zuma's "coalition of the wounded" were several senior ANC figures who had been close to Mbeki but had fallen out with him or felt that he had marginalized them within the party or discarded them. Many had been part of the same tight Mbeki-Zuma exile clique that had so successfully taken control of the movement upon its return to South Africa in the early 1990s and that had assumed the key roles in the country's security apparatus: one, Billy Masetlha, had been Mbeki's head of intelligence; another, Siphiwe Nyanda, had been chief of the South African Defence Force. As with Nzimande and Vavi, their motivation to dispense with Mbeki seemed to be driven by personal grievance: by the way they—like Zuma himself— had been hurt personally or believed that Mbeki had abused their loyalty, or compromised their dignity, or even wrecked their lives.

This was another consequence of the ANC's peculiar heritage; of the way it functioned as a family or extended clan rather than a modern political party. As Matthews Phosa would later say about the ANC's fervent support for Zuma: "We are not an organization that turns its back on people, we are family and we stay in the house with those who are bravely suffering through all sorts of accusations and conspiracies."[10] There was a strong sentiment, even among those who did not particularly support Zuma, that Mbeki had at the very least stood by while his old comrade was victimized. This was contrary to the comradely principles of the ANC "family," and sharply exemplified the negative leadership that Mbeki was accused of having brought into the former liberation movement.

In the months and years to come, it was open season on Mbeki's reputation: from the songs sung at COSATU conferences deriding him as a "big ugly dog," to the burning of T-shirts and posters bearing his likeness, to the hemorrhaging of key loyalists away from his inner circle, to the way that he was jeered and insulted at events in the Zuma heartland of KwaZulu-Natal. Zuma supporters wore T-shirts declaring themselves to be, as Zuma himself had once allegedly described himself, "100% Zuluboy." This led to a deep anxiety among Zuma's critics: would the Zuma ascendancy upset the political stability forged during the Mandela-Mbeki years and bring ethnic strife to one of the few African countries which had managed to avoid it? In his campaign against Zuma, Mbeki would attempt to activate his own home base, the Xhosa-speaking Eastern Cape, but his failure to do so effectively would reveal a significant truth of the Zuma "tsunami": Although Zulu-speaking South Africans were solidly behind Zuma and he was in many respects the successor to Chief Buthelezi as the standard-bearer of Zulu nationalism, his support base cut significantly across ethnic lines. Those on the ground who preferred Zuma to Mbeki did so because he seemed, unlike Mbeki, to be rooted in his home culture, to come from *somewhere*, and thus seemed to understand the needs of ordinary people, even if this somewhere was a Zulu rather than a Xhosa or a Sotho one.

The attacks on Mbeki and on his legacy from 2005 onward went far beyond Zuma partisanship and ANC factionalism: The crisis prized open a space, in broader society, for unprecedentedly robust criticism of the leadership of the liberation movement that had brought freedom just over a decade earlier. This was healthy, and many of the criticisms were legitimate—such as of his AIDS policy, or his seeming inability to act against compromised or ineffective members of his own government. But even so, the pitch of the discourse often seemed fueled by a sense of anger and betrayal leveled at someone who had been vested with a responsibility far greater than mere executive office. Suddenly, Mbeki became a lightening rod for so many frustrations. It was as if, by voting him into office, South Africans had charged him with nothing less than the custody of their dreams—and with every violent crime, with every unemployed high school graduate, with every AIDS death, he stood accused of shattering them.

Jacob Zuma's 2007 defeat of Thabo Mbeki took place at the ANC's yearly national congress, traditionally held on the long weekend in the middle of December that heralds the beginning of the annual Christmas holidays. This year, sharing the Great North Road with the overloaded communal taxis and pickup trucks transporting people and goods to the densely populated rural areas of Limpopo province, were buses bursting with singing comrades and arrogant cavalcades of cabinet ministers in German luxury cars, all making their way to the provincial capital of Polokwane (formerly Pietersburg) for the conference. "Polokwane" has come to stand, in the South African lexicon, as shorthand not only for Mbeki's ignominious defeat (a tropical Waterloo), but for a threshold in the country's political life; a turning-point almost as significant as Nelson Mandela's 1994 victory and the transition to democracy.

The conference took place in a vast marquee erected over the playing fields of the University of Limpopo, once the blacks-only university that had been the primary incubator of the Black Consciousness movement three decades earlier. Built in monumental apartheid style, the university looms incongruously over the hardscrabble peri-urban sprawl of the former bantustan settlement that surrounds it, on the outskirts of Polokwane. Here, around 4,000 delegates gathered—observed by a similar number of journalists, businesspeople, and others—determined to put an end to the Mbeki-Zuma crisis by voting one of them into office and rejecting the other definitively.

According to the South African constitution, presidents are limited to two terms of five years each, but there are no such proscriptions on ANC leadership. Traditionally, the person elected ANC president at its conference heads the party electoral list and becomes the president of the country after the general elections just over a year later. But as it became clearer that Zuma was determined to contest the ANC presidency despite (or perhaps even because of) the charges against him, Mbeki let it be known that he would be available for reelection too, even though he would not be able to be the country's president again. Were he to be successful, he would have the power to prevent Zuma from becoming the country's president. As party chief, he would select his own successor and, presumably, continue to pull the strings from Luthuli House, the ANC headquarters.

Mbeki believed Zuma's play for the presidency to be part of a strategy to avoid prosecution; he also worried that Zuma and his backers had no respect for the rule of law and the South African constitution. The battle with Zuma so compromised Mbeki that not even his strongest supporters believed that he should continue as president of the ANC. But because many felt that Mbeki was perhaps the only ANC leader who stood a chance of defeating Zuma and of keeping South Africa stable, he was nominated for the presidency of the ANC. He accepted the nomination and so, for the better part of 2007, much other activity was suspended—including the running of the state—as the two factions campaigned for support.

About 60 percent of the delegates were pledged to Zuma as a result of provincial nomination conferences. But because delegates were entitled to vote their conscience by secret ballot, the Mbeki campaign sought to get many to change their minds, by painting the Zuma camp as adventurist parvenus who neither knew nor respected ANC traditions. Zuma's supporters retaliated: It was Mbeki himself who had compromised the great South African experiment in democracy and under their man, the ANC would once more return to the value system of Nelson Mandela and would become accountable and responsible, the property of its grassroots membership rather than the small elite of self-serving technocrats around Mbeki.

What damaged Mbeki most was the perception that he was unwilling to step down from power. Even if Zuma did lack the judgment and the skills to be South Africa's president, did Mbeki really believe that he was the only person who could stand against him and defeat him? His decision to make himself available for a third term as ANC president mobilized support against him by people who were at best ambivalent about Zuma, but who were determined that the ANC should not fall victim to that graveyard of African democracies, the ruler-for-life syndrome. Many in the ANC—and in the broader South African society (and particularly among black commentators in the media)—were furious with Mbeki for fighting a battle he was obviously going to lose. In so doing, Mbeki was handing the presidency to a deeply compromised man and preventing a viable "third way" candidate from coming to the fore.

This desire for renewal and accountability in the ANC was captured by the eloquent sign language that characterized the Polokwane conference: One of the delegates' favorites was the rolling of hands—soccer code for "substitute the player." And while the Mbeki supporters' salute was a three-fingered one, suggesting three terms, the Zuma supporters responded with two fingers: two terms for Mbeki, two for Zuma. The message was clear, and appeared to be a blow for democracy and accountability: Zuma would be held to account exactly as Mbeki had. Once it was announced that he had defeated Mbeki, Zuma would draw the loudest applause from the delegates for acknowledging this: "[We] accept the mandate you have given us with a full understanding that you can withdraw it at any time . . ." he said. "That is the essence of democracy. Leaders lead through the will and graciousness of the people."[11] But such promises rang hollow in the way Zuma failed to stem or even criticize the fervent personality cult that developed around him—with some supporters saying that they would kill to keep him out of jail and with Zuma himself prone to declare that the ANC would rule until the Second Coming.

Balanced against this development of a personality cult around Zuma, however, was one of the most significant outcomes of the contest: Despite a fervently partisan nucleus in each camp (larger in the Zuma camp than in the Mbeki one), the votes were negatively driven. Very few of those who voted for Mbeki actually wanted him to remain the ANC president; most voted to keep Zuma out. Similarly, a significant proportion of the Zuma votes was a protest against Mbeki. Previously, the ANC leadership was a pantheon of demigods beyond reproach. Now both candidates were seen as flawed and compromised; the choice was between the lesser of two evils. In the final event, Mbeki won 1,505 votes to Zuma's 2,329. This was not by any means a landslide: 60 percent of the delegates did not want Mbeki, and 40 percent did not want Zuma. A new era of contestation was heralded at Polokwane, one that would change South African politics forever.

Watching Thabo Mbeki's performance at Polokwane, I could not stop thinking of *Coriolanus*, Shakespeare's darkest political thriller and one of Mbeki's favorite works of literature. Mbeki, remember, had discovered Coriolanus while studying at the Lenin Institute in Moscow in 1969 and had written to his Sussex friend Rhiannon Gooding that he found the tragedy's eponymous hero—conventionally seen as a vainglorious protofascist—to be the very model for a twentieth-century revolutionary, not unlike Che Guevara, full of "truthfulness, courage, self-sacrifice, absence of self-seeking, brotherliness, heroism, optimism." As a fired-up young communist, Thabo Mbeki saw him as a revolutionary role model precisely because he was prepared to go to war against his own people, who had become a "rabble," an "unthinking mob, with its cowardice, its lying, its ordinary people-ness."[12] Rome had to be purged of its rot, and Coriolanus would kill his own mother in the process if he had to.

One of the reasons for the Roman general's exile in the first place had been that, upon returning to the city after a victorious battle, he had refused to boast about his war wounds; he would not swagger or take part in the "heroic" performance of the returning conqueror. He would not dissemble: "Would you have me false to my nature?...I play the man I am."[13] This assertion became Mbeki's mantra: from his refusal to spin the media, to his refusal to compromise on positions that he believed were principled, such as the toxicity of antiretroviral drugs, or the right of Zimbabwe to remain in the global community of nations. But Mbeki is a careful and subtle reader: Why, then, could he not understand that one of Coriolanus's tragic flaws was precisely his inability to find a way of casting the image of himself that the people wanted, that was expected of him, while remaining true to his principles?

I thought of this as I watched Mbeki deliver his political report to the Polokwane conference, the day before delegates were to vote. In what was a state of the nation address more appropriate for parliament than for a political congress, he spoke for three hours, stupefying delegates with facts and figures that demonstrated the achievements of his term but failing dismally to connect with the very people whose votes he was canvassing. Certainly he was talking to his legacy as much as to the people in front of him, laying down his achievements and setting a standard by which Zuma would be judged should he win. But this was also a campaign speech: Mbeki was, after all, standing for reelection in the battle of his political life.

Indeed, the speech had been calculated to demonstrate Mbeki's erudition and his precision, in sharp counterpoint to Zuma, who spoke in broad brushstrokes and who had already developed the reputation of being all things to all people, telling each audience what he thought it wanted to hear. Mbeki wished to prove, in contrast, that he spoke the truth, no matter how unpalatable. And so, Coriolanus-like, he performed the spectacularly self-destructive feat of telling the very people whom he wished to vote him back into office that they were a rabble, not worthy of being at the conference in the first place—suggesting that they had been easily misled and manipulated because they did not have "the necessary political maturity" and because they had "very little familiarity with the history and traditions of the ANC."[14] Thus did he confirm to the delegates what the Zuma camp had already told them: He was aloof and high-handed, an elitist who was contemptuous of them because they were not as educated as he.

Toward the end of the speech, Mbeki finally addressed the schism in the ANC: "If we are divided, what divides us?" he asked. "You!" came the answer, shouted—somewhat uneasily—from various corners of the floor. Mbeki looked up, a flicker registering across his habitually impassive features. He tried his question another way: "If we are divided, what should we do to address this challenge...?" Awakened now, the delegates were prepared. They gave Mbeki his answer: "Go! Go!" A few minutes later, as he finished his marathon speech, there was respectful, if restrained, applause—and then open rebellion. A song ignited across the floor: "*Umshini Wam!*" (Bring me my machine gun!)—an old war chant from the struggle days that Zuma had appropriated as his anthem. Mbeki's supporters had decried the use of this song in a time of peace and development—and in a society trying desperately to overcome a gun-driven violent crime epidemic. But with its symbolic call to arms, *"Umshini Wam!"* never failed to arouse the passions of those who felt alienated from the technocratic workings of a liberation movement that was now a ruling political party; who felt that despite the achievements Mbeki had detailed, they had not reaped the benefits of freedom.

In the front of the congress hall, a bloc of loyalists jumped to their feet and tried unsuccessfully to counter the Zuma anthem with songs praising Mbeki. The president himself remained impassive as he took his seat next to Zuma, but his color was ashen. Traditionally, at the end of the leader's speech, an ANC gathering erupts into a mass of stamping feet, praise song, and ululation. That day the party leadership behind Mbeki and Zuma on the stage remained seated, as did the majority of delegates, seemingly stunned by what they had just witnessed—even though most of them were already pledged to vote against Mbeki.

I felt similarly stunned. I had been an ANC supporter myself since finding my own politics in my early 20s, and like everyone else present, I recognized that South African politics would never be the same. I had witnessed one of those tectonic shifts that moves a country from one epoch into another, but it would take months, or even years, to understand exactly what this meant. *"Umshini Wam!"* was sung again and again during the weeklong conference: after it was announced that Zuma had defeated Mbeki and then in the vote for the new National executive Committee, after an "Mbeki list" was routed and much of Mbeki's cabinet—including several venerable struggle icons—was voted out of the ANC leadership. Zuma closed the conference by singing it himself after his acceptance speech, adopting his trademark martial pose, miming the carrying of an AK-47 as he led the crowd in his deep baritone. It was the final humiliation of Thabo Mbeki, for there was little doubt on whom the machine gun was trained. Mbeki was persuaded to stand on stage with Zuma to demonstrate that he accepted the democratic process, but his bleak countenance revealed just how devastated he was. His belief against all evidence to the contrary that he would prevail was a vindication of one of the most trenchant critiques of his administration: his disconnection from his electorate, exacerbated by the insulation that inevitably comes with high office.

Mbeki and his supporters had characterized the Zuma crowd as "howlers," as "hooligans," as an "unruly mob." The way this mob was behaving, I heard repeatedly from his supporters, was "against the tradition of the ANC." Mbeki's tragedy was that he was unable to see that these traditions, honed in the ANC in exile, no longer applied in free, democratic South Africa. Zuma came from the same traditions, but he was a canny intelligence operative: His victory was based on his ability to have his ears to the ground and thus to adapt and understand contemporary South African politics, and to project himself as responsive, accountable, a man of the people.

Mbeki's behavior after the conference only increased the perception of disconnect. He retreated into sullen isolation, all but disappearing from the public eye during the last lame-duck lap of his term, scheduled to last just over a year, until the 2009 elections. It had been expected that he might step down voluntarily or at the very least draw the new ANC leadership into government in some kind of intraparty coalition. But he did neither, and instead continued to govern with only the minimum consultation necessary with his new "political" leaders over at Luthuli House. Most contentiously, he went ahead with the controversial appointment of a new board to the South African Broadcasting Corporation (SABC), the public broadcaster that, Zuma's supporters alleged—not without evidence—was biased in Mbeki's favor.

Mbeki also appeared to retreat from public life in South Africa, particularly during two crises that wracked the nation in early 2008: a power crisis that left much of the country dark over long periods for several weeks and played havoc with the economy, and a wave of xenophobic violence, fueled by frustration with slow delivery of services and with the high unemployment rate, which left at least 42 dead and tens of thousands more displaced. The victims of this violence were largely Zimbabweans, of whom an estimated three million now lived in South Africa as economic refugees, and who stood accused of stealing scarce local resources and jobs from locals. Because of Mbeki's inability to resolve the Zimbabwean crisis and his appeasement of Robert Mugabe, he too found himself accused by many— somewhat unfairly—for having contributed to the cause of violence.

Mbeki did, in fact, apologize publicly for the power crisis—it was a consequence of bad planning and coordination on the part of his government—and he also made a very strong statement against the xenophobic attacks. But in both cases, his response was late, and distant, and executive authority was barely discernible. Unlike Zuma, for example, he did not visit the affected areas of the violence, leaving the country instead to address a conference entitled "Towards A Vibrant Africa: A Continent of Hope and Opportunity" in Japan. More tangibly, his decision to call in the military came several days too late. There is a strong case to be made that the state could have done more to stop this wave of random violence on a scale not seen since the destabilizing days before the 1994 elections, and the moment of intense national gloom and shame that followed.

When, in Shakespeare's play, Coriolanus is banished from Rome by the tribunes—much as Mbeki was banished from the ANC by its delegates— the war hero responds by calling them a "common cry of curs" and storming off into exile with the words "I banish *you*! And here remain with your uncertainty.... There is a world elsewhere."[15] Mbeki's absence from public life for weeks on end after Polokwane, particularly during the crises, had hints of Coriolanus. His "world elsewhere," perhaps, was a refuge he had sought, from domestic criticism, throughout his tenure, in the arena of global diplomacy. He spent much of his time in Zimbabwe, and in his singular obsession to solve that country's crisis—particularly given the very hostile reaction he attracted for his refusal to condemn Robert Mugabe after the effective coup that followed the June 2008 elections—he seemed determined to salvage his legacy on the international stage, as a counterweight to his domestic rejection.

"And here remain with your uncertainty": 2008 became the darkest year yet in postapartheid South Africa: because of the power crisis, because of the xenophobic violence, because of a gathering recession that began to hit consumers even before the international credit crisis of September. Property prices plummeted, the rand fell, and there was an evidence of the greatest emigration wave since the early 1990s. This exacerbated the already-intense skills crisis that was one of the greatest challenges facing the South African economy. After a decade and a half of political stability, the uncertainty arising from Mbeki's defeat at Polokwane played a significant part in this upheaval. South Africa had entered a second transition, a period not unlike the transition to democracy in the early 1990s: huge expectations from one sector of the population, great anxiety from another; an old executive under Mbeki that appeared to have lost its will to govern, a new one in the wings under Zuma trying to assert its authority and needing to reassure jittery markets.

But if 2008 was an intense and unsettling interregnum, it was nonetheless illuminated by the possibilities of a Prague Spring. Cyril Ramaphosa said that the ANC after Polokwane was "almost like a breath of fresh air" where there were "no holy cows,"[16] and the nature of public discourse in broader society seemed to reflect this too: there seemed to be a spate of public forums and debates, and a marked new energy to the media. Not yet locked down by the exigencies of having to run the state, the new ANC leadership appeared to be open and approachable, willing to talk—and listen—to anyone. This was in marked contrast to the defensive and often paranoid posture of the Mbeki government.

Most noticeable was the changing profile of the country's legislature. Mbeki still ran the government, but the ANC controlled parliament and cannily realized that the one way it could assert its authority over the president was through this body's constitutionally prescribed role of executive oversight. The ANC swiftly changed the personnel in parliament to replace Mbeki loyalists with Zuma ones. Miraculously, the ANC caucus, which had been nothing more than a rubber stamp to the executive authority of Mbeki for years, began doing its job—even to a fault: sending back draft legislation, challenging executive appointments, demanding accountability from cabinet ministers and senior bureaucrats.

Had ANC legislators finally found their voices now that the oppressive lid of Mbeki's political control was removed, or were they merely acting as the blunt instrument of Zuma's newfound power, setting out to limit and even humiliate Mbeki? At times it seemed as if the new activism of the legislature heralded a dawn of openness and accountability in South African politics. But it was hard not to feel that the elected officials—silent for so long—were merely following the new leadership as slavishly as they had the old, and that this was merely a sign of the changing of the guard, as new systems of patronage established themselves and loyalties shifted from one group of leaders to another. One pessimistic indicator was the way parliament in 2008 implemented a decision, taken at Polokwane, to disband the Directorate of Special Operations (known as "the Scorpions")—the elite combined prosecution and investigation unit, championed by Mbeki, that had led the investigation into Zuma and into several other high-profile ANC leaders. Established according to international best practices, the Scorpions appeared to have earned a significant success rate. They may indeed have been used by Mbeki to target his adversaries, as the new ANC claimed, and as a judge would later concur. But ANC parliamentarians failed to offer any compelling reasons why they had disbanded the unit entirely rather than immunizing it from political interference. The widely held perception was that parliament had merely become the instrument of the Zuma-led ANC and would do whatever it took to prevent its new leader from prosecution.

Thus did the ANC make a decision that would ensure that it entered the post-Mbeki era morally compromised: rather than dispensing with Zuma, it made his problems its own by insisting on him as the country's next president. As Lindiwe Sisulu put it in January, the ANC had no choice but to get "involved" in trying to squash the case against Zuma, as the ANC was "de facto" affected by it, by virtue of his leadership of the party.[17]

Thabo Mbeki's term was to have expired in April 2009, but many in the ANC felt that he needed to leave office sooner. Finally, in September 2008, they were handed their smoking gun: Chris Nicholson, a High Court judge with good human rights credentials, dismissed the corruption charges against Jacob Zuma on the basis of a technicality and found that Zuma had had grounds to allege a political conspiracy against him, as the evidence was strong that Mbeki had meddled in his case. Zuma himself did not escape criticism—he was described by Nicholson as behaving "like a blinded Samson" who threatened "to make sure the temple collapses with him" through his "dark mutterings" that he would take others down with him. But the focus of the judgment was on Mbeki, and it was harsh: Through "political meddling," the president and his cabinet had criminally compromised the independence of the prosecutor, in a way reminiscent of the workings of the old apartheid order. Nicholson also saw fit to criticize Mbeki for running for a third term as party president and for firing Zuma in 2005: Although not strictly illegal, this latter action had been "unfair and unjust."[18]

The National Prosecuting Authority appealed the judgment, and four months later, in January 2009, the Supreme Court of Appeals [SCA] overturned it in the harshest possible terms, ruling that Nicholson had made "gratuitous findings," had failed "to distinguish between allegation, fact and suspicion," and had overstepped his role as judge. The SCA ruling very carefully excluded any assessment of whether Mbeki had meddled politically in Zuma's case, stating simply that it was not within Nicholson's remit as a judge even to consider the matter.[19] The charges were reinstated against Zuma, and Mbeki put out a statement that his own objections to the judgment were "vindicated."[20] It was, however, too late for Mbeki: Whether judicially correct or not, the Nicholson judgment had changed the course of South African history, for the ANC had used it to oust Mbeki from the presidency of the country.

Immediately following Nicholson's September 2008 judgment, a special meeting of the National Executive Committee had been called, and it was decided, after 14 hours of debate, to "recall" the president. Zuma himself had been opposed to the action: Mbeki's term would end in seven months; why beat "a dead snake"? he asked publicly.[21] Privately he argued that Mbeki should be allowed to depart with dignity and that his remaining in place was necessary for a smooth transition. But he and other more moderate ANC elders had been unable to prevent the putsch. Emotion and a desire for vengeance had trumped reason, and leading the charge were other ANC leaders who had been personal victims of Mbeki's machinations, including the three men accused of plotting a coup against him in 2001: Cyril Ramaphosa, Tokyo Sexwale, and Matthews Phosa. It could be read as just desserts or as base hypocrisy: By firing Mbeki before the Nicholson judgment could even be appealed, the ANC was doing to Mbeki exactly what it had accused Mbeki of doing to Zuma: using an incomplete legal process to justify what was in essence a political decision.

Strictly speaking, the ANC had no right to "recall" Mbeki: The only body that could do that was parliament, through a no-confidence vote or an impeachment process. But since the ANC controlled parliament anyway, Mbeki had decided to accede to his party's demands and to leave without a high-profile fight. Although dignified and accepting of his fate in his live televised resignation speech, he nonetheless returned repeatedly to what he described as the time-honored values of the ANC—"selflessness," "sacrifice," and "service" rather than individual desire—so as to underscore his belief that the way he had been treated showed that these values had been abandoned.[22] About a third of Mbeki's cabinet resigned in sympathy with him, but most adhered to the ANC injunction to remain in office in the interests of stability, at least until the 2009 elections. When Mbeki's office let it be known that Trevor Manuel, the finance minister, was one of those resigned, the markets dipped dramatically—and Manuel was compelled to announce that he would remain in office.[23]

Fascinatingly, Zuma did not step immediately into Mbeki's presidential shoes. The ANC announced that while its president would be leading the ANC's election campaign for 2009, a caretaker administration would be set up by the man who had been elected his deputy at Polokwane, Kgalema Motlanthe. Motlanthe is a modest and considered man who, although a decade younger than Zuma and Mbeki, comes from the same tradition: He knows no other life than that of the struggle and the ANC. He spent time in jail on Robben Island, and after the ANC was unbanned in 1990 he was "deployed" by the ANC to run the behemoth National Union of Mineworkers before going to work full time for the party. He had, in fact, been the hero of Polokwane, restoring order when Zuma supporters were particularly disruptive, and he was not historically a "Zuma man": His ascendancy in the ANC had been as an Mbeki acolyte, particularly around economic policy, and he had done Mbeki's bidding, as ANC secretary-general, in the firing of Zuma. But he and Mbeki had fallen out too, over an arcane spy-versus-spy drama involving allegedly fake e-mails, and he shared the Zuma camp's harsh criticism of Mbeki's leadership style. Lobbied intensively by both sides, he had, in the end, chosen Zuma's, but he still drew respect from most quarters for his fairness and principle and for his willingness—unlike Zuma himself—to rebuke publicly the ANC president's more shrill supporters. After a rushed inauguration, he handled the transition deftly, making at least one inspired new cabinet appointment—veteran activist and parliamentarian Barbara Hogan to replace the reviled health minister Manto Tshabalala-Msimang—and projecting an image of calm confidence and continuity that reassured both markets and ordinary South Africans.

Why, after so intense a leadership battle, had Zuma not taken the job himself once Mbeki was fired? The line that he needed to be free to run the ANC's election campaign was only part of the story: he accepted, as did his fellow-leaders, that a smoother transition would be possible if a more neutral figure took the post. Also, at the time of Mbeki's firing, Zuma was by no means fully in control of the party he now led (evidenced by the way he lost the battle over firing Mbeki in the first place). And the new "Zuma camp" that led the ANC was trying to manage its own fault lines: between those who would, as they publicly said, kill for the new president and those who had backed him to get rid of Mbeki but now worried that they were saddled with a candidate too compromised to run the country effectively. Zuma, too, was strangely ambivalent: although he desperately wanted to be ANC president to vindicate his honor, he was, according to some confidants, insecure himself about his capabilities as a chief executive, and worried about taking on the presidency of the country with the corruption charges against him unresolved. Still, he led the ANC into the 2009 elections with his name not yet cleared. South Africa's new president could well stand trial while still in office; only if found guilty would he need to step down.

This uncertainty about South Africa's political future in late 2008 was exacerbated by the single most dramatic effect of the firing of Mbeki: the birth of a new political party, the Congress of the People (COPE), established by a group of pro-Mbeki ANC dissidents led by the former defense minister, Mosiuoa Lekota (known as "Terror," a nickname from his soccer days), and the former premier of Gauteng province, Mbhazima Shilowa. Both were ex-freedom fighters with impeccable ANC credentials; they launched their new party at a vibrant meeting in early November attended by over 6,000 delegates—most of whom were also ANC dissidents who had supported Mbeki over Zuma, and were enraged at how the party had treated their man. This common grievance was a blessing and a curse: It guaranteed the new party a ready base (remember, Mbeki had won 40 percent of the vote at Polokwane), but it hamstrung it, too, with the limitations of Mbeki's own legacy. Lekota and Shilowa had lost their leadership positions at Polokwane: they and their supporters also struggled to overcome the accusation that they were disgruntled partisans who had left an ANC that no longer wanted them so as to be able to remain in politics. When he quit the ANC, Shilowa commented that the new party could not be formed on anger alone. But COPE began its election campaign with little substance save an opposition to Zuma's ANC. And not many senior ANC leaders actually joined him and Lekota: many felt constrained by an allegiance to the "family" or an unwillingness to be identified with a movement that did not yet have a clear identity.

"The Congress of the People" was the ANC-led convention in 1955 that adopted the Freedom Charter, the touchstone of the South African democracy and the prototype for the country's exemplary constitution. By taking on this name—over fierce opposition from the ANC—the new party sought to lay claim to a struggle legacy it accused the Zuma-led ANC of having abandoned. But its aspiration was to balance this call to struggle tradition with a modernizing high-tech approach—no more talk of "comrades" and "National Democratic Revolutions"—that would appeal to the "born-free" generation of South Africans: young people who had no lived experience of apartheid oppression and therefore much less emotional attachment to the freedom struggle.

This, then, was one of the best possible legacies of the political turmoil arising out of Mbeki's ousting: the collapse of the de facto one-party state and its replacement by a real choice for black South African voters. The initial shrillness and anger with which ANC leaders and members responded to the new party—ranging from vicious verbal attacks to physical disruption—signaled how threatened the ruling party was: not only, of course, by the possibility of a significantly reduced majority, but because it could no longer lay claim to being sole legitimate representative of black South Africans; the days of its old struggle hegemony were finally over. The psychological break had been made, regardless of how well the new party would fare in the elections.

In response to COPE, the ANC doggedly asserted itself as the party of the poor and the working class. Populist appeals to the poor often combine political radicalism with social conservatism, and Zuma articulated the latter strongly in the early stages of the campaign, calling for prayer in schools, the withdrawal of constitutional rights to those accused of rape and murder, and even the separation of teenage mothers from their children and their placement in forced education camps. He also suggested holding a referendum over the death penalty, outlawed in South Africa. Meanwhile, COPE wooed the burgeoning black middle class with a discourse of political tolerance, respect for the rule of law, and the protection of human rights. As one astute commentator observed, the difference between the two parties was more about style than about substance: The ANC would increasingly "come across as a grassroots-style liberation-type party, while the new party will offer a middle-class alternative for those who prefer their politics leavened with a healthy dose of liberal-style values."[24]

Certainly, in the ANC, the left—which had put Zuma into power—was on the ascendancy. But while the ANC's alliance partners, COSATU and the SACP, insisted that there would be a significant shift in economic policy away from the fiscal conservatism of the Mbeki era and toward the kind of state investment that would allegedly improve social services and create jobs, ANC leaders such as Zuma and Motlanthe went out of their way to assert that there would be continuity to the country's economic policies. This was not just because they felt compelled to reassure jittery markets that now worried about economic populism (particularly in the face of the global crisis), but also because they had come to see that they had little room to maneuver if they wished to continue being able to provide social services even at current levels. While the left was correct that the gap between rich and poor was growing in South Africa, real poverty levels actually declined significantly due to state investment in the Mbeki era. This was due largely to the Mbeki government's social welfare policies, which put more than 12 million people—one-quarter of the population—into the welfare net, usually as beneficiaries of child care grants or old-age pensions. According to the government's own statistics in 2008, 4 million households in South Africa had no other form of income.[25]

Under Zuma, the ANC pledged to increase the welfare net. But in 2009, as in the mid-1990s, the state of the world placed a significant constraint on economic experimentation. The fundamental disagreement in the ANC— over economic policy—seemed set to continue, into the post-Mbeki era.

What can be said about the state in which Thabo Mbeki left South Africa when he was forced from office? Writing this epilogue in early 2009, it seems too early to pass easy judgment on a legacy that is complex and multivalent. Certainly, as I hope this book has demonstrated, Mbeki played a primary role in the attainment of South Africa's freedom, leading the ANC to understand that because military conquest was out of the question, a negotiated settlement with the oppressors of black South Africans was the only viable option; and that the holy cows of statism and nationalization needed to be replaced, after the fall of the Berlin Wall, with a reckoning with capitalism and an understanding of South Africa's position in the newly globalized economy. His greatest legacy was the way he seduced not only the West (even Ronald Reagan's Washington) into accepting the ANC as a legitimate liberation movement rather than a Moscow-funded terrorist outfit, but white South Africans away from their support of a doomed apartheid regime and into the acceptance of a black-led ANC that would guarantee their security. He led the ANC in exile back into South Africa after F. W. de Klerk unbanned the liberation movements in 1990 and was the ANC's chief negotiator until he was deposed, in something of a palace coup, by Cyril Ramaphosa and his supporters in 1991, because he was perceived to be too accommodating of the other side. Nonetheless, the role that he played—along with Jacob Zuma—in preventing civil war in those taut years is inestimable.

After the ANC won the 1994 elections, Mandela wanted Ramaphosa to be his deputy but was persuaded by his fellow ANC leaders—most notably Walter Sisulu—to select Mbeki instead. Mbeki became Mandela's de facto prime minister, designing and running the newly democratic South Africa while Mandela occupied himself with "National Reconciliation" and with making all South Africans, particularly whites, feel that they belonged in the new democracy. Mbeki was a primary architect of this official ideology, although he would come to believe that it had serious pitfalls; his determination to confront racism would lead to the accusation that he had a racial chip on his shoulder. Once he became president, he was clearly driven by the need to prove, to a skeptical world, that black people were capable of self-determination. This led to his own official ideology of an "African Renaissance," the first serious envisioning of an emancipated Africa since the *uhuru* ("freedom") generation of people such as Julius Nyerere and Kwame Nkrumah. The result was a dogged overhaul of the continent's moribund institutions into an African Union (AU), and Mbeki's leadership of the New Partnership for Africa's Development (NEPAD), which put him into the global forefront as an African leader and gave him unparalleled access to Group of Eight (G8) leaders such George W. Bush, Tony Blair, and Jacques Chirac.

Mbeki's strategy was to leverage South Africa into the position of the continent's superpower and thus into permanent positions on bodies such as the UN Security Council; South Africa, too, would be the portal through which the developed world could invest in the continent. Despite the steady rollout of democracy on the African continent, neither of these aspirations fully materialized: Mbeki found himself trapped between, on the one hand, a developed world that had limited interest in Africa beyond the pillage of energy resources and, on the other, fellow Africans who were so entrenched in their kleptocratic tyrannies that *they* had little interest in the democratic orders that were the precondition for his vision of a New Africa.

Mbeki's primary motivation, during his tenure, seemed to be to prove that Africans could take care of their own problems, and he thus set himself up as the continent's preeminent peacemaker. This led him, while he was deputy president, into the advocacy of a disastrous multimillion-rand arms deal, which may well have regenerated an obsolete South African National Defence Force but which also became the poisoned well of South African politics, leading to the investigations that would cause the prosecution of Jacob Zuma, the fallout between himself and Zuma, and ultimately his own ousting. It also led him into serial rounds of peacemaking negotiations: He and his South African teams were highly successful in resolving the Central African "Great Lakes" crisis of the late 1990s and bringing stability to the Democratic Republic of Congo; they also played significant roles in bringing about peace in Burundi and Liberia. They were less successful in Sani Abacha's Nigeria, in Cote d'Ivoire, in the Sudan, and, most notoriously, in Robert Mugabe's Zimbabwe; in each case, Mbeki stood accused of siding with those in power against their opponents. Much of the motivation for this approach came from the seeming belief that, if he was seen to be critical of a sitting African head of state, he would be playing into the hands of racists who believed that Africans were incapable of governing themselves.

Nowhere was this dynamic revealed more sharply than in Zimbabwe. Although his policy of quiet diplomacy had its merits in the beginning, he held onto it for far too long, even approving obviously rigged elections and giving Robert Mugabe cover to continue a regime of tyranny that led to the economic ruin of the country and the misery of its citizens. Much of the criticism of Mbeki's role in Zimbabwe is unfair in the impossible expectations it put on him: South Africa could neither invade its neighbor nor easily turn off the electrical power and thus force Mugabe from office, as was often demanded. And from the beginning of the crisis, in 2000, Mbeki was highly critical, privately, of Mugabe.[26] But his strategy entailed engineering an internal transfer of power within Mugabe's ruling party rather than allowing the opposition Movement for Democratic Change into office. This strategy saw him ignoring the democratic rights of the Zimbabwean people themselves and rendered his own notions of an African Renaissance, driven by democracy, something of a hollow vessel. Despite Mbeki's own earlier modernization of the ANC, he clung to the anachronistic belief that the MDC was an agent of the old colonial powers—specifically Britain and the United States—rather than of the aspirations of the Zimbabwean people themselves. Finally, after Mugabe stole power following elections in a coup by stealth in 2008, Mbeki enforced a landmark peace accord, which would bring about an interim power-sharing arrangement, on September 20, 2008. It was Mbeki's greatest moment—and it came, ironically, just a day before the Nicholson judgment in the Zuma case, which led to his ousting. By early 2009, there was no evidence that this accord would have any effect, and Zimbabwe's destiny was bleaker than ever. Domestically, too, Mbeki's deployment of what critics have called the politics of nativism[27] led him to dismiss white critics as racists and the growing number of black ones as Uncle Toms. He thereby created the impression—both inside and outside his ruling party—that he did not tolerate dissent. This preoccupation with viewing any criticism as a slight on his (and therefore the black African's) ability to govern also saw him underplay the severity of the crime epidemic, even suggesting that concerns about it were a function of white fear and racism.[28]

And it also led him to embrace an AIDS dissident position. There are, as the book's chapter on AIDS elaborates, many reasons why Thabo Mbeki decided to question the scientific orthodoxies of this epidemic, but at the root of it was his conviction that AIDS was being used as yet another weapon in the arsenal of Afro-pessimism, trained particularly on black men, who were accused of spreading the virus because they could not control their sexuality. By questioning the etiology of AIDS in this way he confused the science of AIDS with the politics of self-determination. The result was a mixed message from government that undoubtedly compromised its own safer-sex programming, that promoted unproved holistic and alternative treatments at the expense of antiretroviral treatments, and, most catastrophically, that delayed the rollout of a drug program. One recent credible study, comparing South African statistics with those of neighboring countries that provided timely antiretroviral therapy, estimated that this delay could have caused the premature deaths of 330,000 people.[29] For this alone Mbeki—whatever his other achievements—will be held forever accountable.

Ultimately, Thabo Mbeki changed the face of South Africa in several significant and indisputable ways, even if the effects of these changes are open to debate. His twin policies of aggressive affirmative action and black economic empowerment, implemented during a period of economic growth, created a vibrant new black middle class—numbering a fraction of a percentile when the ANC came to power in 1994 and now estimated to be anywhere between 300,000 and two million people, out of a total population of 50 million.[30] Meanwhile, his government's social welfare policies have made a significant impact on the deep poverty, exacerbated by unemployment, of the majority of South Africans. Some analysts blame the Mbeki government for—as author Brian Pottinger puts it—encouraging "the growth of the dependency society," and Pottinger sees this "baleful" effect not only among welfare recipients but also among middle-class blacks, many of whom are recipients of state largesse due to affirmative action.[31] But the growth of this new middle class—educated, upwardly mobile, and fiercely protective of its new position in society—is the best possible insurance South Africa has in the defense of its democracy.

. The area around which there is the most contention, when it comes to Mbeki's legacy, is that of economic policy. He and his financial managers insist that they stabilized the economy in 1996 with their Growth, Employment and Redistribution (GEAR) policy and staved off a crash that would have forced the country to take out the begging bowl before the International Monetary Fund and the World Bank. They cite, as evidence of their correct policies, the unprecedented era of economic growth over which Mbeki presided (an average of 4.5 percent per annum over a decade), the dramatic increase in the efficiency of tax collection, and the fact that, by 2004, South Africa was able to spend more per capita on social services than almost any other developing country. 2.7 million new houses were built, there was a dramatic improvement in access to electrification and sanitation, and, most significantly, there was the extension of the welfare net described above. But despite the fact that there has been a steady decline in the unemployment rate since 1999, it still remains unacceptably high despite the growth, hovering at around 30 percent in 2008.[32] There is consensus among social analysts that this has fueled the crime rate, which has rendered South Africa one of the most violent societies in the world.[33] And the country has slipped on many credible international scales, including the UN's Human Development index. Reasons proffered for this slippage include the dramatic decline of the manufacturing sector, ineffective regulation, inefficient health and education services despite huge investments in these sectors, the increasing skills shortage, and the collapse of the criminal justice system.

These are all serious problems; many openly acknowledged by the new leadership of the ANC. Yet, fascinatingly, this leadership—brought to power in large part through the grievances of the leftist SACP and COSATU—goes out of its way to trumpet the economic growth achieved during the Mbeki years. Indeed, much of the policy that forms the basis of the ANC election manifesto is simply a sharper restatement of policies to which the Mbeki administration already committed itself as it made the shift toward increased expenditure and "the developmental state." Certainly the ANC's left allies will advocate some positions strongly, such as the nationalization of key industries and the termination of practices such as inflation targeting (keeping inflation down by raising interest rates). But the emphasis by Zuma,

Motlanthe, and other ANC leaders on continuity pointed, in the Motlanthe interregnum at least, to a grudging acceptance of the Mbeki legacy on economic policy, and of the fact that solutions to many of South Africa's problems would be found by creating a more efficient state rather than a larger one.

Of course, the growing consensus on the positive effect of Mbeki's economic policies does not absolve him from the allegations of poor management and planning—and, particularly, his seeming inability to take action against corruption and cronyism. Perhaps the most notorious—and instructive—example of this dynamic was the way he intervened in a matter between Jackie Selebi, his police commissioner, and Vusi Pikoli, his national director of public prosecutions, in 2007. Both Selebi and Pikoli were from the same small, tight returned-exile clique as Mbeki and Zuma. Both were hand-picked by Mbeki, and both were close comrades in exile. But now Pikoli was presented with evidence that Selebi had been taking kickbacks for protecting friends in the criminal underworld. He informed Mbeki, who appears to have instead chosen to believe Selebi's story, which was that he was the victim of a turf war between the Scorpions and the police.

Mbeki suspended Pikoli on trumped-up charges, and appointed a Commission of Inquiry into whether Pikoli was fit to hold office. Pikoli alleged before the commission that Mbeki had instructed him to drop the case against Selebi and that he had been suspended for disobeying the president; it also became evident that Mbeki had lied publicly about the extent to which Pikoli had informed him of the Selebi investigation. Why did Mbeki go so far to protect his police chief? Some believe that Selebi must have had dirt on his boss, possibly relating to the arms deal or activities in exile; others think Mbeki was more focused on winning the ANC presidency at Polokwane than on running the state, and that he needed Selebi's support more than he needed Pikoli's.[34]

Whichever the case, Mbeki's support of Selebi is one of the darkest marks against him, for it demonstrated that he could not or would not put his own high ideals about corruption into practice, particularly when it came to members of his own "family." It also seemed to support an allegation that Zuma and his supporters liked to make: that Mbeki eroded the organs of state, particularly its vital security apparatus, in order to fight his own battles. It demonstrated, ultimately, the profound contradiction that Mbeki was unable to resolve as president: between being, on the one hand, the technocrat, an avatar of modernity and efficiency; and on the other, the paterfamilias, bound inextricably into the atavistic politics of family and struggle.

In November 2008, Thabo Mbeki's office leaked a letter that the ex-president had written to Jacob Zuma after he was fired, in which he finally allowed his grievance and personal hurt to show publicly. Although it was an open secret that Mbeki quietly supported the COPE breakaway, the stated purpose of the letter was to tell Zuma that he would not become involved in the campaigns of either party, because "I refuse absolutely to rule from beyond the grave." As a way of smoking out Mbeki's true allegiance, Zuma had said publicly that the ex-president would be compelled to campaign for the ANC. Now Mbeki asked tartly why the ANC would even want him to be associated with its brand, given that it had just expressed so little confidence in him that it had fired him as president.

The real reason for the letter seemed to have been to offer his old comrade and protégé a lesson on the perils of leadership, and specifically on the personality cult that was now growing around Zuma: "Both of us," he wrote, "have grown up in a political atmosphere in which we fully respected and honoured our leaders, our heroines and our heroes, without reservation. However, for me personally, at no point did this translate into 'hero worship' and therefore the progression to the phenomenon of the 'cult of personality.'"[35] The implication was that Zuma had allowed himself to succumb to this—although of course, the way his detractors saw it, Mbeki's determination to remain on as ANC president was precisely an articulation of this cult of personality; one that stifled dissent around him and encouraged the notion that he was the only man able to continue running the show.

As I read Mbeki's letter, I thought of how assiduously he had cultivated the image of the antihero throughout his long career—particularly in contrast to Nelson Mandela, whom he actually cites in his letter as the one "exceptional circumstance" when the ANC has been "enslaved in a cult of the individual." But I thought, too, of that letter to Rhiannon Gooding about Coriolanus in 1969, in which he had written that while they, sixties kids, might "shrink at 'hero-worship,'" "revolutionary struggle" actually depended on the "heroic feats of individuals" such as Coriolanus: such people were "infinitely preferable to the existential non-hero."[36]

I also remembered my very first interview with Mbeki, a decade earlier, when I had asked him how to escape the fate of Coriolanus. His answer had been fascinating, and not a little chilling: Change society, not yourself. While studying at the Lenin Institute, he told me, he had become enamored of a Soviet critic who argued that the reason why Shakespeare's heroes always die is not because of their tragic flaws but rather because this is the way the playwright illuminated society's imperfection: "The person who does good, and does it honestly, must expect to be overpowered by forces of evil," Mbeki had said to me. "But it would be incorrect not to do good just because you know death is coming." Now, in November 2008, reading Mbeki's letter to Zuma, I had no doubt that he considered his actions against Zuma over the previous years to be heroic in this very respect; and thus the consequences of these actions to be tragic—in the sense that *he* understood tragedy, as the consequence of losing the battle of good against evil.

But Mbeki's real tragedy is, actually, the way that this Manichean struggle of good versus evil—as he sees it—takes place not on a battlefield of warring strangers but among former comrades in arms, within the family of revolutionaries. Once more *Coriolanus* gives us a clue to the particular nature of this tragedy, as it might resonate within Mbeki: After the war hero is banished from Rome, he finds common cause with his former enemies, the Volscians, and leads them back to Rome with the intention of sacking his home city—and the mindless rabble with it. But at the city's gates, he is confronted with his family: his mother, his wife, and his infant child. He succumbs to their pleas and chooses not to destroy the city from which he has been exiled. This infuriates his new allies, who kill him. Shakespeare thus allows an interpretation that Coriolanus's fatal flaw is not his excessive pride. Rather, it is his vulnerability to his mother's arguments, a weakness borne of placing ties of blood before the politics of principle.

In the family Mbeki forged out of struggle, Jacob Zuma became the equivalent of a blood relative, as did Jackie Selebi, the man he defended, and Vusi Pikoli, the man he did not. The ultimate purpose of Mbeki's final letter to Zuma is to let him know that even though he has been "a member of the ANC for 52 years" and is thus unable to repudiate it publicly the way COPE's founders have, he will not succumb to the injunctions of a family that has so brutally cast him out. He will attempt to avoid Coriolanus's fate by living with neither the Romans of his blood or the Volscians of his convictions. He even says this in his letter: "I have considered carefully what I should do as a private South African and African citizen...[to] ensure that whatever I do in no way involves me in the internal politics of the ANC or the functioning of the government of South Africa."[37]

After following Thabo Mbeki for a decade and immersing myself in his lifelong denial of the subjective and the personal, these are surprisingly tough lines to read. I conclude this book knowing that he is truly alone. He has been forced at last, at 66 years of age, to consider his subjectivity.

Notes

Please consult the Bibliographical Notes at the end of this book for additional information on where to obtain documents cited here, and on suggestions for further reading.

INTRODUCTION

1. T. Mbeki, Statement at opening of debate in National Assembly on Reconciliation and Nation Building, Cape Town, May 29, 1998.
2. L. Hughes, "Harlem" and "Same in Blues" in *Selected Poems* (London: Pluto Press, 1986), pp. 268, 271.
3. T. Mbeki, Letter to M. Gevisser, February 24, 2008.
4. Quoted in P. Fabricius, "Obama inspired at college by meeting SA exiles," *Sunday Independent* (South Africa), November 9, 2008.
5. B. Obama, *Dreams of My Father* (Edinburgh: Canongate, 2007), p. 106.

1   THE MBEKIS

1. J. Ayliff and J. Whiteside, *History of the Abambo: generally known as Fingoes* (Cape Town: Struik, 1962), p. 17, cited in C. Bundy, *The Rise and Fall of the South African Peasantry* (Cape Town: David Philip, 1988), p. 34.
2. C. Higgs, *The Ghost of Equality: The Public Lives of DDT Jabavu of South Africa 1885–1959* (Cape Town: Mayibuye, 1997), p. 20.
3. B. Head, Foreword in S. Plaatje, *Native Life in South Africa, Before and Since the European War and Boer Rebellion* (Johannesburg: Ravan Press, 1982), p. ix.
4. C. Bundy, "Schooled for Life? The Early Years and Education of Govan Mbeki," unpublished paper, 1994, pp. 1–2.
5. Ibid., p. 2.
6. See X. Mangcu, *To the Brink: The State of Democracy in South Africa* (Durba: UKZN Press, 2008).

2   THE MOERANES

1. M. Arbousset, "Notice on Zachee Mokhanoi," *Journal des Missions Evangéliques* 19 (1888): 72; Morija Archives, Lesotho, p. 183.
2. M. T. Moerane, "I Chose Freedom: The Autobiography of MT Moerane of South Africa," undated, Norah Moerane Personal Collection, p. 6.
3. C. Bundy, " 'Waking from a Midnight Slumber': Govan Mbeki in the Transkei in the 1940s," unpublished paper, p. 21.

3 THE NEW AFRICANS

1. C. Bundy, "Schooled for Life: The Early Education of Govan Mbeki," unpublished paper, pp. 17–18.
2. P. Walshe, *The Rise of African Nationalism in South Africa: The ANC 1912–1952* (Los Angeles: University of California Press, 1970), p. 147.
3. T. Couzens, *The New African: A Study of the Life and Work of HIE Dhlomo* (Johannesburg: Ravan Press, 1985), pp. 33–34.
4. T. Mbeki, "The African Renaissance," in T. Mbeki, *Africa: The Time Has Come* (Cape Town: Tafelberg and Mafube, 1998), p. 72.
5. B. Thompson, interview with G. Mbeki for "Heart of Stone," Mayibuye Archives, RIM-084, University of the Western Cape, Cape Town.
6. Bundy, "Schooled for Life," p. 14.
7. T. Lodge, *Black Politics in South Africa Since 1945* (London: Longman, 1983), p. 21.
8. T. Karis and G. Carter, eds., *From Protest to Challenge*, Vol. 1 (Stanford: Hoover Institution Press, 1973), pp. 69–71.
9. T. Mbeki, "I Am an African," quoted in T. Mbeki, *Africa: The Time Has Come*, p. 32.
10. G. Gerhart, *Black Power in South Africa* (Berkeley: University of California Press, 1978), p. 58.
11. G. Mbeki, "The Cries Answered," *The Territorial Magazine* (January 1939), cited in C. Bundy, " 'Waking from a Midnight Slumber': Govan Mbeki in the Transkei in the 1940s," unpublished paper, p. 15.
12. G. Mbeki, "Gallery of African Heroes," *Inkundla ya Bantu* (May 1941): 3.
13. B. Bunting, *Moses Kotane: South African Revolutionary* (London: Inkululeko Publications, 1975), p. 89.
14. A. G. Cobley, *Class and Consciousness* (London: Greenwood Press, 1990), p. 41.
15. Walshe, *The Rise of African Nationalism in South Africa: The ANC, 1912–1952* (Los Angeles: University of California Press, 1970), p. 143.
16. R. J. Southall, *South Africa's Transkei: The Political Economy of an Independent Bantustan* (London: Heinemann Educational Books, 1982), pp. 79–84.
17. "African Co-operative Store," *Inkundla ya Bantu* (October 1941): p. 3.

4 MBEWULENI

1. T. Mbeki, "We Still Feel the Prick of Van Riebeeck's Thorns," *Sunday Times* (Johannesburg), February 28, 1999.
2. E. S. Haines, "The Transkei Trader," *South African Journal of Economics* 1, no. 2 (1933): 201–216.
3. C. Bundy, "Land and Liberation: Popular Rural Protest and National Liberation" in S. Marks and S. Trapido, *The Politics of Race, Class and Nationalism in Twentieth Century South Africa* (London: Longman, 1987), p. 270.
4. "Biographical Sketch of Thabo Mbeki" in T. Mbeki, *Africa: The Time Has Come*, (Cape Town: Tafelberg and Mafube, 1998), p. v.

5 FAMILY

1. C. Bundy, "Land and Liberation: Popular Rural Protest and National Liberation," in S. Marks and S. Trapido, *The Politics of Race, Class and Nationalism in Twentieth Century South Africa* (London: Longman, 1987),

p. 271. "Bliss was it that dawn to be alive, but to be young was very heaven!" W. Wordsworth, *The Prelude* (New York: Norton, 1979).

2. B. Thompson, interview with Govan Mbeki for "Heart of Stone," Mayibuye Archives, RIM-084, University of the Western Cape, Cape Town. The actual poem, titled "Up-Hill" (1861), reads:

> Does the road wind uphill all the way?
> Yes, to the very end.
> Will the day's journey take the whole long day?
> From morn to night, my friend.

The poem is available in C. Rossetti, *The Complete Poems* (London: Penguin, 2001).

3. B. Thompson, interview with Govan Mbeki.

4. A. Sampson, *Mandela* (Johannesburg: Jonathan Ball, 1999), p. 581.

5. Stock footage of ANC leaders departing for Lusaka, January 15, 1990, South African Broadcasting Corporation Archives, Johannesburg.

6. H. Bernstein, *The Rift* (London: Jonathan Cape, 1994), p. 448.

7. A. Hadland and J. Rantao, *The Life and Times of Thabo Mbeki* (Rivonia: Zebra Press, 1999), p. 17; H. Serfontein, *Breaking the Fetters*, documentary film, Fokus Suid Productions (1987).

8. "Biographical Sketch" in T. Mbeki, *Africa: The Time Has Come* (Cape Town: Tafelberg, 1998), p. vi.

6 QUEENSTOWN

1. D. Coplan, *In Township Tonight!* (London: Longman, 1985), p. 96.

2. T. Matshikiza, "Jazz Comes to Joburg!" *Drum* (July 1957), p. 39.

3. G. Mbeki, "An Unholy Alliance," *New Age*, August 3, 1961.

4. A. Hadland and J. Rantao, *The Life and Times of Thabo Mbeki* (Johannesburg: Zebra Press, 1999), p. 20.

7 LOVEDALE

1. P. Christie, *The Right to Learn* (Johannesburg: Ravan Press, 1991), p. 12.

2. R. H. W. Shepherd, *Lovedale: South Africa 1824–1955* (Lovedale, South Africa: Lovedale Press, 1971), p. 3.

3. G. Mbeki, "The Rape of Lovedale," *New Age*, July 30, 1959, p. 5.

4. J. Jabulani [T. Mbeki], "Why I Joined the Communist Party," *African Communist*, 1st Quarter, 1971, pp. 79–82.

5. T. Mbeki, statement at the Memorial Service for the late Mwalimu Julius Nyerere, October 18, 1999, www.anc.org.za.

8 FATHERHOOD

1. O. Mpahlwa, testimony before the Human Rights Violation Hearings of the Truth and Reconciliation Commission, Port Elizabeth, May 23, 1996. www.doj.gov.za/trc/.

2. Ibid.

3. "Cracks in Unity as FW, Mbeki Clash," *Weekend Argus* (Cape Town), June 12, 1994.

9 JOHANNESBURG

1. G. Mbeki, "Fort Hare, Healdtown and Lovedale Closed Down," *New Age*, June 8, 1961, p. 5.
2. ."Minutes of Committee Meeting," March 28, 1960, SACHED Archives, Johannesburg.
3. O. Britzius, "Principal's Report...14 November, 1960," and "Principal's Report to be Submitted to the Meeting to Be Held on 6th February 1961," SACHED Archives.
4. "Minutes of Committee Meeting," SACHED Archives.
5. M. Horrell, *A Survey of Race Relations 1962* (Johannesburg: South African Institute of Race Relations, 1963), p. 109, and M. Horrell, *A Survey of Race Relations 1961* (Johannesburg: South African Institute of Race Relations, 1962), p. 128.
6. "Dube—Symbol of Comfort and Respectability," *Star*, August 18, 1961; P. Bonner and L. Segal, *Soweto: A History* (Cape Town: Maskew Miller Longman, 1998).
7. "Publication of List in Terms of Section 27 (3) of the Internal Security Act, 1982 (Act 74 of 1982)," Department of Justice, No. 1679, *Government Gazette*, August 7, 1987, South African National Archives, Pretoria.
8. L. Nkosi, "An Obituary on Can Themba" in C. Themba, *A Will to Die* (Cape Town: David Philip, 1982), p. 24.
9. N. Nakasa, "Fringe Country: Where There Is No Colour Bar," *Drum* (March 1961): 23–27.
10. M. Horrell, *A Survey of Race Relations 1966* (Johannesburg: South African Institute of Race Relations, 1967).
11. L. Nkosi, "Obituary on Can Themba," pp. vii–viii.

10 BECOMING A COMMUNIST

1. T. Mbeki, "African Students Have a Mission," *New Age*, January 4, 1962.
2. J. Jabulani [T. Mbeki], "Why I Joined the Communist Party," *African Communist*, 1st Quarter 1971, pp. 79–82.
3. R. Bernstein, *Memory Against Forgetting* (New York: Viking, 1999), p. 124.

11 INTO EXILE

1. "Concern as 'Students' Move Out," *Star* (Johannesburg), November 15, 1962.
2. V. P. Mahali, "Contradiction, Conflict and Convergence of Class and Nation in Black South African Politics, 1925–1985," Ph.D. thesis, University of Illinois, 1995, pp. 297, 330.
3. Ibid, p. 312.

12 SUSSEX MAN

1. "Where the Bright Girls Go," *Sunday Times* (London), April 3, 1966.
2. "Versus the Press," *Wine Press* (Brighton), February 7, 1966.
3. T. Mbeki, Letter to D. Gunby, July 1963.
4. T. Mbeki, Letter to R. Gooding, August 22, 1969.

5. T. Mbeki, "Resistance Against Apartheid," *Wine Press* (Brighton), May 6, 1963.
6. University of Sussex, BA Preliminary Examination, The Economic and Social Framework, March 22, 1963, courtesy of T. Barna.
7. "Biographical Sketch of Thabo Mbeki" in T. Mbeki, *Africa: The Time has Come* (Cape Town: Tafelberg, 1998) p. x.
8. Mbeki, Letter to Gunby, July 1963.
9. Ibid.
10. T. Mbeki, Statement to UN Special Committee Against Apartheid, April 16, 1963, in *Africa: The Time has Come*, pp. 5–6.
11. "Thabo Will Lead Night March on London," *Evening Argus* (Brighton), June 11, 1964.
12. "Wet and Weary but Trekkers Plod On," *Evening Argus* (Brighton), June 13, 1964.
13. D. Gunby, Letter to J. Gunby, undated.
14. " 'Free Rivonia Eight' Rally," *Daily Worker* (London), June 15, 1964.
15. Ibid.
16. Independent Television News (London), June 14, 1964.
17. T. Mbeki, Letter to J. J. Hadebe, November 8, 1964, ANC Morogoro office; Thabo Mbeki, SASA; 1964–65, ANC Archives, Fort Hare, Alice, South Africa.

13 FAVORITE SON

1. A. Tambo, "My Son, My President, and My Comrade, Thabo," in T. Mbeki, *Africa: Define Yourself* (Cape Town: Tafelberg , 2002), pp. 320–321.
2. T. Mbeki, Letter to A. Kgogong, July 12, 1966, ANC Morogoro office; Thabo Mbeki; SASA 1964–65, ANC Archives, University of Fort Hare, Alice, South Africa.
3. T. Mbeki, "Report on April Visit to the USSR 1968," ANC Collection, MCH12/15, p. 7, Mayibuye Archives, University of the Western Cape, Cape Town.
4. T. Mbeki, Letter to "The Reps, Dar Es Salaam," undated, ANC Morogoro office; Thabo Mbeki; SASA 1964–65, ANC Archives, Fort Hare.
5. J. Hadebe, Letter to T. Mbeki, November 30, 1964, ANC Morogoro office; Thabo Mbeki; SASA 1964–65, ANC Archives, Fort Hare.
6. T. Mbeki, Letter to Mazwi, May 11, 1966, ANC Morogoro office; Thabo Mbeki; SASA 1964–5, ANC Archives, Fort Hare.
7. R. Attenborough, Speech in *Official Publication: Honorary Degree Ceremony for Thabo Mbeki at the University of Sussex*, October 6, 1995. Sussex University Library, Brighton.

14 SWINGING LONDON

1. "Great Britain: You Can Walk across It on the Grass," *TIME*, April 15, 1966.
2. R. Kasrils, *Armed and Dangerous* (Oxford: Heinemann, 1993), p. 100.
3. L. Nkosi, "Jazz in Exile," 1966, cited in I. Harris and S. Douglas, "Bebop and Beyond the Blues," JazzUSA.com. 6, no. 6 (June 2002).
4. "Biographical Sketch of Thabo Mbeki" in T. Mbeki, *Africa: Your Time Has Come* (Cape Town: Tafelberg, 1998), p. xi.

5. "Statement by the ANC (SA) on the Situation in Czechoslovakia," ANC Archives, Lusaka Mission Collection, Box 92, University of Fort Hare, Alice, South Africa.
6. "Biographical Sketch of Thabo Mbeki," p. xii.
7. I. Berlin, "The Hedgehog and the Fox," in I. Berlin, *Russian Thinkers* (London: Penguin, 1978), p. 22.
8. T. Mbeki, Letter to R. Gooding, August 22, 1969.

15 MOSCOW MAN

1. T. Mbeki, Letter to R. Gooding, August 22, 1969.
2. See "An Observer," *Message from Moscow* (New York: Vintage, 1971), pp. 325–330.
3. A. Hadland and J. Rantao, *The Life and Times of Thabo Mbeki* (Johannesburg: Zebra Press, 1999), p. 37.
4. "The Battle for South Africa," CBS (USA), 1979, Mayibuye Archives.
5. [C. Hani], Memorandum, 1969. Courtesy of J. Smith and B. Tromp. Another version of the document is cited in V. Shubin, *ANC: A View from Moscow* (Cape Town: Mayibuye Books, 1999), p. 87.
6. T. Mbeki, Letter to R. Gooding, October 1969.
7. T. Mbeki, Letters to R. Gooding, August 22, 1969, October 1969, May 1970.

16 "NOT QUITE HOME"

1. H. Barrell, Interview with J. Slovo, August 12–16, 1989, courtesy of H. Barrell.
2. M. Gevisser, "The Outsiders," *Leadership* (Cape Town), April/May 1991.
3. "Report of Subcommittee on Marriages Set Up by NWC Decision Taken At Meeting of 01/11/88," ANC Collection, Mayibuye Archives, University of the Western Cape, South Africa.

17 SWAZILAND

1. P. Seme, "The Regeneration of Africa," April 5, 1906, in T. Karis and C. Carter, *From Protest to Challenge*, Vol. 1 (Stanford: Hoover Institution Press, 1973), p. 69.
2. "Manifesto of the Africanist Movement" in Karis and Carter, *From Protest to Challenge*, Vol. 3, pp. 517–524.
3. T. Mbeki, "Problems of the Development of the Armed Struggle in SA," Youth and Students Seminar, August 1–14, 1971, pp. 7–8, ANC Archives, Lusaka Mission Collection, Box 5, University of Fort Hare, Alice, South Africa.
4. Karis and Gerhart, *From Protest to Challenge*, vol. 5 (Pretoria: Unisa Press, 1997), p. 147.
5. H. Barrell, Interview with M. Maharaj, November 20, 1990, courtesy of H. Barrell. See P. O'Malley, *Shades of Difference: Mac Maharaj and the Struggle for South Africa* (London: Penguin, 2007), for a more recent published account of this incident.
6. H. Barrell interview with Mac Maharaj.

18 GOVAN AND EPAINETTE

1. E. Mbeki, Letter to G. Mbeki, October 13, 1975, Govan Mbeki Collection, MCH48–1, Mayibuye Archives, University of the Western Cape, Cape Town.
2. L. Jiba, Letter to G. Mbeki, October 24, 1975; L. Jiba, Letter to G. Mbeki, November 10, 1975, MCH48–1, Mayibuye Archives. Translated from isiXhosa by Simpiwe Yako.
3. E. Mbeki, Letter to G. Mbeki, July 14, 1975, MCH48–1, Mayibuye Archives.
4. "Mrs E Mbeki," IDAF Collection, Mayibuye Archives.
5. E. Mbeki, Letter to G. Mbeki, July 14, 1975, MCH 48–1, Mayibuye Archives.
6. E. Mbeki, Letter to G. Mbeki, August 25, 1975, MCH 48–1, Mayibuye Archives. Translated from isiXhosa by Simpiwe Yako.
7. E. Mbeki, Letter to G. Mbeki, November 10, 1975; L. Jiba, Letter to G. Mbeki, November 10, 1975, MCH48–1, Mayibuye Archives. Translated from isiXhosa by Simpiwe Yako.
8. E. Mbeki, Letter to G. Mbeki, November 10, 1982, MCH48–1, Mayibuye Archives.
9. E. Mbeki, Letter to G. Mbeki, August 25, 1975. MCH48–1, Mayibuye Archives.
10. Ibid.
11. E. Mbeki, Letter to G. Mbeki, June 4, 1982; E. Mbeki, Letter to G. Mbeki, September 7, 1982, MCH58–1, Mayibuye Archives.
12. E. Mbeki, Letter to T. Mbeki, December 9, 1965, ANC Morogoro office, Mbeki; Thabo; SASA; 1964–5, ANC Archives, University of Fort Hare, Alice, South Africa.
13. Ibid.
14. E. Mbeki, Letter to T. Mbeki, April 21, 1966, ANC Morogoro office, Mbeki; Thabo; SASA; 1964–5, ANC Archives, Fort Hare.
15. L. Jiba, Letter to G. Mbeki, May 13, 1982, MCH48–1, Mayibuye Archives. Translated from isiXhosa by Simpiwe Yako.
16. M. Maharaj, *Reflections in Prison* (Cape Town: Zebra Press 2001), p. 129.
17. T. Mkhwanazi, "My Years on Robben Island," *Weekly Mail* (Johannesburg), August 21–27, 1987.
18. A. Kathrada, *Memoirs* (Cape Town: Zebra Press, 2004), p. 280.
19. T. Mbeki, Statement before a Delegation of the United Nations Special Committee Against Apartheid, London, April 13, 1964, in T. Mbeki, *Africa: Define Yourself* (Cape Town: Tafelberg 2002), p. 5.

19 THE DISAPPEARANCE OF JAMA MBEKI

1. The interviews for this chapter were conducted by Mzilikazi wa Afrika of the *Sunday Times* (Johannesburg), 2003.
2. "Attorney Mbeki Is Dead," *Botswana Daily News* (Gaborone), April 10, 1989.
3. "Cracks in Unity as FW, Mbeki Clash," *Weekend Argus* (Cape Town), June 12, 1994.

20 NIGERIA

1. "The Significance of the Lagos Conference," *Sechaba* (London: African National Congress), First Quarter 1978, p. 13.

2. V. Shubin, *ANC: A View from Moscow* (Cape Town: Mayibye, 1999), p. 194.
3. "Who Is Tsietsi Mashinini, and What Does He Stand For?" ANC Archives, SMFC, Box R3, Folder 189, University of Fort Hare, Alice, South Africa.
4. G. Gerhart et al., *From Protest to Challenge*, vol. 4, forthcoming second edition (Johannesburg: Jacana, 2009).
5. T. Mbeki, e-mail to M. Gevisser, December 17, 2004.

21 THE NATIONAL INTERFERER

1. T. Lodge, "State of Exile: The African National Congress of South Africa, 1976–1986," *Third World Quarterly* 9, No. 1 (January 1986): 5–6; "Memorandum Submitted by the African National Congress of South Africa to S.I.D.A. in Support of a Request for Assistance for the Year 1977–1978," April 14, 1977, Nordic Africa Institute; T. Nkobi, Letter to Alfred Nzo, "Re: 1985/1986 Requisition to the USSR," May 27, 1985, ANC Archives, Lusaka Mission Collection, Box B49, University of Fort Hare, Alice, South Africa.
2. "President's Draft Report," May 1979, ANC Archives, Lusaka Mission Collection, Box 92, Fort Hare.
3. Anonymous letter to "Comrade Mbeki," undated, ANC Archives, O. Tambo Collection, C3.15.1, Fort Hare.
4. "Classification of Offences and Penalties," undated, ANC Collection, Mayibuye Archives; "ANC Statement to the Truth and Reconciliation Commission," August 1996, Truth and Reconciliation Commission Archives, National Archives, Pretoria.
5. T. Mbeki, "Reconciliation and Social Change Must Go Together," *ANC Today* (Johannesburg), January 23–29, 2004, ANC website.
6. M. Twala and E. Bernard, *Mbokodo* (Johannesburg: Jonathan Ball, 1994), p. 52.
7. Lodge, "State of Exile," pp. 26–27.

22 PARTY MAN

1. O. Tambo, wire-bound writing pad used during Vietnam visit, undated, ANC Archives, Oliver Tambo Collection, A11.3.4, p. 50, University of Fort Hare, Alice, South Africa.
2. "South Africa, Squeezing the ANC," *Africa Confidential* (London), August 25, 1989.
3. O. Mabandla, "Comrades Against Apartheid: A Response by Co-Author Oyama Mabandla (Tsepo Sechaba) to a Review by Jeremy Cronin," unpublished letter to *Work in Progress* (Johannesburg), 1981. Courtesy of Gail Gerhart.
4. M. Mini [Thabo Mbeki], "Class Struggle and African Unity—10 Years of the OAU," *African Communist* (Third Quarter 1973): 39.
5. B. Bunting, *Moses Kotane, South African Revolutionary* (London: Inkululeko Publications, 1975), p. 89.
6. E. Sisulu, *Walter and Albertina Sisulu* (Cape Town: David Philip, 2002), pp. 11, 23.
7. "Special Resolution: Party Work in the Fraternal Organisations," undated, Jack Simons/Ray Alexander Papers, University of Cape Town.
8. T. Mbeki, "The Fatton Thesis: A Rejoinder," *Canadian Journal of African Studies* 18, No. 3 (1984): 609–611.

23 THE DIPLOMAT

1. T. Sellström, Interview with Thabo Mbeki, 1995, in T. Sellström, ed. *Liberation in Southern Africa: Regional and Swedish Voices* (Uppsala, Sweden: Nordic Africa Institute, 1999), pp. 153–154.

2. V. Shubin, *ANC: A View from Moscow* (Cape Town: Mayibuye Books, 1999), pp. 304–305.

3. Shubin, *ANC: A View from Moscow.*

4. O. Tambo, Statement at meeting of UN Special Committee Against Apartheid, New York, June 11, 1981, www.anc.org.za.

5. T. Karis, "Oliver Tambo, June 12, 1981, UN Plaza Hotel," and T. Karis, "Revolution in the Making: Black Politics in South Africa," *Foreign Affairs* 62, No. 2 (1984), p. 400.

6. J. Makatini, Letter to T. Mbeki, undated, ANC Archives, Oliver Tambo Collection, O.R.T. 7.1.2., University of Fort Hare, Alice, South Africa.

7. T. Mbeki, "Reforming Apartheid Doesn't End Slavery," *New York Times*, July 18, 1983, and T. Mbeki, "Peaceful Struggle Is Futile," *New York Times*, August 13, 1985.

8. "Statement of the ANC on Chester Crocker's Testimony Before the US Senate Sub-Committee on Security and Terrorism," March 22, 1982, Karis-Gerhart Collection, Folder 42, Wits University, Johannesburg.

9. Taped response by Thabo Mbeki to questions posed by Luli Callinicos, January 20, 2002, courtesy of Luli Callinicos and Thabo Mbeki.

10. T. Mbeki, interview with Simon Marks, South African Broadcasting Corporation/Government Communication and Information System, June 11, 2004.

11. "Loss of Bases in Mozambique Is Severe Test for S. African Rebels," *Washington Post*, April 16, 1984.

12. A. Sampson, *Black and Gold* (New York: Pantheon, 1987), p. 218.

24 THE SEDUCER

1. R. Rosenthal, *Mission Improbable: A Piece of the South African Story* (Cape Town: David Philip, 1998), p. 108.

2. P. Waldmeir, *Anatomy of a Miracle* (New Brunswick, NJ: Rutgers University Press, 2001), p. 68.

3. A. Sparks, *Beyond the Miracle* (Johannesburg: Jonathan Ball, 2003), p. 260.

4. M. Du Preez, *Pale Native* (Cape Town: Zebra, 2004), p. 143.

5. ANC, "The Green Book" (August 1979), www.anc.org.za.

6. G. Frankel, "S. African Rebels Make Comeback," *Washington Post*, January 1, 1984.

7. A. Sparks, "ANC Sets the Scene for United Front," *Observer* (London), March 2, 1986.

8. A. H. Bloom, "Notes of a Meeting at Mfuwe Game Lodge," September 13, 1985, pp. 28–30. Courtesy of A.H. Bloom.

9. F. Van Zyl Slabbert, *Tough Choices* (Cape Town: Tafelberg, 2000), p. 103.

10. ANC press statement, February 7, 1986, www.anc.org.za.

11. Waldmeir, *Anatomy of a Miracle*, p. 63.

12. "South Africa under Siege," KQED (USA), March 26, 1986.

13. "Pretoria Foes Reach Out to the West," *New York Times*, January 20, 1987.

14. Waldmeir, *Anatomy of a Miracle*, pp. 67–68.
15. Du Preez, *Pale Native*, p. 148.
16. H. Serfontein, *Breaking the Fetters*, documentary film, Fokus Suid Productions, 1987; T. Mbeki, "I Am an African," in T. Mbeki, *Africa: The Time has Come* (Cape Town: Tafelberg 1998), p. 32.
17. Du Preez, *Pale Native*, p. 156.
18. H. Serfontein, *Breaking the Fetters*.
19. A. Sparks, "Whites Elated by Black Africa's Jubilant Welcome," *Observer* (London), July 19, 1987.
20. Serfontein, *Breaking the Fetters*.
21. Sparks, "Whites Elated by Black Africa's Jubilant Welcome."
22. Slabbert, *Tough Choices*, p. 111.
23. Du Preez, *Pale Native*, p. 164.
24. M. Du Preez, "Mbeki, The Old Charmer Is Back," *Star* (Johannesburg), March 25, 2004.
25. M. Du Preez, "Longing for Mbeki the Human Being, Not the Intellectual," *Star* (Johannesburg), October 2, 2003.
26. Du Preez, *Pale Native*, p. 151.
27. Ibid., p. 265.
28. Slabbert also recounts this story, slightly differently, in his 2005 memoir, *The Other Side of History* (Johannesburg: Jonathan Ball, 2006), p. 58.
29. S. Biko, "The Quest for True Humanity" in S. Biko, *I Write What I Like* (San Francisco: Harper & Row, 1987).

25 PARALLEL PATHS TO POWER

1. V. Shubin, *ANC: A View from Moscow* (Cape Town: Mayibuye Books, 1999), p. 322.
2. Minutes of Mells Park Meeting, Somerset, United Kingdom, February 9–11, 1990, courtesy of T. Trew.
3. "Bermuda: Where Nats and ANC Agreed on the Tricky Topic of Violence," *Weekly Mail* (Johannesburg), April 13, 1989.
4. "The Path to Power," Programme of the South African Communist Party as adopted at the Seventh Congress, 1989, www.sacp.org.za.
5. Minutes of Mells Park Meeting, April 24, 1989.
6. Minutes of Mells Park Meeting, August 22, 1988.
7. P. Waldmeir, *Anatomy of a Miracle* (New Brunswick, NJ: Rutgers, 2001), p. 130.
8. "Broeders to Meet ANC," *Sunday Times* (Johannesburg), October 1, 1989.
9. "FW Dissociates Govt. From ANC Talks," *Business Day* (Johannesburg), October 3, 1989.
10. "Statement of Intent by the African National Congress (SA): A Proposed Constitution for a Liberated SA," 1987, ANC Archives, Lusaka Mission Collection, Box 94, University of Fort Hare, Alice, South Africa.
11. Stock footage of "In-house seminar on constitutional guidelines in a Democratic South Africa," Lusaka, March 1–4, 1988, ANC Film and Video Archives, Johannesburg.
12. "Declaration of the OAU Ad-Hoc Committee on Southern Africa on the Question of South Africa" ("Harare Declaration"), August 21, 1989, www.anc.org.za.

13. "Minutes of NEC Meeting 22nd February 1988," ANC Collection, MCH01, Box 51.2, Mayibuye Archives, University of the Western Cape, Cape Town.

14. "Thabo Mbeki: Smooth Operator," *Financial Mail* (Johannesburg), January 26, 1990.

15. "Reconvened Meeting of the NEC—26/10/89," ANC Collection, MCH01, Box 51.3, Mayibuye Archives.

16. "Minutes of Emergency Meeting of the NEC Held on 26/10/89" and "Resumed Meeting of the NEC, Friday 27/10/1989," ANC Collection, MCH01, Box 51.3, Mayibuye Archives.

17. "Minutes Meeting of the NEC—16/10/89," ANC Collection, MCH01, Box 51.3, Mayibuye Archives.

18. "Reconvened Meeting of the NEC—26/10/89."

19. "Emergency Meeting of the NEC Held on 25/10/89" and "Resumed Meeting of the NEC, Friday 27/10/89," ANC Collection, MCH01, Box 51.3, Mayibuye Archives.

20. "Resumed Meeting of the NEC, Friday 27/10/89," ANC Collection, MCH01, Box 51.3, Mayibuye Archives.

26   REUNIONS

1. E. Sisulu, *Walter and Albertina Sisulu* (Cape Town: David Phillip, 2002), p. 405.

2. Stock footage, January 15, 1990, South African Broadcasting Corporation, Johannesburg.

3. Sisulu, *Walter and Albertina Sisulu*, p. 405.

4. "What Happens after Mandela Is Free?" *Nightline*, ABC (USA), February 8, 1990.

5. A. Sparks, *Tomorrow Is Another Country* (Johannesburg: Struik 1994), p. 121.

6. M. Meredith, *Nelson Mandela: A Biography* (London: Penguin Books, 1997), p. 412.

27   COMING HOME

1. N. Mandela, *Long Walk to Freedom* (Johannesburg: Macdonald Purnell, 1994), p. 568.

2. "How Foolish We All Were…Not to Do This Ages Ago," *Weekly Mail* (Johannesburg), May 10, 1990.

3. "Good Flavour at Talks," *Cape Times* (Cape Town), May 4, 1990.

4. A. Hadland and J. Rantao, *The Life and Times of Thabo Mbeki* (Rivonia: Zebra Press, 1999), p. 70.

5. "Why the Exile Was Elevated Above the Activist," *Star* (Johannesburg), May 20, 1994.

6. In a 1997 case, *Kerzner v. Greenblo*, Kerzner claimed that this money had been given to the ANC for "voter education" and not for its own electoral campaigns.

7. C. Smith, "Lavish Surprise Party as Mbeki Turns 50," *Sunday Times* (Johannesburg), June 21, 1992.

8. T. Mbeki, "The Historical Injustice," in T. Mbeki, *Africa: The Time Has Come* (Cape Town: Tafelberg, 1999), p. x.

9. See C. Reddy, "BEE Deal Flow," *BusinessMap: Annual Report* (Johannesburg: BusinessMap: 2006), p. 18.

10. M. Mbeki, "What Is Transformation? The White Roots of BEE," speech given at Wits University, April 26, 2006.
11. T. Mbeki, "African Renaissance Statement," August 13, 1998. www.anc. org.za.
12. T. Mbeki, *Africa: Define Yourself* (Cape Town: Tafelberg, 2002), p. 76.
13. "Man Who May Succeed Madiba," *Star* (Johannesburg), April 26, 1995.
14. Ibid.

28 SIDELINING

1. "A Close Call," *Finance Week* (Johannesburg), July 17, 1991.
2. "ANC Elects National Executive Committee," *Southern African Political Economy Monthly* (July 1991): 35.
3. "ANC 'Cabinet' Take Control," *Star* (Johannesburg), July 20, 1991.
4. P. Waldmeir, *Anatomy of a Miracle* (New Brunswick, NJ: Rutgers, 2001) pp. 186–188.
5. Ibid., p. 189.
6. "The Winter of Discontent," *Negotiation News* (Cape Town), August 7, 1992.
7. Ibid.

29 INTO POWER

1. See "Two Faces of Mandela," *Mail & Guardian* (Johannesburg), June 20, 2002, and "Mokaba Issue Still on the Boil," *Weekly Mail* (Johannesburg), June 6, 1991.
2. "The Long Journey of Thabo Mbeki," *Leadership* (Cape Town), September 30, 1993.
3. "The ANC's New Chief," *Sunday Nation* (Johannesburg), September 12, 1993.
4. M. Du Preez, "Finger on the Trigger of War," *Sunday Independent* (Johannesburg), March 25, 2001.
5. Ibid.
6. A. Nzo, "The People's Programme," *Sechaba* (London), September 1980, p. 6.
7. O. Tambo, Statement at a press conference, July 23, 1980, ANC weekly news briefings, July 25, 1980, www.anc.org.za.
8. P. Waldmeir, *Anatomy of a Miracle* (New Brunswick, NJ: Rutgers University Press, 2001), p. 68.
9. A. Sparks, A *Tomorrow Is Another Country* (Johannesburg: Struik, 1994), p. 224.
10. C. Ramaphosa, "Secretary-General's Report to the ANC 49th Congress," December 17–22, 1994, www.anc.org.za.

30 TRANSITION

1. N. Mandela, Statement at Presidential Inauguration, Union Buildings, Pretoria, May 10, 1994, www.anc.org.za.
2. L. Hughes, "Harlem," in L. Hughes, *Selected Poems of Langston Hughes* (New York: Random House/Vintage, 1974), p. 268. T. Mbeki, Statement at Opening of Debate in National Assembly on Reconciliation and Nation-Building, Cape Town, May 29, 1998, www.anc.org.za.
3. See L. Camerer, *Costly Crimes: Commercial Crime and Corruption in South Africa* (Pretoria: Institute of Security Studies, 1997); COSATU press statement on the 1997 budget, March 12, 1997; and "Public Finances" in *Budget 1998*, South African National Treasury, South African Government Web site.

4. "Looking to Be on the Cutting Edge," *TIME*, September 16, 1996.
5. "The Press Must Rethink Its Role—Mbeki," *Citizen* (Johannesburg), August 20, 1994.
6. "Man Who May Succeed Madiba," *Star* (Johannesburg), April 26, 1995.
7. "Mr Fix-It Turns to Mr Fluff It," *Mail & Guardian* (Johannesburg), May 4, 1995.
8. "Unmandated Reflections. From Resistance to Reconstruction: Tasks of the ANC in the New Epoch of the Democratic Transformation," August 9, 1994, pp. 16–23, www.anc.org.za. See also "ANC Takes Long Look at Itself in the Mirror," *Star* (Johannesburg), September 2, 1994.
9. "Mandela Reassures Whites in Plea for Conciliation," *Sunday Times* (Johannesburg), May 1, 1994.
10. See, for example, P. Green, "The Outsider Who Measured Vision Against Reality," *Business Report* (Johannesburg), February 16, 2006.
11. See T. Mbeki, Statement at 10th Congress of the SACP, July 2, 1998, www.anc.org.za.
12. Ibid.
13. See R. Jacobs and R. Calland, *Thabo Mbeki's World: The Politics and Ideology of the South African President* (London: Zed Books, 2002), p. 33; W. Gumede, *Thabo Mbeki and the Battle for the Soul of the ANC* (Cape Town: Zebra, 2005), p. 95; N. S. Makgetla, "The Post Apartheid Economy," *Review of African Political Economy*, No. 100 (2004); H. Marais, *South Africa: Limits to Change* (Cape Town: University of Cape Town Press, 2001), pp. 160–172.
14. J. Netshitenzhe, "There Is Virtue in Strength and Certainty," *Sunday Times* (Johannesburg), April 4, 2004.
15. "Striking a Balance," *Mail & Guardian* (Johannesburg), August 1, 1996.

31   THE ARMS DEAL

1. See P. Holden, *The Arms Deal in Your Pocket* (Johannesburg: Jonathan Ball, 2008), p. 26–28.
2. T. Mbeki, "The Truth Stands in the Way of the Arms Accusers," *ANC Today* 1, No. 43, November 16–22, 2001.
3. See A. Feinstein, *After the Party* (Johannesburg: Jonathan Ball, 2007).
4. T. Mbeki, "Our Country Needs Facts, Not Groundless Allegations," *ANC Today* 3, No. 21, May 30–June 5, 2003; Mbeki, "The Truth Stands in the Way," www.anc.org.za.
5. "First Accused's Answering Affidavit, in the High Court of South Africa Natal Provincial Division in the matter between the State and Jacob Gedleyihlekisa Zuma and Others," Case No. CC358/2005, and "Zuma Drags President into the Fray," *Star* (Johannesburg), August 2, 2006.
6. Mbeki, "Our Country Needs Facts."
7. P. Govender, "Experiments in a Politics of Love and Courage," *Network News* (Cape Town), July 2004, p. 9; W. Gumede, *Thabo Mbeki and the Struggle for the Soul of the ANC* (Cape Town: Zebra, 2005), p. 139.
8. "Arms Suppliers Owe SA Billions, says Leon," *Independent OnLine* (Johannesburg), September 15, 2006, www.iol.co.za; "R104bn Arms Side-Deals Unenforceable—Heath," *Independent OnLine* (Johannesburg), January 23, 2001; "Were the Arms Deal 'Offsets' a Cloak for Fraud?" *Pretoria News* (Pretoria), October 7, 2006.

9. J. Nicholson, Judgment in the High Court of South Africa (Natal Provincial Division) in the Matter Between Jacob Gedleyihelkisa Zuma and National Director of Public Prosecutions, Case No. 8652/08, paragraph 33.

32 MANDELA AND MBEKI

1. Stock footage of the ANC National Conference, Mafikeng, December 20, 1997, South African Broadcasting Corporation, Johannesburg.
2. "Closing Address by Outgoing ANC President Nelson Mandela," *African National Congress 50th National Conference Report* (December 1997), p. 59. Mandela's speech on the ANC Web site has been edited to excise these comments.
3. N. Mandela, *Long Walk to Freedom* (Johannesburg: Macdonald Purnell, 1994), p. 11
4. "Mbeki on Black Press: Vital Role in Transforming SA," *The Leader* (Johannesburg), September 22, 1995.
5. T. Mbeki, Speech to Annual Banquet of the South African Chamber of Business, September 14, 1995, in T. T. Corrigan, *Mbeki, His Time Has Come: An Introduction to South Africa's New President* (Johannesburg: South African Institute of Race Relations, 1999), p. 35.
6. M. Gevisser, "SA's Reconciliation in Motion," *Mail & Guardian* (Johannesburg), May 19, 1994.
7. "Mbeki Votes in Laudium," *Star* (Johannesburg), April 29, 1994.
8. "Get Angry About the Past, Says Mbeki," *Sunday Times* (Johannesburg), March 28, 1999.
9. "Currency Markets Sound a Warning," *Sunday Times* (Johannesburg), February 18, 1996.
10. N. Mandela, "Don't Praise Me to Damn the Rest," *Sunday Times* (Johannesburg), November 25, 1996.
11. T. Mbeki, "Questions that Demand Answers," *ANC Today* 4, No. 36, September 10–16, 2004, www.anc.org.za.
12. T. Mbeki, "Statement . . . on the TRC," October 31, 1998, www.anc.org.za; "Mbeki Takes on Tutu in Public Spat," *Citizen* (Johannesburg), October 31, 1998.
13. T. Mbeki, Speech to the National Council of Provinces, Cape Town, November 10, 1998, www.anc.org.za.
14. "The Long Journey of Thabo Mbeki," *Leadership* (Cape Town) 12, No. 4, June 30, 1993.
15. "Mbeki Rules the Country—Mandela," *Business Day* (Johannesburg), July 1997.
16. "Mbeki Faces Open Revolt from Angry ANC, Allies," *Business Day* (Johannesburg), May 26, 2006; "Presidency Is Too Powerful—SACP," *South African Press Association*, May 22, 2006; ' "ANC Following in Zanu-PF's Footsteps,' " *Sunday Independent* (Johannesburg), March 25, 2007.
17. D. Tutu, "Look to the Rock from Which You Were Hewn," Nelson Mandela Lecture, Johannesburg, November 2004.
18. T. Mbeki, "Aluta Continua!" *ANC Today* 4, No. 47, November 26–December 2, 2004, www.anc.org.za.
19. J. Cronin, "What Kind of Presidency?" *Mail & Guardian* (Johannesburg), May 27, 2006.
20. *Bua Komanisi!* 5, No. 1 (May 2006), Special Edition, www.sacp.org.za.
21. A. Feinstein, "Arms Deal Returns to Haunt ANC," *Mail & Guardian* (Johannesburg), February 11, 2007.

22. T. Mbeki, Toast to President Nelson Mandela on the Occasion of His Eightieth Birthday, Gallagher Estate, Midrand, July 19, 1998, www.anc.org.za. See also W. Shakespeare, *King Lear* (Bristol: Bristol Classical Press, 1987), Act 4, Scene 3, Lines 6–13.

23. D. Accone, "Doomed Lear Not the Best Birthday Guest," *Sunday Independent* (Johannesburg), July 26, 1998.

24. Mbeki, Toast to Mandela.

25. "Mandela Blasts Mugabe," *Sunday Times* (Johannesburg), May 7, 2000.

26. "Mandela Condemns ANC Graft Arrogance," *Citizen* (Johannesburg), March 3, 2001.

27. "Mandela: The Living Legend," BBC (London), May 5, 2003.

28. T. Mbeki, "He's God's Gift to the World," in "Madiba at 85," *Star* (Johannesburg), July 18, 2003, supplement.

33 MBEKI AND AIDS

1. "On the Record": Interview with Thabo Mbeki by Debra Patta, e-tv, April 24, 2001.

2. All these statistics, with the exception of the lost one, are from official South African government studies. See www.avert.org/safricastats.htm for a summary.

3. P. Chigwedere et al, "Estimating the Lost Benefits of Antiretroviral Drug Use in South Africa," *Journal of Acquired Immune Deficiency Syndromes*, Harvard, October 16, 2008.

4. M. Crewe, *AIDS in South Africa* (London: Penguin Forum Series, Penguin Books, 1992), p. 48.

5. "Death Watch: South Africa's Advances Jeopardized by AIDS," *Washington Post*, July 6, 2000.

6. See "Mbeki Brokered Deal with Warring Virodene Camps," *Business Day* (Johannesburg), December 12, 1997; "Dear Thabo...Love Olga," *Mail & Guardian* (Johannesburg), July 11, 2002; "Virodene May Activate AIDS Virus," *Mail & Guardian* (Johannesburg), March 26, 1998; W. Gumede, *Thabo Mbeki and the Battle for the Soul of the ANC* (Johannesburg: Zebra, 2005), pp. 154–155.

7. T. Mbeki, "Declaration of Partnership against AIDS," October 9, 1998, www. anc.org.za.

8. See "It Needs a Politician with the Real Thing," *Natal Witness* (Pietermaritzburg), October 17, 1998; W. Gumede, *Thabo Mbeki*; E. Cameron, *Witness to AIDS* (Cape Town: Tafelberg, 2005); A. Sparks, *Beyond the Miracle* (Johannesburg: Jonathan Ball, 2003).

9. T. Mbeki, Address to the National Council of Provinces, Cape Town, October 28, 1999, www.anc.org.za.

10. C. Smith, "Rape Victims Are Not Statistics...We Are People," *Mail & Guardian* (Johannesburg), April 9, 1999.

11. T. Mbeki, Speech at Open Ministerial Meeting, 12th Non-Aligned Movement Summit, Durban, August 31, 1998, www.anc.org.za.

12. T. Mbeki, Keynote address to the National General Council, Port Elizabeth, July 12, 2000, www.anc.org.za.

13. M. W. Makgoba, Letter to Thabo Mbeki, January 25, 2000.

14. "AIDS Researchers Decry Mbeki's Views on HIV," *Science*, April 28, 2000; M. W. Makgoba, "HIV/AIDS: The Perils of Pseudoscience," *Science*, May 19, 2000.

15. D. Rasnick, "Talked with President Thabo Mbeki," March 2, 2000, www.virusmyth.net.

16. Ibid.

17. T. Mbeki, State of the Nation address, National Assembly, Cape Town, February 4, 2000, www.anc.org.za.

18. T. Mbeki, "Invitation," March 2000, www.virusmyth.net.

19. N. Nattrass, "AIDS, Science and Governance: The Battle Over Antiretroval Therapy in Post Apartheid South Africa," March 9, 2006, www.aidstruth.org.

20. T. Mbeki, Letter to G8 Leaders and Kofi Annan, April 3, 2000, www.virusmyth.net.

21. "AIDS Deemed a 'National Security' Threat by US as South African President Challenges Medical Orthodoxy," *Natural Healthline*, May 1, 2000, www.virusmyth.net.

22. See, for example, R. Malan, "AIDS in Africa: In Search of Truth," *Rolling Stone*, November 22, 2001.

23. C. L. Geshekter, "AIDS in Africa: Myths of AIDS and Sex," 2001 (reprint), in *Jenda: A Journal of Culture and African Women Studies* 1, No. 2. See www.virusmyth.net.

24. See, for example, D. Fassin, *When Bodies Remember: Experiences and Politics of AIDS in South Africa* (Berkeley: University of California Press, 2007); A. Katz, "AIDS, Individual Behaviour and the Unexplained Remaining Variation," *African Journal of AIDS Research* 1, No. 2 (2002), pp. 87–149; E. Stillwaggon, *AIDS and the Ecology of Poverty* (New York: Oxford University Press, 2005).

25. T. Mbeki, Speech at opening of the 13th International AIDS Conference, Durban, July 9, 2000, www.anc.org.za.

26. "The Durban Declaration," *Nature* 406, July 6, 2000.

27. T. Mbeki, "Health, Human Dignity and Partners for Poverty Reduction," *ANC Today* 2, No. 14, April 11–15, 2002, www.anc.org.za.

28. C. Geshekter, "Reappraising AIDS in Africa: Underdevelopment and Racial Stereotypes," in *Reappraising AIDS* (September/October 1997), www.virusmyth.net.

29. C. Smith, "Their Deaths, His Doubts, My Fears," *Washington Post*, June 4, 2000.

30. "AIDS: Mbeki versus Leon," *Sunday Times* (South Africa), July 9, 2000.

31. "What Leon and Mbeki Had to Say," *Mail & Guardian* (South Africa), October 6, 2000.

32. T. Mbeki, "A Hundred Flowers Under the African Sun," *ANC Today* 3, No. 30, August 1–7, 2003, www.anc.org.za.

33. T. Mbeki, "He Awakened to His Responsibilities," University of Fort Hare, October 12, 2001, www.anc.org.za.

34. "Castro Hlongwane…" (March 2002), www.virusmyth.net.

35. Ibid.

36. Mbeki, "Health, Human Dignity and Partners for Poverty Reduction."

37. See, for example, S. Epstein, *Impure Science: AIDS, Activism, and the Politics of Knowledge* (Berkeley: University of California Press, 1996).

38. Fassin, *When Bodies Remember*, p. 120.

39. "Is Thabo Mbeki Fit to Rule?" *Mail & Guardian* (Johannesburg), May 23, 1996; "Is Mbeki Fit to Rule?" *Mail & Guardian* (Johannesburg), April 25, 2001.

40. Boehringer Ingelheim claims that it never planned to use the facility to conduct trials and that it—rather than the state—had pulled the plug on the project because of the controversy around AIDS in South Africa.

41. N. Mandela, Closing address at the 8th International AIDS Conference, Durban, July 14, 2000, www.anc.org.za.

42. "'Stop AIDS Nonsense': Mandela Tells Mbeki's Government to Halt Debates and Fight the War," *Sunday Times* (Johannesburg), February 17, 2002.

43. "Mbeki Fingers CIA in AIDS Conspiracy," *Mail & Guardian* (Johannesburg), October 6, 2000.

44. "Now I Must Poison My People, says Dr No," *Independent OnLine* (Johannesburg), July 8, 2002, www.iol.co.za.

45. "Mbeki, Mandela Sort Out Problems, Bury the Hatchet," *Sunday Independent* (Johannesburg), May 2, 2002.

46. Cameron, *Witness to AIDS*, p. 130.

47. See, for example, K. Cullinan, "Health Minister Promotes Nutritional Alternatives to ARV Roll-out," Health-E News (Cape Town), May 30, 2005.

48. "I really don't know anybody who has died of AIDS, Says Mbeki," *Cape Times* (Cape Town), September 26, 2003.

49. "Castro Hlongwane...," (April 2002, and later somewhat expanded), p. 189. Courtesy of T. Mbeki.

50. T. Mbeki, Fourth Annual Nelson Mandela Lecture, Wits University, July 29, 2006, www.anc.org.za.

34 MBEKI AND ZIMBABWE

1. See "MDC Refutes Mbeki's Word on Polls," South African Press Association, February 2, 2004; "MDC Leader Mystified by Mbeki's Comments," February 8, 2006, www.zimonline.co.za.

2. "No Crisis in Zimbabwe, Says Mbeki," *Mail & Guardian Online* (Johannesburg), April 12, 2008.

3. P. Godwin, "Soccer 1, Mugabe 0," *New York Times*, June 24, 2008.

4. See "After Eight Debate," SAFM, SA Broadcasting Corporation (Johannesburg), April 14, 2003.

5. T. Sellström, *Sweden and National Liberation in Southern Africa*, vol. 2 (Uppsala: Nordic Africa Institute, 2002), p. 681.

6. Ibid., pp. 683–684.

7. Mbeki publicly stated this twice. The first time was before a public lecture in Abuja after he lost the battle to get Zimbabwe readmitted to the Commonwealth in December 2003. The second was at a land reform conference. See "Put Land Reform in the Context of a Continuing Struggle, Mbeki," *BuaNews* (Johannesburg), July 29, 2005.

8. T. Mbeki, "We Will Resist the Upside-Down View of Africa," *ANC Today* 3, No. 49, December 12, 2003, www.anc.org.za.

9. Ibid.

10. A. Sparks, *Beyond the Miracle* (Johannesburg: Jonathan Ball, 2003), p. 327.

35 HOME

1. J. Zuma, Oration at Govan Mbeki's funeral service, September 8, 2001, author's transcription.

2. Ibid.

3. "Marchers Lash Out at Black Elite," *Pretoria News* (Pretoria), August 17, 2001.

4. M. Gevisser, "Unflagging Spirit in Face of Need Sums Up Oom Gov's Message," *Sunday Independent* (Johannesburg), September, 9 2001.

5. See "Mbeki Takes on the 'Ultra Left,'" *Sunday Independent* (Johannesburg), September 29, 2002; T. Mbeki, Statement at ANC Policy Conference, September 27, 2002; D. Makhaye, "Left Factionalism and the Democratic Revolution," *ANC Today* 2, No. 48, November 29, 2002, www.anc.org.za.

6. COSATU Central Executive Committee, "Final Political Report," November 5–7, 2002, pp. 21–23, www.cosatu.org.za.

7. T. Mbeki, Address at opening of the 51st National Conference of the ANC, Stellenbosch, December 16, 2002, www.anc.org.za.

8. "Mbeki's Extreme Makeover," *Sunday Times* (Johannesburg), April 11, 2004.

9. See "Returning to Its Roots," *Mail & Guardian* (Johannesburg), January 12, 2004; "Mbeki Sheds Aloof Image," *Independent OnLine* (Johannesburg), April 5, 2004, www.iol.co.za.

10. See The Presidency: Republic of South Africa, *Development Indicators 2008*, www.thepresidency.gov.za.

11. M. Linklater, "We Have to Deal with the Real South Africa: Interview: Thabo Mbeki," *The Times* (London), May 31, 2001.

12. "Ma Mbeki to Back Plans for ANC Split," *Independent OnLine* (Johannesburg), September 23, 2008.

13. X. Mangcu, *To the Brink: The State of Democracy in South Africa*, (Durban: UKZN Press, 2008).

14. E. Said, *Reflections on Exile and Other Literary and Cultural Essays* (New Delhi: Penguin India, 2001), p. 181.

EPILOGUE

1. "Statement by the President of the African National Congress, Cde Jacob Zuma, to the closing of the 52nd National Congress of the ANC," Polokwane, South Africa, December 20, 2007, www.anc.org.za.

2. This information was divulged by Penuell Maduna to the ANC's National Executive Committee in November 2005.

3. "Zuma case unwinnable, says Scorpions Boss," *The Star* (Johannesburg), August 23, 2003.

4. J. Netshitenzhe, "Arms deal saga: separating the wheat from the chaff," *The Star* (Johannesburg), August 28, 2003.

5. J. Zuma, "Attempts to destabilise the ANC," press statement, April 3, 2001.

6. See J. Squires, "Judgement on the matter between The State and Schabir Shaik et al," May 31, 2005, available at www.armsdeal-vpo.co.za.

7. See "Timeline of the Jacob Zuma rape trial," *Mail & Guardian Online*, March 21, 2006, and M. Motsei, *The Kanga and the Kangaroo Court: The Rape Trial of Jacob Zuma* (Johannesburg: Jacana, 2007).

8. "A dissonance in the Zuma choir," *The Star* (Johannesburg), October 28, 2005.

9. ANC, "2009 Manifesto," www.anc.org.za.

10. "ANC holds faith with Zuma as lists take shape," *Business Day* (Johannesburg), January 19, 2009.

11. "Statement by the President of the African National Congress, Cde Jacob Zuma, to the closing of the 52nd National Congress of the ANC," Polokwane, South Africa, December 20, 2007, www.anc.org.za.

12. T. Mbeki, Letter to R. Gooding, October 1969.

13. W. Shakespeare, *Coriolanus*, Act III, Scene 2, ll. 14–16. (London: Penguin, 2005).

14. "Opening Address and Political Report of the President of the African National Congress, Thabo Mbeki, to the 52nd National Conference of the ANC: University of Limpopo, December 16, 2007," www.anc.org.za.

15. W. Shakespeare, *Coriolanus*, Act III, Scene 3, ll. 120–135.

16. "Dissidents Want To Cling To Power," *Sunday Independent* (Johannesburg), October 26, 2008.

17. "All-out bid to save Zuma," *Sunday Independent* (Johannesburg), January 18, 2009.

18. Justice C. Nicholson, "Judgement in the matter between Jacob Gedleyihlekisa Zuma and National Director of Public Prosecutions," September 11, 2008, paragraphs 32, 41, 158. Available at www.news24.com.

19. The Supreme Court of Appeal, Republic of South Africa, "Judgement: National Director of Public Prosecutions and Jacob Gedleyihlekisa Zuma, 12 January 2009. Available at www.mg.co.za.

20. T. Mbeki, "Mbeki welcomes SCA findings," www.politicsweb.co.za, January 13, 2009.

21. "Mbeki Regime a 'Dead Snake,'" *The Star* (Johannesburg), September 15, 2008.

22. T. Mbeki, "Address to the National by the South African President," September 21, 2008, www.thepresidency.gov.za.

23. Manuel claimed subsequently that he had never planned to resign but was simply acting procedurally, as all ministers serve at the pleasure of the president.

24. P. Bulger, "The (Very) Last Remake of the New Democratic SA," *Business Day* (Johannesburg), November 3, 2008.

25. See The Presidency of South Africa, *Development Indicators*, www.thepresidency.gov.za.

26. See "Mbeki sends stern letter to Mugabe," *Cape Times* (Cape Town), June 6, 2001.

27. See X. Mangcu, *To the Brink: The State of Democracy in South Africa* (Durban: UKZN Press, 2008).

28. See T. Mbeki, "Freedom from racism—a fundamental human right," *ANC Today*, March 16–22, 2007, www.anc.org.za; "Crime: Experts say Mbeki is out of touch," *Mail & Guardian* (Johannesburg), January 17, 2007.

29. See C. Dugger, "Study Cites Toll of AIDS Policy in South Africa," *New York Times*, November 26, 2008.

30. B. Pottinger, *The Mbeki Legacy* (Cape Town: Zebra, 2008), p. 212.

31. Ibid. p. 5

32. See The Presidency: Republic of South Africa, *Development Indicators*, www.thepresidency.gov.za.

33. See A. Altbeker, *A Country at War with Itself: South Africa's Crisis of Crime* (Johannesburg: Jonathan Ball, 2007).

34. The Ginwala Commission found, in December 2008, that Pikoli was fit to hold office, and that he should not have been suspended, but also cleared Mbeki by finding that his suspension was not related to the investigation of Selebi.

The commission did find that Pikoli was insensitive to "national security," and Kgalema Motlanthe—who was by this point the president—chose to recommend to parliament that Pikoli be dismissed on these grounds. Pikoli had been a determined advocate for the prosecution of Jacob Zuma, and it seemed possible that Motlanthe's action was part of the ANC's strategy for protecting its new president. At the time of publication, parliament was deliberating on the dismissal of Pikoli, and seemed set to uphold Pikoli's recommendation. See S. Sole, "How Ginwala Blew It," www.mg.co.za, December 12, 2008.

35. T. Mbeki, letter to Jacob Zuma, October 31, 2008. Available at www.politicsweb.co.za.
36. T. Mbeki, letter to Rhiannon Gooding, October 1969.
37. T. Mbeki, letter to Jacob Zuma, October 31, 2008.

BIBLIOGRAPHICAL NOTES

ARCHIVES

This book draws, primarily, on three South African historical archives: The ANC Archives at the University of Fort Hare, Alice (http://liberation.ufh.ac.za); the Karis-Gerhart Collection at University, Johannesburg (www.wits.ac.za/histp); and several collections at the UWC-Robben Island Mayibuye Archives, University of the Western Cape, Cape Town (www.robben-island.org.za). Please note, though, that the ANC collection at the Mayibuye Archives has been moved to the ANC's own archives in Johannesburg, and the accession numbers listed in this book may no longer be applicable. Other archives consulted were the National Archives, Pretoria; the Jack Simons and Ray Alexander Papers at the University of Cape Town; the Julie Frederickse Collection at the South African History Archive; the Lovedale Collection at Rhodes University, the Nordiska Afrikainstitutet in Uppsala, Sweden; and the Sached Collection at Wits University. Web sites consulted include: the ANC (www.anc.org.za), the South African Presidency (www.thepresidency.gov.za), South African Government OnLine (www.gov.za), the South African Communist Party (www.sacp.org.za); the Truth and Reconciliation Commission Archives (www.doj.gov.za/trc); and the Congress of South African Trade Unions (www.cosatu.org.za).

Copies of all materials cited from the above sources, as well as from personal collections, are available in the Mark Gevisser Thabo Mbeki Collection at the South African History Archive at Wits University (www.saha.org.za). All recorded interviews and transcripts, except those not for the record, can also be found in this collection.

SECONDARY READINGS

The full citations for all materials and books that directly quoted are to be found in the notes. Following are some of the sources that provided me with facts, figures and contextual information, and which are recommended for further reading:

On early South African history: W. Beinart, *Hidden Struggles in Rural South Africa: Politics and Popular Movements in the Transkei and Eastern Cape 1890–1930* (London: J. Currey, 1987); C. Bundy, *The Rise and Fall of the South African Peasantry* (London: J. Currey, 1988); T. Couzens, *The New African: A Study of the Life and Work of HIE Dhlomo* (Johannesburg: Ravan, 1985); R. Davenport and C. Saunders, *South Africa, A Modern History* (London: Macmillan 2000), C. Higgs, *The Ghost of Equality: The Public Lives of DDT Jabavu of South Africa 1885–1959* (Cape Town: Mayibuye, 1997), T. Karis and G. Carter, eds., *From Protest to Challenge (Volume 1)*; M. Mbeki, "The African Middle Class and Political Change in South Africa, 1884–1964," MA thesis, University of Warwick, 1981; N. Mostert, *Frontiers: The Epic of South Africa's Creation and the Tragedy of the Xhosa People* (London: Pimlico, 1993), P. Ntantala, *A Life's Mosaic* (Cape Town: David Philip, 1992).

On the ANC and the liberation struggle: H. Barrell, *MK: The ANC's Armed Struggle* (London: Penguin, 1990); H. Barrell, "Conscripts to Their Age: African National Congress Operational Strategy, 1976–1986," D.Phil thesis, Oxford University, 1993; H. Bernstein, *The Rift* (London: Jonathan Cape, 1994); R. Bernstein *Memory Against Forgetting* (New York: Viking, 1999); F. Buntman, *Robben Island and Prisoner Resistance to Apartheid*, Cambridge: Cambridge University Press, 2003); L. Callinicos, *Oliver Tambo: Beyond the Engeli Mountains* (Cape Town: David Philip, 2004); S. Clingman, *Bram Fischer* (Cape Town: David Philip, 1998); S. Dubow, *The African National Congress* (Stroud, UK: Sutton, 2000); S. Ellis and T. Sechaba, *Comrades Against Apartheid* (London: J. Currey, 1992); G. Gerhart, *Black Power in South Africa*, (Berkeley, University of California Press, 1978); T. Karis and G. Carter, eds., *From Protest to Challenge, Volume 2* (Stanford: Hoover Institution Press, 1973); T. Karis, G. Carter and G. Gerhart, eds., *From Protest to Challenge, Volumes 3–4* (Stanford: Hoover Institution Press, 1973); T. Karis and G. Gerhart, eds., *From Protest to Challenge, Volume 5* (Pretoria: Unisa Press, 1997); T. Lodge *Black Politics in South Africa Since 1945* (London: Longman, 1983); T. Lodge *Black Politics in South Africa in the 1980s,* (Cape Town: David Philip, 1991); N. Mandela, *Long Walk to Freedom* (Johannesburg: Macdonald Purnell, 1994); P. O'Malley, *Shades of Difference: Mac Maharaj and the Struggle for South Africa* (London: Penguin, 2007); South African Democracy Education Trust, *The Road to Democracy in South Africa, Vol. 1 (1960–1970)* (Cape Town: Zebra, 2004); A. Sampson, *Mandela* (Johannesburg: Jonathan Ball, 1999); V. Shubin, *ANC: A View from Moscow* (Cape Town: Mayibuye Books, 1999); P. Walshe, *The Rise of African Nationalism in South Africa: The ANC 1912–1952* (Los Angeles: University of California Press, 1970).

On the South African transition to democracy: M. Du Preez, *Pale Native* (Cape Town: Zebra, 2004); R. Harvey, *The Fall of Apartheid: The Inside Story from Smuts to Mbeki* (Hampshire, UK: Palgrave, 2001); A. Krog, *Country of My Skull* (Johannesburg: Random House, 1998); A. Sparks, *Tomorrow Is Another Country* (Johannesburg: Struik, 1994); B. Temkin, *Buthelezi: A Biography*, (London: Frank Cass, 2002); P. Waldmeir, *Anatomy of a Miracle* (New Brunswick NJ: Rutgers University Press, 2001).

On postapartheid South Africa: R. Calland, *Anatomy of South Africa: Who Holds the Power?* (Cape Town: Zebra, 2006); R. Calland and S. Jacobs, *Thabo Mbeki's World: The Politics and Ideology of the South African President* (London: Zed Books, 2002); E. Cameron, *Witness to AIDS* (Cape Town: Tafelberg, 2005); J. Daniel, A. Habib and R. Southall, *State of the Nation: South Africa 2003–2004* (Cape Town: HSRC Press, 2003); A. Feinstein, *After the Party: A Personal and Political Journey Inside the ANC* (Johannesburg: Jonathan Ball, 2007); W. M. Gumede, *Thabo Mbeki and the Battle for the Soul of the ANC* (Cape Town: Zebra, 2005); A. Hirsch, *Season of Hope: Economic Reform Under Mandela and Mbeki* (Durban: UKZN Press, 2005), P. Holden, *The Arms Deal in Your Pocket* (Johannesburg: Jonathan Ball, 2008); C. Landsberg, *The Quiet Diplomacy of Liberation: International Politics and South Africa's Transition* (Johannesburg: Jacana, 2004); T. Lodge, *Politics in South Africa: From Mandela To Mbeki* (Cape Town: David Philip, 2002); X. Mangcu, *To the Brink: The State of Democracy in South Africa* (Durban: UKZN Press, 2008); H. Marais, *South Africa: Limits to Change* (Cape Town: University of Cape Town Press, 2001); N. Nattrass, *Combat: AIDS Denialism and the Struggle for Antiretrovirals in South Africa* (Durban: UKZN Press, 2007); B. Pottinger, *The Mbeki Legacy* (Cape Town: Zebra, 2008); Presidency, Republic of South Africa, *Development Indicators* (www.thepresidency.gov.za); M. Ramphele, *Laying Ghosts to Rest: Dilemmas of Transformation in South Africa* (Cape Town: Tafelberg, 2008); A. Sparks, *Beyond the Miracle* (Johannesburg: Jonathan Ball, 2003).

INTERVIEWS

The following is a list of those interviewed for this project. It does not, of course, include those who requested to remain anonymous:

Goolam Aboobaker, Ray Alexander, Ken Andrew, Richard Attenborough, Tibor Barna, Niël Barnard, Howard Barrell, Rusty Bernstein, Paul Bjarnason, Anders Bjurner, Allan Boesak, Pik Botha, Joan Brickhill, Allan Brooks, Asa Briggs, Richard Brown, Brian Bunting, Robert Cabelly, Jan Cedergren, Edwin Cameron, Mamisa Chabula, Lebenya Chakela, Frank Chikane, Mark Chona, Andrei Chuzakin, Piet Coetzer, Stan and Ruth Cohen, Colin Coleman, Judy Crichton, Jeremy Cronin, G. G. Darah, Apollon Davidson, Lionel Davis, Wimpie De Klerk, Pieter De Lange, Albert Dhlomo, Oscar Dhlomo, Nkosazana Dlamini-Zuma, Pam dos Santos, Sigqibo Dwane, Theuns Eloff, Alec Erwin, Willie Esterhuyse, Patrick Fitzgerald, Jendayi Fraser, Geraldine Fraser-Moleketi, Jakes Gerwel, David Gil, Frene Ginwala, Dennis Goldberg, Mel and Rhiannon Gooding, Derek Gunby, Jonas Gwangwa, Tony and Eve Hall, Barbara Harmel, Fink Haysom, Alan Hirsch, Philippa Ingram, Josiah Jele, Linda Jiba, Lena Johannson, Shaun Johnson, Pallo Jordan, Ronnie Kasrils, Ahmed Kathrada, Rod Kedward, Richard Ketley, Keorapetse Kgositsile, Gay Khaile, Baba Gana Kingibe, Josiah Kizito, Wolfie Kodesh, Jürgen Kögl, Malebo Kotu-Rammopo, Mazisi Kunene, Mandla Langa, Peter Lawrence, Vladimir Lebedev, Tony Leon, David Lewis, Veronica Linklater, Isaac Mabindisa, Tiksie Mabizela, Fezeka Mabona, Lindiwe Mabuza, Hugh Macmillan, Saki Macozoma Penuell Maduna, Eric Mafuna, Vincent Mahali, Sipo Makalima, Sipho Makana, Neva Makgetla, Malegapuru Makgoba, Bobby Makwetla, Mosebejane Malatsi, Reddy Mampane, Jackie Mankogoama, Nelson Mandela, Trevor Manuel, Tshepiso Manyelo, Fonti Maphethe, Howard Maqgaza, Gill Marcus, Barbara Masekela, Mphu Matete, Joe Matthews, Vusi Mavimbela, Lizo Mazwai, Richard Mbali, Govan Mbeki, Epainette Mbeki, Moeletsi Mbeki, Thabo Mbeki, Zizi Mbeki, Roelf Meyer, Adrian and Celia Mitchell, Sindiso Mfenyana, Zamukulungisa Mfeti, Sobizana Mngqikana, Victor Moche, Billy Modise, Joe Modise, Hilda Moerane, Majalla Moerane, Mofelehetsi Moerane, Norah Moerane, Sophie Moerane, Barney Mokgatle, Gabriel Mokgoko, Solly Mokoetle, Kgalema Motlanthe, Olive Mpahlwa, Vezikhaya Mpahlwa, Mendi Msimang, Sankie Mthembi-Mahanyele, Phumla Mtyeku, Sydney Mufamadi, Mike Muller, Piet Muller, Hugh Murray, Vernon Mwaanga, Indres Naidoo, Mickey Nama, Cyril Ndebele, Harry Nengwekhulu, Joel Netshitenzhe, Makonza Ngampu, Smuts Ngonyama, Joe Nhlanhla, Welile Nhlapo, Ann Nicholson, Khetani Nkabinde, Wiseman Nkuhlu, Tiny Nokwe, Carin Norberg, Thami Ntenteni, Blade Nzimande, Ann Page, Essop Pahad, Meg Pahad, Kenny Parker, Seth Phalatse, Motsoko Pheko, David Phiri, Pundy Pillay, Vella Pillay, Barney Pityana, Cyril Ramaphosa, Robin Renwick, Shura Rodionova, Andre Roux, Anthony Sampson, Bengt Save-Soderberg, Pierre Schori, Jackie Sedibe, Ronald Segal, Jackie Selebi, Tor Sellström, Reg September, Sipho Shezi, Mbhazima Shilowa, Olive Shisana, Vladimir Shubin, Birgitte Silen, Lindiwe Sisulu, Max Sisulu, Vassily Solodovnikov, Maritz Spaarwater, Michael Spicer, Adelaide Tambo, Vyacheslav Tetyokin, Carl Tham, Tony Trew, Vladimir Trofimov, Manto Tshabalala-Msimang, Ben Turok, Andrei Urnov, H. V. Van Der Merwe, Neil Van Heerden, Frederik Van Zyl Slabbert, Zweliyanyikima Vena, Constand Viljoen, Gunilla Von Bahr-Tidbeck, Per Wastberg, Ruth White, Ann Wilkens, Ann Welsh Yates, Mike Yates, Michael Young, and Jacob Zuma.

INDEX